# AMERICAN GOVERNOR

Chris Christie's Bridge to Redemption

## MATT KATZ

**THRESHOLD EDITIONS**

New York   London   Toronto   Sydney   New Delhi

Threshold Editions
An Imprint of Simon & Schuster, Inc.
1230 Avenue of the Americas
New York, NY 10020

First Threshold Editions hardcover edition January 2016

THRESHOLD EDITIONS and colophon are trademarks of Simon & Schuster, Inc.

For information about special discounts for bulk purchases, please contact Simon & Schuster Special Sales at 1-866-506-1949 or business@simonandschuster.com.

The Simon & Schuster Speakers Bureau can bring authors to your live event. For more information or to book an event, contact the Simon & Schuster Speakers Bureau at 1-866-248-3049 or visit our website at www.simonspeakers.com.

Interior design by Jaime Putorti

Manufactured in the United States of America

10  9  8  7  6  5  4  3  2  1

Library of Congress Cataloging-in-Publication Data
Names: Katz, Matt (Reporter), author.
Title: American governor / Matt Katz.
Description: First Threshold Editions hardcover edition. | New York : Threshold Editions, 2016.
Identifiers: LCCN 2015044712 | Subjects: LCSH: Christie, Chris. | Governors—New Jersey—Biography. | New Jersey—Politics and government—1951– | Presidential candidates—United States—Biography.
Classification: LCC F140.22.C47 K37 2016 | DDC 974.9/044092—dc23 LC record available at http://lccn.loc.gov/2015044712

ISBN 978-1-4767-8266-9
ISBN 978-1-4767-8268-3 (ebook)

*For Deborah.*
*The best thing that ever happened to me*
*was falling in love with a Jersey girl.*

# CONTENTS

# INTRODUCTION

# MOVING THE CONES

"I worked the cones actually, Matt," he said. "Unbeknownst to everybody I was actually the guy out there. I was in overalls *and a hat.* . . . You *really* are not serious with that question."

I really was serious with that question.

Christopher J. Christie, the fifty-fifth governor of the state of New Jersey, loomed from behind a massive wooden podium in the ornate ceremonial meeting room of his office at the state capitol in Trenton. His predecessors lined the walls in oil paintings, gubernatorial ghosts that warned of mediocre political fortune. Just one governor of New Jersey had gone on to become president of the United States: Woodrow Wilson. That was in 1913, exactly one hundred years ago.

Christie was poised to recapture the White House for New Jersey. He had just won a landslide reelection as a Republican in one of the most Democratic states in the country. He had come to personify New Jersey not just in the political sphere but also as a national cultural figure, as likely to pop up on E! as on FOX News. And he was beating all the other Republicans in the polls for the next presidential election in 2016—and even tied with Democrat Hillary Clinton, the presumptive Democratic candidate. Years of buzz about his political future had now turned into a full-on clarion call to every pragmatic Republican through the land: Christie had arrived to save the GOP. Exit polls showed that he knew how to win over independents, women, and the majority of Latinos.

Today was Christie's first press conference back at the Statehouse after his reelection win. He was cocky and combative, as always. So when Christie deflected my question, it was just the kind of ribbing sarcasm we were all used to.

CHRISTIE'S PRESENCE, ALREADY physically large, was magnified by the high perch he took behind the podium, above the reporters who sat packed together, shoulder to shoulder, laptops running hot on our thighs, eye level not with Christie but rather with the state seal.

A disembodied horse head was pictured at the center of that seal. "Liberty and Prosperity," it read.

There was a fireplace behind the podium, but it was never lit. Plainclothes state troopers and top Christie staffers were stationed around the room like sentries, expressionless and seemingly wary of our existence. The room was cold, always, and the wifi was poor, usually.

Reporters shall raise their hands. Permission must be sought before a follow-up can be asked. Keep the questions short. And reading off a notepad, computer screen, or iPhone invites mockery.

With no applause, the governor busted through a tall wooden door next to the fireplace. "All right, all right," he began. "Good afternoon, everybody."

A half hour into that press conference, he called on me.

The scandal that I asked him about had been brewing for months. Something bizarre about access lanes from the little town of Fort Lee to the George Washington Bridge. Word was that the governor's people had closed the lanes to cause massive morning traffic jams for five consecutive days that gridlocked commuters, school buses, and ambulances. Apparently (and this sounded impossibly preposterous) the traffic jams were created to seek revenge on the Fort Lee mayor, who hadn't endorsed Christie's reelection.

This was December, and the lanes closed back in September. Christie's Democratic opponent in the election brought the incident up during a recent debate. She said it showed that Christie and his people were a bunch of bullies.

New Jersey seemed to like the bullying, from the time he instructed the media to "take the bat out" on a seventy-eight-year-old state senator (he meant it journalistically, he later explained) to the time he went after congressional Republicans for blocking billions of dollars in relief money for the biggest natural disaster in New Jersey history.

So when I asked him, "Governor, did you have anything to do with these lane closures in September outside the GW Bridge?" his "I worked the cones" made the crowd, his senior staffers—and maybe a few reporters—laugh.

This was not my first time getting Christie's sarcastic shiv—after all, I had been covering him for three years at this point—so I persisted. The governor likes to grapple, and challenging him sometimes draws out better answers, ekes out some more truth-telling. And I wasn't peddling some cuckoo conspiracy theory here—this bridge thing was now the subject of hearings in the state legislature. Documents were being sought. Articles had been written. This was, without question, a news story.

The governor didn't think so. He did not want to be talking about what I was asking him to talk about. He was going to shut this down right now, and he planned to never hear about it again.

Christie stood by the explanation that the Port Authority of New York and New Jersey, which runs the bridge, had already given: The lanes were closed for a traffic study. He went on to say that he was instructing the Port Authority to "review that entire policy" of having "three dedicated lanes" for Fort Lee. "Because I've sat in that traffic," he said, "before I was governor." He looked at me and winked. He no longer sat in traffic; for him, as governor, they shut down part of the Lincoln Tunnel to Manhattan.

"The fact that one town has three lanes dedicated to it? That kind of gets me sauced," he said. And then he attacked the Democratic legislators who had become the lead antagonists on the whole issue.

"I don't get involved in lane closures. I didn't work the cones, just so we're clear on that, that was sarcastic," he said, to laughter. The Democratic inquiries were just "politics," he said. "They're just looking for something, you know? And that's what they do."

Before he became governor, Christie was the U.S. Attorney for New Jersey—the chief federal prosecutor for the entire state, best known for winning corruption cases against 130 dirty politicians. He ran for governor as the anticorruption candidate, the one who was going to clean up the notoriously shady halls of the Statehouse in Trenton. That's what made the scandal—Bridgegate—so shocking. If his top aides conspired to punish enemies with a traffic jam, was the guy who had fought corruption so valiantly now in bed with the very kind of people he was supposed to protect us from?

Christie had proven to be Teflon to controversy. So there was little reason to imagine he wouldn't get past this bridge situation, either.

Yet the next question proved to be clairvoyant. It came from Michael Aron, reporter for NJTV and the dean of the Trenton political press corps.

"Governor, you're frequently described as the front-runner for the

Republican presidential nomination," Aron said. "I wonder how comfortable a position that is three years ahead of an election. . . . How do you respond to that appellation"—front-runner—"in front of your name all the time?"

"It doesn't matter to me. It's meaningless. It's December 2013. . . . It will change any number of times between now and then."

It sure would.

I BEGAN COVERING Chris Christie in January 2011 for my newspaper, the *Philadelphia Inquirer*. My editor, Mike Topel, wanted a "body man" on Christie—someone who would follow him around the state and around the country, capturing every extraordinary moment and utterance for a blog and the newspaper. The governor was the most dynamic political figure in the region, Topel told me, and I would become the expert on him.

No, I told Topel. I wasn't interested.

Thing was, this should've been a dream job. I had always wanted to cover politics on a big stage—I was a political communication major at George Washington University, around the corner from the White House. For the next decade I covered local politics in New Jersey for three different newspapers, and I came to enjoy watchdogging school boards and telling stories about unusual personalities. I was briefly in Afghanistan, embedded with American troops, and when the Christie job opened up I was in the best beat I ever had—covering Camden, a city where politicians had repeatedly failed its people.

But Christie—Christie!—this guy kept making news. And so I took the job, moving my office to press row at the Statehouse in Trenton. On the *Inquirer's* website I created a blog with the mediocre but satisfyingly alliterative name "Christie Chronicles." Over the first few weeks on the beat I reported on Christie calling state workers "stupid," threatening to commit suicide if anyone asked him if he was running for president, and comparing New Jersey under his first year of leadership to the 1980 "Miracle On Ice" American hockey team. "Look around," he had said. "Much like that band of hard-charging, take-no-prisoners college kids did in Lake Placid thirty-one years ago, New Jersey is inspiring the nation."

Who in the world did this guy think he was? I was fascinated.

Months into the job, even though I had asked Christie questions at press conferences, I had yet to formally meet him. He worked downstairs and across the hall from my office in the Statehouse, but getting an audience with him required patience and persistence. One day in March, his spokesman, Michael Drewniak, stopped by press row.

"Do you want to meet the governor?" he asked. "I'm not guaranteeing anything."

We went downstairs, past several layers of state troopers, and into his outer office. We waited. Finally we got the nod to come in.

"Governor," I said, "nice to meet you." We shook hands. His are fleshy, and his grip is strong. Very strong. My hand hurt for a few minutes afterward.

Christie is five feet eleven inches tall and round in the middle—that's the first thing you notice. He fills out his suit—which is always dark, with a New Jersey–shaped American flag pin on the lapel. Under the suit is invariably a white cuff-linked shirt, monogrammed "CJC," and a colorful, conservative tie. His skin tone is Sicilian beige with a touch of red, prone to grayness when he's tired or under the weather. His nose slopes down like a short but steep double diamond to a bulbous end. He talks close to you, if you're both standing. He tilts his head slightly downward, and his bright blue eyes peer so intently at yours that it looks as if he is penetrating your soul and deciding it bores him.

But he also downshifts. Maybe you're sitting down together, as we were in his office that day in 2011. He leaned back in his chair, crossed his hands behind his head, and smiled, charmingly and casually. "So, how did you pull the short straw and have to start following me around?" he asked, with a self-deprecation I hadn't expected.

I told him that I was instructed to "cover him as if he was the president of the world." I wasn't sure what that meant, exactly, but he laughed.

"Well," he said, "we're going to do our best to keep you entertained."

He joked that he had been clicking on the Christie Chronicles one hundred times a day, and he acknowledged that he couldn't handle the comments under the online posts—"it's not good for the psyche."

Years later Christie recounted this moment in a speech at the annual Trenton Legislative Correspondents Club dinner. "He came in to see me. Sat down in my office with me. I said, 'Man, this is gonna be the crappiest job you've ever gotten in your entire life! We're gonna be boring, man, there's nothing you're going to have to cover.' Now Matt Katz is on TV more than I am!"

When I appeared as a guest on cable news shows, I was there only because everyone wanted to talk about the "potential presidential candidate" I covered. He was a politician approaching liftoff, and we were all watching to see where he went.

Christie watched me watching him. Sometimes, he'd privately let me know what he thought about my reporting, pontificating and live-tweeting. But almost all of our conversations took place in public, with an audience, which is an odd way to get to know someone. These interactions were usually respectful, sometimes funny, and fundamentally adversarial.

He read his own press, at least he did in the first term. One way he responded was by putting me in the "Penalty Box" without explanation for an unspecified period of time. "Sorry," a Christie source once texted me, "not allowed to talk to you right now."

Other times he reacted more directly. After a campaign event one day at a diner, Christie muttered to me as I walked by: "Come see me after." He did not look happy.

I went outside and waited under a steady rain by his pair of SUVs.

Christie bounded out of the diner. "Dan, put him in the car," the governor said to his personal aide, Dan Robles, who had traveled with him everywhere since the first campaign. Dan opened the door, and I got in the back. Dan stayed outside. Christie came around and sat in the passenger seat, next to a state police trooper who looked forward, and remained silent, for the next ten minutes. In one singular motion Christie turned around toward me and extended his index finger.

There were no formalities as the governor effectively communicated his problem with something I reported.

When I stepped out of the SUV ten minutes later, Dan was still standing there, in the rain. He was very wet when he took my place in the backseat.

FOR THE FIRST of two interviews the governor agreed to do for this book I met him at an expensive Midtown Manhattan restaurant in the dead of a weekday afternoon. During the interview my pen busted, spilling black ink on my hands. The governor didn't notice.

But he did. A few minutes later, as I questioned one of his stories—saying I hadn't found people to corroborate it—he came back with a quick jab. "Well of course they're not going to tell you!" he said. "C'mon, you've got ink all over your hands, they're not going to tell you anything! Amazing I'm still at the table after that performance."

Team Christie packaged that sharp-edged personality into digestible digital formats, distilling his gubernatorial id to build his brand for a future presidential campaign. Beginning with a viral video of an argument the first-year governor got into with an elementary school art teacher—thrilling, to some, to see an elected official put a union employee in her place—Christie became the first bona fide American YouTube politician. He had an unusual physical appearance and sound bites galore—a perfect man for this digital moment. Without YouTube, his closest advisers told me, Christie would have never become a "potential presidential candidate" as quickly as he did.

One of the first videos to go viral was in May 2010, at the start of his term, after Tom Moran, the editorial page editor at the state's largest paper, the *Star-Ledger*, asked Christie how he'd get anything done with such a "confrontational tone."

Christie went off, using a line that became his most famous put-down of a reporter: "Ya know, Tom? You must be the thinnest-skinned guy in America. You think that's confrontational, you should see me when I'm *really* pissed!" Christie said politicians were meant to argue—that was the point. "This is who I am," he told reporters. "Like it or not you guys are stuck with me for four years. And I'm going to say things directly. When you guys ask me questions I am going to answer them directly, straightly, bluntly. And nobody in New Jersey is gonna have to wonder where I am on an issue."

In reality Christie dodged when asked for reactions to hot-button national issues that he didn't want to talk about. And he often weaved when asked about possibly corrupt political allies. But Republicans nonetheless loved the "you must be the thinnest-skinned guy in America" shot against the media, with commentator Glenn Beck calling it "conservative porn."

"I never found him erotic before," Beck said, as orgasm sounds played on his radio show, "but now all of a sudden . . ."

Bill Palatucci, Christie's longest-serving political confidant, told me that for months afterward, as the men traveled the country in Christie's new role as campaigner for GOP candidates, folks repeated those words to him. *You must be the thinnest-skinned guy in America.* Through that one line, they felt "like they got to know this guy and got to understand him," Palatucci said.

In the beginning of his term, Christie communications director Maria Comella couldn't get the governor on *Meet the Press*. YouTube fixed that. Christie doubled his communications staff—reaching a taxpayer-funded payroll of about $1.4 million a year—so staffers could be dispatched to every public event armed with video cameras, boom mics, and laptops, cutting and clipping Christie's appearances into mini-movies emailed out to the world before reporters could even file their stories to their editors.

The videos attracted the attention of news shows, which invited Christie on set in New York, where he'd sit for interviews that created more YouTube moments. Comella picked her spots, using TV for when her boss had a message to sell, like a big budget initiative, and preferring to bunch the appearances into single mornings—four interviews on four networks in fewer than four hours had the potential to dominate a single news cycle. He'd cross the tunnel into Manhattan the night before, get a room at a hotel in Midtown so he could sleep a little extra, and then get up while it was still dark to head to the green rooms. The exercise was critical to preparing to be a presidential candidate.

Comella soon brought on a digital director, Lauren Fritts. They commuted together every day from their apartments in Manhattan—ninety minutes to Trenton and ninety minutes back, tucked in a Toyota Prius talking shop and choreographing Christie. The videos they produced were ostensibly about promoting specific issues, but they were also about promoting the man, capturing the eyes of network producers and the ears of conservative talk radio hosts.

Before the governor's 2012 budget address they created a mock movie trailer that began in black-and-white on Route 295 outside Trenton. It's a stormy day, and the music is ominous.

Then Christie emerges from the SUV at the Statehouse and wind chimes play in the score, signaling optimism. He is at work—in a cabinet meeting, shaking hands at a construction site, speaking at a farm, walking the boardwalk, saluting a soldier. "Sometimes you may look at me and think I'm spoiling for a fight," he says. "Not all the time, but I'll tell you this: I'm going to fight for the things that are worth fighting for . . . ladies and gentlemen, this is it. What you see is what you get."

He wasn't a governor. He was *The Governor*. That's how every one of his 2013 reelection campaign commercials ended: "Chris Christie, The Governor." They did a poll in Connecticut once. "Who's the Connecticut governor?" they asked. "Chris Christie," most said. The aura from New Jersey was beginning to seep into America.

The videos alone didn't do the trick. Distribution was key. Christie's office maintained a contact list of people who received the videos every day. I thought the list, created by government employees, should be public information. Christie's lawyers disagreed.

"You guys want everything," Christie told us once. "You're not entitled to everything."

When I left the *Philadelphia Inquirer* in 2013 and moved over to WNYC, the National Public Radio member station, we sued for the You-Tube press list. We got it, four and a half years after the initial request. It contained email addresses for twenty-five hundred journalists and TV producers, broken into tiers for national columnists, Sunday show producers, Spanish language TV, and more. At eighty-eight contacts, FOX News was most represented. For when something had to get out there quickly, there was a "push list" of reporters active on Twitter, like me. Comedy Central's *The Daily Show* was on the list, as was the conservative opposition research group America Rising.

Controlling the message. That's what carefully creating this list—and keeping it from me—was all about.

The culture of secrecy was enforced across all state agencies. Overtime costs for state troopers were kept under wraps. Budgetary information readily available in prior administrations was no longer released. The names of those who flew on Christie's helicopter, visited the governor's mansion, and attended Giants and Jets games in the gubernatorial suite were all state secrets. The amount it cost taxpayers to subsidize his political travels around the country could never be fully accounted for because the administration refused to release complete records, citing security reasons.

It wasn't supposed to be like this. Less than six minutes into his inaugural address, Christie's very first policy promise was this: "Today a new era of accountability and transparency is here."

Christie had other priorities. Comella mandated her staff reach annual goals on increasing the governor's Twitter followers and Facebook likes. My tweets about Christie were flagged by a $55,000-a-year "research analyst" in the governor's office and emailed to outside political advisers. I got more complaints from Christie's people over my quickly scribed tweets than from the long stories in the newspaper or on the radio that I had worked on for weeks. Team Christie knew that quickly disseminating information it liked—and quietly stifling information it didn't—was the name of the political communication game, now and always.

**SOON ENOUGH CHRISTIE** got famous. He and his wife, Mary Pat, were going on double dates with the likes of Mr. and Mrs. Howard Stern and Mr. and Mrs. Matt Lauer. At the annual White House Correspondents' Dinner, Christie was lampooned more than any other governor but then partied until the wee hours with George Clooney. There he was, "Dad dancing" on stage with Jimmy Fallon, and at a party in the Hamptons, gyrating on the dance floor with actor Jamie Foxx.

Christie crashed at Jon Bon Jovi's pad that night in the Hamptons. He also had sleepovers at Facebook founder Mark Zuckerberg's house.

"I've never had trouble making friends, of any kind, in my life," Christie told me. For twenty years, Christie organized his class's high school reunions. "For people who are important to me in my life, I pay attention to them," he said. "Now that I'm a celebrity, celebrities are no different than anyone else."

He spends so much time at friendships that it bothered his wife, Mary Pat. "But I'm better at it than she is," he told me. "I think that's what really frustrates her. I have a lot more friends than she does."

Christie is always on his iPhone with one friend or another. "So when Bono got in his accident, I texted him right away, 'How are you doing, are you doing okay? You need anything?'" he said. "But if my friend Bill Giuliano from high school had gotten into an accident, I would've done the same thing."

Christie and U2 front man Bono met in 2011, in the kingdom of Jordan, where they partied with Jordanian king Abdullah II. Christie met Abdullah through New York mayor Michael Bloomberg at a men-only dinner party Bloomberg threw in 2010, attended by the likes of former British prime minister Tony Blair and the Rolling Stones' Mick Jagger. "It was pretty amazing," Christie said.

Abdullah and Christie soon realized that they each had four children, two girls and two boys, all about the same age. "So we started talking about kids, and this and that," Christie said, and thereafter he got a note from Abdullah inviting the Christies to Jordan. So in 2012, on the back end of a government trip to Israel, the whole Christie family was picked up by the Jordanian army and flown to the king's home at the Red Sea, across from Israel and Egypt and next door to Saudi Arabia. They were taken to the five-star Kempinski Hotel in Aqaba—the royal family picked up the tab—and that night, a dinner was thrown for the Christies. Then Bono came by.

The Christies, the Abdullahs, and Bono spent the weekend together.

The next day they barbecued by the Red Sea at the royal pool as all the kids jet-skied and maneuvered Segways around the property. At night, they flew out to Wadi Rum, the geological spectacle where much of *Lawrence of Arabia* was filmed, and the king threw a party as the kids rode ATVs through the desert.

At some point, Bono and Christie shared the mic. They dueted "Hotel California." In the desert. In front of the king. When Christie told me about this moment, there was a glimmer in his eye, like: *Can you believe how awesome my life is?*

"He needs to be in the action all the time," one longtime intimate told me. "He's addicted to the attention."

Christie had become the American Governor—personifying a media-focused, celebrity-obsessed, blunt-talking U.S. of A. This Christie phenomenon was no longer about the state that had created him.

On the last morning of his visit to Jordan, the king himself drove Christie to the helicopters, where he flew to a private jet—paid for by Sheldon Adelson, the casino magnate and pro-Israel GOP kingmaker. A few years later Christie would draw front-page scrutiny for the conflicts of interest inherent in his journey to the desert, but that was part of the deal with Christie. He had long enjoyed perks—and long gotten into trouble for them.

As U.S. Attorney, the federal Office of the Inspector General found that he spent more money on travel than any of his colleagues, exceeding the maximum government rate twenty-three times.

"I try to squeeze all the juice out of the orange that I can," he once said.

# PART ONE

# THE CHRISTIE MYSTIQUE

# 1

# A PERENNIAL CANDIDATE

In 1666 the greater Newark area was purchased by Puritan settlers from a group of Native Americans for 100 bars of lead, 20 axes, 10 swords, 4 blankets, 4 barrels of beer, 50 knives, 20 hoes, 20 gallons of booze, 3 coats, and a whole lot of shell beads.

Settlers erected log cabins out of the oak trees in the northern New Jersey forest. Land was harvested, dead trees were carved into drainpipes, and a church was built. During Sunday services two armed men stood on guard to watch for invading Native Americans. Town meetings were held, a cemetery was created, and a tax collector was appointed. Men ignited controlled fires to clear brush and build roads deeper into the woods. A tavern, a grist mill, and a school opened.

In the 1700s the first of dozens of tanneries went into business, establishing Newark as a manufacturing center that soon produced cider, shoes, and carriages. The town ballooned from fewer than one thousand people in 1776 to thirty-nine thousand in 1850—thanks in part to an influx of Germans who arrived following a revolution in the German state known as the Grand Duchy of Baden.

Despite the shadow of New York City to its east, Newark became a place on the map—a draw for immigrants and a center of the Industrial Revolution. When Thomas Edison moved there and started making telegraphs, Christie's ancestors began arriving from Germany, Scotland, Ireland, and Italy.

They came from small towns. They were all Catholic, and they crossed the Atlantic Ocean to settle in Newark during a span of about fifty years, from the 1860s to the early twentieth century. They lacked schooling but learned to speak and read English within a generation, census records show.

Women were homemakers. Men toiled in hard, calluses-on-your-hands physical labor, factory work in plastics, leather, beer, and sheet iron, for minimal wages.

That's when there was work—for stretches, young men in his family went unemployed. Struggles lasted two, sometimes three generations.

For a century, Newark was home.

CHRISTINE, A YOUNG girl six years old from the Grand Duchy of Baden, her maiden name lost to history, found herself in this bustling place on the Passaic River with its very own German newspaper. She learned to speak, read, and write English. She married a milk dealer named Charles Winter, who hailed from the same region in southwest Germany. Together they had ten children, including a boy named John.

Zeriak Lott was a tanner who came over from Germany on a ship called the *Labrador*. He married Walburgh Ernst in 1853. They, too, had ten children, seven of whom survived and were baptized at St. Benedict's Church, which served Germans in eastern Newark. In a picture from the late 1800s, the children are in black frocks while Zeriak wears a thick dark suit and sports an unruly goatee that reaches toward the middle of his chest. Walburgh has a cherubic face that is vaguely reminiscent of the future governor's.

The Lotts' daughter, Carolyn, married the Winters' son, John. Their daughter Carrie went to school until the eighth grade and married, at eighteen, James Christie, the son of an Irish mother and Scottish father, whose alcoholism led to unemployment and, eventually, to a Newark boarding-house. James dropped out of school in the sixth grade and supported his family at a factory, making belts used in manufacturing. He worked all the time.

"Dad was a serious dude," his son, Wilbur, said.

Wilbur Christie, the governor's father, first met Sondra Grasso, the governor's mother, in middle school at the end of World War II. She was a flag twirler at West Side High School. He was a cheerleader at Hillside High.

But Sondra, at age nineteen, married another man, who beat her. They never had children, and in 1960 their nine-year marriage ended in divorce. Shortly after that she reunited with Wilbur at a dance, they married, and by 1962 she was pregnant with Wilbur's first son.

Wilbur was an honors student who went to work at seventeen to support his family after his father died. He served in the U.S. Army during the Korean War and then tried out broadcasting in 1955, taking classes at Columbia University on the GI Bill. Once a week, he worked at NBC in Midtown Manhattan. When broadcasting didn't work out he transferred to Rutgers University, making ends meet at Newark's Breyers Ice Cream plant as a salesman and sign-shop supervisor. After college, he became an accountant.

At least that's how Wilbur tells the story to interviewers.

To hear Christie tell his father's life story—and it's one of his favorite life stories to tell—Wilbur's attainment of the American Dream begins with an older guy on the line at the Breyers factory who personally brought the elder Christie to Newark's Rutgers University campus to sign him up for classes. "You're a smart young guy, what are you gonna do with your life?" the man said to Wilbur.

"I like this job, it's a good job. I like working at the ice cream plant."

"Son, this ice cream plant ain't going to be here forever. You're too smart to do this. Go to college. You're a veteran. Take advantage of the GI Bill. Go to college at night."

Wilbur took night classes at Rutgers for seven years, the first in his family to go to college. In June 1962, he graduated, and the Christies took a family picture—Wilbur wore his cap and gown, and Sondra was six months pregnant with Christopher.

FIFTY-TWO YEARS LATER, the spring of 2014, and the baby in that belly was at another college graduation in New Jersey. The governor was giving the commencement address at Rowan University. But there was a rainstorm, forcing graduation into several smaller indoor ceremonies. Christie got the engineering students. The auditorium was half filled. Still, he delivered the most moving speech of his political life, telling the story of his mother's side of the family.

Christie said that Sondra's mother, Anne Grasso, was born on a boat immigrating from Sicily to the United States. Anne's parents, Salvatore and Minnie Scavone, were old-school disciplinarians who selected Anne's husband in an arranged marriage to Philip Grasso, a chauffeur and factory worker. They had three kids. Then she found out he was being unfaithful. "Now at that time, in that culture, that was something women were expected to accept," Christie told the students. "But this woman had absolutely no intention of accepting that. In fact she did the exact *opposite*. She kicked him out of the house, and filed for divorce. In *1942*."

Records show their union dissolved, at least officially, in 1945. The divorce papers blamed Philip for "desertion." "She was thirty-three years old," Christie remembered. "She had no education at all past middle school. She now had three children to raise on her own because the family she had been arranged into said it was a disgrace that she filed for divorce. And there were no laws at that time forcing them, or her husband, to support them or her children. So what did she do? She went out and looked for a job."

Anne, all five feet of her, got a job at the War Department, and then a lawyer's office, and finally as a customer service representative at the Internal Revenue Service in Bloomfield, two hours and three buses away from Newark, Christie explained. She left at 6:00 a.m. every day and didn't come home until 7:00 p.m.

"Every year at Christmas, they rewrapped the gift they had gotten the year before, and that's what they were given for Christmas because they had no money," he told the engineering students. "Many nights they went to bed hungry—but no nights did they go to bed alone. They had each other. This woman worked without a support system except for her own belief in herself."

Growing up, Chris was closer to Nani, as he called her, than anyone. He'd stay at her apartments on weekends. They'd go to the library—Nani got three books for herself, Chris got one—and he was allowed to watch two shows: college football on Saturday and *Meet the Press* on Sunday.

"She taught me that your life is not determined by what you don't have, but by what you are willing to do," he said. "She never remarried. Yet she had a full life."

Nani, a fan of Democratic president Franklin Delano Roosevelt, took Chris on jaunts to New York City, where they went to the opera ("Imagine me at the opera—even then it seemed incredible") and to the Museum of Broadcasting, where he once watched a video of the inaugural address of the first Catholic president, Democrat John F. Kennedy. Young Chris remembered the words he heard JFK say that day: "Let us never negotiate out of fear, but let us never fear to negotiate."

Christie recounted to the rapt audience of graduates, many of them children of immigrants, what Nani told him on her deathbed: "I was born on a boat coming over here, no education, nothing but my own hard work and what I was able to create for myself through the grace of this country— and now *you're* being appointed to something by the president of the United States. My life is full."

Census records, Italian ship manifestos, and Anne's own obituary indicate that Nani was almost certainly born in Brooklyn in 1909—not on the boat from Italy, as he claimed she told him as she died. He later confirmed this factual error through an intermediary, and then in subsequent speeches changed the story so Anne's ex-husband, Philip Grasso, the son of Italian immigrants Santo and Santa Grasso, became the one born on the boat from Italy. This claim also couldn't be confirmed by census records, but it is far more plausible.

So did Nani really take three buses each way to work? Did they really rewrap old Christmas gifts? And does it matter, really? For rhetorical flourish or just because of familial memory lapses, Christie added drama to an already dramatic story.

Christie told the graduates that his story is their story. "Because of everything else you've achieved here, I believe you too will experience a great American life," he said. "Just like my grandmother did. Just like I have. Though very different, they're both great American lives. And you will now write your own story."

Christie had already written Anne's American story. Now he had to finish writing his own.

CHRISTIE ONCE RUMINATED on his beginnings to a New Jersey crowd at a town hall meeting. "I don't know what my mother and father were thinking the day they brought me home from the hospital, but I can bet that they weren't thinking: 'There sits the fifty-fifth governor of the state of New Jersey.' Probably not. They were still mortified they named me Chris Christie."

Christopher James Christie was born September 6, 1962, at Beth Israel Hospital in Newark, surprising his parents, who were expecting a little girl. They were going to name him James Christopher—after Wilbur's dad—but Wilbur's older brother, James Christopher, Jr., was also expecting a child who was to be named James Christopher III. So Wilbur flipped the names around to Christopher James. Not until Nani got to the hospital and said, "Look at little Chris Christie!" did his parents realize what they had done.

The Christies came home from the hospital to a fourth-floor walk-up apartment at South Orange Avenue and South Fourteenth Street in Newark, across from West Side High School, his mother's alma mater. By the time Christie became governor nearly five decades later, his childhood home was a trash-strewn vacant lot next to a bombed-out apartment building. Walking along Route 510 takes you through increasingly well-off suburbs—

to Livingston, where the Christies would soon move, to Morristown, the Morris County seat where he would serve in his first elected office, to tony Mendham, his eventual home. To get from his first apartment to the mansion where he would be living when launching his presidential bid—to go from one America to another America—it's just twenty-two miles and one left turn.

IN THE FALL of 1966, Newark was an increasingly diverse city undergoing economic collapse—twenty thousand manufacturing jobs, which had brought so many southern blacks up north, evaporated. Civic unrest was spreading through the nation's cities, the temperature on Newark's streets was rising, and the Christies were leaving.

On September 2, 1966, Wilbur and Sondra signed the paperwork to buy their first home in suburban Livingston. Christopher turned four years old days later.

The following summer the arrest of a black taxicab driver in Newark and rumors that the driver had been murdered by the cops set off six days of clashes with police. The resulting violence ended in twenty-six deaths, more than $15 million in property damage, and the acceleration of white flight to the nearby suburbs. Mid-twentieth-century demographic changes happened more rapidly in Newark than in all but two cities in the country.

Government helped the Christies bounce from working class to middle class. Wilbur, a military veteran who went to college on the GI Bill, landed a $22,500 Veterans Administration mortgage, records show. He and Sondra borrowed $1,000 each from their mothers—including Nani, who had a government job. That got them almost all of the way to the $25,000 price tag for their house in Livingston.

Livingston's population, which tripled between 1950 and 1970, was almost entirely white. The Christies' black neighbors from Newark did not follow to Livingston, likely due to racist mortgage practices and discriminatory zoning. Newark withered over the next decades, suffering from depopulation and economic depression. Livingston thrived, with the value of Christie's childhood home appreciating at two and a half times the rate of inflation.

Christie has often said that he would have never become governor if his parents had stayed in Newark.

• • •

**THE HOUSE AT** 327 West Northfield Road was just thirteen hundred square feet, with a fenced-in backyard and an above-ground pool. Christie's brother, Todd, was two years younger, and they would be as close as brothers can be, deeply protective of each other. Chris has a story about knocking a kid out who messed with Todd, and someone who knew both men told me Todd was "the most loyal brother I ever met, and lived entirely to promote his brother's well-being."

Loyalty was bred in the small bedroom they shared. They talked every night before bed. They both loved sports, but they retained their identities in part by picking their own teams. Todd rooted for the St. Louis Cardinals in baseball, and Chris became a Dallas Cowboys fan after watching Roger Staubach throw the football on TV in the 1970s.

Eventually, it wasn't just Chris and Todd. After Sondra had three miscarriages, the Christies adopted a little girl, Dawn. The social worker first brought over a picture of Dawn in a Raggedy Ann dress, and noted that she was half Puerto Rican. That didn't matter. "I want her," Sondra said. "This is our daughter."

Dawn was never the "adopted sister"—"she's our sister," they would say. Chris, ten years older, became her second father. All three kids would each go on to have four children of their own, settling down in the same town in northwestern New Jersey.

Wilbur was an accountant at Wall Street investment firms, eventually becoming a partner. Sondra took a job as a receptionist at the offices of the Livingston school district, a post she had for twenty-five years, during which time she was a member of the same teachers' union that her son would become famous for lambasting as governor. Chris went to work, too, as a teenager. First at a gas station, then at a shoe store.

The house was strict, and things could get loud. The family put it all out there—hugging big and hard, and fighting big and hard.

Sondra, they called her Sandy, and Wilbur, they called him Bill, argued about all kinds of things, constantly pushing each other's buttons. Their fights could be frivolous, or serious: Sandy's brother once told interviewers that Bill took a secret second mortgage out to cover a big loss in the stock market.

Yelling reverberated through the walls of the boys' bedroom. At night they lay in their twin beds maybe fifteen feet from their parents, talking to each other and listening during the fighting. "The milk was sour, they would yell at each other," Christie remembered. "That was just the personalities they had."

Relatives have said Chris was the mediator in the parental disputes, often taking his mother's side and consoling his younger siblings.

Chris attributed his mother's personality to her Sicilian descent, which "has made me not unfamiliar with conflict."

"You had to learn how to argue or you got run over," he said. For his father, he used a different metaphor: "A passenger in the automobile of life."

Mom was the driver. "I think because the women in my life have been the predominant influence, that it makes me that much more comfortable with my own emotions," Christie once told a reporter. "I think, in general, women are better at that."

As an adult Christie got visibly amped up by confrontation, quick with a return jab to any perceived slight. But he did not yell with regularity. The threat of his wrath was powerful enough.

"You're a kid who grows up in that atmosphere you either become a yeller and screamer, like you mimic," Christie said. "Or you go like, 'Uhhh, not me.' And I have the capacity to do it when I want to, but most of the time I do it for effect."

To explain himself to New Jerseyans, to let people know *why he is the way he is*—why he isn't a "blow-dried politician"—he talks about his mom.

"The greatest lesson Mom ever taught me. . . . She told me there would be times in your life when you have to choose between being loved and being respected," he said. "She said to always pick being respected, that love without respect was always fleeting—but that respect could grow into real, lasting love."

"Now of course she was talking about women," he quipped, before adding: "I believe we"—politicians—"have become paralyzed by our desire to be loved."

ONE DAY AT Meadowbrook Little League Field in Livingston there was a new kid on the team, a boy who had missed half the baseball season due to a bout of rheumatic fever.

The catcher walked over to the boy and introduced himself as Chris Christie. "Harlan Coben, how are ya?" Chris asked. "Nice to have you back."

Coben, who later became a best-selling novelist, remembered a young boy who acted like a charming adult. He said that young Chris did impressions of their teachers and was "the glue" on their intramural basketball team at Heritage Junior High, encouraging poor players. "If you were to ask who in our class would end up being governor," Corben reminisced to me, "most people would tell you Chris Christie."

Teammates from his Little League and high school baseball years called him a player-coach who knew who to pat on the butt and who to kick in the butt. "If I whiffed or something, or had a little bit of a bad day, he would put his arm around me and say, 'Hey, Jules, you'll get 'em next time,'" remembered Bill "Jules" Giuliano. That continued later in life. "He would be the first person people would turn to for advice. . . . Whether it was something they wanted to hear or didn't want to hear, he had a way of pressing the right buttons."

Baseball was his sport. He once won MVP on a youth baseball team after being hit by a pitch with the bases loaded in a championship game. Another year he wrote a letter to the weekly Livingston newspaper to publicly thank his two coaches.

Chris was starting catcher on the high school team. He wasn't fleet of foot (he once got picked off third while celebrating a triple that probably should have been an inside-the-park home run), but he had pop in his bat and he called a good game.

His senior year, a catcher headed for pro ball transferred to Livingston High. Now that kid was *really* good, and Christie was demoted to the bench and a designated hitter role.

The Christie family considered legal action. "It was one of the first real disappointments in life I had to deal with," Christie said. "But it was a great lesson for me."

One way he dealt with it: He had a good cry, according to the team's star pitcher. "He was just crushed," Scott Parsons said. "But to his credit, he didn't leave the team." Not just that, Chris was elected captain, and the Livingston Lancers became state champs.

At a banquet to celebrate the championship, the Livingston High tennis coach got up and referenced Christie's selflessness: "I want a kid like that on all of our teams every year."

Chris got a standing ovation.

**IN EIGHTH GRADE** Christie lost a bid for student council president of Heritage Junior High by just two votes. Why? Not only didn't he vote for himself—he voted for the girl he was running against. "I thought at that time that it was conceited to vote for myself," he said.

When he ran for class president of the ninth grade, he voted for himself and won. Then it was off to Livingston High School, where Chris was president of his class in tenth, eleventh, and twelfth grades. He was an active president, too, credited with organizing the prom, moving graduation to the football field, and lobbying for off-campus lunch. "Great Hopes make Great Men" was his yearbook quote, and he wrote this message to his girlfriend: *To Melina. You've taken my life into your heart. Our special love will live in my heart forever.*

Not only wasn't it forever, it didn't last until the end of senior year. They went to the prom with other dates. But decades later Melina had only fond memories of the boy who sometimes sent her flowers and cards. "He was a romantic, but we were also good buddies," she told me. "We were very comfortable around one another—he's an easy guy to be comfortable with."

At Livingston High each year, seniors painted their graduation year on the school roof—"80" for 1980. The point was to make it visible from the stands at the football field.

Wilbur, helping with the tradition, bought the paint. Then Chris led the surreptitious charge to the roof so he and his buddies could write "80."

The new school principal wasn't happy. He had the roof painted over, and he summoned Chris to his office. "I would hope you would provide the leadership necessary to let your classmates know that this is not acceptable," the principal said.

Christie agreed, left the office, and found his buddies. That weekend, they repainted "80" on the roof.

**"CHRIS WANTED TO** be a politician," his uncle once said, "when he was a baby."

In second grade Chris ran out the front door of Squiretown Elementary and over to the flagpole. He took Old Glory down for the night and looked up and saw his classmate's mother. "Mrs. Cushman," Chris said, "some day I'm going to be president."

By the third grade Chris was speaking at PTA meetings about field trips and fund-raisers.

In fifth grade he told his grandmother that he wanted a law book for

Christmas. "Oh, *chiacchierone*, this kid is going to be president one day!" Nani said.

At Heritage Junior High School one day in February 1977, the local legislator, Assemblyman Tom Kean, Sr., came in to speak. "The things he was saying, I kind of gut-agreed with," Christie later recalled.

Chris went home and told his mother about his interest in Kean's campaign. So Sandy ordered fourteen-year-old Chris into the car and together they drove to the estate of the Kean family. Chris was nervous.

"What's the worst that could happen?" Sandy said.

Chris got out of the car, knocked on the door of the fancy politician's house, and Kean himself answered. "Sir, I want to get involved in politics and I don't know how to do it, and my mother says I gotta ask you," Chris said.

Kean responded: "I'm thinking of running for governor. If you want to find out, get in the car. I'm going up to Bergen County. Come with me and see if you like it."

They went up to the Oradell VFW Hall, where Chris distributed fliers for Kean before his speech. "I don't remember much else about the evening, except that I just knew I was in the middle of a race for governor," he said. "I was watching it happen, and I thought it was really cool."

That May, a group of Livingston High School students attended a Kean rally in Trenton. The group included Christie and David Wildstein, a Livingston native who would one day order lanes at the George Washington Bridge to be shut down for political revenge.

Christie, Wildstein, and their friends handed out Styrofoam hats that read "Byrned Up? Let's Raise Kean," in reference to Democratic governor Brendan Byrne. On the way home, the boys stopped to buy beer. Chris, fourteen, had his first cold brew after his first political rally.

**AT LIVINGSTON HIGH** School Chris's interest in politics ballooned. He went on a class trip to Washington, D.C., where he took pictures of the White House. One year he was selected to attend the Boys State leadership conference, where he ran for "governor," lost in the primary, and nabbed a senate seat instead. Later he was selected as one of two high school seniors in all of New Jersey to participate in the United States Senate Youth Program. On one hand he got to meet President Jimmy Carter; on the other hand, he got a firsthand lesson in the corrupt tendencies of his home state.

As part of the program, students were supposed to shadow their state's senators for the week. But just as he arrived in Washington the FBI revealed details of the Abscam political bribery scandal, which ensnared several New Jersey politicians, including Senator Harrison Williams, whom Christie was supposed to spend the week with. When the news broke, Williams pulled his participation in the program, so Christie shadowed Democratic senator Bill Bradley instead.

"We were the butt of jokes all week," Christie remembered. The burden of New Jersey political corruption fell on his shoulders, as it often would.

CHRISTIE AND HIS Livingston High friends hung out at the Heritage Diner on weekend nights, a suburban teenage ritual. They did plenty of talking and laughing but maybe not a whole lot of ordering of food. So the owner kicked 'em all out, and created a new rule: You don't order food, you can't sit here all night."

Chris was furious. "Are you kidding me? Ninety percent of us are ordering food!"

So he organized a boycott. He wrote a letter to the editor of the local paper. And he passed out leaflets. For weeks, the kids stopped going to the Heritage Diner and hung out at another diner in the next town. Business at the Heritage plummeted.

One day, several weeks later, Chris stopped at the diner alone. He sat at the counter. The owner of the diner came over. "Chris, this has to stop!" he pleaded.

They negotiated an agreement: The whole group can stay as long as two teens order food—and tip their waitresses. Deal.

Everyone returned to the Heritage Diner the following weekend. Chris had negotiated his first political deal, and emerged with more power than ever before.

IN THE FALL of 1980, Christie headed to college. He had been rejected by Georgetown University, but he found a college closer to home. The only years of his life when Christie didn't live in New Jersey were spent as a political science major at the nearby University of Delaware. Freshman year, he sent in a mail-in ballot from Harrington E Residence Hall for Ronald Reagan for president. It was his first vote.

In college, Christie took a poetry class. But he was focused on politics. His political science professor, James Magee, said that Christie "took a genuine and very deep interest in" his class on civil rights and liberties.

And while Christie often disagreed with his professor and other classmates, "his responses were sophisticated and respectful of views that differed from his own."

Christie first got involved in student politics helping out a friend and future Christie gubernatorial appointee, Rick Mroz, win the class presidency. Christie then chaired the lobbying committee within student government, organizing opposition to President Reagan's proposed cuts to a student loan program, personally lobbying Delaware senator Joe Biden, the future vice president, in Washington. He also set up phone banks so students could call congressional offices. "Our goal is to tie up the switchboards," he said at the time. When one such effort didn't pan out because only forty-one students turned out to make calls, Christie told the *Review*, the student newspaper, that the lack of involvement was "goddamned terrible."

Christie joined the Resident Student Association and became president of his dorm. On the second day of sophomore year he was visiting a friend in another dorm and met a freshman named Mary Pat Foster. "I introduced myself because I thought she was cute, and she said hello, and that was it," he said.

A year later, they ran into each other at a party. She was a student government geek, too, but they were both dating other people. When he made his own run for president of the Delaware Undergraduate Student Congress, he put her on his ticket as a candidate for class secretary. They ran as the Campus Action Party, with a platform that called for "breaking out of old molds" to deal with problems.

Christie's ticket took the campaign seriously. His brother, Todd, now a student himself at the University of Delaware, was a key volunteer. The campaign distributed fliers, bought ads in the student newspaper, and worked the dorms. When one of Christie's speeches droned on, Todd signaled for him to cut it off by moving his hands to his neck. "Chris is an incredible politician," Todd remembered. "But every politician talks too much."

Displaying a political sophistication well beyond his years, Christie focused on wooing student groups, because their members voted at greater rates, and he became friendly with the editor of the *Review*, which endorsed him: *"Christie's efforts in Washington, D.C. and Dover to campaign for student financial aid were more than admirable for a student carrying a full credit load, and his hard work to try to place a student on the Board of Trustees against impossible odds was, although unsuccessful, nothing short of remarkable."*

"Chris approached it like a professional politician," his opponent, Lee Uniacke, said.

"Like, they had a platform," remembered Kathleen Tregnaghi, who was running for vice president from the opposing party. "There was a debate, and he got dressed. He wore, like, a suit and tie."

One of Christie's top campaign promises was to raffle away free tuition for the spring semester, paid for by the Student Congress. He took out an ad in the personals section of the newspaper: DO YOU WANT A CHANCE AT FREE TUITION? VOTE, CHRIS CHRISTIE FOR DUSC PRESIDENT.

Christie won with 61.7 percent of the vote, and pledged a "productive" year.

That it was. President Christie put a referendum on the ballot to create a ten-dollar-per-semester "student activities fee" to help fund student groups. The measure passed by a five-to-one margin.

Christie quoted John F. Kennedy to successfully push for the creation of teacher evaluations for students to reference in selecting courses. Thirty years later, teacher evaluations would be a centerpiece of the governor's education reforms.

"He was always on," one former classmate told me. "He was always working the room. He was always analyzing the shift of power in a room. He would see it in an instant. It was really impressive. He was really agile. He was really quite smart."

Christie once told a classmate that he had learned "how to tell if someone is going to fuck with me from a hundred yards away." This ability was viewed by that classmate as "a presence-slash-arrogance beyond his years."

When anti-Semitic literature was found distributed on campus, Christie made the kind of bellicose comments he would one day become famous for, calling those responsible "ignorant idiots." Then he followed up with an editorial in the student newspaper citing an incident he had just witnessed at the Student Center: "A white student passed a group of black sorority pledges and grumbled an expletive and the word 'nigger.' . . . If we were to start a movement of understanding, caring, compassion and guts, others would surely follow . . . we must all believe that a campus free of racial prejudice is worth fighting for." Christie then created a diversity committee— made up of Mary Pat, the president of the Gay and Lesbian Student Union, and a women's rights activist, among others—that issued recommendations on "cross-cultural education."

Christie mentored younger student politicians, explaining after meetings what they had done right and wrong, and sharing credit for successes. But he had his critics. He was accused of filling up the student congress with allies (one letter to the editor was headlined, "Christie Cronyism?") and employing a top-down approach that muzzled debate and led five student leaders to quit. When Mary Pat Foster ran unopposed for president in the election to succeed him, Christie boasted: "We're not having an election, we're having a coronation."

For that election, Christie's brother, Todd, as chairman of the Election Committee, proposed cutting the number of days to vote and reducing the number of polling places. As the *Review* put it: "Chris Christie bequeathed to Mary Pat Foster an office he feels has finally gained some respect." The paper said she had "rather large shoes to fill."

Christie told the press, simply: "Mary Pat is a good person."

They were dating by then, of course. The relationship started in February of his senior year, right after Mary Pat had returned from a five-week college session in Europe. Christie was hanging out in a booth with some buddies at the Deer Park Tavern, a bar so old that George Washington himself was said to have slept there. Christie saw a woman on the dance floor with short hair. He didn't recognize her.

"And then she turned around and I was like, 'Great! I actually know her,'" Christie remembered. She had cut her hair short while in Europe. "I thought, 'She really looks good!' And I said, 'Now I'm going to go up and dance with her.' So I went up, started talking, danced with her, asked her out that night to go out to dinner the next night."

MARY PAT FOSTER is the ninth of ten children from a Catholic family in Paoli, a small town in Chester County, Pennsylvania, west of Philadelphia. At first Mary Pat thought Chris was "nerdy—but cute." She was attracted to his "humor and intelligence"—"he's always been amazingly smart." When he walked her home and took her hand one night, "that's when I kind of realized it was something different," she said.

"She was fun in a different way than anyone I had ever experienced," Christie remembered. One night they broke into a cafeteria at night "because we smelled that they were baking doughnuts for the next morning." The baker ended up giving them some of his goods.

Nine months after they started dating Chris and Mary Pat were engaged. Mary Pat stayed on at the University of Delaware for senior year while her boyfriend went back to New Jersey to start Seton Hall Law School in Newark. They married in 1986 on Christie's spring break and honeymooned at Couples in Jamaica. He was twenty-three, she was twenty-two.

The Christies began life in a $600-per-month, one-bedroom apartment above a liquor store in the commuter town of Summit. This wasn't exactly the high life. And it wasn't harmonious, either.

Mary Pat had the misfortune of moving in with a fervent New York Mets fan a few weeks before the start of what was arguably the greatest season the franchise ever had. She realized that her new husband watched Mets games every night. Every. Night.

Christie was working part-time at a law firm while going to law school. Mary Pat had originally been an engineering major, but she switched to finance and began a lucrative career trading bonds in a male-dominated field. She was commuting to New York for work and then coming home to the Mets.

"She'd be like, 'Let's talk about our days,' and I'd be like, 'Yeah, let's talk about it while we're watching the game,'" Christie later told interviewers. "So that did not make me popular, and we had any number of dustups in that first six, seven months, that almost all involved the Mets."

CHRISTIE SAID BECAUSE he and Mary Pat were young when they married, "we weren't very mature. I don't know what either one of us thought marriage was exactly going to be like, but what was happening was not what we thought . . . and we had some fairly challenging times—really challenging times." They waited seven years to have kids because "we wanted to be sure, and we didn't want to bring children into a world and a relationship that we didn't think was good and stable."

They made $30,000 between them when they were first getting started—and had accumulated $35,000 in college and law school debt. They were working all the time.

Divorce loomed in Christie's family. His mother and grandmother had divorced; both of his siblings would, too. The Christies went to counseling to work on their relationship—"and I think we have a better marriage because of that." He recommended counseling to friends having problems in their own marriages. "It's kind of like a demilitarized zone you can go through," he said, where an arbiter can call "foul."

Counseling didn't cure everything. "To this day we still have these moments" of tension, he said. "The test of a marriage is: Do you hang in there? It's not that you don't have problems, and that people don't do and say things that they wished they didn't do or say, but how do you recover from that?"

Seven years in, "finally when we felt like we definitely liked each other, *then* we had kids," he said. "And then had four in ten years."

They vowed not to fight in front of the kids, because it scares them, and he said his home became more peaceful than the one he knew back in Livingston. "We argue with each other pretty well, but we have a much different house than the one I grew up in," he told me.

When they need to "air it out" they go to Mary Pat's walk-in closet, the farthest away from the children's rooms. He bemoaned that as governor he couldn't fight in front of the children *or* the state troopers who follow him around, so "it's getting really restricting."

"Think about this: you go to some party with your wife, right? And this invariably happens to every married couple . . . something happens at the party, whatever, that pisses you off. The great moment is when you get in the car and go, *'Are you fucking kidding me?'* And you have it out. So by the time you get home it's washed out. Would you want to do that in front of a New Jersey state trooper?"

No, I told him, I would not. And neither would my wife.

"So what happens is you seethe, you're staring at each other. And then we usually go into her closet to fight."

AFTER THEIR APARTMENT above the liquor store in Summit, the Christies moved to an apartment in a house—this one had a front lawn. They soon bought another house for $160,000, sold it two years later for $140,000 (bad investment), built a new house, sold that, and then moved into a palatial spread hidden by trees off a quiet, winding street in Mendham, Morris County. Children came every few years—Andrew in 1993, and then Sarah, Patrick, and Bridget. The two working parents raised four kids with help from a live-in nanny, a cleaning service, and, eventually, state troopers.

Mary Pat has long maintained that her husband is the same way he is at home as he is in public. "He really is, gosh, he's so forthright and frank," she told an interviewer. "And he's that way with our family. You never have to wonder where he stands, even if it's, 'Can Patrick go to a hockey game at eight o'clock on a Sunday night?' He'll say yes or no, and nine times out of ten we agree."

Mary Pat is a good cook, known for her Dr. Bird Cake—pineapple, apple, walnut. She would also become the family breadwinner, and an important political fund-raiser. A bond trader with a master's in business administration, she earned as much as $475,000 annually as a managing director at the investment firm Angelo, Gordon & Co.

"Listen, I just have three words for you: joint checking account," Christie liked to say. "That money all lands in the same place, baby. It's fine by me."

Weekends at the Christies' always involved sports. They went to Saturday University of Delaware football games, cheering on the Blue Hens with college buddies at the ten-yard line. The festivities started in the lot, for tailgating. Chris brought the Cinnabons, and Mary Pat took over the grill. At some point or another, early on, Christie began a tradition where they all walked to their seats in the stadium in a conga line, waving maracas. "I think we had too much to drink one time, and it became a tradition," Christie said. "Everybody would cheer for us."

Sundays often began with Mass down the road from their home at St. Joseph's Catholic Church, a parish focused on aiding the less fortunate. Mary Pat attended more often than her husband, even teaching Sunday school for a spell. On the Sunday after he was elected governor, Christie brought along state troopers who took communion.

Sunday afternoons meant more sports—often New York Mets games. Christie was such a big fan he brought his lunch to work in a giveaway lunchbox that he got at a game, and he later became friends with the team's owners. But he also threw himself into his kids' athletic events, and was known to razz the refs at his sons' hockey games with barbs like: "You lose your whistle?"

Their oldest, Andrew, was a catcher on his high school varsity squad, like his father. Senior year he was captain, batting an impressive .389. He went on to play baseball at Princeton University, down the road from the governor's mansion.

By the time Christie became a presidential candidate, Sarah was in college, too, at Notre Dame. When she left freshman year Christie wrote her a five- or six-page letter—"about the things I wanted to say to her but couldn't because I knew I would cry."

CHRISTIE WAS WORKING as a commercial litigation attorney when he entered politics for the first time in the early 1990s, at the age of thirty.

He had been registered as a voter in Morris County for just six months. But he was primed with a couple of connections and some personal cash to make an aggressive first move—a run for the state Senate against John

Dorsey, an eighteen-year lawmaker. Christie presented himself as a moderate Republican reformer, pledging to get rid of perks for lawmakers and control political donations.

Some sentences in his campaign materials would sound, twenty years later, downright liberal: "A state legislature in Trenton dominated by men should not be passing laws restricting the rights of women."

In addition to being pro-choice, Christie was antigun: "The issue which has energized me to get into this race is the recent attempt by certain Republican legislators to repeal New Jersey's ban on assault weapons. In today's society, no one needs a semiautomatic assault weapon."

Christie collected 111 signatures to get on the ballot. But Dorsey alleged that most of the signatures were invalid, because they came from non-Republicans or people living in the wrong district. Dorsey dismissed Christie as a "young man" who "doesn't seem to understand the rules of the law."

Defending himself to the *Star-Ledger*, Christie previewed an ad hominem style that would mark his political career. "This is just a perfect example of John Dorsey," Christie said. "He thinks that he has a birthright to this seat and he doesn't want anybody to run against him."

The matter went all the way up to the appellate court, where Christie lost 3–0. And just like that, his first attempt at a political campaign had ended. It lasted nine days.

**THE 1776 NEW** Jersey Constitution said every representative to county government must own property, or "freehold." From there on, despite the unwieldy nature of the word—and the elimination of the property-owning requirement—county representatives in New Jersey would be known as "chosen freeholders."

No other states have such things.

The year after he lost his Senate bid Christie spent $60,000 of his own money to run for the Morris County Board of Chosen Freeholders by promising the same thing that he'd promise voters for decades: saving money by cleaning up government. He partnered with a mentor, Jack O'Keefe, who found Christie "almost magical in his ability to get approval from people."

Christie pledged to eliminate medical coverage for part-time public workers and emphasized his opposition to the practice known as pay-to-play, in which government contractors are chosen by freeholders based on political contributions. Christie accused the incumbent freeholders of giving contracts to cronies, and then paid for an ad during a New Jersey Devils–New York Rangers playoff game in which he personally accused his opponent, a mother of ten named Cecilia "Cissy" Laureys, of "being investigated" for corruption.

In the ad, Christie sits on his couch helping Mary Pat bottle-feed Andrew. Christie wears a tie and no jacket, as if he has just walked in from a long day at the office: "Hi. My name is Chris Christie. . . . The *Daily Record* has called the current incumbents fumbling, bumbling amateurs. And now, they're being investigated by the Morris County prosecutor."

The "investigation" that he claimed his opponents were under was really just "an inquiry" that began over meeting minutes that Laureys claimed didn't exist. There were indeed minutes; Laureys said she made a mistake.

"She knew damn well what I was asking for," Christie said.

No charges or sanctions were filed. Laureys compared Christie to Joseph Goebbels, Hitler's propaganda minister. Decades later Christopher Laureys, Cissy's son, told the *New Yorker*: "This was beyond the pale of what anyone had ever done in politics in Morris County."

But Christie learned a lesson: Attacks work. Christie came in first place in the GOP primary a few days after the ad aired. Laureys sued Christie for defamation, and as part of a settlement Christie published a letter in the newspaper acknowledging the ad was "not accurate." He promised to be "much more sensitive of the impact of such tactics" in future campaigns.

With the primary victory secured in the overwhelmingly Republican county, Christie went on to score his first newspaper endorsement in the general election in Morris County's *Daily Record*. His desire to "conduct county business more openly and make other ethical reforms" was cited. Ethics would become his calling, and his strategy.

Christie nonetheless accepted $6,000 in campaign donations from law firms and engineers that did work for Morris County government on his way to becoming the highest vote-getter in the general election. At his freeholder swearing-in ceremony in January 1995 Christie quoted former Democratic presidential candidate Adlai Stevenson and called on freeholders to take pay cuts and eliminate their health benefits. To set an example he redirected 25 percent of his salary to a local drug treatment facility.

A new, strict code of ethics was needed immediately, he said. Contractors were already trying to bribe him with golf outings, he alleged, so there should be a ban on employees accepting gifts—yes, a ban was already in place, but Christie insisted there was a loophole. Said one veteran politico who watched him on the otherwise staid Morris County freeholder board: "Chris thrives on chaos, and when there isn't any he creates it. There was no ethics issue."

At one freeholder meeting Christie's ethics crusade ended in "an angry name-calling argument," according to a newspaper dispatch.

Eventually, Christie won a small victory: A ban was passed on accepting gifts of more than minimal value from government contractors.

But his attempt to forbid no-bid government contracts failed, and Christie went on to vote for at least 440 no-bid contracts worth more than $10 million. Then he received $17,000 in political contributions from recipients of those contracts.

Nonetheless, he continued to talk tough. When Christie took aim at another recipient of a no-bid contract—the architect of the county jail, whom he implied overcharged the county for his services—Christie was sued for defamation. *Again*. The suit was eventually withdrawn, but Christie got stuck with legal bills.

**A MONTH AFTER** he was sworn in as Morris County freeholder, Christie announced his candidacy for the state assembly, running again on an ethics platform. Christie faced incumbent Republican assemblyman Anthony Bucco, who had just supported Christie's run for freeholder. Christie sought to hold both elected positions simultaneously, and his tactic was to run to Bucco's left on social issues. He called Bucco's support of a repeal of an assault-weapons ban "dangerous," "crazy," and a "radical plan." A Christie campaign flier read: "Vote for safer streets."

Christie also framed himself as a fiscal conservative, even as his claim that he voted against a county budget was debunked by the local paper.

Bucco castigated Christie as a "perennial candidate" who practiced "dirty tricks" and "will say or do anything to get elected."

"If all you need to be a legislator is a lot of money and uncontrolled ambition, then I think the state is in trouble," Bucco said.

Things soon got weird, with Christie denying that he was a millionaire and Bucco denying that he was a Marxist. In one attack ad Christie was depicted as an infant. In another, three men, portraying Christie, literally threw mud all over each other.

Morris County politics didn't normally get like this. "We'll be glad when Tuesday's primary is behind us," bemoaned the *Daily Record* editorial board.

On Election Day interviews at the polls showed that local Republicans had problems with Christie's style. "Christie and his partner, they just gave you a bad taste," one Republican said.

Christie lost. He finished fourth, in last place.

TWO YEARS AFTER the Assembly defeat, Christie ran for reelection as freeholder, and lost. Morris County was done with the brash kid who came out of nowhere, ran for a bunch of offices, caused some havoc on the freeholder board, and kept getting sued.

Local establishment Republicans ignored his concession speech as he delivered it. After he got off stage a local councilman tugged at his sleeve, blew him a kiss, and said: "That's just me kissing your fucking career good-bye."

Christie sued his former opponents in the race for defamation, saying they had falsely accused him of using government funds to defend himself in the *other* defamation suit involving the architect. "I want my reputation back," Christie said.

As part of the settlement, the opponents released a statement clarifying their language. Christie was thrilled, telling a reporter: "We've been able to drag them, kicking and screaming, to the truth."

"The ink wasn't dry on the settlement and Christie was on the phone to the newspapers," griped one of his opponents, John Murphy. "The gloves are off again."

If you're keeping score, that's four elections in four years that triggered four court cases.

"I pretty much decided I would never run for anything again," Christie later said. "I thought to myself, you know, maybe I was not cut out for this. . . . Maybe I have to find another way to be involved in public issues and public life."

But Christie has patience for playing the long game. He would rebuild many of these relationships before his comeback. Former nemeses Laureys and Murphy endorsed him for governor. Even the wife of the man who kissed his fucking career good-bye ended up campaigning for him.

BEFORE, AFTER, AND during his stints in politics, Christie was developing a lucrative legal business. He was working at a small North Jersey law firm, Dughi & Hewit, defending doctors in malpractice cases and handling investment and securities cases. His brother and wife, both Wall Street traders, referred him clients.

Christie also handled appellate matters, which involved taking questions from a panel of judges. This, said former law partner Bill Palatucci, is what helped Christie build the expertise to be so deft at handling questions from reporters and constituents.

Palatucci was a successful New Jersey politico running President George H. W. Bush's 1992 campaign in New Jersey when he first met Christie, a volunteer. The men started a two-man lobbying operation handling a range of policy areas, including banking, Christie's area of expertise. On behalf of the Securities Industry Association they opposed an effort to have securities fraud included in the state's Consumer Fraud Act. Clients included Edison Schools, a for-profit manager of public schools that wanted to increase charter schools in poor New Jersey districts, and the University of Phoenix, a for-profit college that was trying to obtain a higher education license. Christie and Palatucci advocated for energy deregulation and jail privatization.

Palatucci knew his way around the moneyed political world and his was fast becoming the most important relationship in Christie's political life. He provided the Rolodex of connections that helped Christie pivot from the 1990s, when he was a failed local politician, to the 2000s, when he was appointed United States Attorney of New Jersey.

SANDY CHRISTIE, THE blooming politician's strongest link to Newark and the immigrant world he came from, lived just long enough to see that happen.

And just long enough to rib him for it.

"If there were any merit to this selection," she told him after President George W. Bush appointed him U.S. Attorney, "it was because you followed my advice."

Sandy Christie was brassy and brash and a ball-buster. She was, in other words, her son's mother.

"If I've got a problem you're gonna hear about it," she would say.

Sandy was seventy-one when she died. Her obituary was headlined, "A Pillar of Livingston," and it recounted her "radiant smile and hearty laugh" as a receptionist working the front desk for Livingston's board of education.

A lifelong smoker, Sandy was diagnosed with breast cancer in 1980, shortly before Chris went to college. He then struggled those first few days of school, dealing with separation anxiety and worrying about his mother. "It was one of the most difficult periods of my life, but it taught me very much that you have to move on," he said. "It didn't teach me how to do it, but it taught me that you had to do it."

Sandy beat the cancer, and she watched him graduate from law school and run for public office. She had a brain aneurism in 1996—she beat that, too. But in 2004, complaining of dizziness, she went to the hospital, where doctors found large tumors on her lungs and on her brain. Before delivering the news to Sandy and Bill, the doctor called their oldest son. "I'm going to give them some news and you need to be there, because they're not going to take this well," the doctor told Christie.

He was there when the doctor gave her the news. Afterward, in the car to take her home, he put his hand on the stick to put the car into gear. She put her hand on his. "I know I'm going to die," she said.

This was a shock to him. "I never heard my mother, ever, ever be defeatist, ever, in her life," he remembered. "This is a woman I thought would beat anything."

He vowed that after she had been with him for so many life moments, he would make sure to be with her when she died.

And he was.

HE HAS A story about that moment, and it might be the most potent in his repertoire, packing laughter and sadness into four minutes that worm their way into your heart. Christie has repeated it hundreds of times to tens of thousands of people in New Jersey and beyond. The story ended almost every town hall meeting he held in New Jersey in his first term as governor, and it would become a staple of his early presidential campaign, acting as a window to understanding his edgy idiosyncrasies. When voters wondered about his temper or his judgment, maybe because of this story they would understand why he is the way he is.

The story, as he tells it, begins with a little background: "I had an Irish father, and I had a Sicilian mother. Now what this means is from a very young age I became adept at conflict resolution."

No matter that his father is of half German ancestry and only a quarter Irish, the laughter begins from there. "See, it's not that my parents argued all the time. It's just that my mother felt there was not any argument *not* worth having," he says. "My mom would tell you whatever was on her mind all the time. And we used to say, 'Mom, why do we need to know that?' And she'd say, 'I need to get it off my chest! There'll be no deathbed confessions in this family! You're hearing it *now*.' "

Then his voice softens. Now he shifts, showing that he has, as he would say, more than one club in the bag. He doesn't just yell at reporters; he also can talk about life's most painful moments. "My mom was diagnosed on Valentine's Day in 2004 with lung cancer. And by the first week of May she was back in a hospital and near death. I was at a conference for U.S. Attorneys in San Diego. And my younger brother called me and said, 'It's gotten much worse, they're starting to give her morphine, so if you want to talk to her again you're going to need to get home right away.' "

He pauses, and adds: "I'm sure there's people in this audience who have gone through exactly the same things, exactly those kind of moments."

Christie took the red-eye home from San Diego and drove to the hospital. It was about 9:30 a.m. when he arrived, and she was sleeping. He sat next to her bed for a bit. They hadn't seen each other in five days.

"She woke up, she looked at me, and she said, 'What day is it?' Not hello or anything else.

"I said, 'It's Friday.'

"She said, 'What time is it?'

"I said, 'It's about nine-thirty.'

"She said, 'Go to work.' "

The chuckling begins again, cautiously. They know what she's like.

"I said, 'Mom, I thought I'd take the day off, and spend the day with you.'

"And she said, 'Christopher. It is a work day. *Go to work!*'

"I said, 'Mom, are you worried about not getting your taxpayers' money's worth? I'll make up the time. *Don't worry about it!* I wanna stay here with you today.'

"She reached over and she took my hand and said, 'Christopher, go to work, it's where you belong. There's nothing left unsaid between us.' "

The silence is cut by the sounds of unsnapping handbags as women dig for tissues. Men's eyes glisten, too, as their minds flash to frames of regrets and memories, love and loss. Like a preacher, Christie taps into common struggles with family and mortality, and in that way he becomes more familiar.

"This was one of the most powerful moments of my life, which will summarize for all of you why I am the way I am," he says. "My mother taught me, say what's on your mind to people you have a trusting relationship with, to not let them wonder what you think and how you feel."

He is signaling that the honesty between Sandy and Chris could be replicated between voters and Christie. Maybe there'd be some yelling—but it'd be real.

"Because of the gifts she gave me I didn't have to say I wish I had said *this* to her, I wish she knew *this* about me or I knew *that* about her," he says. "When she looked at me that morning and said there's nothing left unsaid between us—I knew she was right. And I knew she had taught me the way to live my life."

This was the last conversation Christie ever had with Sandy. She went into a coma the next morning and died the day after that.

"And so, that's why I am the way I am."

# 2

# "IT'S HARD TO BE A SAINT IN THE CITY"

The British crown bequeathed the land that would become New Jersey to two men, John Lord Berkeley and Sir George Carteret, to thank them for their support during the English Civil War. This was the very first instance of mutual back-scratching and transactional politics in state history, but it would foretell the next 350 years.

Because Berkeley and Carteret were a couple of dirty politicians. New Jersey's official historical record notes that Berkeley was "under a cloud" during his public career "in consequence of his being detected in selling of offices, and other corrupt practices." Carteret, meanwhile, was elected and then summarily expelled from the House of Commons after being accused of embezzlement.

Political shenanigans are New Jersey's original sin. Shortly after America won her independence, boys, slaves, Philadelphians, and women were found to have illegally voted in a special election to decide the location of a new courthouse in Essex County. By the early twenty-first century, New Jersey had accumulated so many stories of dirty politics that a book was written, *The Soprano State*, named for the fictional antihero criminal Tony Soprano. The authors thanked Christopher J. Christie, the chief federal prosecutor for the state at the time, for being a corruption fighter "who took on the bad guys." Finally.

Christie made his name prosecuting crooked pols in his seven years in that job as U.S. Attorney, and when the book was turned into a documentary Christie attended the premiere and told a reporter, ominously: "We'll always have a corruption problem in New Jersey."

Even the ones who are supposed to be the toughest on corruption fail New Jersey. Republican governor William Cahill was a former FBI agent, county prosecutor, and deputy attorney general who ran in 1969 on a promise to "search out the corrupters and the corrupt, wherever they exist." But when top advisers started getting in trouble—his secretary of state was convicted of getting campaign donation kickbacks from a highway contractor—Cahill lost his own party's primary for reelection.

New Jersey's reputation for corruption grew due to its propensity for sensational cases. Democratic governor Jim McGreevey was a married father who gave his Israeli boyfriend a job he was wholly unqualified for—homeland security adviser—and moved him to an apartment across some woods from the governor's mansion. Amid threats that the man, Golan Cipel, was going to sue him for sexual harassment, McGreevey called a press conference to resign from office. With his parents and wife at his side, he said: "My truth is that I am a gay American." Later, pundits would argue that McGreevey really resigned to prevent more significant scandals from being revealed.

THE PRESIDENT OF the United States appoints ninety-three U.S. Attorneys as chief federal law enforcement officers in districts around the country. USATs are the prosecutors in federal criminal cases, working with the FBI and other agencies to investigate violations of federal law. They often view themselves as above the political fray, and they are rarely household names.

In New Jersey the U.S. Attorney enjoys a unique kind of notoriety as the only USAT in the state—compared to four in New York. Also, unlike most states, New Jersey's attorney general is an unelected political appointee of the governor, making the U.S. Attorney the most potent check on the governor's power that there is.

Christie's journey to this august responsibility began in 1988, when his future law and lobbying partner Bill Palatucci picked up George W. Bush at Newark International Airport. Bush's father, Vice President George H. W. Bush, was seeking the presidency, and Palatucci, who was running the vice president's New Jersey campaign, drove the cigar-smoking younger Bush around the state. Four years later, Bush was up for reelection and Palatucci was in the same position when Christie joined the presidential campaign as an advance man.

Bush lost his reelection bid (and lost New Jersey), but when the younger Bush became governor of Texas and began building his own candidacy for president, Governor Bush's adviser, Karl Rove, invited Palatucci and his friends to Austin.

In January 1999, Palatucci, Christie, and a handful of other Jersey GOP politicos made the pilgrimage to Bush. Christie became a lawyer for Bush's 2000 presidential campaign in New Jersey and a campaign surrogate, appearing on the trail in New Hampshire and Delaware and on Court TV to analyze the *Bush* v. *Gore* election dispute. Together with Palatucci and future Christie gubernatorial adviser Jon Hanson, Christie raised more than $500,000 for his campaign. Bush affectionately nicknamed him "Big Boy."

"In the context of political life in this country, the way you get to know these people is by supporting them and being involved in their campaigns," Christie explained at the time.

Even before the election was over Christie knew what he wanted from a Bush presidency: the U.S. Attorney gig. "I just kind of thought I would be perfect for the job," he later said. "Now, I don't know in retrospect whether I really had any basis for that or not, but I just—my sense, my gut, was I could do that really well."

He had never worked in criminal law or in a federal courtroom. He had never cross-examined a witness or worked as an assistant prosecutor. But after Bush was elected, Palatucci mailed Christie's resume to Rove, now the top adviser to the president, while Christie conducted an aggressive letter-writing campaign. At one point he stopped the then Republican governor, Donald DiFrancesco, at an event at the Jersey Shore with a letter of recommendation already written from DiFrancesco to the White House; Christie just needed a signature. Christie secured the approval of the Democratic gubernatorial candidate at the time, Jim McGreevey, by promising he had no interest in running for political office.

In July 2001 Christie interviewed for the job. But as word circulated about the new potential nominee, whispers sounded that the process was rigged by the Republican Party establishment. "Everybody in the game wants Christie," an anonymous source told the *New York Times*, "and everybody not in the game is looking for a rational alternative." The article described Christie as a corporate lobbyist who contributed money to Republicans but was otherwise unfit for the job.

On September 10, 2001, at 4:30 p.m., Christie got the call from White House counsel Alberto Gonzales. "Big Boy" would be nominated as the new U.S. Attorney for New Jersey.

LESS THAN EIGHTEEN hours later Christie dropped his kids off at school and came home with his then toddler son, Patrick. Mary Pat and Christie's brother, Todd, were at work in Lower Manhattan. At 8:46 a.m., terrorists piloted the first of two planes into the World Trade Center, and Mary Pat, in her office four blocks away, felt the building shake. She called Chris as the second plane hit.

Phones went down, and Mary Pat and her colleagues were hustled into a basement at the office. She stayed there for two hours before putting a wet T-shirt over her face and navigating desolate streets covered in the vaporized remains of metal, plastic, paper, wire, and human beings. She and her coworkers headed uptown, passing pockets of hysteria—like those fleeing over the Brooklyn Bridge, fearing that someone had blown up the Brooklyn courthouse—and ended up at a bar in Union Square, Pete's Tavern, said to be the oldest continuously operated such establishment in the city. No idle hands on this high-powered financial executive and mother of four, though—Mary Pat began serving food to the masses from Lower Manhattan.

Back in Mendham, Christie didn't know his wife's whereabouts. "What am I going to say to the kids when they get home at two-fifteen?" Christie wondered.

"When it first happened . . . all I could think about was the [U.S. Attorney] job—what is this going to mean? And then, once the second building was hit and I couldn't get her on the phone for hours, I had completely forgotten about the job. And I was like, 'What am I going to do as a father? What am I going to do if she doesn't come home?' "

Mary Pat finally got a call through. Christie told her to take a ferry from the east side of Manhattan to the Jersey Shore; Christie drove the hour to pick her up. Covered in that sand-colored dust, she was deemed "contaminated" and hosed down by firefighters. She was given a blanket. She wrapped herself in it.

"I'm standing on the corner watching people walking down the street from the boat slip and every second person seemed to be soaking wet," Christie said. "They were all in a trance."

"I saw Chris and I just hugged him," Mary Pat said. "I was shaking."

Later that night, Christie returned to the port to pick up his brother. The county where the Christies lived, Morris, is a well-off bedroom community less than an hour's drive from Manhattan, and there were lots of financial sector workers in Lower Manhattan who were from the county. The Christies visited a friend that night whose husband hadn't yet come home. He never would come home. Two people at the Christies' church, three parents of their children's classmates, and, in all, sixty-four residents of their county died in the attacks.

Christie's nomination, meanwhile, was in limbo. Given the national crisis there weren't enough FBI agents available to do a background check. "The job I accepted on the tenth had now become 180 degrees different," Christie said. "You are now going to be U.S. Attorney when terrorism is going to be the main focus."

When President Bush finally announced the appointment in December, the New Jersey papers pounced. The *Asbury Park Press* wrote: "The ability to raise money for candidates should not be a qualification for the top federal prosecutor for New Jersey." The paper called on the Democratic senator, Jon Corzine, to play one of the strongest hands in American politics—senatorial courtesy—and block the appointment.

If only. Instead, Corzine, who would one day lose his own job to Christie, acquiesced. The second senator from New Jersey, Robert Torricelli, also agreed to sign off on the appointment—but only if Christie hired a Torricelli ally as the number two in the U.S. Attorney's Office. Christie agreed, and when Christie got into the position he also did one other thing: He demoted the prosecutor who had led a corruption investigation into Torricelli.

**AT THE U.S.** Attorney offices at the Rodino Federal Office Building on Broad Street in Newark, there was skepticism about whether Christie could properly oversee a drug bust in Newark, let alone prevent terrorism and prosecute political corruption.

U.S. Attorneys typically rose from their own federal prosecutor ranks—they weren't partisan fund-raisers without criminal law experience. The man he was replacing, Robert Cleary, had prosecuted the Unabomber, for godsakes. But Christie wasn't anything like that—he wasn't "a case guy." And the case guys were offended. The state's federal bar association passed a resolution opposing Christie's nomination, and Cleary refused to let Christie come to the office to talk before his confirmation.

Christie got home to Mendham after his first day on the job. "How did it go?" Mary Pat asked.

"I know I am going to be able to do this job very well," he said, "but I am also the only person in the office that knows it."

Christie might not have known much about federal criminal law. But his natural flair for leadership, instinctual managerial skills, and shared sympathy with New Jerseyans weary over political corruption would shade over many deficiencies. At least in the beginning.

First Christie did what he could to assuage concerns. He scheduled individual meetings with the office's 120 prosecutors. He asked what he didn't know, and what he could do differently. Christie tapped three veteran prosecutors as his top assistants, rearranged the office to more quickly move cases, and boosted the public corruption, narcotics, and counterterrorism units. Notably, he was credited for hiring with diversity in mind, bringing on more black lawyers.

After some time, younger prosecutors found themselves drawn to his office. "People walk out of there and feel like they met with Jesus," a former employee told me. Early on Christie attended a Black History Month event at the federal courthouse. This was an annual program for court staff. A spread of food was put out. The U.S. Attorney was expected to give a perfunctory speech, as his predecessors had. Instead, said someone in the room, Christie launched into a moving account of the scourge of gang violence in the inner cities. Women in the audience cried. The attorneys who worked for him had never seen anything like it.

Christie's staff soon learned that the boss made decisions quickly and confidently, and he flexed his upper hand with the necessary muscle. After not being briefed about a big corruption case, Christie pulled the chief investigator aside, pointed to the *Christopher J. Christie* name etched in gold on his office door, and said: "You see whose name is on the door? As long as you see my name there, you tell me what's going on!"

"There were a lot of ugly meetings," Christie said, "and I got really angry if things weren't going the way I asked or people didn't have answers."

"CONGRATULATIONS," ATTORNEY GENERAL John Ashcroft told Christie when he was confirmed. "Remember, over seven hundred people in your district were murdered. It's the single largest loss of life in any one district in the country. It's your job to make sure it never happens again."

Here Christie was, an unsuccessful former local politician, a thirty-nine-year-old securities lawyer not only leading a major law enforcement agency but now on the hunt for terrorists. Christie had not served in the military. His travel out of the country had been limited. But for the next seven years he would make thorny decisions about protecting Americans, and he was doing so in a region where the physical and emotional trauma of September 11 was still fresh. One of the hijacked planes came from Newark

International Airport. In the months before the attacks the terrorists lived above a bodega in Paterson, rented cars in Wayne, and took in "Jersey Style table dancing" at Nardone's strip club in Elizabeth. The smoky ruins of the World Trade Center were right across the river, visible from the seventh-floor conference room of his Newark office.

In the beginning, almost every week Christie met those who were widowed or left without a parent due to the attacks. "They look to you now to say are we safe," he said. "We were intent as prosecutors—and I'm sure the agents felt this way, too—on making sure it wasn't going to happen again."

The Justice Department's new mission wasn't to bust people *after* they committed terrorism, it was to prevent another attack from happening on American soil. Christie called this a "brand-new mandate from the president" and a "sea change" in federal law enforcement.

One week during his weekly terrorism briefing, Christie was told about an informant who had a bead on a possible international arms dealer. The ensuing investigation would become one of the most significant terrorism cases in the nation after September 11.

> On the NewsHour tonight . . . British Airways today suspended all its flights to Saudi Arabia. Britain's Department for Transport said it had received credible intelligence of a serious threat to British interests in the kingdom. . . . Two more American soldiers were killed in Iraq . . . 59 U.S. soldiers have died from hostile fire. . . . It was a bloody day in Afghanistan, where an estimated 60 people were killed in violent incidents.

On August 13, 2003, less than two years after September 11, the drip-drop of bad news about the seemingly endless War On Terrorism was continuing to assault the American psyche. But there was a glimmer of good news after that opening on PBS's *NewsHour* that night. Christie appeared on the screen and revealed that federal prosecutors had arraigned a suspected terrorist, caught him before he had a chance to attack.

In Pakistan in the 1990s a hustler named Mohammed Habib Rehman made a lot of money working as an informant for the U.S. Drug Enforcement Agency. When someone tried to kill Rehman the feds moved him to New York, where he became a paid informant on terrorism cases for the FBI. Despite questions about his credibility from his former DEA handler, Rehman stayed on the FBI payroll and went to work reeling in an Indian-born British Hindu named Hemant Lakhani, who made himself out to be an international man of mystery. Lakhani promised Rehman that he could obtain weapons and a whole lot more for terrorist attacks against Americans: antiaircraft missiles, radioactive suitcase bombs, plutonium for nukes—and submarines.

Turned out Lakhani was full of it. Sixteen months passed, and Lakhani had yet to provide the informant anything. He had no connections to arms dealers at all.

Eventually, Lakhani made contact with some Russians to try to get weapons. The Russian Federal Security Service found out and tipped off their American counterparts. Working with the Americans, the Russians sold Lakhani a dummy missile. Lakhani then delivered the missile to Rehman in a room at the Wyndham Hotel at the Newark International Airport, two miles from Christie's office. The missile was placed on the sofa. Moments later, federal agents stormed the room and took Lakhani to jail.

At trial, one juror held out: "He was never going to get no missile. And they knew he was never going to get one either—that's why they bought it, and set it right there on his lap." But in the end that juror went along with the conviction.

"Today is a triumph for the Justice Department in the War Against Terror," Christie said outside the federal courthouse in Newark. "I don't know anyone can say that the state of New Jersey and this country is not a safer place without Hemant Lakhani trotting around the globe attempting to broker arms deals."

But reporter John Martin of the *Star-Ledger* reviewed one hundred taped conversations in the case. He concluded that Lakhani was "little more than a sixty-eight-year-old failed clothing merchant who, desperate for money and full of bluster, stumbled into a highly orchestrated sting at a time when the United States was eager for success against terrorism."

Christie defended his decision on the public radio show *This American Life*, saying Lakhani had brokered an arms deal in the past, had been recorded praising Osama bin Laden, and had mused about the optimal time to take down American planes. Lakhani knew exactly what the man he was selling the missile to planned to use it for.

Lakhani was sentenced to forty-seven years in prison.

"The fact that we were able to sting this guy is a pretty good example of what we're doing in order to protect the American people," President Bush said.

.            .            .

**TWO YEARS AFTER** Lakhani was convicted U.S. Attorney Christie announced that another terrorist plot had been foiled. Six foreign-born Muslims allegedly plotted to attack Fort Dix, a massive military installation in South Jersey, and kill U.S. soldiers with rocket-propelled grenades and automatic weapons. The plot had been revealed after a Circuit City clerk reported to police that a customer wanted to make DVDs of his jihad-training videos. One of the defendants was caught saying that when someone "attacks your religion, your way of life, then you go jihad." The feds infiltrated the group and arrested the alleged terrorists.

"The threat that was being brought against Fort Dix has been taken care of," Christie declared.

Yet as the case wore on, questions grew about the significance of that threat. As in the Lakhani case, the feds used a known criminal as an informant—two, in fact. They were paid a combined $390,000 for their assistance. As in the Lakhani case, the informants had to help the alleged plotters get weapons. And just as in the Lakhani case, the Fort Dix crew lacked connections to terrorist groups like al-Qaeda.

At trial it was revealed that there was no plan about what an attack at Fort Dix would be like, nor much urgency to do anything at all. An informant asked one of the alleged terrorists 197 times to set up a meeting to discuss the plot. The meeting never happened.

But Christie led a successful prosecution. Four were sentenced to life in prison. A federal appeals court later rejected a claim from the defendants that Christie misapplied the Patriot Act, the controversial post-9/11 law that gave the federal government extraordinary investigative powers. This was one of at least two Christie terrorism cases in which the Patriot Act was employed.

Christie said that the Fort Dix case gave him "the most gratification" of any matter he dealt with as U.S. Attorney. He said the government "saved American lives."

*January 24, 2002—The mayor of Paterson was indicted today on federal charges of taking cash, gifts, 14 vacation trips, home improvements and payments for "female companionship" from city vendors in return for contracts. . . . Christopher J. Christie, the United States attorney for New Jersey, said the many gifts that Mr. Barnes is accused of accepting from city contractors showed him to be "a mayor more interested in serving himself than serving the people."*

***May 8, 2002***—*A businessman and Democratic fund-raiser was charged today with extorting payoffs from gambling operations in West New York while claiming to represent a high-level official. . . . "Public officials need to know that this investigation is ongoing," Mr. Christie said. "Today is another opportunity for us to send that message out."*

***June 6, 2002***—*The former top administrator of the Hudson County township of North Bergen was indicted today on federal charges of illegally receiving $35,000 in home improvements and cash from a contractor who in turn received municipal contracts totaling $2.5 million. . . . Official misconduct like that charged in the North Bergen case, [Christie] said, "is rampant throughout the state". . . .*

Christie's first six months as U.S. Attorney were dominated by a series of indictments of politicians, dutifully documented by the press. This, more than trapping terrorists or rooting out drug gangs, would be his law enforcement legacy and his springboard back to politics.

Sure, Christie handled other cases. Every year of his term from 2002 to 2007, the number of criminal prosecutions increased. But prosecutors who worked with him told me that Christie was most interested in nabbing dirty politicians. How could he not be? Christie benefited from a target-rich environment of elected officials who sought a little extra cash on the side.

One of the most prominent Republicans in the state was Christie's first scalp. In his third month on the job federal investigators raided the offices of James Treffinger, the top elected official in Essex County and the next likely Republican nominee for U.S. Senate. This move set the tone that Christie sought for his tenure—despite a partisan pedigree, he was now just a party-blind prosecutor, out for justice alone.

As politicos whispered about the side benefits for Christie in taking out a guy ahead of him in the line of New Jersey Republican ascension, Christie indicted Treffinger for using public workers for campaign purposes, awarding public contracts to a company that donated to his campaign, and giving no-show jobs to people like his barber.

Treffinger had offered to surrender, but one day while walking his dog he was surrounded by seven police cruisers and frisked as his picture was taken by the *Star-Ledger*. Treffinger was put in leg irons for two and a half hours and handcuffs for six. The fact that Treffinger was caught on wire-tap calling Christie a "fat fuck who knew more about cookbooks than law books" may or may not have had something to do with his treatment.

Christie had no regrets about making a very public example of the county executive. "We'll never be able to deter all of it, but the job here is get whatever percentage of the people you can get," Christie said. "And scare the hell out of the rest of them."

Christie revealed that the feds recorded Treffinger angling to become U.S. Attorney instead of Christie—Treffinger said he wanted the gig because once he got it, the investigation into him "goes away." "Plenty of mobsters to go after; you don't have to go after all these poor politicians plying their trade," Treffinger said.

There it was, the political trade in New Jersey, with corruption in the job description.

"The time to treat violent criminals and white-collar criminals as two different classes of people is over," Christie told reporters.

Treffinger wasn't the only top county official whom Christie put away that year. Robert Janiszewski, a Democrat who led Hudson County as the county executive, pleaded guilty to taking more than $100,000 in bribes.

Christie, the new sheriff, had arrived in town. Neither Republicans nor Democrats were safe.

"I AM PUTTING each and every one of you on notice," Christie told a conference for local mayors in Atlantic City. He wanted it to be clear that political corruption was his target. "We are going to root this stuff out, and I expect all of you to help me."

Christie went after the political bosses, like John Lynch in Middlesex County, once the most powerful Democratic legislator in the state, for running a shady political action committee that moved campaign donations from government contractors to politicians. And he nabbed the biggest mayor in the state, Newark mayor Sharpe James—a Rolls-Royce-driving, yacht-owning epitome of flamboyance who raked in cash through public jobs and pensions as mayor, state senator, and county college professor. James was investigated over and again, but it wasn't until Christie sub-poenaed his travel records—first-class trips around the world, billed to Newark taxpayers for $58,000—that his illicit house of cards collapsed.

"He was supposed to be [Newark residents'] protector. He was sup-posed to be their champion," Christie said when he indicted James in July

2007. "All he protected was his wallet and all he championed was his own lavish lifestyle, and that's just strictly wrong."

"I made Governor Christie," James later said. "I was his poster boy."

CHRISTIE CULTIVATED HIS corruption-busting image as he traveled the state to senior citizen groups and Chamber of Commerce luncheons to deliver humorous lectures about political corruption as New Jersey's great scourge. During his seven years in that office he collected $20,000 in mileage reimbursements from the federal government—traveling 106,000 miles by car in his last three years alone, barnstorming his state in a display of the indefatigable spirit that would later prove one of his strengths as a political campaigner.

The Christopher J. Christie name was catching on. The first national newspaper profile came out in the *Washington Post* in November 2002, ten months into the job. It was headlined, "In N.J., a Crusader Confounds Skeptics." From the high school class president who had a front-row seat to the Abscam scandal, to the hard-charging but reform-minded freeholder, to the corruption-busting U.S. Attorney, Christie was a good bull in a dirty Jersey china shop. Those early press clips portray an air of inevitability to his political rise—the feeling that either because of innate ability or sheer ambition, he was going places. Even if he told the *New York Times* in 2003: "I don't have any political ambitions, I just don't."

IN 2006 AND 2007 Christie had more corruption convictions than any other U.S. Attorney in the nation. Over his seven-year tenure Christie oversaw indictments and guilty pleas from more than 130 elected and appointed political officials—including five state legislators, eighteen mayors, and fifteen municipal-level officials—without a single acquittal.

The joke in political circles was that the worst thing a shady politician can hear is this: "It's Chris Christie for you on line one."

At a convention for local politicians, the U.S. Attorney was introduced as "a corrupt public official's worst nightmare." Christie took to the podium and taunted the mayors and council members in front of him: "If over the next couple of days someone approaches you with an envelope of cash looking to seek a favor from you—unless it is your *mommy*—turn and run for the ocean." Because, he said, "it's probably us."

Not so obliquely telegraphing his own career plans, Christie said this "crisis" would require not just justice, but new leadership throughout the state.

.        .        .

**ON SEPTEMBER 8,** 2006, less than two months before the U.S. Senate election in New Jersey, a blockbuster story dropped in the *Star-Ledger*. Federal investigators—according to four anonymous sources—had subpoenaed records on a rental deal between Senator Robert Menendez of New Jersey and a small New Jersey nonprofit. Menendez, then in the middle of a heated campaign to hold on to his seat, leased a property he owned to a social services agency, collecting $329,353 in rent while helping it land millions of dollars in federal grants.

Who were these four sources dishing this confidential information to the *Star-Ledger*? Everyone in politics assumed one of them *had* to be Christie. Who else would drop allegations in the middle of a Senate campaign that had the potential to tip the balance of the entire Senate to Republicans?

As Menendez's opponent in the upcoming election, State Senator Tom Kean, Jr., reconfigured his campaign to focus on Menendez's alleged corruption—repeatedly referring to Menendez as "under federal criminal investigation"—Menendez accused Christie of leaking the material to try to help a Republican win in the Senate seat. "Suddenly, sixty-one days before the election, a prosecutor appointed by George Bush decides to take an interest and, not coincidentally, leaks to the press," Menendez said.

Several sources claimed Christie was a compulsive leaker. He always denied it. A few weeks after the Menendez scoop, Christie was asked by a reporter how politics might have a role in his investigations. Christie "visibly reddened and stepped forward," the reporter wrote, and said: "I don't get involved in politics, the silly season—that's for politicians, not for prosecutors."

Christie was in fact both a politician and a prosecutor. In his U.S. Attorney office he kept a political cartoon depicting President Bush reviewing his resume, which listed "Bush Fund-raiser" as his sole qualification, and a picture of him and Bush, taken by Rove, in front of a painting of the Last Stand at the Alamo at the Texas governor's mansion. Christie was known to meet with the state's GOP leaders and he once made the news when he had a power lunch with a former chairman of the Republican National Committee at a Trenton steak joint where political brokers went to be seen.

Christie was so ferociously focused on political corruption that he cut a deal to greatly reduce the sentence of an alleged sex trafficker in exchange for information about a corrupt mayor in a town of just eleven thousand people. The sex trafficker got probation but avoided jail time, while the mayor got thirty-six months in the big house. Christie attended the trial, in which the deputy chief of staff to the sitting governor, Jon Corzine, testified about his involvement in the shady matter. That led to that aide's resignation—an embarrassment for Corzine, Christie's future opponent in the governor's race.

So when suspicions arose that the Menendez leak was a way to force the Democrat out of the race, questions were whispered. Was this whole thing a way of helping Kean, whose father had inspired young Chris to enter politics? Was this a gesture to his GOP patrons?

There was one other wrinkle. The same year Christie decided to take on a sitting Democratic senator, the Bush White House had put Christie on two lists of U.S. Attorneys it was considering firing for alleged lack of loyalty to the administration. Shortly after the existence of the Menendez subpoenas was leaked, though, Christie's name was taken off the list. Was this to-be-fired list what prompted Christie to investigate a Democratic senator? Was Christie spooked after his friend U.S. Attorney Debra Wong Yang of Los Angeles was rumored to have been pushed out of her job for probing a Republican congressman?

Menendez beat Kean Jr. on Election Day, the Democrats secured a single-vote majority in the Senate, and five years later, the Menendez investigation was quietly closed, as per a letter from federal prosecutors leaked to the press.

Christie claims he had no idea that he was on a to-be-fired list until a few months after the Menendez reelection when a senior official from the Justice Department called to give him a heads-up. He described being "speechless," and theorized that perhaps he was targeted for firing because of his personality: "Some of my colleagues told me I said things in a very Jersey way—with not a lot of varnish."

Christie was put on the chopping block by his own Republicans even as Democrats accused him of trying to steal an election from them. Independent, and despised by everyone—that was the message he would sell to weary New Jerseyans. He was fighting corruption on their behalf, politics be damned—first as prosecutor, and soon, as governor.

Not that he was thinking about that now, of course. "The future," Christie said at the time, "will take care of itself."

# 3

# "EVERYBODY IN NEW JERSEY WAS ARRESTED TODAY"

They called it "The Christie Project," a stealth operation by Christie friends and relatives to quietly build hype for a gubernatorial campaign. Christie's adoring younger brother, Todd, was a face of this precampaign. Todd had made millions when his stock specialist firm was bought by Goldman Sachs, so he had thrown some campaign money around in recent years to Republican county chairmen and the Republican National Committee. In 2004 Todd set up a vending cart to give out "Christie's Popcorn" at an annual New Jersey Republican gala.

"I'm not shy in saying I'm one of the people who chirps in his ear that I think he would make a great governor," Todd said at the time. "Does he want it? Who wouldn't want to be the most powerful governor in the country?"

Christie held at least one secret political meeting in 2004 about jumping into the 2005 gubernatorial race, according to an attendee. He ultimately turned down the chance, deciding he liked his current job too much. Then rumors about Christie running in the 2009 gubernatorial election turned into buzz, so Democrats threw a brush-back pitch. Democratic congressman Frank Pallone challenged Christie to sign an affidavit saying he hadn't engaged in political activities. Christie ignored it.

In November 2008, Christie finally resigned. Barack Obama had just won election and would replace Bush's U.S. Attorney appointees anyway.

Christie left quietly—as quietly as he could. He released his resignation letter without holding a press conference but couldn't resist the urge to walk to lunch that day. Sans overcoat on a brisk afternoon Christie left the U.S. Attorney's Office in Newark to what he knew would be a bank of cameras. He was flanked by two of his top deputies, Jeff Chiesa and Michele

Brown, both of whom would follow Christie to the governor's office. Chiesa and Brown wore tight-lipped smiles as the cameras followed them from the office to the restaurant. Christie smirked, barely able to contain his bemusement over the attention.

**A LITTLE MORE** than a week after he quit Christie showed up on MSNBC and FOX News, where he pontificated about the corruption investigation of the sitting Illinois governor. He then went to Jamaica with his family and returned ready to start telling reporters that he was running for governor.

On February 4, 2009, Christie boarded a black campaign bus with a Bruce Springsteen concert playing on the TV inside and set off on a two-day tour to spread word of his candidacy. He began with a kick-off speech that had few laugh lines. He looked stiff. But he loosened as he headed south, literally saluting the Statehouse as the bus rolled past Trenton to Haddon Heights, where he offered a surprising promise to the suburban crowd at a former five-and-dime store: "In order to grow our economy and improve our state, I will propose a plan to renew our cities," with a focus on "public safety, economic growth, improved public education, and housing that working men and women can afford.

"We have to do it," he added. "It's a moral imperative. It's an economic imperative."

Christie first had to beat back three opponents in the GOP primary, including Steve Lonegan, a former mayor and head of the state chapter of Americans For Prosperity, a Tea Party group backed by the powerful conservative Koch brothers. Christie did not dazzle in the debates—he was stuck deep in the policy weeds. He had not yet honed his storytelling style of speaking. But he was perceived as a quintessential moderate New Jersey Republican, in the mold of former governors Tom Kean and Christine Todd Whitman, and so he handily won the race.

In the general election Christie faced Corzine, who had been the CEO of Goldman Sachs before walking away with $400 million and spending $60 million to finance a Democratic campaign for the U.S. Senate in 2000. Corzine handed money to every Democratic political boss around, which gave him the juice he needed to switch over and get elected governor in 2005.

Corzine, bearded and dull, wasn't very popular, either with the electorate or the political class. He lacked the wily wherewithal to control the legislature, Democrats included. Still, a Republican would have to do something pretty extraordinary to win in a state that had hundreds of thousands more Democrats.

Corzine went to battle against Christie armed with a 760-page opposition research file. In Christie's greatest strength, Corzine sensed a vulnerability: ethics, in the form of multimillion-dollar legal contracts that Christie gave out to friends and associates as U.S. Attorney.

*A million lawyers to choose from,* the narrator said in the Corzine attack ad, *but it's Christie's three pals who got millions.*

Corzine was zeroing in on Christie's use of Deferred Prosecution Agreements, a new kind of legal vehicle that allowed companies to avoid prosecution in exchange for a fine and a federal monitor. Christie said such agreements prevented job losses that happen after a company is prosecuted. But Christie chose curious people to be federal monitors, such as former attorney general John Ashcroft, Christie's ex-boss in the Justice Department, whose firm was paid as much as $52 million for legal fees, private jets, and other expenses over eighteen months. Three executives of the firm, including Ashcroft himself, made $750,000 a month. Ashcroft would later become a Christie campaign donor.

David Samson, one of Christie's closest confidants, landed a monitor contract shortly before he began raising money for Christie's gubernatorial candidacy. His law firm would go on to earn millions in outside legal work for the Christie administration—and millions more lobbying the administration for private clients—before Samson became ensnared in Christie's second-term scandals.

The matter of David Kelley was deep with intrigue. He had been the U.S. Attorney in Manhattan—Christie's colleague—when a case involving Christie's brother, Todd, came across his desk. A federal investigation into twenty Wall Street traders ensnared Todd, but when the indictments came Todd and four others were spared criminal charges. Todd was found to have only violated stock exchange rules on "inappropriate trading," and his firm paid a fine. Later, Christie named Kelley as a federal monitor as part of a DPA. Christie denied ever talking to Kelley about his brother's case and said the allegation "hurts" him. For his part, Kelley said the decision on the indictments was based solely on the evidence.

Revelations about these contracts damaged Christie's reputation among the prosecutors in his office. "We need to toil in the trenches every day and we have to be seen as nonpartisan," one told me. "This seems partisan, and this seems based on friendship."

To that end, in 2008 the website *PolitickerNJ* named Christie political "boss of the year" for doling out sweet deals to friends. Officials in Washington were said to be concerned about this "boss" in their U.S. Attorney's Office in New Jersey, and as a result the Justice Department under President Obama subsequently changed its rules so a top official in Washington would have to approve all monitor contracts going forward.

This was the context in which Christie was summoned to Washington in June 2009 to testify before a Democratic-controlled congressional committee about these contracts.

Despite being in the middle of a gubernatorial campaign, there he was in front of a little black microphone in a Capitol Hill hearing room. His hands were clasped, his eyebrows were in the air, and his wide shoulders leaned in, looking as if he was wearing linebackers' shoulder pads underneath his dark suit.

His tone was initially respectful. But things escalated when Steve Cohen, a Democratic congressman from Tennessee, asked Christie whether the companies that entered into deferred prosecution agreements had any say in choosing their federal monitors. The subtext was that Christie was blackmailing the companies—hire my friends, or face criminal charges.

"The bottom line is you made them an offer they couldn't refuse," Cohen said.

"I don't agree with that, sir," Christie responded.

"That is what happened, sir, I believe."

Christie and Cohen went back and forth. Six *sirs* were exchanged.

"Sir, you have said that I 'gave them an offer you couldn't refuse,'" Christie said.

"That is right," Cohen replied.

"First of all, it is an ethnically insensitive comment by you, first of all, to an Italian-American."

"I have no idea and I—"

Christie moved on. But the pick-off move threw Cohen off balance. The congressman may have been expecting a defensive witness; instead, he got a prosecutor playing offense.

*The Godfather* is Christie's favorite movie, and he regularly makes mob references about himself. So was Christie really upset by Cohen's comment? Or did he just see an opportunity?

At every turn, Republican congressmen on the panel defended Christie. One said he would endorse his candidacy for governor. As Christie's second hour in the congressional hot seat stretched into three, Christie denied any instance of political bribery for the final time and dropped the congressional mic.

"Mr. Chairman, I just would like to let you know, as I said to you in the letter I sent to you, I have to depart at one-thirty because of pressing business I have back in New Jersey. So I don't want to cut anybody off, but I need to go and catch a train, sir."

Democratic congressman Brad Sherman wasn't having it.

"Mr. Christie, what time is your train?"

"My train is a little bit before two, sir, and I have to go."

"You are not going to make a two o'clock, so—"

"Well, sir, I am. . . . Sir, I am going. I said I had to leave at one-thirty and I will."

So Christopher J. Christie did just that. He left a vacant chair behind as he hustled to Union Station. But not before telling reporters in the hallway: "It's unfortunate that they're using the money of the taxpayers of the United States to perform this kind of political circus."

*EVERYBODY IN NEW Jersey Was Arrested Today*, ran the headline on *Gawker* on July 23, 2009.

Not exactly. Forty-four people were arrested en masse and hauled into federal court, including three mayors, one deputy mayor, two assemblymen—and five rabbis. The charges involved political corruption and money laundering across Israel, Switzerland, Brooklyn, and the Jersey Shore—plus the selling of human kidneys on the black market.

For Corzine, this could not have come at a worse time. This was a sensational political corruption case in the middle of a political campaign that the *other* guy was trying to make about corruption, and among those busted were several Democrats tied to him.

Christie had triggered this investigation when he was U.S. Attorney. He authorized the use of a con man, Solomon Dwek, to set up stings against politicians. Christie quit the U.S. Attorney's Office to run for governor while the Dwek operation was still in motion, but his old lieutenants executed the arrests the following summer, just as the Christie-Corzine gubernatorial race was heating up.

Corzine watched the drama unfold on TV from his Hoboken apartment alongside traumatized advisers who would remember this as the day the campaign collapsed.

"Is there anyone there we *don't* know?" Corzine asked, incredulously watching as the Democratic politicos were hauled away.

"Maybe the rabbis?" someone responded.

It would get worse. One of Corzine's top cabinet members, Department of Community Affairs Commissioner Joseph Doria, was ensnared in this mess. Dwek had claimed he had given $40,000 to a middleman to bribe Doria, so ten federal agents went to Doria's house, woke him up, searched his house, and emerged two hours later with nothing but the empty boxes they brought in with them. There was no evidence to take.

Yet pictures of box-carrying agents in front of Doria's house did *not* look good on the front page of newspapers the next day. Hours later, Corzine asked Doria to resign.

"You guys are young," Doria told two of Corzine's aides as he left Trenton. "Get out of this business while you still can."

Doria was never charged with anything. Like his fellow Democrat, Senator Menendez, more than two years later Doria got an official letter from the U.S. Attorney's Office saying he was no longer under investigation.

CHRISTIE WENT HOME the night of the Dwek arrests and told his wife that they might actually win this thing.

"Really?" Mary Pat said. "You know, I think you're right."

Mary Pat was raising money through her Wall Street connections. The campaign was also collecting government dollars through the state's campaign matching fund, and the Republican Governors Association pumped in millions.

Top political operatives for Obama were alarmed that Democrats might lose a governor's seat in a blue state so soon after the president's historic election. So the president's chief political adviser, David Axelrod, convened a meeting at Corzine's girlfriend's apartment in Manhattan to discuss their "concerns." Obama, who was still widely popular in the state, did three campaign events to help Corzine that summer and fall.

Corzine also tried to turn the page by picking Senator Loretta Weinberg, a tough Bergen County Democrat, as a running mate. Often described with the shorthand "feisty Jewish grandmother," Weinberg's persistence later helped to trigger the Bridgegate probe.

Christie had already chosen his running mate: the sheriff of Monmouth County, Kim Guadagno, another former federal prosecutor. She was not intended to be a game-changer, but she gender-balanced the ticket and reinforced the law-and-order shtick that Christie was running on. "Now imagine this: Two former federal corruption prosecutors walking up the front steps of the Statehouse in Trenton, New Jersey, with the keys to the front office," Christie told cheering supporters. "They're shaking already!"

In the closing days of the campaign, at a rally at the Morristown Green, where General George Washington twice encamped, Christie name-dropped the politicians he had indicted for corruption. He then called out "naysayers" who didn't think he could clean up the state: "Well, let me tell you for those people who said that eight years ago, tell them this morning to give Sharpe James a call! Tell them to give Wayne Bryant a call! Tell them to give John Lynch a call! Tell them to give Joe Coniglio a call! Tell them to call the latest fella, Joe Ferriero up in Bergen County!"

The Corzine campaign got desperate, capitalizing on a juicy story about a top female prosecutor in the U.S. Attorney's Office, Michele Brown. As one of Christie's chief assistants, Brown traveled with Christie, along with others, on trips around the state and even abroad. She became a close friend and confidante. They were neighbors, too, and were known to carpool to work together. When Brown's husband lost her job and got into some credit card debt, Christie and Mary Pat loaned them $46,000.

Corzine seized on news reports about this questionable arrangement. Brown worked for Christie, first of all, which made it inappropriate at best and possibly unethical. Christie also failed to disclose the loan on his tax returns and financial disclosure forms. Approached one hot day in August by NJN reporter Zach Fink, Christie called it an "honest mistake" because he didn't view a loan to a friend as an investment. He also didn't think the arrangement was unusual, since he and Mary Pat had loaned money to friends before.

"I just believe that if you have friends who are in need, that you help them, whether they work with you, or whether they're friends of yours from outside the work realm," he said. "We were happy to help and they've been great about repaying the loan."

That didn't quell the controversy. A Corzine attack ad opened with Christie in sepia tone, waving his arms, perhaps yelling at someone. It went on to a freeze-frame color image of Christie with an angry face. The narrator said: "While he was U.S. Attorney Republican Chris Christie gave one of his supporters a $46,000 loan, and even though it is required under federal and state laws, Christie never reported the loan. . . . When he was caught, Christie said it was a mistake. But he prosecuted people who did the same thing. Chris Christie: one set of rules for himself, one set of rules for everyone else."

A Christie spokesman said the loan was settled two months after it was disclosed—either because Christie had forgiven the balance or Brown had suddenly come into enough cash to pay it all off. Brown went on to have some of the most important and lucrative posts in the Christie administration, and yet once in office neither she nor Christie reported the loan in financial disclosure forms they were required to file as government employees. They therefore avoided detailing how the finances were sorted out.

Corzine's campaign operatives also highlighted how Christie was a poor driver—very poor, amassing thirteen tickets and six accidents. A Corzine spokesperson said Christie was "a complete menace to society on the highways of New Jersey" and charged that he had improperly used his position as U.S. Attorney after driving the wrong way down a one-way street and colliding with a motorcycle, sending the biker to the emergency room.

In that incident, as he had done one other time, Christie identified himself to police as the U.S. Attorney. He avoided a ticket. Christie also initially said there was no resulting lawsuit, which wasn't true. The parties settled out of court.

Corzine was trying to put a little tarnish on the image of a guy who literally had a bottle of Mr. Clean with his face on it sitting on his desk at the U.S. Attorney's Office. Corzine's message: Hey, Jersey, this guy's a fraud.

THE WEEKEND BEFORE Election Day, Corzine told the New York Times in an ill-advised interview that he might revisit his plan to sell the New Jersey Turnpike to raise money. This had been the single least popular policy proposal from his term. Now here he was, bringing it up again.

Word got back to the Corzine camp that after the article ran, they were high-fiving in Christie's campaign bus, on the road to victory.

ON ELECTION DAY Christie went to Peterpank Diner in Middlesex County to do some last-minute campaigning. The owner came up to Christie and told him a story, about a lucky silver dollar that he carried in his pocket until he gave it to his nephew when the nephew joined the military and went to Iraq. Wouldn't you know it, the nephew came home safe and returned the coin to his uncle. Then the nephew was suddenly deployed to Afghanistan, and he asked his uncle for the coin back, but his uncle couldn't get down to Fort Dix in time to hand it over. Wouldn't you know it, the nephew was wounded in Afghanistan.

"So I really think this good luck charm works," the diner owner told Christie. "And I really want you to win. So I want to give it to you. Carry it with you until Election Day, and you'll win."

The diner owner handed Christie the coin. As Christie retells this story to me, he drops the coin on the table between us. *Clank*.

"And then I was completely freaked out," Christie says.

That's because the diner owner's coin was identical to a Morgan Silver Dollar given to him by a Sussex County freeholder earlier that year, when the campaign first began. The freeholder had told Christie: "Every time I've run for office I've carried this coin in my pocket, and I never lost, and I really want you to win so carry it with you every day. And if you do, you're gonna win."

Christie thought: "What the heck? I can use every edge I can get in this race."

And so from the beginning of the campaign, Christie carried that silver dollar in his right pocket. Now here at the end of the campaign was someone else handing him the same kind of silver dollar and promising him the same kind of good luck.

So Christie put that second silver dollar in his left pocket.

One coin is from 1883; the other is from 1886. These are large coins that collectors specifically say are not intended to be carried in pockets. But from that point on, through his election and his entire time as governor, every morning Christie put each coin in its respective pocket.

Christie got lucky immediately. He garnered 48.5 percent of the vote on Election Night, enough to win the race. Corzine had 44.9 percent and a third-party independent candidate, Chris Daggett, took 5.8 percent.

"Hey New Jersey, we did it!" Christie screamed to a crowd in Parsippany. He was flanked by his wife, the new lieutenant governor, and their families.

"At the end of these four years I promise you one thing: That we will restore your *hope*, and your *faith*, and your *trust*, in New Jersey."

Thirteen days before the end of those four years, that promise would be gravely tested.

PART TWO

# GOVERNOR

# 4

# BIG STEVE, JOE D., & CORY B.

The Republican prosecutor had beaten the millionaire Democrat. Now, Chris Christie wanted to go to the hood.

On no sleep, fueled by a hotel breakfast with his family and the extraordinary thrill of being elected governor of the state of his birth, Christie bounded into an SUV driven by a man now charged with protecting his life. They left Christie's base in the leafy suburbs of Morris County where he had declared victory the night before and snaked their way to the state's most significant Democratic stronghold, Newark.

They pulled up to a place called the Robert Treat Academy, a charter school and the capital of North Jersey's Democratic empire. Republican Christie was welcomed with screams, kisses, backslaps, and handshakes. Christie parted the masses of enthusiasm just enough to greet the master of this domain: legendary political boss Steve Adubato, Sr.

Adubato hugged Christie the way they do in the old country, all body and soul, and together they walked into a student assembly where four hundred black and Latino students blew two hundred newly purchased whistles. They waved tiny American flags, held aloft "Gov. Chris" signs, and chanted, "Hip hip hooray!" Adubato then presented the sleep-deprived Republican a freshly embroidered "Governor Christie" fleece, which would one day make an improbable cameo on *Saturday Night Live*.

Christie had campaigned on expanding charter schools as part of a whole education reform agenda. So it made sense to visit a premier charter like this one. Bearing the distinctive hoarseness of a victorious politician the morning after, the governor-elect took the lectern and told a story about a mother whose son won admission to the Robert Treat Academy via lottery. Christie said he asked this mother what it felt like. And she said this: "I was sitting there thinking to myself whether my son gets his number picked out of this bin is the difference between him going to college—or jail."

But all that was really the second reason why this was Christie's first stop on this most meaningful day. The primary reason was Adubato. They called him "Big Steve."

STEVE ADUBATO, SR.'S nickname came not from his size, which was smallish, but from his political power, which in North Jersey had been unmatched for generations. Adubato's political operation was built through a portfolio of nonprofits including a senior citizens' medical center, a job-training program, the largest (free) preschool for poor children in the state, and the Robert Treat Academy K–8 charter school. Collectively headquartered out of a nineteenth-century mansion on a hill, the North Ward Center, as it was called, symbiotically churned philanthropy and politics.

Adubato was known for keeping not one but three pictures of Machiavelli in his office. He was ruthless and relentless, and unabashed about both. Through his nonprofits, and the patronage jobs and public money that went along with them, Adubato built a rep for burnishing alliances, spurning enemies, and driving turnout on Election Day for approved candidates. Generously funded by the Adubato-favored politicians in county and state government, the North Ward Center became a bountiful source of employment for generations of Newarkers who in turn become campaign foot soldiers—planting candidates' lawn signs, manning polls on Election Day, and picking up senior citizens to go vote.

The Robert Treat Academy was a required stop for all Democrats and many Republicans. Before Cory Booker, the future U.S. senator, even moved to Newark to make a bid for city council he stopped by to pay homage to Adubato. Former governor Jon Corzine donated more than $1 million to Adubato's operations. And when then-governor Richard Codey ran into Adubato at an event ("Steve, I haven't seen you in a few months"), Adubato responded with classic candor ("I know, I got everything I wanted from you a few months ago").

As for Christie, he was long familiar with this place. He had been visiting since he was U.S. Attorney.

POLITICAL BOSSES LIKE Adubato are New Jersey's way of giving messy democracy a little bit of order. There are so many elected positions in the Garden State that I couldn't find a single person who actually knows the total, but my best estimation is a whopping 8,927. That's one politician for every 100 people, presiding over a labyrinthine 565 municipalities, 537 school boards, 21 counties, and 185 fire districts.

The average citizen does not keep up with such government. Voter turnout in some local elections can get as low as 0.6 percent. Political bosses therefore step in to control the political parties that decide candidate placement on ballots. This is critically important, because the favored politicians who go in the top spots almost always win.

Bosses amass their power over parties through campaign donations, which come almost entirely from unions and companies that have (or want) government contracts. With nearly fifteen hundred local tax-collecting entities hiring attorneys, accountants, engineers, planners, and other assorted vendors, that's a lot of potential contributions. Individual candidates are only allowed to take $2,600 maximum donations, but political action committees run by bosses can bring in $37,000 checks. From there bosses are expected to return the favors by securing zoning approvals for developers, contracts for government work, and generous benefits for unionized workers.

"In New Jersey, you contribute money not for access but results," one big North Jersey political consultant said of the boss-run campaign system. "Anybody who doesn't admit that is lying."

Bosses trade up, too. From the governor, they want their allies picked as some of the 6,235 appointees, from advisory committees to the Supreme Court, at more than 500 state entities. In return, bosses deliver votes on bills from legislators they control.

Former governor Jim McGreevey wrote a book, *Confession*, after he resigned amid scandal, revealing how he was beholden to Middlesex County Democratic boss John Lynch: "Lynch and the other bosses had been a political compromise that I'd accepted in order to advance my career. I had my people strike back room deals I kept myself in the dark about or forced from my mind if I learned too much."

*If I learned too much.*

ADUBATO GOT INVOLVED in local Democratic politics in the 1960s by splitting from the white establishment and carving his own identity as a champion of the increasingly diverse and economically troubled North Ward of Newark. His power soon grew to the rest of Newark, surrounding Essex County and then North Jersey. They called him "a local warlord."

"Look, I'm not a nice guy," Adubato once told a reporter. "I'm not Mother Teresa. Do I use politics to help me do my work? More than you think. Is that wrong? That's for you to decide."

Through his North Ward Center, Adubato had an indisputably positive effect on his poor, mostly minority community. But his political operation has also had brushes with the law—as when a patronage employee in the elections office pleaded guilty to fraud after submitting phony absentee ballots for a favorite Adubato candidate.

A "combo of a do-gooder and a ne'er do well," a reporter who covered Adubato told me.

After U.S. Attorney Christie took down Lynch on corruption charges in 2006, it was thought that the era of the bosses might be over. His gubernatorial victory provided further hope that he'd have the gumption to work around the boss system.

But Christie had a new job now, and it was time for new friendships. He didn't care about perception. He was trying to be governor. To accomplish anything he would need support from a legislature controlled by Democrats, and the fastest way to Democratic hearts was through the bosses.

In his speech at the North Ward Center that first day after the election, the governor-elect signaled that he'd be working with the bosses and not against them. "When I had to decide what I was going to do with my day, the day I was elected governor, there was no place else I wanted to be than here with all of you," Christie told the crowd.

Adubato was pleased. "He came to the strongest bastion of Democratic power in the state," Adubato said. "That's a governor who's governor of everybody."

Big Steve was the first of three political partnerships that the Republican cultivated with Democratic party bosses. All brought an intriguing back story. In Big Steve's case, U.S. Attorney Christie had investigated a $95,000 no-bid government grant that the North Ward Center received from a political ally. The case closed without an indictment.

That was then. Now, Adubato was leading students in a chant of "show me the money!" to governor-elect Christie, who was amused.

Christie had seen Adubato's outstretched hand before. "Thanks for that 'show me the money' thing," Christie said. "It's always one of my favorite parts about coming to visit."

Afterward Christie held a press conference where he declared, almost angrily, that bipartisanship was why he had come to Newark. "This stuff of

Republicans and Democrats thinking that we have to be mutually exclusive has just got to be over because the problems are too big," he said.

Asked how he would turn around the perception that Republicans only care about white suburbanites, Christie said: "I'm *here*. I mean I don't know how the hell else I'm going to address it. I'm *here*." He talked about having had campaign offices in Paterson and Newark, and about campaigning in Trenton and Camden. "I was trying to send a signal to the people who live in the cities that I care about their problems. And whatever they thought about Republicans before, they're dealing with a different kind of Republican now."

**HANGING ON TO** Christie during this visit was Joseph "Joe D." DiVincenzo, a long-ago high school quarterback in Newark who tried to play pro ball but ended up as the athletic director at the North Ward Center. He was taken under Adubato's wing and elected director of the Essex County Freeholders, where he voted for funding for the North Ward Center. In 2002 he became the top elected official in Essex County—the county executive—with no Republicans even coming close to challenging him. He didn't work in the legislature, but by virtue of his alliance with Adubato and his two decades in elected office he held sway over his county's representatives. And now he was about to become Christie's Democratic point person in North Jersey, the link between a Republican governor and a major Democratic voting bloc.

Big Steve was getting old. His memory wasn't what it used to be, and Joe D.—Adubato's self-described "other son"—was now taking over much of his political operation.

The relationship between DiVincenzo and Christie began in 2002 after Christie was appointed U.S. Attorney and DiVincenzo was in the middle of a tumultuous race for county executive. "Scared shit of him!" DiVincenzo told a reporter who asked what he thought of Christie at the time. "The guy was on a mission."

But when DiVincenzo's opponent ran an ad that insinuated he was under federal investigation, Christie did Joe D. a solid, declaring in a letter that he wasn't a target of an investigation. DiVincenzo won the election, and Christie won a political friend for life.

After the 2002 election DiVincenzo brought U.S. Attorney Christie into his office to run ethics trainings, and credited him with restoring public confidence in a dirty county government. On the day after Christie resigned as U.S. Attorney, Joe D. held a ceremony honoring him with a badge from the Essex County Sheriff's Department and a New York Mets jacket.

The following year, DiVincenzo called Christie on the night of his gubernatorial election. "I'm going to be there with you," Joe D. said. "You're always going to be my friend."

"Let's see what we can do together," Christie said.

Making that phone call was the right play. "I think he was happy that I called to show him respect," DiVincenzo later said.

AFTER ADUBATO AND Joe D., a third Democratic political boss backed Christie: George Norcross in South Jersey, perhaps the most powerful boss of them all.

Joe D. envied Norcross's control in the legislature. He once gushed to the *New Yorker* that while he only controlled two senators and five assembly members, Norcross had seven in the senate and twelve in the assembly. "George has seven and twelve!

"His people control the assembly, and they control the senators," Joe D. said. "He controls their campaigns, he funds their campaigns. They don't always all get along, but, when it comes down to a vote, they'll all be together."

Shortly before Christie got into office, Norcross and Joe D. amassed their power, cementing a plan while attending the U.S. Open tennis tournament in Queens. One of the assemblywomen in Joe D.'s corner, Sheila Oliver of Newark, would lead the lower house of the legislature as the Speaker of the assembly. Norcross's childhood friend, Steve Sweeney, would represent the southern part of the state as the president of the state senate.

This would be the legislative leadership of Christie's first term. DiVincenzo's North Jersey votes and Norcross's South Jersey votes—plus Christie's Republicans—composed the magic formula that Christie needed to get most policies through. There would be no more Republicans and Democrats. There would just be Christiecrats.

There were pressures on this alliance, particularly when the Democratic legislators faced backlash from their liberal constituencies, such as public employee unions, over certain Christie policies. "That's when you call in the personal relationships—when people get weak in the knees," Christie told me.

He'd say: "Knock it off, guys, c'mon . . . we have a deal, we got to stick to the deal . . . Don't worry about these people, you'll be fine." He'd take calls from allied Democrats regardless of where he was—at Patrick's Little League games, or at dinner with Mary Pat, or hanging at his brother's house.

"Joe D. calling me at six in the morning three times a week," Christie said. "Waking me up, whatever his topic of the day is, he has no compunction about calling me any time. And if the first time he did it I picked up and said, 'Never call me at this time again, ever,' it probably wouldn't help develop the relationship. . . . My wife's not thrilled when she gets woken up at six in the morning and I'm laying in bed talking to Joe D. That's one of the sacrifices of the job."

He meant that, when he said "sacrifices." He liked Joe D., sure. But this was transactional and temporary. "Joe D. and I are not about politics," Christie said. "We're about getting things done."

Joe D. was also honest about what he wanted in return for his loyalty to the Front Office. "The person who controls the budget is the governor," DiVincenzo said. When $3 million in state funds and a $7.7 million grant from the Port Authority came through to build soccer fields and walkways on the waterfront in Newark, DiVincenzo said: "This project would have been dead on arrival with anybody else in the position, but [Christie's] done it." Christie was at the groundbreaking ceremony, and he moved a bit of dirt with a ceremonial shovel, front and center next to Joe D.

Republicans, DiVincenzo later said, "get upset because they feel Joe D. gets everything."

Christie also provided some cover for DiVincenzo. In 2011, Joe D. faced scrutiny for collecting both a public salary and a public pension at the same time—the kind of maneuver that would normally anger Christie. But when asked about it, Christie went after reporters for not scrutinizing another Democrat for doing something similar.

Later a *Star-Ledger* investigation found that DiVincenzo had reimbursed himself with $250,000 from his campaign account through the years, with some of that money going to gym memberships, parking tickets, a tuxedo, and two trips to Puerto Rico billed as political meetings. Christie told us what Joe D. was doing was "appropriate."

BEYOND BIG STEVE and Joe D., yet another major Democrat showed up in Newark to greet the governor-elect on his first morning in Newark—the city's mayor, probably the most popular Democrat in the state, Cory Booker. Booker grew up as one of the few black kids in his suburban North Jersey town, then went to Stanford University, where he was a tight end on the football team, then Oxford University, where he was a Rhodes Scholar and cofounder of a Jewish club called the L'Chaim Society (even though he was Baptist), and then on to Yale Law School, where he graduated from while living in the projects in Newark.

With idealistic progressive values tempered by a coziness with Wall Street and a soft spot for the education reform movement—plus youthful looks and a preacher's knack for the spoken word—Booker had come to Newark to save it. Once, he even busted into a neighbor's house to rescue her from a fire.

Booker was a media sensation. If Christie would become the YouTube governor, Booker was already the first politician to master the art of stoking publicity and performing constituent service via the tweet. He used Twitter like a bat signal, responding to complaints about out-of-service streetlights and unplowed walkways. He mixed in self-help aphorisms, quotations from civil rights leaders, and poetry.

Booker was in Newark that day with the rest of the North Jersey Democratic machine to fete the new Republican governor. But as with all of Christie's key Democratic relationships, the foundation had been laid years earlier, during Christie's U.S. Attorney days. Christie had provided federal monitors on the streets to protect against election fraud when Booker first ran for mayor in 2002. When Booker was finally elected in 2006, he asked U.S. Attorney Christie for help addressing crime, and Christie put resources toward Newark and other urban areas. Later, Booker gave Christie the evidence that he needed to bring in one of his biggest corruption cases—Sharpe James, Booker's predecessor.

Booker and Christie texted with each other, right on through Christie's election campaign against Governor Jon Corzine, whom Booker was supporting.

On Election Night, Booker took a call from an operative on the ground. "You're hearing from Camden to Bergen that it's pretty much over? In the other counties, Christie is pretty much crushing? Uh-oh. That's horrible."

Booker met with his staff. "It's a whole new world," he told them. "And now it's about figuring how to work with Governor Christie. That to me is critical. And everybody has got to understand this is a great opportunity."

And so the next day, Booker was at Adubato's headquarters, ready to meet the new governor. And a few weeks afterward they were together again, just the two of them. They got in the back of a Chevy Tahoe for what was billed as a "safety patrol" through the nighttime streets of Newark. They stopped in Christie's old neighborhood, now one of the roughest places in the city. There, in the back of the Tahoe, they made a commitment to each other that they'd work together on a huge area of agreement and mutual interest: education in Newark. Booker had little choice—under a controversial takeover statute, the state ran the school district and gave it most of its money every year.

"Politics is over," the mayor declared. "I've got to find partners for progress."

Of course politics wasn't over. But the state of play was changing dramatically.

THE CHRISTIE-BOOKER BROMANCE went public. We watched in real time as two politicians who viewed themselves as political mavericks made the bipartisan decision to tackle New Jersey's property taxes, which were the highest in the nation and the bane of New Jerseyans' existence. Christie's plan was to institute a 2 percent cap on the annual tax increases levied by towns and school districts.

Booker not only endorsed the 2 percent cap, but he did so very publicly, appearing with Christie at a joint press conference in Newark to embrace the governor's property tax reduction agenda.

Taxes weren't really capped at 2 percent—there were exceptions built into the law, and Christie concurrently cut tax rebates—but taxes would end up increasing at a slower rate than they had before. The cap became a bipartisan, if not incremental, success.

"The governor is a Republican, I'm a Democrat," Booker said that day, using a line that he would recycle in the coming years. "The governor likes steak, I like tofu. The governor is bold, I am bald. But we both recognize that we have common ground between us."

Bipartisanship also meant that when Christie cut funds to Newark, as he did to all municipalities, Booker did not speak up to criticize the governor—even though the cuts meant deep reductions to his own city's police force. I asked for an interview about Christie's empty campaign promises to cities, but Booker strung me along for weeks. Instead, I quoted Mayor J. Christian Bollwage of Elizabeth, the state's fourth-largest city: "Too many mayors in this state will not speak the truth for fear of angering the governor."

On the morning that my article ran, Booker wrote me a direct message via Twitter: "Sorry, I'm on the road, not really having the chance to talk to reporters but I look forward to the opportunity to talk in the future."

**BOOKER WAS A** star of political New Jersey, with leading roles in an award-winning documentary about his first mayoral campaign and two reality TV seasons about his life as mayor. In no small part due to his celebrity Booker had developed business connections that would come in handy as he and Christie joined together for their next big policy initiative.

Booker presented the governor a confidential plan for reforming Newark schools that called for expanding charters, breaking teacher unions, and soliciting philanthropic dollars. Shortly thereafter Booker dined with Facebook founder Mark Zuckerberg in Idaho at an exclusive conference for billionaire media and tech titans. During an after-dinner stroll Zuckerberg told Booker that he wanted to get involved in improving urban schools. A month later Booker presented Zuckerberg with his plan to do just that, and he asked for $100 million to execute it.

Booker called Christie, who was flabbergasted at the price tag that Booker was floating.

"Governor, I believe I can close this deal. I really do. I need you, though," he said.

A meeting was scheduled at the Continental Airlines Presidents Club at Newark Liberty International Airport, where Booker and Christie sold Zuckerberg and his wife on the plan. Their next stop was Oprah Winfrey's studio in Chicago, where this bombshell announcement was dropped.

"So, Mayor Booker, for those who don't know, what's the big *neeeews*?" Winfrey asked, with her trademark lilt.

Zuckerberg was handing over a $100 million challenge grant—Booker and Christie would have to raise another $100 million—and Oprah was stoked. "One. Hundred. Million. Dollars! Yo, yo, yo, yo, yo-oh!"

The whole audience, led by Winfrey, Booker, and Christie, then stood to give Zuckerberg a standing ovation. Why did you choose to make such a generous gift, Winfrey asked.

"Really just because I believe in these guys," Zuckerberg said as the cameras turned to humble-faced Christie and Booker. "Running a company, the main thing I have to do is find people who are really great leaders, and invest in them. And that's what we're doing here."

U.S. education secretary Arne Duncan chimed in via satellite: "I'm really proud of these guys."

Winfrey gave her seal of approval. "I think that is so fantastic. In this age of red states and blue states and everybody being so partisan about everything, the fact that you would all come together. Did that ever enter into it, the politics, that you're a Republican and he's a Democrat?"

"No," Christie said, "it's about the children." Big applause. "What I'm committing to is changing the schools in the city where I was born."

THE MEDIA ROLL-OUT reflected both politicians' proclivity toward celebrity. Winfrey had long run in Booker's social circles. And Christie was now developing an unlikely friendship with Zuckerberg, who would soon host his first-ever political fund-raiser at his home for the New Jersey governor.

But the celebration with Winfrey would prove to be premature. A nonprofit set up to manage the Facebook money spent the first $1 million on a community survey. Then $4.2 million was given to political and educational consultants to lay the groundwork for the plan. Some consultants charged $1,000 a day. Eventually $20 million went to companies for public relations, data analysis, and the creation of teacher evaluations.

The community, an increasingly loud mix of teachers' union activists, parents, students, ex-politicians, and old-time radicals, was not involved in the decision-making process for how the money would be spent. As they demanded answers, the nonprofit set up to manage the Facebook money wouldn't tell reporters how much it paid its CEO.

Still, things were happening: Four new high schools opened, schools extended their hours, and a call center for parents was created. The city got fifty new principals.

And, most expensively, the teachers had a new contract. That's what the bulk of the Facebook money funded—raises for teachers. The contract was agreed to by Christie and the national president of the American Federation of Teachers union, Randi Weingarten, as part of a historic agreement that altered the long-standing teacher tenure system. The contract instituted merit pay for good teachers instead of basing salary increases solely on seniority and advanced degrees while providing $31 million in back pay for teachers who had gone two years without raises.

This wasn't everything Christie, Booker, and Zuckerberg wanted. There would be no buyouts for bad teachers, as originally sought. But the contract was progress, and Christie and Weingarten appeared together on MSNBC's *Morning Joe* to tout it.

"So, Chris, what are you doing here?" host Joe Scarborough asked.

"My job," Christie said, not skipping a beat. He said he was doing what

Zuckerberg wanted—crafting a teachers' union contract that "would be an example for the country."

After the contract was signed, Zuckerberg texted Christie: *Thank you. You kept your end of the bargain now I'm keeping mine.*

Yet local politics undermined the successes. At the behest of Adubato, who wanted to avoid political unrest before the next set of local elections, the selection of a leader for the Newark schools was delayed for months. When Superintendent Cami Anderson was finally hired, she had a brief honeymoon before she laid off two hundred clerical workers, janitors, and security guards—mostly Newark residents—to begin to close a $57 million budget gap. At the same time, $60 million in Facebook money was being spent on charter schools.

Booker already had a foot out the door—he had lost substantial political capital in the community due in part to his education reform agenda and he was now in his waning days as mayor, often traveling the country doing paid speeches. Soon, he would be elected as a U.S. senator.

Any improvements in the schools, like modest gains in test scores and the graduation rate, were overshadowed by Anderson's plan to replace neighborhood-based schooling with a citywide admissions system created through a computer algorithm. This gave students choices and accommodated the new charter schools, but it was a logistical failure. A third of the city's schools were suddenly slated to be closed or relocated, displacing thousands of students. The plan didn't provide transportation to accommodate those who needed to traverse dangerous neighborhoods to get to their new schools, and siblings found themselves scattered to separate parts of town. The reformers, led by Booker and Christie, were shockingly naïve about how closing schools with little public input would upend the daily lives of Newarkers.

School board meetings turned into protests while students staged sit-ins in Anderson's office. Anderson moved out of Newark for her safety. There were concerns about wider unrest as protesters began showing up at Christie's town hall meetings across the state.

Out of this rose a new mayor, Ras Baraka, a public high-school principal and longtime activist who was elected largely due to his opposition to outside control of Newark schools. By then, Christie was eyeing national office and avoiding local controversies, so he wiped his hands clean. He ultimately made a deal with Baraka to nudge Anderson toward an immediate resignation and gradually return the Newark schools back to the city.

By the beginning of his second term, Christie's on-the-ground attempt to rescue the city of his birth was largely over, and he stopped visiting almost entirely. He had another troubled city, this one in South Jersey, where he was spending more and more time.

Camden, not Newark, would be where the Republican governor could try to become an urban savior. But his methods—Democratic alliances and deals of mutual benefit—would be familiar.

# 5

# CONQUERING CAMDEN

C hris Christie remembered it as the hottest press conference he had ever attended. He stood behind the gubernatorial podium in June 2011 on a sad-looking street in Camden—the most physically and financially distressed city in New Jersey, and one of the most dangerous and impoverished in the country. A plan to hold the press conference inside the auditorium of the 136-year-old Lanning Square elementary school behind him was nixed because it was actually cooler *outside*, at well over ninety degrees.

Across the street, a woman living in one of two or three houses still inhabited on the block looked on from a front stoop protected by iron bars. They called these "bird cages." All around us were sagging two- and three-story row houses interspersed with trash-strewn vacant lots where tiny heroin baggies blew like tumbleweeds.

Fifty-seven percent of children in this city were living in poverty; Camden had an unemployment rate more than twice the national average. One-hundred-seventy-five open-air drug markets were counted through a city that's just nine square miles, tucked around two bridges that lead over the Delaware River to Philadelphia.

Christie arrived in Camden in this, his second year on the job, in order to save it.

AS U.S. ATTORNEY, Christie pushed through a plan to allow fugitives to turn themselves in at Camden churches in exchange for possible leniency, drug counseling, and employment services. He publicly feuded with a recalcitrant Supreme Court chief justice who blocked his plan, but he won in the end and the program was the second most successful of its kind in the country.

As a gubernatorial candidate he campaigned in Camden and other cities, which was unusual for a Republican, and even filmed a campaign ad at Camden's sprawling, self-governing Tent City of homeless veterans and addicts.

But over the first twenty months of his term he pursued just one of eleven campaign promises for helping cities. To balance the state budget Christie nipped and tucked from discretionary items such as after-school programs and legal aid for poor people. His budget meant fewer police officers in Camden, Newark, and Trenton—among the most dangerous medium-sized cities in the country. Statewide urban poverty continued unabated, with some of the worst unemployment and home foreclosure rates in the country. Christie's Department of Transportation cleared that Tent City in Camden and put a $45,000 fence around it, but many of those displaced moved across the street, creating an even larger Tent City.

New Jersey was one of the most unaffordable states to live in, with a quarter of renters paying half of their income toward housing. Yet Christie took aggressive steps to dismantle the state's housing safety net, which through the years had created sixty thousand new homes for those with low and moderate incomes, senior citizens, and the disabled. Christie saw the system as fundamentally unfair because it was created by unelected Supreme Court justices who preempted local zoning laws to require affordable housing. Christie thought the law increased property taxes, as towns were forced to accept more residents and associated costs for education and municipal services.

In Christie's second month in office he issued an executive order suspending affordable housing regulations in the state for ninety days. Later he tried to seize $160 million from towns' affordable housing trust funds, which funded homes for the poor and elderly. He even dissolved the state agency in charge of issuing housing regulations.

At every step, he was sued by the Fair Share Housing Center, an advocacy group. The state Supreme Court regularly ruled against him, and in the end he did little more than delay construction of affordable housing for several years.

Christie vetoed a bill to raise the minimum wage to $8.50 an hour because of a provision to tie the increases to the rate of inflation. (The increase was later approved by a ballot referendum.) And he blocked a bill to increase home heating-and-cooling subsidies in order to qualify the poor for more federal food stamp dollars. Meanwhile, the federal government ranked New Jersey second worst in the country for processing applications for food stamps in a timely manner and threatened to take away millions of dollars in funding if the state didn't improve its system.

In 2012, I crunched the data to reveal that the number of general assistance welfare recipients had quietly plummeted under Christie, with thousands denied monthly cash benefits of about two hundred dollars because of a tweak in requirements. Applicants had to, as always, attend job training or show proof that they were looking for work, but now they also had to attend four weekly appointments at the welfare office before they could receive their first checks. Advocates said this put undue strain on those desperate enough to seek aid—they were already dealing with extreme poverty, homelessness, mental illness, or addiction.

Sure enough, I interviewed a nineteen-year-old homeless woman suffering from multiple mental illnesses who managed to take two buses to the welfare office in downtown Camden for three weeks in a row to hand in paperwork showing she was looking for a job. But when she missed the fourth week, she had to start the process all over again. In eight months, five thousand applicants failed to meet the new requirement, helping to save $9 million. The change was a fiscal success.

Christie was more pragmatic than ideological on these issues. Even as he lampooned Obamacare, the federal health care law loathed by Republicans, and rejected its provision to create a state health exchange, he accepted one key element of the law: federal funds to make 175,000 more New Jerseyans eligible for Medicaid. Christie's state treasurer later revealed to us that under this Obamacare provision New Jersey saved $150 million in health care costs in a single year. Christie didn't talk about that.

WHEN CHRISTIE FINALLY started speaking up about urban issues, well into his first term, it was generally in the context of education reform. Inner-city children, he said, were "enslaved" by a public school system run by corrupt teachers' unions that prioritized rich contractual benefits over children's education.

Which was why the governor was here under the Camden sun to announce a major education initiative. There would be a new kind of school rising in urban areas, he said, run by private entities but paid for by taxpayers in some sort of public-private partnership—like a charter school, but not. The plan was sketchy, really, but Christie revealed that a bill would be introduced in the legislature the following week to create these schools. He did not say who would sponsor the bill, but he vowed to sign it.

I asked him: Would one of these new schools come to Camden?

He said that would be up to local school board members.

Then why are you here, in Camden?

This place, he said, symbolized the failure of government to deliver quality schools for its poorest children.

Christie failed to mention that earlier in the year, he canceled construction of a new public school in Camden at the very spot where he was speaking.

FOR NINE YEARS, this Camden neighborhood called Lanning Square had been promised a new school. A few years earlier former governor Jon Corzine promised a modern $42.4 million Lanning Square School. Construction would begin in 2010, Corzine said, because it was "inconceivable" that children were still learning in a school from the 1800s, a place where pieces of the stone veneer at the entrance fell to the sidewalk below, regularly and without warning.

To make way for the new Lanning Square School, the Corzine administration purchased under the threat of eminent domain thirty-four properties, some occupied and some vacant, and knocked them down. Furniture and a color scheme for the new school were chosen.

The new elementary school meant that Hilda Vera-Luciano would finally have to move. She had lived on her little block for thirty-seven years, and raised her family here. But the block was designated as "blighted" by the city, which meant that her home could be seized for redevelopment. She got so many letters through the years threatening eminent domain that she left packed boxes in her living room, stacked up, ready to go. Vera-Luciano, now a great-grandmother, wasn't reluctant to leave, but she was insulted by the cold indifference from the powerful. "I'm just getting tired of going up and down like a yo-yo," she told me.

In 2009, someone from the city finally came and gave her a $64,000 check. In came the bulldozers, turning the family home into rubble. She moved elsewhere in Camden, got a small three-bedroom for $52,000.

The politicians defended what they had done. Progress, imperfect as it was, was happening. The kids would get the school. Vera-Luciano would get a new place and some extra dough. The ground of the city would be rejuvenated. Camden was on its way back.

Not so fast, Carlton Soudan, a third-generation Camden resident, warned me. He had seen it all before. Politicians "do the bait-and-switch on you," he said. "Same old song."

And sure enough, a new school wouldn't replace Vera-Luciano's house any time soon.

Because when Christie came into office in 2010, the hard-charging governor, frustrated with years of Democratic waste at the state's school construction authority, froze almost all construction funding for the state's poorest school districts. The agency had been deeply mismanaged and was now broke; by the time Christie got into office it was not building promised schools for New Jersey's poor children. The new governor needed time to look at the books and figure out how to proceed, he said, prudently and cost-effectively. The perfect problem for a corruption buster with fiscal sense.

In his second year Christie announced that he had determined that the state simply couldn't build all the schools it had promised. So he restructured the school construction program to ensure that schools weren't green-lit based on "political whim." Just ten schools throughout New Jersey would get built now, instead of fifty-two. The lucky ten would be selected through a new, complicated formula.

When the results came back, it was bad news for Camden: Construction on the Lanning Square School was canceled, indefinitely. Lanning Square finished eleventh on the list of ten schools. Officials said that although it qualified under the criteria of the school construction agency, it failed under a separate rubric created by the state Department of Education. Camden lost bureaucracy's game.

Years later, Christie officials refused to provide me details about how they came up with the final score, saying it was "deliberative and therefore will not be provided." In other words: protected under the state's strong secrecy laws. Two more school construction lists came out in the coming months and years, but Lanning Square still somehow failed to make the cut.

"Shocked," the Camden school district's construction official said when the project was canceled. This was a huge priority for the city, the centerpiece of a redevelopment plan to revitalize the whole neighborhood. The state had already spent at least $5.8 million clearing the land and buying property, such as Vera-Luciano's home, to make way for the school. Now what?

The conventional wisdom in the city was that the white Republican governor had abandoned his black and Latino constituents. Of course he had, they said. The betrayal was felt more severely when it was revealed that the land where the school was supposed to go would become a construction staging area for a new medical school being built nearby by Cooper University Hospital, whose chairman was none other than South Jersey political boss George E. Norcross III.

OUT OF THE corner of my eye, I saw him, Norcross himself. A smallish and elegantly appointed man in his fifties, Norcross was standing at the back of that 2011 press conference as Christie, under the Camden heat, said this: "I believe that Camden is a place that has bipartisan leadership, folks who care little about party, and much more about getting the results."

Now things were coming together. Christie made that comment in reference to Norcross, the legendary unelected leader of the Democrats in these parts of Jersey. Norcross was said to control everything from the Statehouse in Trenton to the hospital in Camden, like a political Wizard of Garden State Oz.

"Folks" who care about "getting the results"? Norcross has a sign reading "CAN DO CLUB" on his office desk.

"Second place is first loser," Norcross once said. "I love that."

I could not believe Norcross himself was standing on the curb in Camden, watching a Christie news conference. I had only once or twice seen the man at a public event. For a decade, he had been a Democrat in the shadows.

Now, after Christie stepped down from the podium and returned to his gubernatorial SUV, Norcross held an unprecedented, impromptu press conference of his own. Here he was, sweatless in a perfectly cropped suit as if he were in an air-conditioned space all his own. His driver idled nearby.

Norcross told us Camden public schools were "juvenile prisons" and said that tax dollars to Camden were going down the "sewer." Then he pointed to the sewer, for emphasis. "See that sewer drain?" he said. "That's what it would be like to give the school board ten cents." We were standing down the block from a growing piece of his empire, Cooper University Hospital. And we were next door to a brand-new building now rising—Cooper Medical School of Rowan University, essentially gifted to Norcross in 2009 by former governor Corzine in a surprise, late-night executive order.

Norcross didn't need another crumbling public school next to his expanding medical empire; he wanted one of these new schools, the ones that Christie had just promised. Norcross then talked about creating schools throughout the city—effectively replacing a chunk of the school system in the state's lowest-performing district. He said this would be "the most important thing to happen in Camden in twenty years."

Norcross later told me he didn't know anything about Christie's plans for new schools until the Camden press conference. But Norcross and Christie had quietly developed an unusual and fruitful political friendship. The unelected Democratic power broker and the future Republican presidential candidate had just gone to a Phillies–Mets game together, in fact. Norcross said he didn't recall if they even talked about Camden and education.

And yet after the press conference, Norcross's younger brother—Donald Norcross, a state senator and soon-to-be congressman—sponsored a bill in the legislature to create "renaissance schools," which would use private dollars to construct and manage public schools. These new types of schools would be run by for-profit entities not subject to public bidding and disclosure laws. Norcross's renaissance schools bill moved through the system faster than almost any Democratic legislation during the Christie era. Months later Christie held the bill signing in Camden, back at the old Lanning Square School.

"It is unconscionable to me to see what is going on in this city," Christie said, flanked by Senator Norcross. "I can no longer sit by as governor and allow these children's voices to be silenced."

Soon, not one but *five* new Camden renaissance schools would be planned. All would have the Norcross family name on them—The KIPP Cooper Norcross Academy. The Norcrosses didn't fund the schools, but they provided something more important in New Jersey: political muscle. The KIPP Cooper Norcross Academy would rise right where the Lanning Square School was supposed to go, and it would benefit from millions in tax dollars already spent on the scuttled public school project.

The day of the bill signing I called up a former school board member, Jose Delgado, who was worried about this newfangled renaissance school—worried about public money headed to the private sector, about the loss of local control, about who would be making money off these public dollars. There shouldn't be a bill signing today, Delgado said. "The affair that should be occurring on this day is the opening of a school," he said.

But to others, this seemed like a good deal. The schools would be 5 percent cheaper per student for the taxpayers, and unlike charter schools they were required to educate all students in the neighborhoods where they sat. They would be incentivized to cater to special education students and non–English speakers, the kinds of students who critics said were sometimes left behind by charters because they cost too much to educate and brought down test scores.

Technically, the plan had to be approved by the Camden School Board, which deadlocked 4–4, rendering it dead. But the Norcrosses had serious sway over the board, and two months later the school board came back, met behind closed doors, made a minor adjustment to the plan, and voted yes.

For Christie, the arrangement meant he saved tens of millions of dollars in further school construction costs, because renaissance schools had to use private financing to build their facilities. Plus, by injecting the philosophies of the private sector into urban education, Christie got a chance to do something he actually believed in. Years earlier Christie had worked as a lobbyist for Edison, a large for-profit manager of schools, and he even appointed the company's CEO as his education commissioner. Signing a bill like this was in keeping with his ideological pedigree.

For Norcross, the school was a chance to build a positive legacy for his family name with an institution that would also buffer his medical school in downtown Camden.

There was nothing, Christie later told me, that was unholy about how this went down. The governor said he had never discussed the idea of ending construction of the Lanning Square public school in order to turn the project over to KIPP.

Regardless, what effectively happened was clear: A future Republican presidential candidate handed the state's top Democratic political boss a major educational operation on six acres of a revitalizing downtown in the heart of South Jersey.

This deal was just one piece of the larger puzzle. Norcross controlled more votes in the legislature than anyone else. Not only was his childhood friend, Stephen Sweeney, the senate president, and not only was his brother, Donald, an important senator, but several other senators and assembly members throughout South Jersey and beyond owed their political lives to Norcross.

By working with Norcross—by dealing with him—Christie could infuse his term as governor with near limitless potential.

AS A KID, George E. Norcross III donned a bow tie and tagged along to meetings with his father, who as president of the four-county Regional Council of the AFL-CIO Central Labor Union was a major South Jersey political power player. The boy was instructed: "Don't say anything. You can learn just by observing." After the meetings, father explained to son how to read those rooms.

Norcross went to Rutgers University in Camden but dropped out after listening to a political science professor drone on. "He knew less about how politics is actually practiced than I did," Norcross later told *Philadelphia* magazine. So he started an insurance business in downtown Camden and built a practice boosted by political connections and government contracts. In 1978, at the age of twenty-two, he got a patronage job as the head of the Camden Parking Authority and ran in political circles with Angelo Errichetti, the Camden mayor, state senator, and South Jersey political boss of his time.

Errichetti would soon get caught up in the corruption scandal known as Abscam, and the twenty-five-year-old Norcross became the campaign finance chairman for his successor in the mayor's office, Randy Primas. By the end of the eighties Norcross was Primas's primary financial backer.

Norcross ascended to the chairmanship of the Camden County Democratic Party in 1989, the only official job he would ever have in politics. He raised campaign cash through engineers, lawyers, and accountants who did business with the local government; in 1990, a political action committee associated with him funded $145,000 of the winning mayoral candidate's $170,000 war chest. He shocked local politicos by taking out TV ads in a low-profile campaign against a Republican state senator who had once denied a political appointment to his father.

Norcross didn't invent the game, but he played it better than damn near everyone, and his influence spread from Camden City to Camden County and then to all of South Jersey. As Christie was getting off to a stumbling start in politics in North Jersey, Norcross was cementing political control in the South. He was professionalizing local politics with pollsters, strategists, and a moderate message. He successfully ran women, minorities, and a high school football coach for office, developing one of the most diverse political coalitions around.

Government contractors funded the operation. Companies were

instructed on how much money to contribute to which campaigns and political action committees by the number of invitations they received for fund-raisers; you need not attend, just send checks. Political fund-raisers were staged in Atlantic City casinos and exclusive golf clubs. They were called birthday parties or barbecues, lobster fests or clambakes, but they all fueled the Democratic machine.

When Norcross's insurance company was absorbed by Commerce Bank, his fortune grew financially and politically. With Norcross as one of the executives at Commerce, the bank started doing business with hundreds of local governments and funding local candidates for office. Norcross's power extended statewide, and he was said to regularly call Governor Jim McGreevey's office with "instructions on hiring, contracts, and policy decisions."

"The McGreeveys, the Corzines, they're all going to be with me," Norcross once said. "Because not that they like me, but because they have no choice."

Buoyed by the influence that their flush campaign coffers bought, Norcross's South Jersey Democrats ascended to leadership positions throughout the legislature. This is what drove Norcross—the belief that the southern part of the state had been shafted by the wealthier, more populous north when it came to governmental largesse. South Jersey would finally get its fair share, and Norcross would be the broker to make it happen. "For years, there has been a political order in this state, and we're now rearranging the seats at the table," Norcross said in 2002. "South Jersey Democrats are coming to have a presence, and many in the north don't like it."

Case in point: When Norcross made a rare trip to the Statehouse to personally seal a deal giving South Jersey a minor league hockey arena and civic center, he ended up in a legendary shoving match with Republican Senate copresident John Bennett, who was stalling the plan. Norcross uttered this, allegedly: "I will fucking destroy you."

Bennett lost his reelection bid.

"He has those who stand in his way defeated or removed," Bennett said. "I will never seek public office again."

Norcross explained: "There have been times when my passion and intensity have gotten the better of me, and I've acted in ways that would not have made my mother proud." But he said his motives were pure—he was fighting for South Jersey.

"No one will ever, *ever again*, not include or look down or double-cross

South Jersey," Norcross once said. "Never again will that happen. Because they know we put up the gun and we pulled the trigger and *we blew their brains out."*

Norcross's juice came in part from his association with the trade unions, which provided a wealth of political contributions and a farm team for future politicians. George's brother, Donald, succeeded their father as the leader of the eighty-five-thousand-strong South Jersey AFL-CIO and the union's legendary get-out-the-vote operation. Donald would soon be appointed to a seat in the Assembly (the assemblywoman who stepped aside got a library named after her) before heading over to the state Senate and shortly thereafter to Congress.

A third brother, Philip, formed the last piece of a three-headed political machine—he was a highly paid lobbyist whose law firm earned millions in government contracts. He was known as the policy wonk in the family, helping with writing legislation.

All of this has long been viewed warily by the government do-gooders who work in newsrooms and ivory towers. Norcross "combines the smoothness and outward style of a business leader with the wiles and savvy of an old-time political boss," political scientist Ross K. Baker told the *New York Times.* "Then he has a volcanic temper, which is the sheathed sword that makes many people afraid to cross him. It's a very formidable combination."

In the legislature, rather than uttering his name, Democratic staffers used a euphemism that referred to Norcross's impressive silver mane. "The gray-haired uncle," they would say, "wants this done."

The hair is thicker than thick, combed and classy—and it is the first thing you notice about him. When he smiles, it's a toothy smile, a little strained. He sometimes juts out his bottom jaw, as if he's about to crack his knuckles and punch you in the gut.

The perception of power is Norcross's greatest weapon, backed by a personality that can be charming and threatening in the span of a single conversation.

**IT HAS BEEN** written that Christie met Norcross in early 2003, when they dined together at Panico's in New Brunswick. Christie was U.S. Attorney at the time, and Norcross was coming into his own as the South Jersey Democratic leader. The intermediary was Michael Critchley, a prominent defense attorney who would one day represent Bridget Kelly, the woman at the center of the Bridgegate scandal.

Norcross sought the meeting, Christie told me. Christie obliged because he was "trying to get to know prominent people." "He's a significant businessman and operator, political operator, in the state. He wants to meet me? Sure, why not," Christie thought. All it was, he said, was a "get-to-know-you dinner," two hours about their respective backgrounds and families. It was, Christie said, "small talk."

Norcross had a different recollection. He told me the men actually first met in the nineties, and their 2003 dinner was about something substantial—new federal regulations on health care compliance that he was dealing with at Cooper University Hospital, where he was the vice chairman at the time.

Soon enough, Norcross found himself dealing with a lot more than just compliance issues. The Securities and Exchange Commission was looking into a business partnership involving Norcross and the top assemblyman in New Jersey. At about the same time Christie himself as U.S. Attorney announced that his feds were probing a billboard company that had done business with Norcross and aides to Governor McGreevey.

As these investigations swirled, U.S. Attorney Christie was asked by *Philadelphia Inquirer* columnist Monica Yant Kinney if he would dine again with Norcross considering his most recent legal issues. He said: "Anything I do or say, is only good for the moment."

At the end of their conversation Christie randomly quoted his favorite rock star, Bruce Springsteen, from the song "Badlands": "Poor man wanna be rich, rich man wanna be king, / And a king ain't satisfied till he rules everything." Christie's criminal investigators were now looking into the Norcross empire. All direct communication, according to both men, ceased. Norcross lowered his profile and tried to keep his name out of the papers. He wasn't successful.

"I WANT YOU to fire that fuck. You need to get this fuck Rosenberg for me and teach this jerk-off a lesson. He has to be punished . . . Rosenberg is history and he is done and anything I can do to crush his ass, I wanna do because I just think he's just done, an evil fuck."

Norcross's most infamous moment—and closest brush with the law—came when a part-time councilman in tiny Palmyra Township started recording their conversations. John Gural's tapes, which were later publicly released by the New Jersey Attorney General's Office, included Norcross's brutal takedown of Ted Rosenberg, a Democratic lawyer who opposed him. The tapes also depicted Norcross explaining how he kept a political serf in line: "I sat him down and said . . . 'Don't fuck with me on this one . . . if you ever do that and I catch you one more time doing it, you're gonna get your fucking balls cut off.' He got the message."

After going through hundreds of hours of these tapes the New Jersey attorney general, a Democratic appointee, decided not to indict, instead kicking the case to U.S. Attorney Christie. In July 2005, Christie said he was investigating the matter. Gural and Rosenberg were hopeful that this political-corruption-busting prosecutor would rid South Jersey of Norcross. But Christie never called them to testify before a grand jury, and they soon told the press that they were worried that Christie was protecting Norcross.

The following month, January 2006, Christie dropped the case.

And he didn't do it quietly. In an extraordinarily public move Christie wrote a six-page, seven-point letter explaining that he couldn't pursue the investigation because the New Jersey Attorney General's Office had, in so many words, screwed it up—perhaps intentionally, for "the protection of political figures."

This was unusual, for a federal prosecutor to publicly lambaste state investigators. The attorney general at the time called Christie's allegations "utter nonsense."

By accusing others of politicizing the Norcross investigation, Christie was "freed of any responsibility for letting George Norcross get off of the hook," Rosenberg said. "Chris Christie is first and foremost a political animal."

A decade later, I asked Christie why he gave up on the Norcross case. "I'm not going to talk a lot about it, because I still feel under some ethical restrictions to discuss publicly a lot of the stuff that happened when I was U.S. Attorney that isn't completely public," he said. He also wouldn't get into what he found out about why some of the Norcross tapes were deleted by the Attorney General's Office. "There was no evidence to conclude what definitely happened. All I know is the investigation got messed up at the state AG's office."

The authorities did nail three people on tax fraud and campaign finance violations as part of the investigation, but illegalities were not pinned on

Norcross himself. In the end, much of the recordings was determined to be little more than juicy gossip and political bravado.

"Christie, as I've come to know him now, is somebody who if he has a head shot he will take it," Norcross later said. "If I had done something illegal, he would've indicted me. No doubt about it in my mind." The fact that the Christie letter did not explicitly pronounce his innocence "disappointed" him.

The dropping of the Norcross case became a much-discussed riddle in the Trenton political world. Did Christie agree not to indict Norcross in order to establish a partnership with a man he could later make deals with as governor? Those who worked with Christie at the U.S. Attorney's Office, even his detractors, doubt this—they say he wanted as many political indictments as possible. They do note, however, that if he didn't think he could *convict* Norcross, if he thought this über-smart and carefully coiffed millionaire would woo a jury enough to avoid prison, Christie wouldn't have gone after him. Taking a swing at Norcross and missing was ill-advised.

Asked about the Norcross investigation that he dropped, the governor seemed to get about as honest as he could get in explaining it to *Philadelphia* magazine. "You change roles. Um, I'm now—here I was the United States Attorney, a prosecutor, and I was doing my job as I saw it. And now I'm the governor. And now I'm a political leader, on top of being a governmental leader. And so certain things that I couldn't do as a prosecutor, I can do now, and I'm really obligated to do, and certain things that I could do as a prosecutor I can't do anymore. So, you know, your power is in some ways expanded and your power in some ways is limited, as the governor, as compared to being U.S. Attorney."

ON SEPTEMBER 11, 2001, a seventh grader at Sacred Heart School in Camden was asked if he was afraid.

"I'm not afraid," the boy said, "because if the terrorists fly over Camden, they'll think they have done it already."

I heard that anecdote, told by Monsignor Michael Doyle, a longtime Camden civil rights crusader, when I first began covering Camden for the *Courier-Post* in South Jersey. It is still the saddest thing about Camden that I've ever heard. The feeling of abandonment—by people, by business, and mostly by government—was tangible. Camden had lost 70 percent of its population since 1950, and more than a third of its parcels of land were vacant.

Like Newark, Camden experienced a multidecade, across-the-board collapse in the manufacturing job base. Schools, government, and the police department were woefully underfunded and rife with corruption. Camden became a place to dump what wealthier suburban subdivisions didn't want: waste water treatment plants, trash dumps, and halfway houses. The city became known less as a place to buy a home to raise a family and more as a place to idle your mom's Nissan while you bought strong heroin.

One freezing winter night I visited a shelter in Camden to interview the homeless, and I asked a heroin addict from western Pennsylvania how he ended up here, in South Jersey. "If you liked cheeseburgers, if you really *really* liked cheeseburgers, and you heard that the best cheeseburgers in the world were in Camden," he told me, "wouldn't you be here, too?"

I also wrote about the Gonzalez family, who made enough money cleaning offices in the suburbs to buy a little row house, only to find out that Camden's broken sewerage system was leaking feces into their basement. The city government was too broke to fix it. They put the house up for sale, but there were no takers.

Things weren't supposed to be this way. Several years earlier, South Jersey Democrats had a grand idea to save Camden. Thanks in part to Norcross's muscle in 2002 the state handed Camden $175 million in bonds and loans. There was one catch: The governor would appoint a chief operating officer to run the city and oversee the elected mayor and city council. Longtime Norcross ally Primas, the former mayor Norcross had backed thirty years earlier, was the first COO; the second was another Norcross ally who earned $175,000 a year, the same salary as the governor.

At the time this was the biggest state takeover of a municipality in American history. Camden residents lost democratic rights. In return they were promised more jobs, lower crime, the demolition of vacant properties—and yes, fixed sewers.

But even though the Gonzalezes' sewer was listed as an emergency project, it was never fixed. In fact few of the stated promises were fulfilled. Down the block from the Gonzalezes' house, across the street from a prostitution den, I met George Arroyo, who was cleaning a vacant lot so the local kids wouldn't have to walk through urban detritus to get to school. Arroyo told me a rumor he had heard on the streets: that the $175 million bailout package was sent in an armored truck from the state capital, but the truck got carjacked on the way to Camden.

He was serious. And he didn't realize how right he was.

As I found in a thirteen-month investigation for the *Philadelphia Inquirer*, less than 5 percent of the money to save Camden went to address crime, education, job training, and municipal services. The vast majority of the $175 million was for institutions, like Norcross's Cooper University Hospital, which received more than $25 million to expand, and the local aquarium, which used its $25 million for a new hippo exhibit.

In 2009 Governor Corzine, who had presided over much of this disaster in public policy, was leaving office—and leaving Camden to the next guy.

**"GOVERNOR-ELECT CHRISTIE FOR** sure."

On election night 2009, Norcross emailed Bill Palatucci, Christie's political aide-de-camp, to tell him the breaking news that Christie had just beaten Corzine. Norcross had seen the early returns. It was three minutes after the polls had closed.

Palatucci burst into the hotel suite where Team Christie was holed up, carrying his BlackBerry with the email aloft. He had a huge smile. Later, as a gift, Norcross gave Christie a framed copy of the "Governor-elect Christie for sure" email.

With a new Republican governor on his way to Trenton, South Jersey legislators sprang to action, working to end the Camden takeover and return control to the city. The so-called "Camden Freedom Act" was rushed through in the last week of Corzine's term, without input from the residents who were supposedly being freed, ending America's biggest state takeover after more than six years.

Meanwhile, Christie called Norcross for a meeting. Just as he had met with Big Steve and Joe D. and Cory in Newark, now here he was meeting with Norcross in Philadelphia, across the river from Camden.

"Listen, I want to find a way for us to work together," Christie told Norcross. "The election's over. I'm the governor. I want to work with you. And it's going to be important for me to have a relationship with you."

Norcross agreed. He found Christie to be a dynamic communicator and terrific political artist.

One Christie adviser told me the takeaway from the meeting was this: "Let's do it—how do we do it? Let's break some heads."

That's how the most consequential relationship in modern New Jersey politics began. The de facto leaders of opposing political parties would never utter an ill word about the other in public. Christie once said that he "can't think of anything off the top of my head that hasn't been laudable" that Norcross has done.

"He has never in his dealings with me ever broken his word to me, ever," Christie told me. "If he tells me he's going to do something, he does it. And if he tells me he can't, he doesn't. And I have had nothing but a fair, even, and honest relationship with him."

IN THE BEGINNING, the new Norcross-Christie relationship had no evident benefits for Camden. Blaming a state deficit, Christie cut $466 million in aid to municipalities when he became governor. That disproportionately affected cities, like Camden, where the state funded more than 80 percent of the city budget.

Camden mayor Dana Redd, a Norcross acolyte, was faced with a slimmed-down budget, but she never spoke out against the governor (as much as I tried to get her to). Turned out, that was the smart play. Some months later Christie came through with another allocation of funds, which meant that Camden faced only an 8 percent cut from the previous year in Trenton money, far better than expected.

Christie promised that the cuts would deepen every year until he could wean Camden off its state subsidies. But Camden was filled with nontaxpaying entities like schools and hospitals—it lacked tax ratables. With Christie's frugality and the economic recession, Redd couldn't make payroll. The cost of the police department alone was more than twice as much as the city's total municipal tax base.

So after failing to negotiate contractual cuts with the unions, and with no state bailout from Christie, she did the unthinkable, laying off 163 of 368 officers—nearly half of the department, rendering the police force in America's most dangerous city nearly impotent with barely more than 200 officers, the lowest level in more than half a century. Sixty firefighters, and 100-plus employees of every department in City Hall, were likewise laid off.

But the cop cuts were the harshest. The entire narcotics unit was eliminated, prompting gangbangers to print T-shirts marking the date when the layoffs would take effect—"JANUARY 18, 2011: It's our time." There were no more property crimes detectives. Car gets stolen? Head to the police headquarters, somehow, and file a futile police report. Car accident? No major injuries, then no police response.

The rate of aggravated assaults and burglaries went up by double-digit percentages. The arrest rate went down 43 percent. Homicides reached forty-seven that year and sixty-seven the next, a city record. The unsolved crime rate skyrocketed.

On the day the layoffs were executed, officers lined the side of Federal Street in Camden with boots they would no longer need. Soon Camden residents started coming by. They wanted to know if the shoes were being given away, because they sure could use a pair.

CHRISTIE DIDN'T SAY much about the public safety crisis. He didn't come to Camden to decry the violence or walk through the white crosses planted in the front of City Hall to memorialize the victims.

For a period, he sent in state police. Invoking his mother's old phrase, he said he didn't have a "money tree" to do more.

But behind the scenes, the powers that be were cooking up a solution. They were going union busting.

Norcross and Christie reasoned that tens of millions of dollars could be saved by severely cutting back on police officers' benefits. The police contract was laden with goodies like "shift differentials" (originally intended for officers who worked overnight shifts, this perk was now used for day shifts, too) and "longevity pay" (which kicked in after just five years).

The proceeds from eliminating the labor agreements, they reasoned, could then be used to hire more officers. But the only way to rip up the contract was to bust the union. The only way to bust the union? Eliminate the police department altogether. So the Republican governor, partnering with a Democratic mayor and a Democratic political boss, agreed to do just that.

The state takeover of Camden had ended, but now the city's primary duty—public safety—would be taken over by the county government. The plan was to replace the city police department with a Camden County Police Department overseen by the Camden County Freeholders, all Democrats who served at Norcross's will.

Around this time I sat down with the governor in his office in Trenton. Bruce Springsteen sang "Wrecking Ball" quite loudly from his office stereo. "We're not trying to break the unions, the unions are trying to break the middle class in New Jersey through the expenses, and they're close to doing it," he said. "And this government, our government, is the only thing that can stand up and fight that."

Protests ensued. Community activists in Camden believed that the original police layoffs, spurred on by Christie's cuts, created a crisis in the murder rate that provided a convenient excuse for yet another takeover by out-of-town politicians. They said Democrats were intentionally sabotaging the city police, breaking the department's budget on things like overtime for officers who did security at the tax-exempt concert arena.

In the end, though, Democrat-backed judges signed off on the dissolution of the city force and the creation of the Camden County Police Department. Christie sent $10 million in state start-up funds. New patrol cars were purchased. Civil service protections were temporarily suspended, allowing the police chief to promote and demote at will. The force had new foot patrols, cameras on street corners, and a gunshot-detecting network of microphones, but it also sought to win hearts by distributing free hot dogs, ice cream, and Christmas presents to kids. The "culture," as Chief Scott Thomson was fond of saying, was reborn.

And in fact, most of the anti-Christie and anti-Norcross community activists I knew said their neighborhoods felt measurably safer. In 2014, the force's first year under the county, homicides were down 51 percent and total violent crime dropped 22 percent.

Christie trumpeted stats like these whenever he could—on national TV, in his State of the State speech, and while traveling the country. Yet the context was cherry-picked. He always compared the progress to 2012, the most violent year in Camden history, when the governor himself allowed the police department to be cut to nearly half of its legally mandated size.

The numbers didn't look as impressive when compared to the pre-layoff years. Under the new force, in 2014, there were thirty-three homicides in Camden. In 2009, before Christie got into office, there were thirty-four.

Camden's public safety success was moving more slowly than Christie's political aspirations. Christie sold the department's techniques as the way to reduce crime, save money, and quell the recent violence between blacks and police around the country. Here was a fiscal conservative, compassionate about an urban area and willing to work across the aisle, all the while cutting onerous union-inflicted work rules and hiring more cops. The Camden story was tailor-made for a nascent presidential campaign.

Privately, Camden County Democratic functionaries griped that Christie's rhetoric about his Camden success overstated his involvement. He did not order the firing of the department, as he claimed on the stump, and instead had signed on to a plan already in progress. As the deal was being finalized, one source said, stretches of time went by when Christie wasn't responsive to local leaders.

But no one dared publicly complain, and a narrative was built of a Camden reborn through bipartisanship. President Obama even came to the city, highlighting it as a model for twenty-first-century policing. In his remarks he thanked Mayor Redd. The president did not mention Christie nor Norcross, who was more responsible for this than anyone.

I HAD REPORTED about each man at different times—Norcross, when I was covering Camden, and Christie, when I was based out of the Statehouse. Now that their political partnership was starting to go public, I was eager to untangle the story, because I knew Christie's partnership with Norcross would be central to understanding him both personally and as a governor.

Then Norcross bought my newspaper.

Norcross and a group of investors announced they were purchasing the *Philadelphia Inquirer*, the *Philadelphia Daily News*, and the joint website, Philly.com, for $55 million.

Someone asked Christie what he thought about that. The governor smiled mischievously and looked at me. "I'd love to have Norcross be Katz's new boss," he said.

As a newly minted newspaper owner, Norcross attended the next Trenton Legislative Correspondents Club dinner. When he showed up he found his table somewhere near the back of the room, but he pulled the power move of all power moves: He proceeded to the head table, greeted the governor, and then sat at the table next to his—in the temporarily vacated seat of Christie's spokesman. Norcross stayed there for the rest of the event. (The following year Norcross skipped all pretense and simply sat with Christie's senior staff.)

I was president of the correspondents' club that year, which meant I sat next to the governor at the dinner—and I roasted the governor. When I was called up to the mic for my speech I left my iPhone at the table with the audio recorder going so my wife could listen to it later if she was interested (she wasn't). Former law enforcement guy that he is, Christie noticed my phone on the table and picked it up. What transpired next I gleaned from my recording.

"He's recording us!" Christie said, feigning outrage as he showed the phone to the lieutenant governor, the Senate president, and the chief justice of the Supreme Court, all of whom were sitting at our table.

Christie left the recorder going. When I opened my roast with an off-color joke about Governor McGreevey's ex-boyfriend, Christie approved. "Wow! Really! That's starting off strong," he said.

Then I moved to zing Christie about Norcross. "Governor, you and I do have something in common," I said. "As many of you know, my newspaper, the *Inquirer*, was bought by George Norcross one year ago. . . . That's right, Governor. You and I have the same boss . . . I don't know what everybody is laughing at. He's your boss, too!"

CHRISTIE'S URBAN NEW Jersey—from Camden to Newark to Paterson and back again—needed a new stimulus. Manufacturing had sustained it over the centuries, now those jobs were long gone, overseas, or obsolete. For a time, information processing—back-end office work for corporations—replaced manufacturing as a good source of middle-class jobs, but now many of those cubicle farms sat empty in sprawling office parks. The national recession in 2008, Superstorm Sandy in 2012, and the collapse of the Atlantic City casino industry in 2014 only compounded the economic problems.

Christie enacted gradual business tax cuts, eventually totaling more than $2 billion. But his only other major effort to create jobs was through generous and highly controversial tax incentives, used to lure businesses to New Jersey or keep them in-state.

He began by trying to restart two stalled mega-projects with jaw-droppingly large tax breaks. First, he earmarked a $261 million tax credit to finish construction of the half-built Revel hotel and casino in Atlantic City, but it went bankrupt on the way to its indefinite closure, leaving a brand-new glistening skyscraper as a vacant symbol of the gambling town that Christie was supposed to save.

Likewise, Christie sought to complete the stalled construction of a massive shopping and entertainment complex at the Meadowlands known as "American Dream"—he pledged $390 million in tax credits—but litigation and other issues delayed its opening until years after the target date of the 2014 Super Bowl, which was played next door.

Some companies were given tax breaks for simply moving from one place in New Jersey to another place in New Jersey—and sometimes, to another place in the same neighborhood. Prudential Financial moved a few blocks away in downtown Newark and won a $211 million tax break. Panasonic was awarded $102 million to move one train stop.

Christie's most significant change to the state's tax incentive program began with the signing of a bill sponsored by Norcross's legislator brother, state senator Norcross, that gave businesses moving to Camden richer incentives than those offered to the rest of the state. So Subaru snagged $118 million in tax incentives to move its headquarters four miles down the highway from suburban Cherry Hill to a Camden office park, promising to create one hundred jobs as part of the move. That's more than $1 million per new job. The multibillion-dollar defense contractor Lockheed Martin got $107 million in tax breaks to relocate from nearby suburban Moorestown to the Camden waterfront; after thirty-five years, if Lockheed is still around, the company will have provided just $249,000 in *total* net economic benefits to the state. That's according to Christie's own figures.

Critics of incentive programs say the short-term political gains of ribbon-cutting ceremonies for new buildings are not worth the long-term shortfalls in the state budget. But boy did the deals look good in the newspapers the next day! A politician's name in a headline that tells of "jobs created" becomes fodder for future campaign ads. Officials made grand pronouncements about Camden's renewal after each tax break. Just as with the state takeover, officials promised a brand-new day for Camden just around the corner.

The Camden tax incentives may have come from Christie but they bore the Norcross name. George served on the board of directors of Holtec International, a nuclear parts manufacturer that landed $260 million in tax breaks to move its plant to Camden's waterfront (net economic benefits over thirty-five years: $155,520). Cooper University Hospital, where George served as chairman, was awarded $40 million in incentives to move two offices from the suburbs to the city (nineteen jobs created). And lawyer-lobbyist brother Philip represented the Philadelphia 76ers in its deal for a new practice facility in Camden with $82 million in incentives. That deal failed to even allow Camden kids to sometimes watch practices or use the gym, and jobs were not guaranteed for Camden residents.

The millions in tax breaks for the 76ers—owned by a billionaire who donated $50,000 to the Republican Governors Association when Christie ran the group—troubled one conservative New Jersey state senator enough that he actually criticized the Christie administration over it. This was a rare betrayal amid the typical obsequiousness of the Republicans in Trenton. And Americans For Prosperity, founded by the conservative financier Koch brothers, slammed the tax breaks as "corporate welfare handouts" that neither bring jobs nor stimulate economic growth. Conservatives said empowering government to pick corporate winners defied the laws of capitalism.

Meanwhile liberals argued that corporations moved to New Jersey for its location, educated workforce, and quality schools—not tax incentives. They spoke of the unfairness of giving breaks to the wealthy corporations while tax relief programs for the working poor were slashed.

The tax deals were hammered out in secret and then approved by the state's Economic Development Authority, which was led by longtime Christie confidant Michele Brown. The details of the 76ers agreement were released on a Monday and then voted on on Tuesday at 10:00 a.m. by a group of gubernatorial appointees in a cramped conference room in Trenton, forty-five minutes from Camden. I stood in the doorway, struggling to listen in on the hearing, as Camden activist Kelly Francis took the mic. He had taken a bus and train to Trenton to ask the 76ers CEO if there'd be entry-level jobs for local residents at the team's new practice facility.

Well, the CEO said, "we need a shooting guard."

The suits laughed and laughed.

Norcross and Christie believed that targeting one small area with nearly unlimited tax incentives would bring in a critical mass of employers for an immediate economic impact. Construction jobs would be created, and the new companies would attract other companies. Lunch places would open and retail stores would follow. Having corporate executives in a downtrodden place would lead to philanthropic efforts. The Christie Republicans and the Norcross Democrats argued that the cynics just couldn't recognize the momentum.

Officials also noted that companies had to make money before they could collect tax breaks. So when Revel closed, for example, the state didn't lose a dime.

In the long term, though, there'd be untold billions of dollars in lost tax revenue, and in the short term there was little improvement in the state economy. While hundreds of thousands of private-sector jobs were added under Christie's watch, New Jersey lagged in job growth compared to the rest of the nation. After his first term New Jersey had recovered just 47 percent of jobs lost during the Great Recession, far fewer than its neighbors and the country as a whole.

NONETHELESS CAMDEN WAS fast becoming Christie's symbol of not just urban renewal but also presidential-caliber bipartisanship—a demonstration of how when Americans lay down their ideological swords and sit down at the same conference table, they can do the impossible.

"For those who examine what's happening in Camden and constantly have critiques of it," Christie said in a speech in the city, "I would say to you this is a place I look forward to doing the business of government." For a time, Christie was visiting Camden more than any other municipality besides Trenton.

Regardless of the policies, when Christie compared New Jersey to Washington, where Congress dissolved into discord each week, he had a strong argument to make. He was most assuredly working with the other side.

But there was more work to be done. Many of these white-collar professionals now coming to Camden for work drove here every day from their homes in the surrounding suburbs. Until Camden had schools that functioned properly, it would never turn those professionals into residents.

Of course, Christie and Norcross had a plan to fix all that, too.

CAMDEN SCHOOLS WERE performing horribly: Twenty-three of the district's twenty-six were considered the worst in the state, and fewer than 20 percent of fourth graders were proficient in language arts. Each student cost an average of $23,709 to educate, $5,000 more than the state per-student average.

The problem wasn't money, Christie said again and again. The problem was leadership.

Even though Christie's state coffers funded 86 percent of the district's $327 million budget, he wasn't allowed to choose the Camden schools superintendent. "I don't want to look back on my time as governor and say, 'I should have done something different, I should have acted more aggressively,' " he later remembered thinking.

So in 2013 Christie took over the school district. Norcross Democrats welcomed Christie's intervention and even thanked him for it. The school board would be reduced to an advisory role, stripped of its powers, and the governor unilaterally appointed the new superintendent—a thirty-two-year-old Iranian American from the Bronx with a background both as a teacher and as an analyst for Goldman Sachs.

In a testament to the near-control Norcross had over the city, this was all met with acquiescence. Just one board member complained about "disenfranchisement" and resigned.

CHRISTIE'S TAKEOVER OF the school district gave him a stage to return to Camden, over and again, to make announcements and declare progress. Each time his PR team shot videos of him adorably mixing with black and brown kids. One afternoon Christie walked through an old community center in North Camden, past a boxing ring and onto a basketball court, where he asked for the ball and went to the foul line. Reporters shadowed him, aware of the potential for an authentic moment.

*Clang.* The gov missed his first free throw shot. *Boom, clang.* Missed again. *Whiff.* Air ball! After one particularly errant throw the ball bounced toward me, almost hitting the microphone I was holding. "If I hit Katz, I would have stopped!" he said.

Because hitting me would've been better than actually landing the shot.

But he didn't stop shooting. And he didn't stop missing. He continued to ask for the ball back again and again. There was a hard-headedness here that seemed unusual—wouldn't most politicians make a self-deprecating joke and move on to the next photo-staged activity? Not this governor.

On the *twelfth* shot, as the cameras clicked, the ball hit the backboard, then the rim, and fell in. He smiled, high-fived Mayor Redd, and proceeded outside to a Little League field to have a catch with a little girl.

"In all the years of previous governors, we were always the forgotten city, they never came to Camden and showed the love that Christie does," an optimistic Emiliano Reyes, Jr., a Camden truck driver, told me that day. "Flowers growing out of concrete, it's awesome."

IN HIS FIRST term the Norcross family quietly brought the Christies to Philadelphia about a half dozen times to watch sports. They sat together in luxury suites at Eagles football and Phillies baseball games. These trips were never on the governor's public schedule.

But by 2013, the Norcross-Christie relationship was very public, affirmed at the grand opening of Norcross's new Cooper Medical School of Rowan University in downtown Camden. The medical school had been the dream of George's father, a onetime Cooper board member.

Had Norcross's political muscle helped him to finally land the $140 million facility? "I sure as hell hope so," Norcross once told a reporter.

Christie took the lectern as keynote speaker. "The son executed the plan of the father," Christie said. "And any of us, *any of us* who have children, who we have dreams for, and then those children begin to execute on those dreams, not only of their own but some of ours . . . we feel a great sense of pride."

He said, "There is fascination in the media about my relationship with George Norcross," but it is nothing more than admiration and friendship. "So now some will run away and write stories, and say, 'Jeez, why was he saying this stuff today about Norcross?' Let 'em write about it. Because from my perspective, whenever my name is in the newspaper it ain't all that bad. And—and—I know whenever I mention George's name *I'm going to be in the newspaper*."

Nearly blinded by the flashes of cameras, the men stood and shook hands as those in the room rose to their feet in applause.

SOME MONTHS LATER, Christie returned for the groundbreaking of yet another Camden milestone: the KIPP Cooper Norcross Academy.

Yes, Lanning Square was finally, now, getting its school.

From the podium, Norcross mentioned that he had recently sponsored an annual charitable run—the Cooper Norcross Run the Bridge Event, which temporarily closed the Ben Franklin Bridge to Philadelphia.

"There's one thing the governor with all his power has not been able to achieve," Norcross said. "*I'm* the one who's able to shut down the bridge."

There it was, the first Bridgegate joke ever publicly told to Christie's face after the scandal erupted. Uncomfortable and then hearty laughter filled the room. The governor smiled broadly. Norcross was the only guy in the world who could get away with saying such a thing, which was exactly the point.

# 6

# "DAMN, MAN, I'M GOVERNOR"

After he was first elected, Christie and his original political mentor, former governor Tom Kean, Sr., met weekly to do tutorials.

"Who's your best friend?" Kean asked.

"My wife," Christie said.

"Not anymore. If you're going to be successful, you've got to make the Senate president your best friend."

So whenever Christie was at the statehouse at the same time as senate president Stephen Sweeney, the governor made it a point to try to meet up, even for just a few minutes, even if just to bullshit about their families or politics. There were frequent phone calls, too, several times a week. "You've got to have human relationships," Christie would say.

Christie's approach contrasted with that of President Obama, who was concurrently dealing with a hostile legislative body. Obama was accused of being uninterested in swimming in the sometimes murky waters of legislative deal-making. Christie, on the other hand, dove right in.

In the beginning of their courtship, early in his term, Sweeney and Christie had a four-hour dinner, drinks included, at one of Sweeney's favorite local haunts, an old-school place called Filomena's Lakeview. They talked about their families. They swapped political war stories. Sweeney picked up the tab, in cash.

When Sweeney's mother died in the middle of Christie's reelection campaign, Christie went to the wake and stayed for hours. The woman running for governor at the time as a Democrat, a colleague of Sweeney's in the Senate, didn't show up at all.

The power brokers who controlled New Jersey spoke a language of loyalty and respect that Christie understood. But Christie connected most naturally with Sweeney. They could be two fifty-something Jersey guys joking around on line at the Big & Tall store; instead, here they were running New Jersey.

Back when he was U.S. Attorney, Christie had a boss who dispensed this advice: "It's harder to hate up close." U.S. Deputy Attorney General James Comey was explaining why he, a George W. Bush appointee, was on his way to meet with the left-leaning *New York Times* editorial board. That became Christie's mantra, the approach he took to dining with Sweeney, visiting black churches, or calling legislators he didn't like all that much.

It worked. Sweeney was the supporting actor in every legislative victory of his term, central to his argument that he was both an effective governor and a future president in the making.

BEHIND SWEENEY WAS George Norcross.

The Sweeneys and the Norcrosses grew up together in Pennsauken, outside Camden. Their fathers were best friends, involved in union and local politics—even sitting on a committee together that sought to get a medical school for Camden in the 1970s. Both fathers had four boys, all the same ages.

"Well, ya know they used to go out drinking, and shit happens," Sweeney joked about how their parents had kids at the same time. "I grew up with them boys."

Sweeney stayed home until age twenty-six, followed his father into the ironworkers' union, married a hairstylist, fathered two children, fell a few stories a couple of times at work, and finally became an instructor to apprentice ironworkers. From there he went into the union's political operations, specializing in steering campaign donations to politicians who created union jobs. He got involved in politics by his own inclination, he says, but his association with Norcross put him on the fast track.

One day after visiting Adubato, Booker, and Joe D. in Newark as the governor-elect, Christie went to South Jersey, to Sweeney's Ironworkers Local Union 399 headquarters. Sweeney sounds like South Jersey and he looks like a tractor trailer barreling down the southern part of the New Jersey Turnpike—a muscular, meaty rectangle of a man. The men sat down.

"Are we going to be able to get anything done?" Christie asked.

"As long as we focus on areas we agree on," Sweeney remembered saying, "we're going to be fine."

They were both pragmatic practitioners of realpolitik. Neither was hell-bent on ideology. And their styles were awfully similar.

"I'm a fighter and I don't make no bones about it," Sweeney once told me. "And I fight hard."

Days after I wrote a long front-page article in the *Philadelphia Inquirer* about a controversial lawsuit that he filed against his own town, Sweeney pulled me aside at the Statehouse to complain about the story. We went into a vestibule out of earshot but in full view of the rest of the press corps and legislative staff. If he was going to dress me down, he wanted to make sure everyone saw it.

Sweeney and Christie had the same moves. No wonder they get along so well.

To become Senate president, Sweeney first had to relegate former governor and longtime senator Dick Codey, Norcross's nemesis, to the back bench. Democratic senators had to be convinced to vote out Codey *and* vote in Sweeney to replace him as the Senate president, and it all had to be done quietly, to catch Codey off guard. Conceived by Norcross and backed by Joe D., the coup was successful. Sweeney relished the victory. He framed two editorial cartoons in his office—one of a decapitated Codey and the other of a monstrous claw, "Sweeney," attacking a shivering, pajama-clad Codey.

DURING THE CAMPAIGN Christie promised that the federal prosecutors who used to work for him at the U.S. Attorney's Office "are watching the newspapers. And, after we win this election, I'm going to take a whole group of them to Trenton with me and put them in every one of the departments."

That he did. Christie populated his senior staff and state departments with those who had worked for him as prosecutors when he was U.S. Attorney. By the time he was done, about twenty former federal prosecutors, including the lieutenant governor, were part of the Christie administration. There was a cynical saying among the Newark-based assistant U.S. Attorneys: "Don't look for truth in Trenton." But they went anyway, some believing they had found truth in Chris Christie himself.

Christie once joked that he had no choice but to hire federal prosecutors in the governor's office because no one else responded to this Help Wanted ad: *People willing to work for a moody, passive-aggressive, demanding, outspoken, unreasonable, fat bully—to make miracles happen in Trenton.*

Christie lured so many federal prosecutors to the Statehouse that at a good-bye party for one Trenton-bound prosecutor at a Brazilian chicken place in Newark, Christie's successor, new U.S. Attorney Paul Fishman, held aloft the thick red directory of New Jersey lawyers. "Chris, there are eighty-seven thousand lawyers in here," he said to the new governor. "If you'd like to hire more people, I'm going to give this to you."

Fishman wasn't just being funny. He had already called Christie and asked him to stop poaching his staff. After all, back when Governor Corzine was hiring away Christie's guys, U.S. Attorney Christie had called Corzine and told him to back off, and Corzine agreed.

Now, Fishman sought the same courtesy. He wouldn't get it.

"Well, you're not me, and I'm not Jon Corzine," said Christie, recounting what he told Fishman. "And Paul understood exactly what I meant by both statements." (Years later, Fishman would regain the upper hand when he opened the Bridgegate investigation.)

The feds who followed Christie to Trenton had a prosecutorial style— loyal, hardworking, secretive, and respectful of the chain of command. They lacked both management and political experience. These prosecutors weren't encumbered by the weighty responsibility of preexisting relationships with lobbyists, legislators, and not least of all, the Statehouse press corps. This was by design, as they would be kept away from media and constituents. They weren't here to make friends. Quite the opposite.

Christie banded the ex-prosecutors together with a few people he grew tight with on the campaign—political types who instilled a certain edge to the administration, like political guru Bill Stepien and communications director Maria Comella. Only the chief of staff, Rich Bagger, came from neither Christie's campaign nor U.S. Attorney circles. He was a former state senator and assemblyman who knew the idiosyncrasies and alliances of Republican legislators. And he supplied balance, with a gentler bedside manner than his boss's.

In what the governor called a two chiefs system, Bagger shared duties with a chief counsel, Jeff Chiesa, who had been with Christie longer than anyone. Chiesa had worked with Christie back at the law firm, then at the U.S. Attorney's Office, where he ran the political corruption unit. One day, Christie would make Chiesa attorney general and then a U.S. senator.

Bagger managed state government and wrote the policy that Chiesa turned into legislation, while a third prosecutor, Kevin O'Dowd, sold that legislation to the Democrats. O'Dowd spoke to all legislators, regardless of station, and developed a particularly strong relationship with Sweeney. His colleagues called him "the resident Democrat" and "the Prime Minister"—that's how much he dealt with Democratic legislators. And everyone knew that when O'Dowd spoke on a bill, he was speaking for the governor himself.

Together, Bagger, Chiesa, and O'Dowd were "the triumvirate."

The triumvirate trumped the cabinet officials. Power was centralized in the governor's office at 50 West State Street, with decisions across a multitude of agencies run up the chain to the governor's senior staffers. Responses to media inquiries from the Treasury and Education departments were funneled through the front office for approval, as were public appearances by cabinet members. Singularity of message was the mission, public focus on anyone other than Christie was discouraged, and leaks were a capital offense.

Christie kept an open-door policy for his senior staff, often using extended lunch hours, post–5:00 p.m. chats, and quarterly sleepover retreats at the governor's mansion to give feedback and build camaraderie. On big issues Christie brought the team together in his office for talks that were part pep rally and part policy briefing.

He demanded that both sides of policy arguments be presented to him in his briefings. At night he asked that a folder—it was purple—be put together with constituent mail most representative of what New Jerseyans were thinking.

His management approach, one former staffer told me, was to delegate down and inform up. He was fine with others making decisions as long as the most important information reached him. The extent of that delegation would come under great scrutiny as scandal enveloped the end of his first term, but in the beginning it worked seamlessly.

WHEN NEW CHRISTIE staffers arrived for their first day in Trenton, the Cs on the keyboards in one of the governor's offices were missing. It was a screw-you from the Corzine folks.

But Christie got to work. On his first full day as governor he issued Executive Order No. 1, freezing 154 proposed government regulations—ones that would not, he promised, affect "public health, safety, or welfare." From there came more executive orders intended to inject capitalistic decision-making into government—there'd be a new task force to cut "red tape," and cost-benefit analyses would now be taken into account when new regulations, such as those on the environment, were enacted.

But the new governor had an immediate problem: The state was in deep, deep debt. The note from the state Office of Management and Budget hit Christie's desk the afternoon of his inaugural: New Jersey was out of money.

Then at the end of his first week, Bagger gave the governor a piece of paper. It was a slide from a briefing that Bagger had attended at Goldman Sachs, the Wall Street firm, indicating that state cash balances had hit zero dollars in December 2009, Corzine's last full month in office. And the trend was going downward. The slide "showed me that if I did not act immediately to stop the planned spending, that New Jersey would not meet its payroll for the second pay period in March," Christie said. "So we acted immediately to use the executive authority of the governorship to impound $2.2 billion in projected spending. *Without* the permission of the legislature. *Without* compromise. Because it was not the time for *compromise*."

Two weeks after getting that piece of paper from Bagger, the new governor issued Executive Order No. 14, declaring a state of fiscal emergency. He convened a joint session of the legislature to announce his plans. When Democrats got word about the speech, they wanted to know what he was going to talk about.

"It's about the budget crisis," Christie told them.

"Can we have a copy of your text?"

"No, no, no. We don't give copies of the text out beforehand."

"No, Governor, you don't understand. It's tradition for you to give the legislature a copy."

"Yes, so you can leak it and attack it before I give it? I'll pass up on that opportunity. This ain't Vegas, and I ain't Wayne Newton. We do one show a night. That's it. You don't get a preview."

Into the chambers of the assembly he went to give his speech. "This morning, I signed an executive order freezing the necessary state spending to balance our budget," he said. Then he got specific, actually listing the line items he was cutting. Such as $32.7 million from the N.J. Transit public transportation system, which was bogged down by "rich union contracts" and "patronage" hiring. He knew these cuts could lead to "service reductions or fare increases." Didn't matter. "The system needs to be made more efficient and effective."

We are simply out of cash, he said. So he stopped $475 million that had been earmarked for school aid. He eliminated the Department of Public

Advocate and took $62 million from colleges. Hospitals lost $13 million. He cut $158 million from a clean-energy fund. He skipped the payment into the pension system, and he reduced property tax rebates.

In the end, 375 budgetary line items were eliminated. A $2.2 billion budget gap had been closed.

Rush Limbaugh noticed. The lion of conservative talk radio read most of Christie's speech on his show and played clips from Christie himself. "Hello, public employee unions!" Limbaugh said. "The day of reckoning has arrived for you in New Jersey! This is not going to be pretty, folks. This is not going to be pretty."

For days, Christie was all Limbaugh could talk about on his show. The first month of his governorship wasn't even over. That's how early the Christie phenomenon began.

"Pow, pow!" Limbaugh said, giddy over Christie's calling out teachers for not paying toward their health benefits. Rush lowered his voice, leaned into the mic, and sounded like Barry White: "I love this guy."

But Rush knew it was a cruel world. "They are going to try to take him out. They are going to try to destroy this guy," he said. "And these stuffed pigs"—he spat the words—"in the Philadelphia and New York media cannot stand hearing the truth, because it's an indictment on everything they believe."

As a member of said "Philadelphia and New York media," I didn't think this was an accurate statement, but I was nonetheless moved by its stridency. Anyway, it was clear why Limbaugh liked Christie. "He stuck to his guns and gave them the what for," Limbaugh said.

For his first national TV interview as governor Christie went on CNBC, where he wowed a panel of financial pundits with his recitation of stats and quick retorts.

"That's going to hurt," one of the pundits said of his cuts.

"Absolutely—that's why they call them hard choices, Carl . . . I know there's real people behind them and I don't like doing them."

So what about raising taxes to pay for some of this deficit?

"I've lost my job, my home's been foreclosed on, and you want more taxes from me? Are you kidding?"

He was then asked about national politics and the then-ascendancy of the Tea Party—in his very first TV interview, he was no longer just a New Jersey governor, he was an American governor, fielding questions from four comers for sixteen nonstop minutes.

He then returned to Trenton to work on his budget proposal for the following fiscal year, which began in July 2010. He was having meetings about that next budget three days a week, for as long as four hours at a time. The meetings went something like this:

"Governor, this program costs this much, what do you want to do?"

"Cut."

Mary Pat had never seen him so tired at the end of each day.

"When I was sitting there doing those things I could see the faces of those people in my mind who were affected," Christie later told Oprah Winfrey. "And it really drained me."

When he released that budget proposal with across-the-board cuts, he returned to CNBC, as promised. One of the hosts told him: "You are making waves with this budget."

"Things are going well," he responded, smiling. He boasted about cutting $9 million *an hour* since he'd become governor.

Another CNBC panelist told him that Americans are "looking for a hero."

Christie kept focused, like a guy who's used to getting compliments. "I was elected by people who were tired of having New Jersey being the economic laughingstock of the nation. I'm gonna change it."

He was already getting the Statehouse portrait afforded every governor, he would say. No matter what, he'll have something to show his grandkids one day when they visit the state capitol. Popularity and reelection wasn't a concern. "Now it's my job to do what I said I was gonna do no matter the garbage I take from folks who write in the newspapers," Christie said, shadowboxing with opponents real and imagined, as he was wont to do.

IN THE OPENING months of his tenure Christie signed three bills into law on his signature issue: cuts to public employee pensions and benefits. They were small measures, but they were first steps with bipartisan support. The new governor was flanked by Democrats and Republicans alike at the bill-signing ceremonies.

The back-slapping wouldn't last long. Given the historic deficit, Democrats sought their own solution to the next budget. Instead of approving drastic cuts, they wanted to renew a temporary tax surcharge on the wealthy. This was known as "the millionaires tax" (although it applied to anyone making $400,000 or more).

"The partisan Democrats in my state believed they had me right where they wanted me," Christie later told conservative crowds. "They put it right down on the table and said they wanted to increase the tax that they love the most. . . . And they told me that if I did not agree they would close down the government. There would be no budget in 2011 without an income tax increase."

The last guy, Corzine, had a cot delivered to his office during one budget stalemate to indicate that he'd stay at work as long as it took to come to an agreement. Not Christie. He called the Democrats into his office and let them know face-to-face that he was calling their bluff.

"This place is under new management," he said. "Listen, if you guys want to pass an income tax increase, you can. That's fine, I'm going to veto it. And if you want to close down the government because of that, that's fine. But I want to tell you something—I'm not moving any cot into this office to sleep in here. If you close down the government I'm getting into those black SUVs with the troopers and going to the governor's residence. I'm going to go upstairs, I'm going to open a beer. I'm going to order a pizza. *I'm going to watch the Mets.* And when you decide to reopen the government, give me a call and I'll come back.

"But don't think I'm sleeping on some cot. Take a look at me, you think I'm sleeping on a cot? Not happening."

The Democrats passed their millionaires tax anyway. Following the party-line vote, Sweeney, trailed by a bunch of reporters, made a show of walking out of Senate chambers. He walked down the hall, took a left, passed the stairwell, and hooked another left into the governor's outer office. Sweeney figured he'd upstage the new guy, show him who runs these halls of Trenton.

Christie was expecting company. Chairs were put out for the press in front of a polished table that held a single pen. The veto message had already been written.

Sweeney and Christie shook hands over the desk. Sweeney handed Christie the tax increase bill.

Christie gave a signed veto message right back to him. "As to Bill 810, I am sending it back to the legislature without my approval," Christie said. He closed his pen cap.

"We'll be back," Sweeney said.

"All right, we'll see ya," Christie said. "Thank you very much."

Of course that's not the way Christie tells the story to Republican crowds. "I handed it right back to him and said, 'Take this back where it came from!' " he says.

The Democrats ultimately approved the budget that Christie sent them, with deep, across-the-board cuts: $820 million for schools, $445 million for municipalities, $33 million for public transit, $173 million for colleges and universities, $5 million for poor children's nutrition programs. A payment into the pension system was skipped and rebates to property-tax payers were suspended.

Every department was affected. A nine percent total spending cut; $3 billion less than the previous year's budget.

"Governor Christie got the Democrats to basically abdicate their role as the majority party in the legislature," said a baffled, thrilled GOP assemblyman, Jay Webber. "Despite our being in the minority, we effectively controlled the budget debate. It was remarkable."

IN CASE ANYONE didn't realize who was now in charge, at the end of his first year in office Christie publicly fired his most well-known cabinet member. This move sent a message to his senior staff, to his cabinet, and to the state of New Jersey. "I told them I always will have their back. I won't throw them under the bus unless they lie to me," Christie said. "Only one lied to me, and he is gone."

Bret Schundler was a unique choice to be commissioner of the Department of Education and run perhaps New Jersey's second most influential state department. An advocate of education reform, Schundler aligned with Christie's thinking on the matter, but unlike other cabinet members, Schundler was something of a political rival, a twice-failed Republican candidate for governor. Schundler's high profile was a potential problem for an administration that concentrated the spotlight on one man. Unlike other cabinet members, Schundler spoke to the media—and also to the hated teachers' union.

President Obama, meanwhile, had some similar ideas about education reform. The federal stimulus bill that he signed in 2009 to jump-start the economy allocated more than $4 billion for the Race To The Top grant program to fund innovative educational initiatives in states. This competition was right up the alley of education reformers, and Schundler put together New Jersey's $399 million application.

The application included a request for $20.5 million to be used in part to implement the new Common Core education standards in language arts and math, which "will transform our educational system." Common Core, the application said, created "a clear and high set of aspirations for students all across the country." This was before conservative backlash caused Common Core to become something of a radioactive policy that 2016 presidential candidates, including Christie, would run away from. For now, Common Core was popular within both parties.

Also included in Schundler's Race To The Top application were proposals that the New Jersey Education Association—the teachers' union, Christie's nemesis—opposed, such as providing merit pay for good teachers. Schundler could have submitted New Jersey's proposal with that provision but in doing so he would've lost union support for the application. The Obama administration awarded points for applications backed by unions, so despite the fact that the NJEA union had just a few days earlier rallied thirty-five thousand against Christie, Schundler went to the union leadership and negotiated. They reached a compromise that moved toward merit pay but did not replace length of tenure as the primary driver of pay increases.

In the newspapers, they called this a "truce" between the governor and the NJEA. Except Christie said he didn't know anything about it.

He woke up the next morning to read about the "truce" and felt the ire immediately from a fired-up host on New Jersey's statewide talk radio station, New Jersey 101.5 FM. Up to this point the station had been unabashedly pro-Christie—with a sort of anti-elitist, antitaxation, angry shtick that embodied the new governor's sensibilities. The station's opposition to Corzine's plan to raise tolls helped to propel Christie into office. But on the morning that the NJEA "truce" was revealed, drive-time host Jim Gearhart concluded that they had all been snookered by the new gov, just like the old gov. "The union won on all counts," Gearhart told his listeners. "You feel like you have been made a total fool of. It's embarrassing." New Jersey, he said, was expecting Christie to actually take on the teachers' union. But "the clash of the titans is over, apparently," Gearhart said. "Apparently the administration has backed down from its policies."

Christie heard this and was steamed. He got Schundler on the phone. They had a long talk.

Schundler would later claim that top Christie staffers knew about the compromise before he announced it, and it was only when Gearhart got on the air that things changed. Christie didn't want to take all that criticism "merely to cave in to the union," Schundler said. The $399 million "was not worth it" to the governor.

And so over a single weekend, the $399 million application that had been worked on for months was changed to reinsert the merit pay provisions that the union opposed. Then Christie took to the microphone at a press conference to announce the changes—and lambaste his own education commissioner for overstepping his authority. "This is my administration, I'm responsible for it, and I make the decisions," the governor declared. He said Schundler did not and would not have the power to make deals on major policy initiatives.

Schundler would keep his job. For now.

"There's nothing subtle about me, OK?" Christie said. "I think Bret and I have an understanding on how communication has to happen from here on. I don't expect we'll have a problem again."

Schundler was forced to prostrate himself before reporters. "I made a mistake," he said. "It's not myself who gets to make final decisions for the state of New Jersey. It's the governor."

Christie put Schundler in the penalty box. He was not allowed to do media events or interviews. Meanwhile Christie called Gearhart to explain that his administration would not be giving in to anyone, let alone teachers' unions.

And so the revised Race To The Top application was submitted.

But New Jersey's final score landed it in eleventh place. Only the top ten states got money. New Jersey got zilch.

The lack of union support had cost New Jersey fourteen points that would have put it into the top ten and qualified it for hundreds of millions of dollars.

There was another problem. In the rush to excise the union-supported compromises, a clerical error was inserted. This was a single item in the 1,299-page application, but enough to cost New Jersey 4.8 points. Again, without that deduction, New Jersey would have won the money.

At a subsequent news conference Christie spent nearly a half hour taking responsibility for the error while also ridiculing bureaucrats in the Obama administration. "If you are a normal, thinking, breathing human being you pick up the phone and say 'Hey, you sent this *one* wrong paper, can we get the information?'"

He added: "This is the stuff, candidly, that drives people crazy about government and crazy about Washington," he said. "Does anybody in

Washington, D.C., have a lick of common sense? Pick up the phone and ask us for the number."

Then he went further, calling federal officials "mindless drones" who are "just down there checking boxes."

"When the president comes back to New Jersey, he's going to have to explain to the people of the state of New Jersey why he's depriving them of $400 million," he said.

Except the president didn't have anything to answer for. Because a video soon surfaced of the final-round interview that Schundler and his team had in Washington with the Obama education officials. In the video, Schundler is in fact asked to clarify an inaccurate budget figure in the application. But he and his team could not come up with the correct figure, so the interviewers moved on, and the penalty was assessed.

Christie viewed the video. He said Schundler had lied, and he immediately fired him.

"I didn't try to hide anything," Schundler claimed. "I didn't try to mislead anyone." He said he was "heartbroken."

The Democrats called legislative hearings. "The accusation that I misled the governor to hide a poor interview performance is utter nonsense," Schundler testified. The blame lay with the governor's desire to play nice with the loudmouths on the radio instead of dealing with the unions, he said.

But as Schundler was testifying, Christie called a news conference on an unrelated announcement. That distracted the press from the Schundler show, and also gave Christie the chance to condescend to Schundler. "I understand his yearning for the spotlight. I really do," Christie said.

Distract and attack—vintage Christie in responding to a crisis.

"The Schundler thing had a chilling effect on the rest of the cabinet," one Trenton insider later told NJ Spotlight, a news site. "The governor didn't just call him on the carpet, he fired him. Everybody knew from that point on: You don't do anything unless you're absolutely sure it's what the governor wants, and that it's what he wants that week, and you have the written approval in your hand."

THAT SPAT WASN'T the only early management snafu.

The state economy in 2010 had been hammered by the national recession. Income tax revenue was down 15 percent and the unemployment rate was tickling the 10 percent line. But the most widespread economic problem may have been something Christie rarely ever talked about: housing. The state was one of the most unaffordable in the country, and New Jersey-ans were reluctantly moving out of state in droves.

People had come to expect not to be able to afford to live in Manhattan. They didn't understand why they should be priced out of no-name towns forty-five minutes away. The state had the highest percentage of mort-gage delinquencies and foreclosures for a good part of Christie's term, and homelessness ticked up 16 percent between Christie's fourth and fifth years as governor.

In this first term New Jersey got $300 million from the federal govern-ment to help those most affected by the recession. Two years later I pub-lished an investigative report in the *Philadelphia Inquirer* about how the Christie administration mishandled the money. Fifteen months after the so-called HomeKeeper program launched to help struggling homeowners, only 10 percent of the $300 million had been spent, with just 750 home-owners assisted. New Jersey had drawn down a lower percentage of federal money than the seventeen other hard-hit states in the program.

Christie's team of former federal prosecutors running state govern-ment, notoriously concerned about fraud, implemented stringent require-ments for distributing the money that disqualified too many people. And an inadequate number of staffers were processing the applications for assistance.

A few weeks after my story appeared a TV reporter from New York got Christie riled up at a press conference when he tried to ask him about the foreclosure situation. Christie blamed the high rate on the end to a brief moratorium on foreclosures; delayed filings were now clogging the system, he said. Housing advocates doubted this theory, but Christie wouldn't take a follow-up question. Instead he tried to get reporter Michael Aron to ask him a question so he could move on—"Michael, please, help me ignore him."

That's when Democrats in the assembly started paying attention. They called a hearing, and a Christie cabinet member actually acknowledged screwing up the distribution of the funds. "Listen, it's indefensible, the program was not being run well," said Department of Community Affairs Commissioner Richard E. Constable III, who had worked with Christie at the U.S. Attorney's Office and who had inherited the program as a midterm appointment. "We did a disservice to the folks that we were supposed to serve."

This was like seeing a unicorn run through the Statehouse—cabinet members never disavowed something the Christie administration had done.

IN 2011 DEMOCRATS in the legislature loaded into their annual budget proposal funding to make their constituencies happy—millions for AIDS patients, mental health services, and tax credits for the poor. They said it could all be paid for with a tax increase. They knew Christie would veto such an increase, of course, but they wanted to force him to be the one to cut the money and face the inevitable political fallout. The governor had mere hours to review their spending plan before the start of the new fiscal year. Otherwise government could shut down.

Sweeney sent a message to Christie through an intermediary. He told the gov, his partner, to be gentle with the cuts. Let's talk about it first. "I know you're mad, you want to teach us a lesson, I got it," Sweeney told him. "But don't do anything to hurt people."

The return message came from the governor's office: Stand by. Christie would call at 2:00 p.m. to negotiate the final budget details.

The call never came. Instead, the governor's staff sent a press release: Christie was holding a news conference at 5:00 p.m. Sweeney went to the news conference, and seethed in the back of the room as Christie announced $913 million would be eliminated from the Democratically approved budget.

"Fuck!" Sweeney thought. "I sat around all day waiting for you to negotiate!"

Christie did the opposite of negotiating, seemingly targeting every spending item, big and small, important to Democrats. Christie ended after-school programs for about six hundred students, reduced legal assistance for the poor, slashed aid for city governments, and, in perhaps his most controversial move, cut $500,000 for Wynona's House in Newark, which cares for physically abused teenagers. He even cut the money that paid the salaries of staffers to legislators, meaning Democratic aides could soon be out of work.

Perhaps Christie hastily crossed out funding for some worthy programs in the chaos of a tight budget deadline. Or perhaps this was a very clear message to the Democrats: *I'm crazy like a fox. Don't mess with me.* Regardless, that'd be the last time the Democrats pulled something like that with Christie.

*Star-Ledger* editorial page editor Tom Moran called Sweeney the morning after the line-item vetoes to see what he thought of his bipartisan part-ner, the man who had made such a big deal about being Sweeney's friend.

"I wanted to punch him in his head," Sweeney told Moran. He called the governor a "bully," "punk," "cruel," and a "rotten prick." Sweeney's quotes ran on the front page of Sunday's *Star-Ledger*. "You know who he reminds me of? Mr. Potter from *It's a Wonderful Life*, the mean old bastard who screws everybody," Sweeney said.

Christie called Sweeney first thing in the morning. "Hey, Steve, this is Chris. I just read the paper," Christie said. "Give me a call."

Sweeney never called back.

The state GOP demanded that Sweeney apologize, which he refused to do.

Christie went on vacation and when he returned he announced that federal dollars would be used to make up for the cuts at Wynona's House. He insisted the administration was aware of this alternative funding source all along, and there was never any danger of losing money. Worried officials at Wynona's House had no idea about such plans.

Christie and Sweeney didn't speak for the entire month of July.

"I like the guy a lot. I think he is brave in a lot of the things he has done politically, and he has always been honest to me," Christie said. "And in politics, that's a pretty good guy to be friends with."

I asked Sweeney about their relationship. "We fight a whole lot, but it doesn't mean I don't like the guy," he said.

Christie even mentioned the "prick" comments at the next State of the State Address. "You may even recall that even some of my friends had some very colorful nicknames for me," he said. He turned to look at Sweeney, who smiled and shrugged. The audience applauded.

"We have similar personalities," Sweeney explained. "The difference between he and I is, I have an off switch and he doesn't. You know, if I knock you down, I'll pick you up, brush the dirt off your back, try to build a rela-tionship and go forward. He knocks you down, like with the teachers, and he'll stomp on you, kick on you until he can kill you."

BACK WHEN DEBORAH Gramiccioni was a prosecutor, she was so tough they called her "The Tornado." Later, investigating political corruption at the U.S. Attorney's Office, her boss, Christie, called her "My Tornado."

Christie brought Gramiccioni to the governor's office to become direc-tor of the Authorities Unit. This was a job that during previous administrations had an office tucked into a lost corner of who-knows-where at the Statehouse.

Christie had different ideas. The way he deployed Gramiccioni reflected how he'd govern. Her job was to comb through meeting minutes of the fifty-five state authorities, boards, and commissions to search for waste, fraud, excessive raises, and questionable perks. Her findings were then backed with gubernatorial muscle: Using his constitutional powers, Christie regularly vetoed agencies' actions—"parental supervision," he called it. This had rarely been done before.

"John!" Christie yelled on the phone to the CEO of one of those agencies, the Delaware River Port Authority, which operates bridges and a commuter train into Philadelphia. "I want the minutes right now, so I can veto them!"

Then Christie hung up the phone and turned to Gramiccioni. "And that, Deb, is one of the best things about being governor," he said. This was 2010, right at the beginning of his term. Christie loved vetoing agencies.

Gramiccioni, whose quick smile belied an aggressive work ethic, explained it more gently. "We ask a lot of questions," she told me at the time. "And, candidly, we don't go away. . . . Angry defiance has become the norm in my world."

What Christie saw in Gramiccioni for this assignment was her ability to withstand that defiance. "I go to sleep at night knowing the next day is going to be another battle," she said. "And I look forward to it."

Everywhere she looked lay some absurd expenditure for Christie to veto, from the New Jersey Redevelopment Authority, which let its employees pick gifts from a catalogue as part of an "Employee Service Awards Program," to the South Jersey Port Corporation, which randomly spent $800 on booze.

Most dramatically Christie went after the Passaic Valley Sewerage Commission, a water treatment facility rife with contract kickbacks, wives on the payroll, and full summers off. "They took the summer off because why work over the summer? It's hot!" Christie said. Christie canned six "self-indulgent and self-interested" commissioners, seventy-one employees, and the $313,000-a-year executive director. Four officials were subsequently arrested.

"You don't hear a lot of people complaining about what we've been doing, except the people whose ox is being gored," Christie said. "Other than that, most people are really jazzed that the governor is spending time overseeing this thing."

Jazzed they were. In rejecting agencies' actions Christie became the governor that New Jersey wanted. He was grabbing hold of government excess and shaking the shenanigans out of it. They saw him tackling shadowy, shady shysters who were taking their hard-earned money.

Democrats argued he was all show, and that instead of issuing high-profile vetoes his administration could've just worked with the agencies to stop actions before they were approved. "You're doing it just for headlines, not for substance," griped Sweeney.

Sure enough, by Christie's second term, he wasn't talking about vetoing agencies anymore. Christie rejected agency actions twenty-four times in his first two years in office but just six times over the next three years. Christie officials explained he had just successfully forced better behavior.

CHRISTIE HAD LOTS of changes he wanted to make to state government. In 2011 he ordered the elimination of the state Commission on Higher Education, despite a provision in the law creating the commission that forbade it from being dissolved by the governor.

Democrats were oddly complacent about this move. We later learned that Christie and the Sweeney-Norcross Democrats were planning big changes to the higher education system that the Commission on Higher Education would've had to sign off on. Eliminating the commission cleared a path to the most dramatic alterations to the university system in modern state history.

Their plan was to have Rutgers University's Camden campus taken over by Rowan University, a former teachers' college a half hour away. The University of Medicine and Dentistry of New Jersey, which Christie had investigated for impropriety when he was U.S. Attorney, would be eliminated, its medical and dental schools absorbed by Rutgers.

Christie vowed that this would turn higher education from "good to great," keeping more talented high school students in-state for college and attracting a greater share of research dollars. Revamping the college system gave Christie another opportunity to do "the big things" and to "turn Trenton upside down," as he had promised to do.

Past governors had tried to revamp the higher education system. All had failed. Asked what was different this time, Christie was terse: "Me."

But as with every other major initiative of Christie's tenure, this Republican governor couldn't have succeeded without the South Jersey Democrats. Rejiggering the colleges happened to be at the top of Norcross's wish list, part of a long-held dream to create a research university in the southern part of the state to bring in new students and dollars. Norcross had personally pitched his ideas to a Christie-appointed panel, and he was intimately involved in final negotiations.

While Norcross was pushing the plan behind the scenes, Sweeney was doing the heavy lifting in the legislature. The opposition was significant, particularly from Assembly Democrats in North Jersey who thought South Jersey was getting too much out of the deal. Meanwhile in the south there was growing grassroots opposition at Rutgers's Camden campus, where professors and students feared marginalization if they were swept up in the takeover.

The opposition peaked one day on Main Street in the little town of Florence, South Jersey, inside a century-old auditorium that once served as an entertainment venue for workers at the nearby steel mill. At a town hall meeting there populated by a pro-Christie crowd, the governor called on a man with a high-and-tight haircut. William Brown, a former Navy SEAL and a second-year law student at Rutgers's Camden campus, complained to Christie about the plan to change his school's name to Rowan University.

Christie told Brown that as a current student, he'd still be able to graduate with a Rutgers degree.

"What about my son? What about my neighbors? What about my friends?" Brown asked.

When Christie tried to respond, Brown interrupted—and oh boy does Christie *hate* interruptions. All went downhill from there.

"Listen, pal, I sat here and listened to your story and your position . . . and if you decide what you want to do is put on a show today, let me tell you something, I can go back and forth with you as much as you want," Christie said.

As the cops moved in to remove Brown, Christie yelled: "If, after you graduate from law school, you conduct yourself like that in a courtroom, your rear end's going to be thrown in jail, *idiot!*"

Brown was removed. "It's freedom of expression," he protested. "This is America!" He was not arrested; instead he held court with a few reporters outside.

I grabbed a few quotes about Christie's being a bully and then returned inside to hear the governor bemoaning the spectacle. "Now it's going to be on YouTube somewhere with me calling him an idiot," he said. It sure would be.

"Damn, man, I'm governor," Christie said. "Can you just shut up for a second?"

The following Monday, we asked Christie if he had any regrets about the incident, which would become a defining moment in his career.

"He acted like an idiot, he is an idiot," he said. "Just because he's a Navy SEAL doesn't give him any reason to be a jerk." He noted that Brown had run for the Assembly as a Democrat, and he just "wanted to try to make me look bad."

The governor's insult highlight reel was filling up. When a Bergen *Record* reporter asked an off-topic question at a press conference once, Christie was furious. "Did I say on topic? Are you stupid? On topic! On topic! Next question." (No more questions were forthcoming.) "Thank you all very much, and I'm sorry for the idiot over there. Take care."

At a joint press conference with Newark mayor Cory Booker, the mayor got a probing question from a reporter. "Here's what you do," Christie said to Booker. "Start yelling at them. It works. Call them names, yell at them a little bit. It all gets squared away."

On *The Daily Show*, Jon Stewart asked Christie about his tendency toward name-calling.

"You grew up in New Jersey," Christie said to Lawrenceville native Stewart, "how many idiots are there?"

Christie then gave as extensive an answer to the whole *why do you yell at people* question that I've ever heard.

"If somebody stands up at a town hall meeting of mine, asks a question, and won't let me answer, and I keep trying to answer and they keep interrupting, well ya know what? There are two ways you can do it," he said. "You can be a phony politician and say, 'Oh jeez, I'm really put off by the way you are treating me.' Or you can say, 'Sit down and shut up, you idiot, and let me answer the question.' That doesn't make me nonhumble, that makes me honest. That makes me say, 'If you're being an idiot, I'm going to call you an idiot, and if you don't like it, then stop acting like an idiot!' "

Huge applause followed. The appeal of this husky guy, almost bursting out of his seat as he won over liberal Stewart, was political gold.

**THE *IDIOT'S* FELLOW** Rutgers-Camden law students dug into their legal books and found that the whole scheme to turn their campus into Rowan might be illegal. Students amassed at public hearings, slowing a bill that was moving through the legislature at high speed. They kept pointing out how no one knew how much this college merger—with new governing bodies and bonding powers—was going to cost. Estimates ranged between $0 and $1.3 billion.

Lingering questions, sympathetic Democratic lawmakers, and public pressure succeeded in stopping Rutgers's Camden campus from being renamed. But the bill that landed on Christie's desk in June 2012 did almost everything else that he, Norcross, and Sweeney sought—including creating a joint Rutgers-Rowan College of Health Sciences in downtown Camden, anchored by Norcross's medical school. Two years later, tuition would be raised to pay for it after all.

Christie could now make a legitimate claim to having reinvigorated the collegiate system, creating new medical and research institutions that would attract funding and students.

But the South Jersey Democrats were the ones who really brought home the spoils. The newly formed Rutgers-Rowan College of Health Sciences, led by a $275,000-a-year chief executive closely aligned with Norcross, was guaranteed annual funding of $2.5 million from each university, effectively giving Norcross a growing pot of money from which to pioneer his self-styled revolution in America's poorest city. Having been shafted for so many years by Rutgers University's main campus up in New Brunswick, South Jersey Democrats got what they coveted.

But just wait, there'd be more.

Seventeen months after signing the bill, Christie had another bill on his desk that would give South Jersey Democrats more unprecedented reach. The bill granted the new Rutgers-Rowan College of Health Sciences board the power of eminent domain, allowing it to seize private property in Camden. If a private property owner refused to sell, it could force a sale.

Rutgers University itself, the huge statewide college system, didn't have such a power.

Republicans were annoyed—and told me so on the record, which was unusual. Shortly after Christie signed the bill, he was asked about it for the first time on a call-in radio show.

"I haven't heard anything to this point about giving eminent domain to a university," he said dismissively. "I don't think that's how it works."

That was exactly how it worked.

ONE OF THE finest perks of the governor's office is frequent and frivolous access to a lakefront mansion on a barrier island at the Jersey Shore, two hundred feet from the Atlantic Ocean. The state-owned Governor's Ocean House is shielded from public view by natural vegetation. Elsewhere on the island sits a house for the governor's guests.

Governor Corzine spent a considerable amount of money fixing the place up, getting a couple of flat-screen TVs, new carpeting, and windows that actually opened. But it was Christie, his family, and his staff who benefited from those improvements, regularly sleeping over in the summers.

Shortly after he signed the higher education restructuring bill, Christie hosted a banquet at the beach house to celebrate the victory with those who had a hand in getting it through. Joe D. and Norcross were there, of course. As were key members of Christie's staff, a handful of Republicans, and the bill's sponsors.

"I did that to thank them for all the hard work," Christie said. Four or five tables were set up on the back patio; everything was informal. This was something he periodically did. "It's a nice way to treat people, to say thank you."

Later in the evening, Cory Booker—then the Newark mayor, soon to be U.S. senator—pulled Christie aside. Booker asked to chat privately. At the time Booker was said to be considering a run against Christie, so their walk raised some eyebrows.

"We walked out to the beach and talked," Christie told me. He refused to shed light on their conversation. "I'm not telling you—that's why he wanted to do it in private."

Booker told the *Star-Ledger*: "It was two guys talking about families and work. He's a great storyteller. He was cracking me up."

Maybe what they talked about didn't matter. Maybe the banquet, on its own, didn't matter. But all of this was about the relationships, which made Trenton turn.

CHRISTIE GRABBED HOLD of the Supreme Court the first chance he got after he was elected. The 1947 New Jersey state constitution calls for each Supreme

Court justice to be nominated by the governor and approved by the Senate for one seven-year term. At that point, the governor is empowered to grant tenure to the justice. And that's what happened, year after year. Never had a justice been denied tenure.

Enter Christie. In his fourth month in office Christie rejected tenure for a Democratic appointee, John Wallace. Democrats were apoplectic. Wallace was the only African American on the court and a South Jersey guy who was friends with Sweeney.

Christie didn't have a beef specifically with Wallace, but he was a Democratic appointee on a Supreme Court that Christie blamed for the highest property taxes in the country. This liberal unelected Supreme Court, he argued, mandated education spending and affordable housing construction that New Jersey simply couldn't afford.

The legal community was gobsmacked, publicly warning the governor that denying tenure without an extraordinary reason would send shivers down the spines of other justices. Tenure was not meant to be wielded as a political threat, they said.

Christie called Sweeney an hour before announcing Wallace's firing to give him a heads-up. "I'm doing my constitutional responsibility," Christie said.

Sweeney promised that whomever he nominated to replace Wallace would not get a Senate hearing. For an appointment to be confirmed, the majority Democratic Senate had to approve the nominee.

Christie's first nominee was Anne Patterson, a mentor of Christie's. Patterson appeared to be an ideological kindred spirit, having helped to establish a probusiness legal precedent as a commercial litigator for gun, lead paint, and tobacco manufacturers. Sweeney held up Patterson's appointment for more than fifteen months, an extraordinarily long time to go with a vacancy on the court. She was then confirmed.

Against the majority party the "governor's cudgel is public opinion," Christie told me, but the "public doesn't care" about Supreme Court nominees.

When two more vacancies arose, Democrats demanded diversity on what was now, post-Wallace, an all-white court. So Christie gave them diversity, and then some. He nominated Chatham mayor Bruce Harris, the only gay African American Republican mayor in the country, and Philip Kwon, a Korean-born registered independent who had worked for Christie at the U.S. Attorney's Office.

Harris, who brought his longtime partner to the press conference announcing the nomination, was in line to become only the seventh gay state Supreme Court justice in the nation. Kwon would become the first Asian American on the New Jersey Supreme Court.

An hour before the announcement Christie called the president of the leading gay rights group in the state to let him know about the Harris nomination, prompting a laudatory press release about Christie's "warmth and responsiveness" to the gay community.

Christie was double-daring Sweeney to confirm his two nominees.

So Sweeney gave them hearings. He had to at least do that. But then he squashed them.

During a marathon confirmation hearing before the Senate judiciary committee—a hearing in which Sweeney was seen poking in and out of the room, whispering with staffers—Democrats grilled Kwon about since-settled civil charges involving bank deposits from his parents' business.

When it was all done, Kwon was voted down, 7–6. It was a historic moment, the first time ever that the legislature had rejected a New Jersey Supreme Court nominee. In fact it was the first time any Christie nominee of any sort—from judges to sewer commission members—had been turned aside.

Christie was pissed. Watching it was "one of my angrier moments as governor," Christie told me. "I just sat there and seethed." Democrats knew Kwon was a friend of his. "They were ruining a guy's reputation for sport, and it really angered me."

Christie's ally, Republican senator Kevin O'Toole—the son of a Korean immigrant—went further: "We didn't have a hearing. We had a lynching."

Two months later Christie's other nominee, Harris, faced the same fate. Vacancies on the state's highest court continued, casting a shadow over the entire judicial system—words like "crisis" were used—as lower-court judges were called up to don the all-important Supreme Court robes.

So Christie had little choice. He decided to deal. To replace Kwon and Harris he chose two moderate Republicans from South Jersey with ties to Norcross Democrats. To get these through, Christie first got rid of Republican justice Helen Hoens, saying she deserved to be renominated for tenure but in doing so she'd have to go through the Democratic Senate and he didn't want to "let her loose to the animals."

Most controversially, Christie renominated the chief justice of the Supreme Court, a Democrat named Stuart Rabner who had become the face of the institution that Christie had railed against for so many years. Christie was violating a promise that he had made not to renominate any sitting justices, but in order to get any of his other nominees through, he believed he had to concede Rabner.

Environmental groups and advocates for the poor praised the governor; Americans For Prosperity, aligned with the conservative financier Koch brothers, said Christie had "waved the white flag of surrender to Steve Sweeney."

I asked Christie about this at a press conference, about remaking the court, as he planned. He had failed, no? The court would never be conservative now, right?

"You beg for bipartisanship!" Christie shot back at me. "Those of you who write opinion, or those of you who mask news and opinion, write all the time about bipartisanship." He then launched into a three-minute diatribe about how leadership requires compromise. His critics lived to be quoted in news articles, he said, while "my job is about the real thing."

He defended his remade Supreme Court as "not the perfect court, but it's a better court today."

The night the final deal was announced I ran into Sweeney at the annual Trenton Legislative Correspondents' Club Dinner. He whispered in my ear.

"I fucking won," he said.

BACK IN 2011, when Sweeney was still giving Christie the silent treatment over his massive budget cuts, I found myself at a farm in a rural corner of Somerset County awaiting a Christie press conference. It was humid, he was late (as usual), and I was texting pictures of the farm's adorable goats to my wife. A half hour passed. Then forty-five minutes. Finally Christie spokesman Michael Drewniak took the podium. This was highly unusual. Drewniak never spoke in front of the cameras. I listened up.

> Governor Christie this morning was having difficulty breathing. And out of an abundance of caution he went to Somerset Medical Center to be checked out. In line with someone dealing from asthma he is being given routine tests as a precautionary measure. And the governor is extremely grateful for the quality of care he is receiving this morning and has nothing but praise for the world-class doctors and nurses and staff who are attending to him.

*He is fine. There is more testing going on. And that's all I can tell you at this time.*

We rushed over to the hospital, all of the New Jersey reporters who follow him around. Soon enough the satellite trucks showed up from New York City. In all, nineteen video cameras were staked out in the parking lot.

The tan SUV that transports the First Lady pulled up. Mary Pat had been at the dentist's. Then Todd, the gubernatorial brother, came by.

Inside the hospital, Christie's cell phone rang. It was Sweeney, who a month earlier had cursed Christie out on the front page of the state's largest paper. He had ignored Christie's calls ever since. This asthma attack brought them back together and restarted the relationship that made New Jersey work.

"We had a nice conversation," Christie said afterward.

"Politics goes out the door at a time like this," Sweeney said.

Christie was at the hospital for eight hours, during which time his asthma attack became national news. "I was lying on this gurney in the emergency room and they said to me we'll just turn on this TV for you to relax," Christie said, at which point he saw his face plastered on MSNBC with speculation about his potentially fatal medical condition.

He emerged from the hospital eight hours after he arrived wearing the suit he came in with. He looked tired. But at a podium set up in the hospital's driveway, he took questions for twenty-eight minutes.

This was a potential crisis in the making—just as he was emerging as a future presidential candidate, his mortality was in question. But in times of intense media scrutiny, Christie lets it all out there. He does what he does best: talk. And talk and talk and talk. On this day, just as he would one day do in the wake of Bridgegate, he answered every single question with calm and grace. Even the personal ones, about why he's so fat.

Christie told us he was on his way to the farm when he felt short of breath and light-headed. He used two inhalers to try to clear up his breathing problems, but they didn't work. He told the state trooper next to him in the SUV that he didn't feel well; the trooper thought he didn't look so hot, either.

So they detoured to the hospital. "I was kind of betwixt and between about whether to come or not . . . when you have four kids, you don't take chances, so I came here," he said. He walked in on his own and was put in a wheelchair and taken in for a variety of tests. His blood pressure was a respectable 118/78.

"I was a little bit scared, but I was never passed out, incapacitated," Christie said, assuring America, for both now and later. This was just asthma, nothing more than asthma—and it was the first time he had been hospitalized for it since law school. He attributed his difficulty to that day's humidity and poor air quality.

He projected cool, joking that Mary Pat "owes me big time" because he got her out of her dentist's appointment. At the hospital he got on the phone with all four of his children and Lieutenant Governor Kim Guadagno. He took texts wishing him the best. And then he watched his New York Mets on TV as they nearly blew a lead in Cincinnati. "They almost sent me to the wrong end here," he deadpanned.

A reporter asked if the attack had anything to do with his weight.

"The weight exacerbates everything," he said. "It's one of the major struggles of my life. I'm working on it. Like many other people across New Jersey and the country, I'm working on it."

And *why*, reporters asked, do you weigh so much?

"I weigh too much because I eat too much," he said. "Despite the well-chronicled issues with my weight, I've been generally healthy by all indicators."

Well-chronicled? And then some.

Christie's heft has been a political issue from the moment he entered politics. As a Morris County freeholder in 1995, Christie read a letter to the editor in his local paper, the *Daily Record*, that charged that he "resembled the Pillsbury Doughboy because he has lots of dough and hot air but little else."

Christie allowed his weight to be part of his early public persona. In 1996 Christie and former Morris County sheriff John Fox, both "portly politicians," as the *Star-Ledger* described them, bet $500 in charitable donations that one could lose more weight than the other. Another freeholder said the weigh-in would have to be held at the county trash transfer station that registered tons instead of pounds.

By 2009, in his campaign for governor, Christie faced questions from curious constituents. "How's your diet?" a man at a senior citizens' center asked the candidate.

"Not as good as it should be, I'm a work in progress," Christie said. Then he smiled: "Thanks for piling on."

The weight was right there, daring anyone to pass personal judgment, and his opponent, Corzine, simply couldn't help himself. The Corzine campaign commissioned a focus group that determined voters were disgusted by Christie's size, and then committed what would turn out to be an epic blunder. Corzine aired a TV ad that depicted Christie getting out of an SUV as a narrator said Christie had been "throwing his weight around." This was supposed to be a reference to the politicization of the U.S. Attorney's Office, but the camera zoomed in on Christie's jiggling belly and went into slow-motion.

Christie responded forcefully. "If you're going to do it, at least man up and say 'I'm fat,' " Christie said. "[Corzine] wusses out and says, 'Oh, no no, I didn't mean that.' Man up, if you say I'm fat, I'm fat. Let's go. Let's talk about it."

Christie portrayed himself as a populist representing those everywhere victimized by fat jokes. "He sat at a conference table and watched that thing, and said, 'I approve it. Go ahead, put it on the air,' " Christie said. "He should be embarrassed for doing it. Because ya know what, there are hundreds of thousands of people in this state who have struggled with their weight, as I have, for most of their lives. And I don't know what the governor's trying to say. Does that disqualify you from holding public office? Because that's what that implies."

Always beefy, Christie was made fun of for his weight as a kid. He kept it under control when he played baseball in high school, but he steadily added pounds as an adult and as a politician. Fat politicians are a rare breed, and this fact about him preoccupied constituents and the media. The *New Republic* and *Politico* both guessed his weight at different junctures, with the former concluding, without evidence, that he was heavier than the heaviest president in American history, William Howard Taft. When Christie went to Israel on an official state trip, the *New York Post* published a photo of him praying at the Wailing Wall under this headline: "Whale at the Wall." After Christie called a *New York Daily News* sports reporter an "idiot," the paper responded with this on the front page: "Who you calling an idiot, fatso?" Inside the paper, the headlines included "ATTACK OF THE BLOB" and "PICK ON SOMEONE YOUR OWN SIZE."

Year after year, the man so often derided as a bully was bullied for his physical appearance more than any other male politician in the country. A former White House doctor told CNN that she was "worried" Christie would have a heart attack or stroke, which prompted Christie's kids to ask him if he was going to die.

In Trenton, Democrats wondered aloud whether he had some sort of fat man complex that made him so aggressive with them. Political activists referred to him as "Krispy Kreme" at government meetings, without rebuke. And some pundits determined that his weight reflected a lack of discipline that precluded him from higher office. "Look, I'm sorry, but New Jersey governor Chris Christie cannot be president: He is just too fat," wrote Michael Kinsley, adding that it was a reflection of poor "behavior."

"The people who pretend to be serious commentators who have written about this are among the most ignorant people I've ever heard in my life," Christie said.

Christie's outrage was tempered with humor. When radio host Don Imus asked how much he weighed, Christie joked: "550 pounds." Imus said he should set a better example.

"I am setting an example, Don," Christie said. "We have to spur our economy. Dunkin Donuts, International House of Pancakes. Those people need work, too."

During an interview on *The Daily Show*, host Jon Stewart complimented him by saying: "The beautiful thing about the Republican Party right now, it is so starved for [your] type of real leadership."

Christie responded: "I think it's really unfair by the way, and I get the import of this, that you look at me and say the word 'starved.' "

Christie's self-deprecating fat jokes gave license to comedians to make their own jokes. At the 2012 White House Correspondents' dinner, host Jimmy Kimmel directed *three* fat jokes at the New Jersey governor, including: "Governor Christie, I think you might be misunderstanding New Jersey's slogan. It's not the Olive Garden State." The other two lines were just as lame, but Christie kept laughing along as the CSPAN camera trained its lens on his reactions.

Later, Christie laughed it all off, saying he was sitting next to bombshell sitcom star Sofia Vergara. "When you have her next to you to console you, let me tell you, you don't care what Jimmy Kimmel says," he said.

But it was David Letterman who most often used Christie's girth for laughs. He once devoted an entire top ten list to Christie fat jokes: *What if Christie was president? Instead of Iraq, we'd invade IHOP.*

In 2012, when Christie finally appeared on the show, he needed a snack. He pulled a doughnut from his suit pocket in the middle of the interview.

"I didn't know this was going to be this long," he said. The crowd loved it. So did Letterman. They both ate. "I'm basically the healthiest fat guy you've ever seen," Christie declared.

There was something uncomfortable about watching a fat man making fun of himself as a fat man for the benefit of others while also defending himself for being a fat man. But it wasn't inauthentic. He has a complicated relationship with weight, as many Americans do.

He told Letterman, for instance, that fat jokes don't bug him. "From my perspective, if the joke is funny, I laugh—even if it's about me," he said. "If it's not funny, I don't laugh."

Ridiculed for his appearance and held to largely arbitrary physical standards, Christie was certainly living a contemporary American life.

When I wrote an article headlined "Is Christie too fat to be president?" it garnered more online comments than anything else I'd ever written. I suggested that just as presidential candidate Barack Obama addressed the issue of his race in a 2008 speech, and just as presidential candidate John F. Kennedy addressed his Catholicism in a 1960 speech, Christie would likewise have to address his weight in a notable way if he intended to run for president. I quoted a pundit who suggested Christie do this in an interview with a female broadcaster, such as Diane Sawyer.

Christie did one better. Less than two months later none other than Oprah Winfrey came to his house for an emotional interview that dealt extensively with weight. Christie's conversation with America about losing weight began right there in his living room with a woman whose own struggle had played out publicly.

Christie told Oprah that in high school, he was thinner. "But I felt fat."

"I think that if you're a chubby little kid, and people tease you about it, and that's when it's hurtful, then that remains with you for the rest of your life if you continue to struggle with your weight like I have," he said.

Winfrey said this was the first time she had spoken to an overweight man about these sorts of struggles. She was fascinated. She told him food was "like a drug" for her; he said it was something similar for him. "There is a certain compulsiveness at times to my eating," he said.

He was seeing a dietitian, he told Oprah. He had a personal trainer for three days a week and he worked out once a week on his own.

All of that, though, didn't work.

BETH DEFALCO, REPORTER for the *New York Post*, called the governor's media gatekeeper, Maria Comella, to get comment on a big scoop: Months earlier in 2013, just days after he ate a doughnut on the Letterman show, the governor underwent lap-band surgery to lose weight.

DeFalco told Comella she had enough to run the story the next day, but she wanted an interview with the governor. Immediately.

At first Comella tried to delay, but DeFalco pushed. She knew Christie had an interview scheduled with NBC's Brian Williams the next day, and she wasn't going to risk the governor leaking it himself. At the last moment, Christie agreed to meet DeFalco at the Tribeca Grand Hotel in Downtown Manhattan. DeFalco was in Albany to cover a New York political story. The last train had left upstate New York, so she took a $350 cab to meet the governor.

The conference room where they met was tense. He was not happy she had somehow gotten the scoop on this, but he had to have known it was inevitable.

DeFalco had covered Christie for years. She knew his moods and rhythms, so she began with a human touch, telling him about her own fluctuations in weight, about her own experiences having different clothes of different sizes in her closet.

The interview went well. DeFalco stayed up all night worrying how the *New York Post*, the nation's most famous tabloid, would handle this story on one of its legendary front pages. But the headline the next morning was perfect and poetic: "The Weight Is Over." DeFalco quoted Christie saying that this decision was about his family—not about getting ready to run for president in 2016. "I know it sounds crazy to say that running for president is minor, but in the grand scheme of things, it was looking at Mary Pat and the kids and going, 'I have to do this for them, even if I don't give a crap about myself,'" Christie said.

DeFalco reported that Christie had used a pseudonym to check himself into the New York University Langone Medical Center—named for the hospital's benefactor, Ken Langone, a billionaire who supported Christie for president. He underwent outpatient laparoscopic adjustable-gastric-band surgery, involving the placement of a silicon tube around the top of the stomach—the "lap-band"—to restrict the quantity of food and create a faster feeling of satiation.

"A week or two ago, I went to a steakhouse and ordered a steak and ate about a third of it and I was full," he told DeFalco.

The secret weight-loss surgery instantly became national news. Here he was, the most American of governors, dramatically dealing with the most American of problems. The day the article came out Christie faced questions from the press at an appearance in Newark.

The press conference went on and on, with questions ranging from the personal to the governmental, like why he hadn't transferred powers to the lieutenant governor while he went under the knife for forty minutes. He answered everything, the way he often did during times of intense scrutiny.

That night, I was scheduled to roast the governor at the annual Trenton Legislative Correspondents Club dinner. For weeks I had worked on a speech that intentionally didn't contain a single joke referencing the governor's weight. But now that the lap-band surgery was breaking news, I *had* to mention it at that night's dinner. I went with this: "I guess Springsteen's no longer the band closest to the governor's heart."

A few days later, Christie was at a Princeton bookstore where MSNBC's Mika Brzezinski, a celebrity friend, was promoting her new book, *Obsessed: America's Food Addiction—and My Own.* Christie addressed the crowd.

"The moments where I would say to myself, 'Why can't I beat this? Why can't I do better?'—it would be when I'd be going out with Mary Pat on a Friday night or Saturday night," Christie said. "I'd be changing out of my professional clothes . . . and would go to casual clothes that I didn't wear a lot, and then something wouldn't fit. That's when I'd really be angry with myself."

Bullied, laughed at, and shamed. But in the end, he was just like every heavy middle-aged man, staring at himself in his bedroom mirror, wanting to look good in khakis again.

# 7

# UNION WARS

In February 2011, at the beginning of his second year in office, Christie went to Washington. If he was going to battle the unions at home, he needed to build some political prominence, get some national TV time, and make some powerful friends.

Showing an early deftness at the D.C. game, Team Christie leaked excerpts of a planned speech to *Politico*'s Mike Allen, the capital's agenda-setting journalist. The resulting headline, "Tough Talking Chris Christie Plans DC Roll Out," created a buzz. What was supposed to be a lunchtime address for a bunch of conservative policy wonks in a conference room at the American Enterprise Institute think tank turned into a coming-out party. Tickets for the speech were snatched up and media calls overwhelmed AEI's lone spokeswoman. The *New York Times* sent a photographer and the *Washington Post* had two columnists handle the job. The speech was streamed live, allowing the cable networks, most importantly FOX News, to drop in fresh footage as the day progressed.

The most significant accomplishments of his first term—such as public worker benefit cuts and teacher tenure reform—were still ahead of him. He was in just the fourteenth month of his governorship. And yet by the fifth sentence of the introduction from AEI vice president Henry Olsen, Christie was being compared to the last New Jersey governor to become president of the United States: "Simply put, he is the most consequential governor of New Jersey in at least a hundred years, since Woodrow Wilson changed his address from Drumthwacket to 1600 Pennsylvania Avenue."

The governor took the podium. Christie's communications chief, Maria Comella, seemed nervous. This was the first time the gov would be describing his fight for public employee union reforms to a national audience.

Christie, on the other hand, felt loose. He told me he gave most of the speech off the cuff. He had a little something extra on his fastball for this speech on this day. His words were tinged with humor, not anger, and as they reverberated through the cramped room his status was affirmed as a legitimate major leaguer in politics.

He described himself as a leader of a bipartisan movement to control benefits for public workers, comparing himself to everyone from liberal California governor Jerry Brown to union-busting conservative Wisconsin governor Scott Walker to middle-of-the-road New York governor Andrew Cuomo, the "son of a liberal icon."

"These are not, in and of themselves, Democratic or Republican issues," Christie said. "Each governor in America is confronting the same things I'm confronting in New Jersey."

Christie said he wanted to make the most significant changes to the benefits system in its history. He wanted to require teachers, cops, firefighters, judges, and every other public worker to make bigger contributions toward both their health coverage and their pensions. He wanted to raise the retirement age required to fully cash in on benefits, and to get rid of automatic cost-of-living raises. Over thirty years, the deficit in the pension system of $54 billion would be nearly cut in half to $28 billion, he promised.

This speech was not just about New Jersey. Christie framed it as talking truth about America. "Pensions and benefits are the equivalent of federal entitlements at the state level," Christie told the crowd. "They are no different. They have no more vocal constituency at the federal level than they do at the state level. Take my word for it."

He described how just three days after he rolled out his reforms, he had gone to the Firefighters Convention in Wildwood, a raucous Jersey Shore town. "Seven thousand, five hundred firefighters at two on a Friday afternoon—I think you know what they had for lunch," Christie recounted to the AEI crowd, to knowing laughter. Christie's proposals hit firefighters hard. And yet there he was, showing up at their party, selling his proposal:

*As I walked into the room and was introduced, I was booed lustily. I made my way up to the stage, they booed some more. I got to the microphone, they booed some more. So I said, "Come on, you can do better than that." And they did! They did. And then I said to them—I took away the prepared notes I had for the speech—I actu-*

*ally took them off of the podium, crumpled them up, and threw them on the ground, so they could see that I would.*

*And I said, "Here's the deal: I understand you're angry, and I understand you're frustrated, and I understand you feel deceived and betrayed. . . . For twenty years, governors have come into this room and lied to you. Promised you benefits that they had no way of paying for, making promises they knew they couldn't keep . . .*

*"Here's what I don't understand. Why are you booing the first guy who came in here and told you the truth? . . .*

*"You may hate me now. But fifteen years from now, when you have a pension to collect because of what I did, you'll be looking for my address on the internet so you can send me a thank you note."*

The AEI crowd delighted in this story. He drew a distinction between his style and the ways of Washington, which wasn't addressing federal entitlement problems. He mocked President Obama for pushing things like high-speed rail, high-speed Internet access, and electric cars, and he knocked Tea Party Republicans who had just taken over Congress for not dealing with the "big things," either.

Since he had campaigned for some of those Republicans, now it was "put up or shut up time." Otherwise: "The next time they'll see me in their district is with my arm around their primary opponent."

Wow, did the audience love that! "We need to say these things and we need to say them out loud," he said.

For the biggest laugh line of the speech, Christie offered some national policy prescriptions: "You're going to have to raise the retirement age for Social Security. Whoa-oh! I just said it! And I'm still standing here! I did not *vaporize into the carpeting.* . . . We have to reform Medicare because it costs too much and it is going to bankrupt us—once again *lightning did not come through the windows* and strike me dead."

The crowd had no idea that Christie had tried out the *I did not vaporize into the carpeting* line over lunch. Christie accepted an enthusiastic standing ovation. People were clapping with their hands over their heads. He gave out some hugs, and then caught a train back home. There were unions to fight back in Jersey.

.     .     .

IN THE VERY first speech of his career before both houses of the legislature, Christie likened his union enemies to children. He said that if they
called his plans for cuts "unfair," they should know that "unfair" was also
the favorite word of his son, Patrick, when he had to do something he knew
was right but didn't want to do.

Patrick was nine at the time. Cameras panned to the audience where
Patrick sat. He smiled and looked at his sister.

Christie, meanwhile, looked up into the rafters of the Assembly chambers, where the lobbyists sit for these legislative speeches. Somewhere, there
were a handful of lobbyists from the union Christie hated most of all—the
New Jersey Education Association. His brow was furrowed, his mouth was
still, and his eyes were fixed upward. He looked intimidating as hell.

"Ya know how they say dogs can smell fear?" Christie later recounted.
"You could feel the air come out of that room."

Christie told of an unnamed retired teacher who paid just $62,000
toward her pension, and nothing—"yes, nothing!"—toward her family's
medical, dental, and vision coverage, and yet still earned *$1.4 million* in
pension benefits, plus an additional $215,000 in health benefit premiums
for her whole family.

"Is it fair," Christie asked, "for all of us, and our children, to pay for that
excess?"

Fairness. He talked about that a lot. He described middle-class private sector workers who were paying so much in property taxes to fund
rich benefits for public employees that they were being forced out of their
homes. Lying "union bosses" used school kids as pawns in their greedy
demands for more money, Christie argued, with "political muscle fueled by
intimidation tactics, political bullying, and smears of public officials who
dare, dare, to disagree."

Christie liked to say that when he got into office he looked around and
"there were a bunch of people on the ground, all bloody and moaning, all
beat up, and there was one person on the schoolyard standing . . . that's the
New Jersey teachers' union."

To sell his plan for reform, Christie memorized a few key stats—like
the $130 million in annual dues that the NJEA collects from teachers' pay-
checks, or the $550,000 in salary and other compensation that the NJEA
executive director collected in one year.

And he told stories. "Every issue has a story," one staffer told me. Even little ones, like about how last week, Christie's pharmacist remarked that the gubernatorial asthma inhaler cost him just $15—down from the $55 that Christie paid when he had federal health benefits as U.S. Attorney.

"That $40 didn't disappear into the ether," he would tell audiences. "I want to thank all of you for paying it."

He portrayed the unions and their wealthy tax-funded benefits as enemies of the New Jersey Dream. "New Jersey is an actor, a player in our lives," he would say. He was proud to raise his kids not far from where he himself had been raised, and take them to the same beaches that he went to as a kid. He was worried, though, that his own kids wouldn't be able to enjoy the same life, that they'd be taxed down Route 95, all in order to pay for some retired teacher's husband's health benefits.

"I don't want our generation to be the one that has to hear about the great North Carolina life that our children and grandchildren have, the great Florida life they have, the great Virginia life they have, and has to wonder, 'If we had done the tough things we needed to do, could they have stayed here?' " he said. "I want this state to be a place where my kids and grandkids can grow up and have the great life that I had."

Once, Christie scolded a middle-aged woman named Gayle who asked why he sent his kids to Catholic schools instead of having skin in the game on public education. If he was passing policy that affected unionized public school teachers, Gayle reasoned, then his own kids should be part of the system.

His response: "Hey, Gayle, ya know what? First off, it's none of your business. I don't ask where *you* send *your* children to school. Don't bother me about where I send mine."

Christie said he and his wife sent their children to parochial school out of a personal belief "that a religious education should be part of a child's everyday education."

And then as if to confirm to New Jerseyans that this was not an unusual outburst, that this was just how he was going to talk to them—that this was just *who he is*, damnit—he repeated, for emphasis: "So in all due respect, Gayle, it's *none of your business.*"

This answer became an example often cited by his enemies of his inappropriate "tone."

Whatever. Never did hear someone ask him that question again.

.    .    .

CHRISTIE TOOK ADVANTAGE of his opponents' blunders. So when the head of the teachers' union in Bergen County circulated an email that said the following, Christie capitalized:

> *Dear Lord this year you have taken away my favorite actor, Patrick Swayze, my favorite actress, Farrah Fawcett, my favorite singer, Michael Jackson, and my favorite salesman, Billy Mays. I just wanted to let you know that Chris Christie is my favorite governor.*

How thrilled must the governor have been to read this email published in the Bergen *Record*! The head of the NJEA, Barbara Keshishian, was forced to walk to the Statehouse to apologize to this governor, *blech*. The conversation did not go well. Keshishian refused to fire the email writer.

Christie looked at Keshishian. The governor pointed to the only other person in the room—Rich Bagger, his chief of staff. "If he did that," Christie said, "he'd be gone this afternoon."

Bagger didn't say a word. He got up and walked Keshishian to the door. "Thank you for coming by," he said.

A half dozen reporters, somehow alerted to this meeting, were lying in wait. Keshishian had been released to the hounds. They followed the vanquished enemy out of Christie's office, down the hall, out the front doors of the Statehouse, and all the way back to the doorstep of union headquarters on State Street.

AT THE OUTSET of his term in office Christie asked local teachers' unions to accept, due to the state's extraordinary fiscal condition and the continuing national recession, a one-year freeze on annual pay increases. On a whim, he laid out a challenge. He told the public that if the unions didn't agree, voters should oppose the school budget in the upcoming April elections.

One of the more unusual things that New Jerseyans vote for are local school board budgets. They usually pass. Now, a governor was suggesting the citizens *vote those budgets down*. Unprecedented.

"You didn't just say that?" Bagger asked Christie after he made the announcement.

"Oh, yeah I did."

"When did we decide that?"

"Oh, right there on the spot."

Christie called his political adviser, Bill Palatucci. "We have to mount a campaign," he told him. Palatucci was confused: It's April—they had *just* mounted a campaign, months ago.

"We have to defeat all the school budgets," Christie said.

"Whaaat?" Palatucci asked.

In the end the majority of districts' budgets, 58 percent, were voted down. The most in thirty-five years, in fact, forcing waves of layoffs and cuts to transportation, after-school activities, and supplies.

"He whipped the public into a frenzy," bemoaned an NJEA spokesman. About ten thousand teachers and support staff saw their jobs eliminated due in part to the resulting funding cuts.

The unions fought back with TV ads featuring soft-spoken teachers criticizing Christie for destroying public education. They wanted a tax on millionaires to make up for the shortfall in school funding. By April 2011, the NJEA had spent $10 million in advertising, including a rented plane that flew a banner up and down the Jersey Shore over Memorial Day promoting MillionairesForChristie.com. The banner featured a monocle-wearing, cigar-chomping cartooned man with a vague likeness to Christie.

AN ELEMENTARY SCHOOL art teacher named Marie Corfield stepped to the microphone at a Christie town hall meeting in Raritan. Corfield once finished second on *Jeopardy!*, which got her a mention in the paper, as did her unusual exhibits in local art shows. On this day in 2010, she was about to reach a whole new level of notoriety.

Every hero and every villain within Chris Christie was wrapped up in what happened next.

"I wonder how your reforms are going to help the middle class when so many middle-class teachers have been laid off this year," Corfield began. "And tons of middle-class teachers are spending tons of money out of their pockets to supplement the budgets that were cut so that they can buy supplies. . . ."

She wasn't done. "And I'd also like to say that New Jersey has some of the best schools in the country and this administration has done nothing but lambaste us, and tell us what horrible schools we have. We have some failing schools, but the majority of our schools are *wonderful* and *fantastic*."

She kept going. "And this school district has MANY OF THEM."

Now she was lecturing. "And I feel like you have alienated so many people with your rhetoric and about how we are bilking this state of all of this money, when *I am a taxpayer.*"

Finally, this: "And because of the budget cuts you have implemented I am going to have a hard time paying my bills this year."

Christie was more patient than normal. Finally, he said he had not "lambasted" the schools.

That's when Corfield dramatically threw her head back and to the side, sarcastically laughing at the governor's denial.

Here it came. "If what you want to do is put on a show and giggle every time I talk, *well then I have no interest in answering your question,*" he said. Applause. "So if you'd like to conduct a respectful conversation I'm happy to do it, and if you don't, please go and sit down and I'll answer the next question. What's your choice?"

For the next seven minutes—and with just one brief interruption from Corfield, who was stuck standing there next to a microphone-minding Christie aide—the governor lectured her about the predicament he was left with after a $1 billion reduction in federal money for education and a selfish refusal by the teachers' unions to take a one-year pay freeze. He talked about private-sector New Jerseyans on the verge of losing their homes to pay taxes so teachers who pay *nothing* toward their benefits could collect full family medical coverage for life.

And then he told the crowd the story of the union leader asking God for him to die. "If they're going to be out there praying for my death, I'm going to say exactly what I think as well and not put any varnish on it either!"

The applause sent Corfield right out of the town hall meeting.

The Christie-Corfield tussle was in the papers the next day as an afterthought. But Christie posted it on his official YouTube channel, where it became his most watched video *ever.*

Three years later, Corfield ran for the Assembly as a Democrat, losing by just one thousand votes. Her Twitter bio said: "That Teacher In That Chris Christie YouTube Video."

CHRISTIE BRANDED HIS thirty-three proposed laws to reduce taxes "The Property Tax Toolkit." These "tools" weakened union power by empowering local government to reduce compensation for cops, firefighters, and teachers.

On two laws, Christie and Stephen Sweeney, the senate president, compromised to cap salaries for public workers. Other proposals died with a lot of Christie bluster but not enough Democratic support.

The most significant Christie-Sweeney accord—the biggest moment in each of their careers to that point—would be what was known as pension-benefit reform, or simply "pen-ben." The proposal called for major rollbacks in health benefits and retiree pensions for all public workers. This was the centerpiece of Christie's political future—the signature achievement that would give him a national platform to run for president. And Democrats would help make it happen—Sweeney at the forefront and George Norcross behind the scenes, securing the votes of legislators under his thumb.

The pen-ben proposal was this: Public workers, from teachers to cops, would pay a higher percentage of their health care premiums and larger contributions toward their pensions. Retirees had to wait until they were sixty-five to collect pensions, and cost-of-living increases would be eliminated.

The unions argued that their right, since 1968, to collectively bargain for health care benefits would be lost under these proposals. As for the pension changes, they said that they had put money aside for their pensions in paycheck after paycheck even though governors, including Christie, sabotaged their savings by skipping mandated contributions from the state.

The Christie strategy was to portray the unions as caring more about their pocketbooks than about poor kids. At one point Republican Party workers, including a former Christie staffer, opted for guerrilla warfare, putting on sweatshirts and knit caps and staking out NJEA headquarters with video cameras asking departing workers: *Do you care about urban schoolchildren?*

But Christie could also downshift his approach. He held meetings with small groups of educators at schools, sans reporters, to make his case. "As I listened to him, I was drawn in," one teacher later said. "He was the snake charmer and I the mesmerized snake. He is truly a master at this craft."

BACK WHEN HE was running, Christie wrote an open letter to cops and fire-fighters calling accusations that he'd cut pensions "inaccurate information" from political opponents. "The false claim states that I would somehow eliminate or diminish your pension benefits. Let me be clear. Nothing could be further from the truth. . . . Your pension will be protected when I am elected governor. . . . It is a sacred trust."

Pen-ben reform would violate that agreement.

Protests on West State Street outside the state capitol ensued. Cops, firefighters, teachers, and state workers came by yellow buses each morning. They brought speakers and inflatable rats and some hard-core union brethren from the Bronx and Yonkers. Whistles blew and air horns wailed. One poster depicted Sweeney as Christie's sex slave, and a top union official told the crowd that just as Hitler had attacked the unions, Christie and his "two generals"—Sweeney and Democratic Assembly Speaker Sheila Oliver—were following suit.

Liberal legislators took to the stage, telling the rally-goers that if Christie really wanted money, he needed to pass their millionaires tax, get some money from the Wall Street tycoons who had led the country down the sewer, and stop picking the meat off the bones of the working men and women of New Jersey.

"What's up with your governor, anyway?" asked Richard Trumka, president of the AFL-CIO, as state workers booed. "They've taken a lot from us, but they can't take our freedom! They can't take our right to bargain for a better way of life!"

This being 2011, in the months after the Tea Party's big wins in Congress, the Tea Partiers showed up at these protests, too, and out on West State Street there were some good arguments to be witnessed between conservatives and union members. Blue lines of cops separated the two sides in small but significant demonstrations of democracy that reflected broader, national ideological wars.

THE DEMOCRATS WERE inclined to support the unions, which were their biggest backer. But Sweeney had long pushed the idea of rollbacks to public employee pensions. As a private-sector union leader, he represented laborers who had steadily seen wages erode even as their taxes increased. There was room for Sweeney and Christie to come to a compromise on this issue.

Christie dropped his pen-ben proposal in September 2010; Sweeney came forward with his own plan the following February. Christie made fun of Sweeney for taking so long. Yeah, he looked at Sweeney's plan "briefly," Christie said, but it "didn't look like much, looks like the special interests wrote it."

"They just talk, talk, talk, talk, talk," Christie said. "The problems are too big, and we've been waiting too long for solutions, so I am impatient."

In reality, Christie and Sweeney were talking all along. They slammed each other behind microphones and in press releases, but behind the scenes,

Christie's point man on all legislation, Kevin O'Dowd, was negotiating with top Democratic staffers.

Hoping to use the federal health benefits system as a model for what could be adopted by New Jersey, O'Dowd told his Democratic counterparts: "Let's get on a train." And there they went—O'Dowd, Christie's state treasurer, and two top Democratic staffers—to Washington, D.C., where they met with the Obama administration's Office of Personnel Management. The meeting, and the information they garnered, helped to break a logjam in the negotiations over the pen-ben bill.

Christie once explained how deals worked with him and Sweeney: "You say what you want in a perfect world. Someone else says what they want in a perfect world. And compromise is in between those two."

A former adversary described the governor's style as going something like this: "Fuck you, no." And again: "Fuck you, no." And then: "Not gonna live with it." More: "Not gonna do it." And finally: "Okay, deal."

It took the Dems a while to realize that "fuck you, no" was just the first round of negotiations, not the last.

At one point Sweeney and Christie negotiated a provision one-on-one—and then gave conflicting reports back to their staffs about what the agreement was. After that, O'Dowd and Sweeney's top policy guy, Andrew Hendry, was always in the room when dealing with the details. A sense of camaraderie and trust was built over pen-ben talks that led to deals on other issues. As negotiations grew deeper, Christie was described to me as being more pleasant than hard-nosed, open about the politics that were forcing his hand.

Christie ultimately agreed to a concession: Employees would be required to pay less for their health benefits than his original proposal called for. And Sweeney accepted that benefit terms would be written into law and not negotiated in collective bargaining.

Sweeney would now have to push this proposal through his Democratic caucus. But Christie had work to do, too.

FROM THE PASSENGER seat of the gubernatorial Chevy Suburban, a back-benching Democratic legislator's phone number is being dialed. "Hey, it's Chris," the governor says. "Happy birthday!"

The governor's staffers put legislators' birthdays (plus cell phone numbers) at the top of Christie's schedule each day. If he had some time on the long ride from Mendham to Trenton, he'd call, talk politics, maybe invite 'em to a Jets game—or better yet, a Giants game—in his government-owned luxury box.

One longtime Trenton staffer told me that the difference in Christie's style from his predecessor's was evident in the opening months of his term. A Democratic Assembly member in a swing district had gotten calls from former governor Jon Corzine's office only if he was desperate for a vote—and even then, the calls often came from a deputy. Yet now, in Christie's first two months, this assemblyman had called the governor's office twice—and both times, the governor himself was put on the phone.

Giving Democrats attention, calling them back, and, yes, wishing them happy birthday, could mean *Yes* votes when they mattered most.

More importantly, I once pointed out to Christie, he also had the backing of the Democratic bosses, Norcross and Joe DiVincenzo.

"I've been able to have bipartisan success primarily because I've worked at it," Christie told me. "And the relationships with George and Joe are the *result* of that work."

CHRISTIE DIDN'T HAVE to work hard to get the Republicans on board with pen-ben reform. They were with him uniformly on almost everything.

Christie vetoed more than one hundred bills in his first two years in office, signing fewer laws than any governor in 164 years. Over his first six years in office, more than fifty times the Democrats tried to get the two-thirds majority of votes needed to override his vetoes. Each time, they failed—because Christie wouldn't let Republicans vote against him. Republicans who sponsored bills that got vetoed by the governor even switched their votes on the override attempts.

When Democrats tried to renew a tax on millionaires, a Republican senator said, flatly: "I can't vote for this. The administration won't let me." During voting sessions, Christie's chief of staff went on the floor of the Senate, as if taking up an enforcer position.

"On legislation that we needed Republicans on, it was easier going to the governor's office than the Republican Senate office," a Democratic staffer told me.

According to a source in on one set of negotiations, Christie said he'd take care of the GOP votes this way: "We'll get within striking distance, and then I'll take out my whipping hand."

·        ·        ·

A PEN-BEN BILL landed on the floors of the legislature. As the bill was debated, two dozen union activists allowed themselves to get mass-arrested as they chanted "Kill the bill!" and "Workers' rights are human rights!" Testimony from Sweeney was interrupted by hisses and heckling.

The bill would gradually increase the mandatory state contributions for the pension fund, raise the retirement age from sixty-two to sixty-five, and eliminate cost of living adjustments until the system was solvent. On health care, employee contributions would increase—those making $105,000 would pay 35 percent of their health plan costs. And the right to collectively bargain for health benefits would be suspended for four years.

Outside, protesters called for his head: "We want Sweeney!"

Meanwhile, Assembly Speaker Sheila Oliver was having trouble wrangling votes. Getting the bill through Sweeney's Senate proved far easier than moving it through the more liberal, more independent-minded state Assembly.

Oliver was desperate, Christie later claimed. So he told her that he'd save her job as the leader of the Assembly by guaranteeing her Republican votes if her position was threatened. He said he even went down the hall to tell the Republicans: "If they take a run at her on the floor, I need all of you to vote for her for Speaker." And that's how he got her to support the bill.

Oliver called the story an outright fabrication. She told us that she was "beginning to wonder if Governor Christie is mentally deranged."

Christie was just myth-making for his Republican friends, Oliver said.

WITH THE CLOCK winding down to the end of the legislative session on June 30, the unions didn't have much time if they wanted to scuttle the bill. So they went nuclear.

The NJEA took out a TV ad that went after Norcross for a provision in the pen-ben bill, later removed, that would have theoretically benefited his insurance business. The ad said: *Apparently, Christie and Sweeney care more about paying off political bosses than protecting taxpayers.*

Christie sat quietly and smiled. Because this ad turned out to be a major miscalculation.

Within hours Norcross responded by convening a press conference at a South Jersey wedding hall. Norcross appeared alongside a number of major New Jersey figures, including a former governor, Jim Florio; the state's most popular politician, Newark mayor Cory Booker; and the most famous religious figure in South Jersey, Monsignor Michael Doyle. They all lauded

Norcross and criticized the NJEA as an obstacle to saving the state's poor children.

The union had pushed too far. Less than an hour after the press conference ended, Christie sent out a statement. He had a deal with Democrats on pen-ben reform.

The unions were neutralized. The governor had slain the dragon. Within weeks, the bill was passed and signed.

PEN-BEN WASN'T EVEN in the bag before he unveiled his next major project to change New Jersey—teacher tenure reform. Christie had his foot on the teachers' unions' throat, and he wasn't about to lift it.

Christie knew how to sell tenure reform. At town hall meetings and in policy conferences, he turned to the audience and he told a story, like this:

"What's your name, sir? John. What's your name, ma'am? Pamela. Okay, John and Pamela are third-grade teachers in my school and I'm a principal, and it's the end of the school year and it's time for me to give them an evaluation." Principal Christie explains that John is an "extraordinary" teacher— stays late, talks to parents over email, and so he is hiring him back for next year and giving him a 4 percent raise.

"You, on the other hand, Pamela, are a disaster," Christie says to laughter. Pamela doesn't return parents' calls, the students don't do nearly as well as John's students, and yet, "We're gonna give you a 4 percent raise."

Christie talked about how he imagined an *honest* back-to-school night, where Principal Christie speaks to the parents: "This year your children have Mrs. Smith, and now to be completely candid with you, Mrs. Smith is a lousy teacher. . . . Here's the problem, though: We have a union contract that's *this thick*. And she has tenure, which means we can't fire her for any reason at all, and so we're stuck with her. Have a great year!"

Christie wanted to implement an educator evaluation system to determine whether a teacher should be granted tenure, as opposed to having it based purely on seniority. These tests would incorporate student test scores and classroom observation. Too many "ineffective" ratings, and a teacher would lose tenure, which made it more likely that he or she would be laid off during budget cuts.

Christie would win this battle, signing a law that marked the most significant changes to teacher tenure rules in one hundred years. Tenure would be linked to performance, it would take longer to earn, and dismissing a low-quality teacher would be easier and cheaper.

Unfortunately for Christie, he wasn't able to implement his plan for merit pay, in which math teachers would earn more than gym teachers, nor did he eliminate seniority protections in tenure—the "last in, first out" system that forced junior teachers to be fired during times of layoffs. Miraculously, though, for his tenure reforms that were enacted by the legislature, Christie got the NJEA to sign on in agreement.

NJEA representatives, scorned by Christie for so long, showed up at the bill signing. Like the bullied kids who finally got a chance to spend a few minutes at the cool lunch table, they even laughed at Christie's jokes. The governor beamed.

# 8

# GLORY DAYS

When he first ran for governor, Christie released a five-minute video that name-dropped President Obama and committed to renewable energy. "I will be New Jersey's number one clean energy advocate," he said, promising solar farms "all across New Jersey." He even won an endorsement from the New Jersey Environmental Federation.

Christie wasn't in office too long before the environmental group regretted its green seal of approval, calling him "either a liar or a flip flopper."

Christie went to court to shut down a Pennsylvania coal facility where emissions were damaging plant life in New Jersey, and he signed a bill requiring utilities to buy more power from solar companies, which angered Tea Party conservatives. But just about everything else Christie did on the environment was viewed by activists as hostile to the earth.

Christie targeted the Department of Environmental Protection as an albatross on the state's economy, a bloated bureaucracy enforcing super-fluous regulations. He appointed an environmental commissioner empowered to unilaterally waive regulations for businesses and train employees in customer relations. Penalties for environmental violations dropped dramatically, as did the number of regulators. Relations with the business community got so cozy that when the number-two environmental official left the DEP she became president of a top New Jersey corporate lobbying group.

On energy, after signing a bill allowing wind farms off the Jersey Shore, Christie's Board of Public Utilities indefinitely delayed construction because it never adopted the necessary regulations to move forward. Christie also rolled back rebates for solar panels, supported a gas pipeline in a protected forest, and took $1.2 billion from utility bill surcharges for clean energy projects to instead backfill the state budget. Likewise, when he settled a long-running suit with ExxonMobil over environmental damage caused by its refineries, Christie collected a quick $225 million to balance his budget. That caused a fury among environmentalists because the state originally wanted $8.9 *billion*. Environmentalists framed this as a crony capitalistic giveaway by a future presidential candidate; Christie insisted he got the best deal possible.

Christie's most notorious move on the environment came when he unilaterally dropped out of the Regional Greenhouse Gas Initiative—a cap-and-trade program for all states in the Northeast. The ten-state treaty was a landmark effort to curb greenhouse gases by essentially billing power plant operators for their carbon emissions. New Jersey would be the first and only state to drop out of the program. Democrats said he sold out the state's environment to conservatives who saw RGGI as a heavy-handed government program that increased costs to energy companies and consumers.

In a very Christie bit of triangulation, the governor announced the RGGI pullout at a press conference in which he spent most of the time talking about . . . protecting the environment.

"Climate change is real and is impacting our state," he said.

THIS WAS SIGNIFICANT, for one of the top Republicans in the country to say this in 2011. Only a year earlier at a town hall meeting Christie had expressed skepticism about global warming. He said he needed more information. Apparently, he got that; he met with academic experts inside the government and elsewhere, and read up on the science. He decided that human beings had a role in the warming of the planet.

"This decade average temperatures have been rising," Christie said. "Temperature changes are affecting weather patterns and our climate."

He talked tough on coal energy, saying he wouldn't allow it in New Jersey, and was committed to expanding wind turbines and solar fields. He even established a committee to examine how to reduce energy costs for the state.

Despite all that, he had concluded that RGGI "is not effective in reducing greenhouse gases." The financial penalties weren't high enough to force conservation, he argued. And he said that with natural gas replacing coal as a cleaner-burning fossil fuel, the market was proving it could do a better job solving environmental problems than the government.

Christie again demonstrated a deft ability to walk the political tightrope, saying for his first time ever that he *did* think human beings caused climate change—while simultaneously tossing out the most consequential climate change policy in the state. Observers were baffled: Was he an authentic political being with a complex belief system—or the most calculating politician in America?

Christie's approach was often to make conservative moves with more moderate rhetoric. So annually rejecting Planned Parenthood funding was about saving money, not restricting abortions, and pulling out of RGGI was about ending a "gimmicky program," not rolling back environmental protections.

**THE KOCH BROTHERS** own the second-largest privately held company in the nation, a conglomerate that does everything from oil refining to commodity trading to paper production. By 2015 they were worth, according to *Forbes*, a combined $86 billion. They spent an estimated $400 million on electing conservatives in the 2012 election.

Christie announced his pullout from RGGI three months after his first meeting with David Koch in New York, and exactly one month before headlining a Koch brothers' conference in Colorado. The meeting was not on his public schedule, and no announcement was made about transferring powers to the lieutenant governor while he was out of state. The meeting was so secretive that "audio speakers around the periphery of the outdoor dining pavilion blasted out static to thwart eavesdroppers."

*Mother Jones* magazine got a recording anyway. Christie called the group "modern-day patriots" and David Koch declared Christie "my kind of guy."

And Koch specifically told the crowd about RGGI. "Another example of Governor Christie's commitment to the free-enterprise system is that only a few weeks ago," Koch told the conservatives, "he announced that New Jersey would be withdrawing from [RGGI], which would have raised energy costs, reduced economic growth, and led to very little, if any, benefit for the environment."

Of course, the fact that the Kochs adamantly opposed government efforts to curtail climate change and have a history of violating environmental regulations in their business dealings was not lost on the environmentalists who smelled collusion between Christie and the Kochs on RGGI.

Christie denied all that. But the courtship between the most exciting Republican in the country and the largest well of Republican money was on.

•           •           •

**IN THE SUMMER** of 2010, the first year of the term, the brand-new governor found himself dining with right-wing talk radio kingpin Rush Limbaugh and FOX News chairman Roger Ailes at Ailes's upstate New York compound, where *New York* magazine reported that Ailes "fell hard" for Christie—and asked him to run for president. This visit came just six months into Christie's first real job in politics.

Christie turned Ailes down (he would turn him down a second time the following year) by joking to them why he wasn't ready: "I still like to go to Burger King."

Summer turned to fall, and the year's newest political rock star began a fifteen-state tour on behalf of local Republican candidates—logging twenty thousand miles and raising more than $8 million. In Portland, Oregon, they played Bruce Springsteen's "Born to Run" for him in a high school gymnasium and a woman handed him a "Christie/Palin 2012" button, for former vice presidential candidate Sarah Palin. The rope line for Christie ran the entire length of the gymnasium.

"I'm watching this going, 'Oh, my god,' " Christie fundraiser Bill Palatucci, who traveled with the governor, later told me. "This is 2010!"

In Ohio the *Star-Ledger* reported young Republicans wanted to fist-pump with him like they did on MTV's bacchanal *Jersey Shore*. One fan drove five hours just to get a look at him. Christie stayed to take pictures even after Congressman John Kasich, the gubernatorial candidate he was actually campaigning for, had left the rally.

"That's when you kind of know that things have changed," Christie told me years later. "Governor candidates, Senate candidates, House candidates. All were calling and asking me to campaign and raise money for them. That was the first time that I really knew from a political perspective that I was going beyond the borders of New Jersey in a fairly significant way."

Radio host Don Imus was the first to ask this inexperienced neophyte governor if he would consider running for president. "No, no. Come on. Look at me. Me for president? Come on, seriously. No way. No way," Christie said, flabbergasted that he was even having this conversation.

That's what he repeated on the *Today* show, too: "No way."

"This is just completely surreal," Christie thought, "and not what I expected."

**IOWA HOLDS THE** first presidential election contest, giving that state's millionaires an outsized role in the presidential nominating process. So it was newsworthy when the news leaked in 2011 that six Iowa businessmen—barons in hogs, ethanol, and real estate—were headed to New Jersey to court Christie to run for president. They scheduled dinner at Drumthwacket, the governor's mansion in Princeton.

Naturally I asked Christie if I could come along.

"You're not from Iowa, you cannot come, and the only non-Iowans there will be real friends of mine, not people I spend a lot of time with, like you," he told me.

Regardless, we all soon learned a lot about that dinner.

Christie's son Andrew was in a baseball playoff game earlier that day for Delbarton School, an elite college preparatory school run by Benedictine monks. The way the governor could catch a few innings of the game and make it to dinner on time was to take a brand-new, $12.5 million, fifty-five-foot-long, white-blue-yellow AgustaWestland state police helicopter to and from the game. Christie landed next to the baseball diamond and got a ride in a state police SUV for the hundred yards to the stands.

A local reporter covering the game snapped a photo of Christie arriving in his taxpayer-funded bird. Christie took this helicopter everywhere, from Trenton to the Hamptons to a GOP fund-raiser in Connecticut. Each year of his first term his chopper use increased—to 106 trips in 2013—but this trip got him into more trouble than any other.

The picture was widely circulated and Coptergate, as it was known, became a national news story. At a news conference a couple of days later reporters peppered Christie with questions for thirty-five minutes.

"I'm governor 24/7, every single day," he said by way of explanation. "But I'm also a father."

Andrew was a junior at the time and a promising athlete. He would go on to play baseball for Princeton University. But after beginning the year on the bench he was now starting catcher—redemption, of sorts, for his father, who had started at catcher on his own high school team only to be benched his senior year.

"So those things are going to end pretty soon, for me and Andrew," Christie continued, growing wistful and intimate, live CNN cameras rolling. "And it's not a good enough excuse for me to say: 'I was governor, you just have to understand.' Because I'll be governor for a lot less of a time than I'll be a father."

Christie felt he needed to be at the game, and in making that argument he was getting at something that you rarely hear from politicians: Real talk about life-work balance, and the decisions plus sacrifices entailed in striving for that balance in modern America. "We try to balance me being governor and the demands on that with my responsibilities as a father," he said. "And I'm always going to balance that as hard as I can toward my responsibilities as a dad. Not just because I feel responsible for it, but also because I want to."

Christie was asked what his seventeen-year-old son thought when Dad landed a helicopter at his baseball game.

"Dad," young Andrew told his old man, "thanks for coming."

Christie agreed to reimburse the state for $2,151.50 to cover not one but two trips he apparently took to Andrew's baseball games, and the state Republican Party covered the flight to Drumthwacket for the dinner with the Iowans. But at the same press conference Christie also went on the offensive, singling out Democratic assemblywoman Valerie Vainieri Huttle, who had issued a statement questioning the "priorities" of a man who leaves his son's baseball game to meet with political donors. "She should really be embarrassed at what a *jerk* she is for saying something like that," Christie said, cameras still rolling.

Vainieri Huttle was right about this point: Half of the reason he took the helicopter that day was so he could meet with people who wanted to fund his candidacy for president. This whole situation was not simply an outgrowth of fatherly love—it was also a direct result of career ambition.

Christie thought he could do both, remain governor while cultivating long-term presidential aspirations. But it kept getting complicated, in part because others had a more accelerated timetable in mind.

**KEN LANGONE, A** mega GOP fund-raiser and cofounder of Home Depot, assembled a few of the most powerful people in the world for breakfast at the exclusive (and men-only) Racquet & Tennis Club in Manhattan. Langone was the leader of the unofficial Ready For Christie 2012 club, and he wanted to make a direct pitch to get him to run for president.

This was no ordinary pitch. Dozens of millionaires and billionaires were seated in rows across from Christie. Guys like Richard Grasso, the former chairman of the New York Stock Exchange, and Charles Schwab, of the eponymous brokerage. David Koch was on speakerphone. Four were on the *Forbes* list of richest Americans.

Christie brought political strategist Mike DuHaime, his communications director Maria Comella, his wife, Mary Pat—and his oldest son, Andrew, who was about to become a high school senior.

Langone began. "Governor, all these people are here today for one reason," he said. "If you're willing to announce for president of the United States, we're with you, and everyone in this room has committed that to me and everyone in this room will raise every dollar you need to have raised to have a successful campaign. You don't have to worry about raising the money."

Then, former secretary of state Henry Kissinger took the mic. Christie and Kissinger had first met at Yankee Stadium—in owner George Steinbrenner's box. Now, Kissinger stood and talked about having known nearly a dozen presidents in his lifetime. "Being a president is about two things, courage and character," Kissinger told Christie. "You have both, and your country needs you."

The room applauded.

"I'm not running," Christie told them, according to a paraphrased account assembled by *Politico*. First, he cited his reluctant wife. Second, he was concerned about not seeing his kids very much, possibly, for ten years. Third, he had made a commitment to the people of New Jersey to at least finish out one term.

But he left them with this: If he ran, he told them, he could win. And then he employed the kind of humor and humility that showed them why he *would* win.

"I brought my oldest son today because, first of all, I wanted him to wake up early. And, second of all, to have to put on his one suit and tie," Christie said. "But I wanted him to listen because if I did run, which I'm *not* going to—but if I did in the future, it's going to affect him. There's six people in the family—I'm just one."

And yet he said that out of respect for them, he'd go back and think about it once more.

Meanwhile the calls kept coming. Like from casino mogul Steve Wynn.

"I got on the phone, and he's like, 'You have to run,' " Christie told me. "I'm like, 'Oh, my God. Really?' "

This was about the time that Obama's people started doing opposition research on him. It was getting that real.

Karl Rove, President George W. Bush's so-called "brain," who had met Christie in Austin back in 1999, came over to the house in Mendham to talk it over, while Barbara Bush, the former First Lady, dialed up Mary Pat at work to reassure her about the effects it would have on the family.

Former president George W. Bush called from Kennebunkport, Maine. He and Christie talked for forty-five minutes. Bush gave advice, but didn't commit to supporting a Christie candidacy. "And he kind of asked me then what was I thinking, what were the impediments in my mind, what were the concerns, so that he could try to play a sounding board for me on that," Christie said. "It was an amazing conversation."

CHRISTIE KEPT DENYING he was running. And sometimes, as in this speech at Princeton University, he was quite thoughtful about it:

> People say to me, "You could win." And I say, "Well yeah, I know I could win." But that's like the dog catching the garbage truck, right? What happens if I actually catch it? . . .
>
> I think that I've been able to govern the way I've governed, aggressively, because I'm not filled with self-doubt. I will tell you that if I were ever at this moment just elevated to the presidency, I would be filled with self-doubt. And you can't lead if you have self-doubt . . .
>
> I can't allow flattery to get in the way of common sense, and I can't allow opportunity to trump my own good judgment. And so that's why I say no. I say no because in my heart, as much as my ego might want to say yes, my heart tells me no.

Denials notwithstanding, demands for Christie to appear around the country were increasing. A fund-raising trip to western states yielded $620,000 for the New Jersey GOP. People from around the country were spending $5,000 for a few minutes with him at a dining room table.

Nothing, though, kept the drums banging about a possible presidential run more than bogus rumors in the press. In August 2011 one respected journalist tweeted that Christie was holding focus groups about a possible candidacy—a scoop that instantly became breaking news, until it was publicly refuted thirty-six minutes later.

In September, things got outrageous. The 2012 presidential election was fourteen months away, but both the Republican establishment and the media seemed to long for different GOP candidates. The *Wall Street*

*Journal* reported that Christie was brushing up on foreign policy by dining with experts. Conservative site *Newsmax* alerted us that "Christie seemed inclined to enter the race," while Christie's mentor, former New Jersey governor Tom Kean, said the odds of Christie running were "better now than they were a couple weeks ago," even as Christie's brother, Todd, said Christie was staying put: "If he's lying to me, I'll be as stunned as I've ever been in my life." But then Todd himself was debunked by ABC News: "A source close to Chris Christie says we should disregard what the New Jersey governor's brother said about Christie's plans."

The *Huffington Post* determined that Christie wasn't running but then cited unnamed sources in the final paragraph saying he *was* indeed running. The *New York Post* reported he was now "giving serious thought" to making an announcement the following Monday before the *Daily Caller* then outscooped the *Post*, saying "potential donors" were told to report to Trenton Thursday for the announcement.

My ears hurt. I texted Palatucci, one of Christie's oldest and closest political advisers, to ask him what the hell was going on.

"I am home watching football, and not the Iowa Jayhawks," he replied coyly, referring to the all-important Iowa presidential caucuses barely three months away.

Perhaps I could be as clever as he, I thought, and ask about the *next* state in the presidential campaign calendar—New Hampshire. I texted back: "Maybe there'll be a University of New Hampshire Wildcats game on some time soon??"

"I didn't know NHU had a football team," Palatucci responded.

I imagined them all sitting there on the couch in Christie's living room, the whole inner circle, laughing over their smartphones as they teased the media via text message.

MARY PAT HAD concerns about how a race would affect the four children, all still under eighteen. And what if he didn't win? What would that mean about his political future, both at home and nationally?

"It was true that she really didn't want me to do it," Christie later said. "But there's a big difference between what she really would want me to do and what she was willing to participate in."

In early September she woke her husband of twenty-five years at 6:00 a.m. "If you want to run, go for it, and don't worry about me and the kids," she told him. "We'll be fine."

Christie couldn't believe it. Mary Pat got out of bed to take a shower. "I was like, 'You've got to come back here!'"

After the shower, he asked her more directly: "Are you telling me you think that I should run? Or are you giving me permission to run?"

"Well, I mean, you definitely have permission to run. And . . . maybe you should run."

Mary Pat said she was tired of the constant speculation and back-and-forth discussions about whether he should get into the race. "I wanted to stop thinking about it. . . . So I was like, 'Okay! Do it. I can't take this anymore, just do it.'"

THIRTY-ONE YEARS AFTER making his first vote for Ronald Reagan via absentee ballot from his dorm room at the University of Delaware, Christie got a letter in the mail from none other than Nancy Reagan herself, the widow of the undisputed most popular Republican in American history. It was hand-written, with some flattering things to say. She wanted him to fly out to Simi Valley, California.

"Oh, my God," Christie thought. "Nancy Reagan is inviting me to come to the Reagan Library to speak?"

When he arrived, he was given a private tour. Then as the sun set and the crowds packed in for his big speech, Chris and Mary Pat were taken to the residence that Reagan maintained on the property.

"Do you realize this is the fastest sellout in our speakers' series history?" Reagan asked.

"No, Mrs. Reagan, I didn't."

"Did you know this is the most media credentials we've given out?" she asked.

"No, Mrs. Reagan, I didn't."

The queen of the Grand Old Party smiled. "You better be good!"

Christie told me that Nancy even described to him what Ronnie would've thought of him, had he been alive. Christie wouldn't tell me what that was, though. "It was nice," is all he said. I asked if he thought it felt like the torch was being passed to a new Reaganite leader. "That's a *little* much," he told me, "even for my ego."

They took pictures, and Christie then escorted Reagan to her seat next to Mary Pat in the front row. This was the hard part. Just one month earlier, before his own speech at the Reagan Library, Florida senator Marco Rubio had nearly dropped Nancy Reagan (some say he saved her; either way, she fell while she was walking with him). This gaffe was in the back of Christie's mind.

"It's your job to walk me in," she teased him. "Don't mess it up."

He didn't. They walked in and sat down in the front row. As he was being introduced, Nancy turned to him and said: "Do you see that podium? That was one of Ronnie's podiums from the White House."

"Really?" Christie asked.

Nancy just smiled.

**HE MOSTLY WROTE** the speech himself, and intended it to be his "statement on the state of our country both at home and around the world." The remarks started with the obligatory homage to the former president, telling his favorite Reagan story—when Reagan stared down striking air traffic controllers, demanded they return to work, and threatened to fire those who refused.

"In the end, thousands refused, thousands were fired." This was his first applause line of the night.

"Reagan was a man who said what he meant and meant what he said. Those who thought he was bluffing were sadly mistaken."

Sound like someone you may know?

The speech veered into the familiar, with Christie touting his bipartisan accomplishments achieved through "leadership and compromise." He called Obama a "bystander in the Oval Office" and he gave nods to the interventionist foreign policy he would later adopt as a presidential candidate.

The twenty-seven-minute speech had soaring rhetoric, constructed in a way that did not sound the way Christie usually talks. "The America I speak of is the America Ronald Reagan challenged us to be every day," he said.

Christie was well received, but Christie's talent is not delivering big speeches. It was in the twenty-seven-minute Q&A that followed that Christie really electrified his audience.

He began by knocking the answer to an immigration question out of the park—offering a vision of the immigrant-fueled American dream while also coming out firmly against college scholarships for children who immigrated illegally. Conciliatory bipartisan and fiery partisan in one breath—vintage Christie.

A second person in the audience took the mic and asked if he was running for president: "You're known as a straight shooter, not one given to playing games. Can you tell us what's going on here? Are you reconsidering, or are you standing firm?"

"You folks are an incredible disappointment as an audience," he began, pausing to let that sink in. "The fact that it took to the *second* question shows you people are off your game. That is *not* American exceptionalism!"

They were in stitches. He told them that his answer was currently on *Politico*'s website, which had compiled a nearly two-minute video of all the times he had said "no" to the "Are you running?" question. "Click on it. Those are the answers. Next question."

His audience was dissatisfied. "Oh, c'mon, grumbling? Okay, since we're having some grumbling. I have rules, too."

He dramatically put down his water glass. And off he went, warning the crowd that "for the purpose of tonight, we're *all* from New Jersey. And what that means is, you give it, you're getting it back."

They were whooping and hollering at this point. As even Christie himself was giggling—when he thinks something is actually funny, when it's not just a polite laugh or a put-on laugh, his shoulders rise and he giggles.

A transplanted New Jerseyan, now living in California, took the mic. "You make us so proud to be New Jerseyans and so proud to be Americans. And my Italian mother, she told me to tell you that you've got to run for president," she said.

"If I make you proud to be a New Jerseyan and proud to be an American, and your Italian mother wants me to run for president, *what the hell are you doing in California?!* Get back to New Jersey, let's go, come home, come home for godsake. What are you doing out here? I got a plane. You can come back now if you want. Meet me by the side, we'll take you home."

The assembled Republicans knew their party was on its way to nominating Mitt Romney, who showed the public neither humor nor much personality. Here—right before them!—was the opposite. Same positions, but sold with soul.

Up in the balcony was a woman with her hand raised. She seemed serious. What happened next was one of the most extraordinary unscripted moments I had seen in politics.

"All kidding aside," she began. "You know how to tell the American people what they need to hear. And I say this from the bottom of my heart, for my daughter who's right here, for my grandchildren who are at home . . . I mean this with all my heart: We can't wait another four years till 2016. And I really implore you to—as a citizen of this country, to please, sir, reconsider. Don't even say anything tonight, of course you wouldn't. Go home and really think about it. Please! Do it for my daughter, do it for our grand-children, do it for our sons."

She concluded: "Please, sir. We need you. Your country needs you. To run for president."

And wouldn't you know it, the whole crowd, hundreds upon hundreds of people in the home of Ronald Reagan, stood up to give Christie extended applause. They were now literally begging him to run for president of the United States of America.

Humility took over. "I hear exactly what you're saying and I feel the passion in which you say it, and it touches me. And it touches me. Because I tell you, I'm just a kid from Jersey who feels like the luckiest guy in the world to have the opportunity to be the governor of my state . . . I'm extraordi-narily honored, and I really appreciate you saying it with the passion that you did. That's why this country is the great place that it is, because of folks like you."

Christie walked out, and the political world shook in his wake. Years later, I met people around the country who fell in love with Chris Christie on this very night. "Ever since I saw his speech at the Reagan Library . . ."

SO MUCH COVERAGE of the New Jersey governor's possible presidential cam-paign, but not enough pundits! Eventually, the TV producers got to my name. A black Suburban picked me up at six one Sunday morning and whisked me to the ABC studios in New York, where I went on the air with *This Week* host Christiane Amanpour.

That very morning, the *New York Times* scooped that Team Christie was "working to determine whether they could move fast enough to set up effective political operations in Iowa and New Hampshire."

In the SUV on my way to the studio I contacted a close political adviser to Christie who told me that the *Times* story was BS. So I went on air and reported that NO preparations had been made.

The truth was everyone close to Christie was reexamining the possi-bility. A poll showed Christie and Obama running even in a hypothetical head-to-head.

Then a Nebraska farmer FedExed a letter to the Christies. The letter was written to Christie's kids, and in it the farmer implored them to urge their father to run, telling them that it was okay if he missed their school concerts and athletic contests in the coming years because the *history books* would remember *them*, the children, as the ones who changed our country. "They're going to write about the fact that the Christie children approached their father on an October weekend . . ."

Mary Pat looked at him: "Chris, we've got to put an end one way or the other."

CHRISTIE TALKED TO his father. "Do you still love your job?" Wilbur asked.

"Yeah."

"Then why are you leaving?"

Christie thought this question was a "very simple but powerful piece of advice."

On the first weekend of October, Christie told his staff not to call him. He needed time to process all of this. He decided that with guaranteed money from the billionaires, he could win the nomination. But his gut told him now wasn't yet his time.

As the story goes, in the SUV on the way home from work the Monday after that weekend, Christie made his final decision—and then he fell asleep for the rest of the drive, relieved. When he got home, he gathered the family and said: "Listen, guys, Dad's made a decision: I'm not running for president."

In the Christie house there was applause.

Next, Christie made twenty phone calls to those who had pushed him to run. His first call was to Langone.

"Yeah? What? You got something to tell me?" Langone asked.

"I'm not doing it, Kenny."

"Oh, Governor. Don't tell me that, Governor. Don't tell me that!"

THE NEXT MORNING, October 4, 2011, Christie's staff alerted the media via email that he was holding a news conference at 1:00 p.m. at the Statehouse. Further deepening the suspense, and coy as always, communications chief Maria Comella didn't say what the press conference was about—was he announcing a run, or simply reiterating, for the umpteenth time, that he wasn't running?

A massive contingent of reporters descended on Trenton, a line of them snaking all the way out the front door of the Statehouse. Reporters who had traveled down from New York City for the show couldn't even get into the room.

The last event to draw this many reporters to the governor's outer office was seven years earlier, when former governor James E. McGreevey resigned from office as a "gay American."

This press conference offered similar suspense. On the way over to Trenton, I learned that FOX News was reporting that the governor was about to announce his candidacy while *Politico* was saying he was not running. Misinformation prevailed until the end.

Christie walked through the door behind his podium and glanced up once at the largest crowd he had ever seen there. He was wearing what he calls his "big speech tie"—a fuchsia paisley number that I once described as the ugliest tie any politician has ever worn on TV.

Christie began without even a "good afternoon."

"For months I've been adamant about the fact that I would not run for president," he said. He only recently reconsidered after "serious people" urged him to run. But, alas: "Now is not my time."

And the sound bite: "So New Jersey, whether you like it or not, you're stuck with me."

"YA KNOW, YOU asked if there was any regret, Marcia. The only regret I have is I've given such great TV exposure to some of the local reporters. I mean, who's gonna have *Katz* on TV now that I'm out of this race? *Nobody* is gonna have *Katz* on TV. He won't be able to get on News 12 for God's sake. That's about the only regret I have, is that."

I was hidden away in a corner of the room. We had yet to make eye contact; he hadn't called on me to ask a question. But here he was, in a live nationally televised moment, in his most high-profile press conference of his career, using me as a comedic foil. He was who he always was, smacktalking the local reporters for a laugh—and, notably, not playing to Iowa or Washington, D.C., where they would have no idea who "Katz" was. He was, in his way, keeping it real . . . while also totally avoiding a question by giving a funny answer.

The press conference on the nonannouncement went on for fifty minutes, and featured Christie at his most hilariously combative with reporters. He was dismissive of a) an out-of-town reporter for interrupting him ("You're new here, you don't know the rules"), b) veteran Trenton columnist Charlie Stile for asking something introspective ("You're so worried about me, we gotta get you some help"), and c) me, when I asked him about the moment that he began to reconsider running ("I didn't mark it down in my *diary*").

Christie said the decision had a lot to do with Jersey, with constituents coming up to him while he was out to dinner with his family, telling him they wanted him to do whatever he wanted to do—but that they'd miss him, here at home. "The people in New Jersey got me back on course," he said.

"I have a commitment to New Jersey that I simply will not abandon. That's the promise I made to the people of this state when I took office twenty months ago, to fix a broken New Jersey, and when I look at what we've accomplished so far, I'm proud, but I know we're not nearly done. . . . I'm just not prepared to walk away."

At the end he was humble, saying it was a "blessing" for just "a regular guy from Jersey" to be considered. "I appreciate all of you coming today, I appreciate the great deference that you've given to me to try to make this decision," he said, perhaps his kindest words ever to the media. "I think you have all done your jobs well, I appreciate the way you've covered this, and I'm going to get back to work. Thank you very much."

MITT ROMNEY DID not waste any time trying to get the biggest name in GOP politics in his camp for the Republican nomination. That Friday night he called Christie to say he was coming through New Jersey the following day and wanted to know if he could come by for a visit.

Christie loves telling this story. He used it throughout the 2012 campaign while stumping for Romney—it was how he explained how a guy like *him* could believe in a guy like *that*. The schlubby raconteur and the math nerd. What do they see in each other? There's an answer. It's seven minutes long, and it goes like this.

"It was Friday night," he begins. "And I spring on my wife that the next president of the United States and his wife are going to come to lunch tomorrow." He pauses. "So we both look at each other in a sense of real horror and say"—he lowers his voice—" 'Okay we gotta clean this house.' "

Christie gives you a sense of himself by making him seem just a bit like you. And the thing is, he *is* just like you. Christie stories are embellished but not contrived; they're familiar, told with pitch-perfect tone and cadence. Most of all, Christie stories have something rare in political stump speeches: plots.

The setup: The Romneys are coming for lunch! The dramatic tension: The Christies live in a house of two working parents, with four kids between the ages of nine and nineteen.

They have a cleaning service, but the housekeepers come only once a week. "We're used to stepping over things, in fact we know where they are, we don't have to look anymore," Christie says. "My sense was that Mitt Romney wouldn't know where to step over, so we had to get moving."

In addition to cleaning up the house, "we gotta have *the talk* with the children." So, after shopping for food to make lunch, "we bring the four of them together and say, 'Listen, Governor Romney and Mrs. Romney are coming. Very important people. We expect you to be on the *best* behavior. We want you to be at the front door when they come. We want you to give them the firm handshake, look them in the eye, introduce yourself *c l e a r l y*, *articulate*, and then . . . make yourself scarce.' "

There was a problem: Romney didn't know that lunch would be served at the Christies'—there had been some sort of misunderstanding between the intermediaries who arranged the details. So the Romneys stopped for lunch at a deli somewhere near the Christies' house in Mendham, delaying their twelve-thirty arrival.

Christie didn't want the Romneys roaming around Mendham, blowing their secret rendezvous. So, as Christie remembers it: "We sent one of the state police to go and find them."

Once the Romneys got to the house, everything went well with the kids during the greeting. Then Andrew, nineteen, and Sarah, sixteen, grabbed a sandwich and went up to their rooms to be scarce, as they were instructed.

But Bridget, nine, and Patrick, twelve . . . uh-oh.

Chris and Mary Pat, Mitt and Ann, they all went to the back patio to eat. They started talking about the campaign. "All of a sudden out of the corner of my eye, I see like a flash," Christie says. "Ya know it's that parental *peripheral* vision that you're only granted like actually during *labor* with your first child, somehow God comes down and says: 'You couldn't see any of this stuff before—but you're going to be able to see it after this.' I see that flash, and I turned and look—and there's my twelve-year-old son, Patrick.

"Now," Christie says, backing up to provide some context, "*every family* has a Patrick. Every one of you have 'em, right? You know who I'm talkin' about. *This is the child* in your family who's the straw that stirs the drink. *This is the child* whose mood determines the mood of the household. *This is the child* who if he's in a good mood, life is great. And if he's in a bad mood, *hell* has descended upon your household."

Here is the set piece, the penultimate moment of our little dramedy.

"I see that flash and I turn and Patrick is going *full* speed, *full* bore, *full* speed, on his rollerblades . . ."

"Uh-ohh!!!" the audience will yell when Christie tells this part. They really yell, every time.

"Headed directly . . ."

"Ahhh!!!"

"For Mitt Romney!"

Audiences will now laugh, hysterically. They will slam their hands together in applause.

Christie pauses. "I know you're going to find this as a *surprise*, but I was sitting in a chair. And at this stage of my life I'm not the most *nimble* guy in the world. So the idea of getting up and throwing my body between Patrick and Governor Romney—you want to talk about bad execution? *This* would be bad execution."

Of course all turns out well. Patrick pulls his rollerblades to a screeching stop two feet from Romney. "How ya doin'?" Patrick asks, smiling, as soon as he stops.

"You rollerblade a lot?" Romney asks.

"Well," Patrick says, "when I'm not ice skating."

"You're ice skating?"

"Yeah, I'm a hockey player."

"Really, what position do you play?"

They took the conversation from there, Romney talking to this twelve-year-old boy about his hockey season, about how many goals he scored, about whether he was in a checking league or a nonchecking league. "Patrick feels like the center of the world," Christie remembers, as the room quiets. "And it was wonderful to watch."

PS: Before long, "Bridget, from the swing set, sees Patrick getting attention from Romney. So you know what happens next . . . through a series of somersaults and cartwheels, Bridget lands"—he spreads his arms wide— "like this! In front of Mitt Romney!"

Bridget looks at Romney. "I do gymnastics!" And all of a sudden Romney is in a whole other conversation.

Now we get to the takeaway of the story. "I watched the real Mitt Romney," Christie says, bringing it all back around. "You can't fake it with children . . . you could tell this guy has been an involved father and an involved grandfather . . . in the end, what matters most is what kind of person is sitting behind that desk."

Christie's gut had spoken. So when Romney told him that day that he wanted his endorsement, Christie already had an answer ready.

"What do I need to get you to be part of our team?" Romney asked. Maybe national campaign chairman?

"Nothing," Christie responded. "I'm in."

"It's Christmas in October!" Romney said.

Christie agreed. He later called his endorsement "an enormous gift."

ABOUT A YEAR earlier, Romney had come to the governor's mansion, Drumthwacket, to dine with Christie and his team, a dozen or more guys like longtime political adviser Bill Palatucci, brother Todd Christie, a few county GOP chairmen, and some top Republican legislators. Romney gave them the sell: He had been down this road before, having run in 2008, and wouldn't make the same mistakes twice. He could raise more money than anyone else. And he wanted Christie as the first big name on his team.

Romney was trying to make an ally before he made an enemy. After dinner Romney retired to the library with Christie and Palatucci for a private chat. The library at Drumthwacket is grand, as you'd imagine, with floor-to-ceiling bookcases and Gothic-style carved stone fireplace. "I'd like to start collecting money and endorsements in New Jersey," an emboldened Romney told Christie.

Palatucci had learned in the 1980s from his old boss, former New Jersey governor Tom Kean, that biding one's time before delivering an endorsement—and simultaneously telling every major GOP donor in New Jersey to do the same—gives an endorsement more impact once it finally happens. Palatucci's advice to Christie was to say this to Romney: "When I deliver my state, I will deliver my state lock, stock, and barrel."

So Christie told Romney to stay away—for now. "Because when I make up my mind, I can deliver. I'll deliver as much of my organization as I can, to whoever I want to."

"You know I'd really like to get started," Romney protested, gently.

"This is my state," Christie countered, "and this is the way I'm going to approach it."

If Romney tried to go over his head and start wooing party leaders and donors in New Jersey, then he might as well say good-bye to Christie's endorsement. The governor of New Jersey was demanding loyalty, and time. It was a "rather tense conversation," Christie later told author Dan Balz. "I heard later from others that he left not very happy with the approach I took."

Authors Mark Halperin and John Heilemann write in their book about the campaign that Romney thought Christie was acting out a scene from *The Sopranos*, and Romney's chief strategist Stuart Stevens asserted that Christie sounded like "the biggest asshole in the world."

But Romney's patience paid off. When Christie finally decided to back Romney after their lunch in Mendham, he held a fund-raiser for the candidate at a Hilton in North Jersey in which 350 major contributors lined up with open checkbooks to get pictures with the presidential candidate and the New Jersey governor. "Everybody thinks they're going to get a picture with the next president and vice president of the United States!" Palatucci remembered. "Easiest fund-raising I've done since Bush ran for president."

After the photo session with the high rollers, Team Christie and Team Romney walked into the ballroom to find the entirety of the Republican Party of New Jersey—every county chairman and all Republican legislators but for one. They raised $1.5 million that night.

"Wow," Romney said, according to Palatucci. "Now I know what you guys were talking about. I'm glad I waited."

CHRISTIE'S BACKING DIDN'T just mean money for Romney. Christie was also there to rally the base.

Christie formally endorsed Romney in New Hampshire, hours before a big debate for the New Hampshire Republican primary. In his endorsement speech Christie assumed the role he would have throughout the campaign— attack dog against both the president and Romney's Republican opponents.

Christie would later claim, repeatedly, that he was the first governor to endorse Romney. That's not true; the governors of Idaho and Nebraska had endorsed him months earlier. But Christie was right in saying that he busted his hump more than almost anyone else. "I traveled literally tens of thousands of miles for him, raised tens of millions of dollars for him, and worked harder, I think, than any other surrogate in America other than Paul Ryan," the eventual vice presidential nominee.

In January 2012, days before the first-in-the-nation presidential primary in New Hampshire, Christie made the trip north and rallied the crowd in a jam-packed high school gymnasium there. The first half of the rally went as planned: Romney quoted from "America the Beautiful"; Christie used a metaphoric American pie to talk about the economy.

But then two women, in the front of the crowd, began yelling: "Christie kills jobs!"

Christie had the mic. His other hand was in his pocket, casually. "Reeeaaally?" he asked, smirking.

Like a hungry Roman Coliseum crowd, these New Hampshire Republicans grew wide-eyed—anticipation hung in the air. They had heard stories about this gladiator—oh! had they heard the stories!—but they had never seen him in person. And now, there he was, poised above in his chariot, spear in hand, about to reach down for the kill.

As the women chanted about the number of jobs in New Jersey "going down," the cops began descending to escort them away. And then Christie said this:

"Something may go down tonight, but it ain't going to be jobs, sweetheart."

The crowd loved that, regardless of the fact that the unemployment rate in New Jersey was (and would remain) higher than the national average. The verbal smackdown had enlivened Christie as he called out one of the women, long after she had been pulled from the arena: "If she wasn't so blinded by her Barack Obama–induced *anger*, she would know that American jobs are coming back when Mitt Romney is the president of the United States! . . . If she wasn't so disoriented by the loss of *'hope and change,'* she'd understand that Mr. Romney is the hope for America's future!"

When a Republican goes to his first Christie event, he hopes Christie does what he does on YouTube—and gets into a fight. I've talked to scores of Republicans around the country, and invariably they know the governor's style more than his substance; they can recite YouTube encounters but not policy positions.

After this YouTube moment, Jean White, a New Hampshire voter, told me she wished it was Christie who was running for president instead. "He's got a lot of spunk, he's awesome," she said.

Back home, though, women were not nearly as thrilled. Some alleged he was being misogynistic for using the term "sweetheart," while still more were upset he had made an oral sex joke.

Wait, what?

Technically, the women had said "going down" first. And the crowd didn't seem to have noticed anything untoward about Christie saying "going down" while talking to a woman. The reporters I was sitting with in the crowd didn't mention anything—and we didn't exchange eyebrow-raised glances, as we often do when ridiculousness emanates from a podium.

Yet a blogger at *Slate* wrote a piece headlined: "N.J. Gov Chris Christie Responds to Female Hecklers With Offensive Oral Sex Joke." And the editorial board of the *Star-Ledger* referenced that time when he called an assemblywoman a "jerk" and the other time he suggested the media "take the bat out" on a female senator. The paper wrote: "For a guy who's had problems with women in the past, Chris Christie sure doesn't choose his words too carefully."

AS CHRISTIE WENT national, he stayed Jersey.

We found that out one beautiful Jersey Shore night when Christie and his family were cursed by a heckler on the boardwalk in Seaside Heights—the very same boardwalk where the cast of MTV's *Jersey Shore* had gallivanted for so many years. Christie had repeatedly blasted the show for unfairly depicting New Jerseyans, and yet what did the gov do when he got yelled at? Exactly the same thing that the characters on the show would've done—he went after the guy. The gov had an ice cream cone in one hand and the beginning of a fist in the other. His security detail shut things down before they escalated, but the video of the moment found its way online and was said to have given Romney pause in deciding whether to choose Christie as his running mate.

Months after the Seaside Heights incident, I talked to Christie about this, about his attitude. "I think I can become better at the way I express myself to the public," the governor told me. "I'm a completely unscripted person most of the time, and sometimes that leads you to say things that in retrospect you wish you had said differently. . . . Those are all things that I have to keep in mind."

From now on, it seemed, we were going to get a kinder and gentler Christie—the man who had once picked fights would now govern by repairing relations. He was more mature, he said. "When you get a significant amount of responsibility and you take it seriously, it matures you, if you're a good person," Christie told me. "And I think I am."

And yet—and yet!—forty-eight hours after he told me this, the same day in which these comments ran in the *Philadelphia Inquirer*, Christie went to New Hampshire and derisively called a female heckler "sweetheart." This was a beautiful moment of journalistic serendipity that indicated Christie hadn't changed a damn bit.

A few short weeks later, Christie called a Democratic assemblyman "numbnuts."

THE CHRISTIE PERSONALITY seemed to embody what the rest of the country thought they knew about Christie. Even though he publicly refuted the state stereotype as personified by televised reality on *Real Housewives of New Jersey* and *Jersey Shore*, he embraced it when traveling around the country. The governor didn't run from Jersey—he *became* Jersey, playing the stereotypes for national laughs, owning it as his brand—even as he disavowed that such a brand exists.

"You think it's funny?" Christie once asked host Jimmy Fallon on late-night TV after Fallon made a New Jersey joke.

The rest of the bit, though, was Christie *himself* making fun of New Jersey. "You know what we do to people like that in New Jersey, Jimmy?" Christie asked, before intimidatingly staring at Fallon.

By the time he began campaigning for Romney, Christie had made the Jersey mob guy shtick a regular feature of his speeches to Republican audiences. On a frigid West Des Moines day in December 2011, Christie warmed up the crowd at a Romney rally with this: "And so listen, I wanna tell ya something. I wanna tell you something really clearly. I'm in a good mood this morning. I'm feeling happy and upbeat. I love being with Mitt and Ann, but let me tell ya: *You people* disappoint me on Tuesday," he said to laughter, "you don't do what you're supposed to do on Tuesday for Mitt Romney, I will be back—*Jersey-style*, people. I will be back!"

Beefy and brawny Christie became Romney's Jersey muscle.

At the Republican convention, I went to an out-of-the-way but packed hotel ballroom somewhere around Tampa, Florida, and watched Christie do the same thing at a breakfast meeting of North Carolina Republicans. His message was that the activists before him had better work to get Republicans elected November 6. "I don't want to get nasty early in the morning," he said to a crowd that was audibly hungry for nasty. "You let me down— I know enough about North Carolina, I know where to find you. And you do *not* want an angry Chris Christie coming back to North Carolina on November 7."

He went on, saying he had a guy who would "name names of who *didn't deliver*. And then we're going to make some rounds. And we're going to give you some *Jersey-style treatment*. You don't want that now."

The speech was so well received that the rest of the event that morning was delayed because no one was listening to the county chairman who was trying to introduce the next speaker. I later asked Christie straight-up if he was invoking *The Sopranos*. He said no. But as I wrote in the *Inquirer* at the time, "Jersey-style treatment" sounded a whole lot like what Christopher did to the Russian in the Pine Barrens in Season 3.

ROMNEY NEEDED SOME Jersey-style. He watched as Christie called Obama the "weakest president I've seen in my lifetime" who was "searching around in a dark room, trying to find the light switch of leadership." He saw how effective those shots were.

That's when Palatucci, the governor's political handler, got a phone call from Beth Myers, the woman leading the search for Romney's running mate.

Just as speculation about Christie running for president had dominated political talk in New Jersey in 2011, now VP speculation was all the rage. When Christie visited West Windsor–Plainsboro North High School's AP history class in Central Jersey, I heard a student asking him if he would consider being Romney's running mate. Nothing unusual there. Christie's normal answer was that he wasn't a good fit to be *anybody's* second in command.

Today, though, he was more blunt (he was often more blunt with kids). Romney "might be able to convince me—he's a convincing guy," Christie said.

I tweeted the quote when I got back to my car, and it sent political reporters scurrying. In short order, this sound bite was national news.

Behind the scenes Romney had been given a list of twenty-four possible running mates, which he cut down to eleven. Research was done on each, and the presumptive nominee then narrowed his list to five, including Christie. Romney adviser Stuart Stevens, who had only months earlier called Christie an "asshole," was now fully on board with Vice President Christopher J. Christie. "We're in a street fight, and he's a street fighter," Stevens said to Romney. "He's the *best* street fighter—and he's comfortable saying things that you're not comfortable saying."

Christie didn't expect to get an offer. They weren't a natural fit. I was told that Christie once made fun of Romney for using "Jiminy Cricket" as an exclamation in a sentence. "Jiminy fucking Cricket, who talks that way?!" Christie wondered.

Christie also didn't act as though he wanted the job that badly. As part of the vetting process, he was asked to hand over information such as tax returns, a medical report, and answers to seventy questions on things like extramarital affairs, mental health issues, and drug use. The governor was resistant to baring his soul outside of his inner circle, and he didn't give Romney's people everything they wanted.

According to the tell-all campaign book *Double Down*, Christie—code-named "Pufferfish" by Romney aides during this secret process—failed to provide the legal settlement from a defamation suit when he was a county freeholder and documentation of the legal status of his household help. Christie said he provided whatever information he had.

Romney's concerns about Christie were wide-ranging: his brother's business dealings, his tardiness to events, his demands for "lavish" food spreads on political trips, his weight (which Romney allegedly made fun of), and the possible steering of U.S. Attorney contracts to friends. Plus, some of his YouTube videos, such as the recent boardwalk incident with the ice cream cone, called into question his "presidential temperament." Together, these controversies worried Romney's team, with one believing that if Christie had decided to run for president, they would have hobbled him so severely with this material that he would have been unable even to win reelection in New Jersey.

In fact, something else altogether may have killed the prospect of Romney/Christie 2012. In the middle of this vetting process, just a few weeks before the Republican convention, Palatucci got a call from Myers, Romney's top vetter. She sounded agitated.

"What's with this SEC rule?" she asked.

Palatucci said he was of course aware of the obscure Securities and Exchange Commission rule that forbade sitting governors from raising money from executives of financial institutions that did business with their states. This rule would clearly apply to Christie, and it meant a lot of reliable and wealthy Republican donors—and personal backers of both candidates—wouldn't be able to write checks to the campaign. More significantly, it might have forced Romney to *return* some of the money he had already collected from Wall Street. No way a losing, underfunded presidential campaign was going to give back huge chunks of change three months before the election.

Neither Christie nor Palatucci had any idea about how to avoid the regulation.

"You guys must've had a work-around in case you were running," Myers said.

"We didn't," Palatucci said.

"Are you telling me I have to tell Mitt Romney that he can't have the guy he wants as vice president because of this SEC rule?" Myers asked Palatucci.

WHAT! Palatucci was floored that Christie was the top choice. He had been jokingly referring to the governor as "Mr. Vice President," just to get used to saying it without cracking up. He immediately called Christie and relayed the conversation with Myers.

"WHAT!" Christie repeated.

Just one way existed to *possibly* get around the SEC rule. Romney called Christie. They discussed setting up separate fund-raising vehicles so each candidate could collect his own money.

Another option was available, too. "Are there any circumstances in which you'd consider resigning to become the nominee?" Romney asked.

Christie laughed. The answer was no.

A couple of weeks later, Christie was flying back from the West Coast, where he was raising money for Romney. The message came through aides: Call Romney when you land.

"I have some news that I think you'll find both disappointing and a relief at the same time," Romney told Christie. "I've decided to go another direction with the vice presidency."

MORE THAN TWO years later Christie and I sat in a back corner of a fancy and overpriced Italian restaurant in Midtown Manhattan. If Romney had offered him the job, I asked, would he have taken it?

Christie answered immediately. "It would have been a very hard decision," he said. "It's very hard for me to believe that you say no if you're asked. But I wasn't asked, so I didn't have to say no."

"Would a Romney/Christie ticket have won?" I asked.

He paused. "Probably not.

"Because I don't think you vote for the vice president, you vote for the president. And I think it probably would've been the same result, yeah, because I don't think *I* would have made the difference. The guy at the top of the ticket is the guy who makes the difference. You're like in Hippocratic oath land as the vice presidential candidate: First, do no harm."

Christie, the bull in the presidential shop, was deemed to hold too much potential for harm to be the running mate.

CHRISTIE GOT A consolation prize: He would be the keynote speaker at the Republican convention that August, getting the same kind of prime-time national audience that Illinois state senator Barack Obama had received back in 2004, launching his national political career.

Christie was psyched. His team launched a special Twitter handle and a Tumblr page, which was essentially a blog of photos of the big week—like a travel journal that could have been entitled, "Chris Christie Goes to a Republican Convention and Gets a Lot of Attention." There he is hugging former secretary of state Condoleezza Rice, laughing with Ohio governor John Kasich, and helping his son, Patrick, get his tie on.

Christie had written more than two dozen drafts of the speech, and rehearsed extensively—including an all-day session at Drumthwacket with his brother and a circle of insiders.

Then Romney's people tried to cut his video.

Christie's media team had created a three-minute homage to the governor that was to air before the speech. Quotes from his former high school baseball coach were coupled with images of the red "Trenton Makes The World Takes" sign on the bridge that goes over the Delaware River to the New Jersey Statehouse. There were snapshots from his office, including a picture of Ronald Reagan, a Fender guitar signed by Bruce Springsteen, and the "it CAN be done" sign on his desk. Out of context but blunt sound bites lay over the images—*"How the hell did this happen?"* and *"I got sent here to do a job, I didn't get sent here to be elected prom king."* It ended with the advice he recounts from his mother: *"Just be yourself, because then tomorrow you're not going to have to worry about remembering who you pretended to be yesterday."*

There wasn't enough time, Romney's people said, to fit in the video. Much of the programming for the convention had been condensed after a hurricane canceled the first day of festivities, and Christie couldn't play a three-minute movie *and* speak for twenty minutes before the networks ended the convention coverage at 11:00 p.m. EST.

Christie guaranteed that he could finish in time.

And if his video was cut, he'd say "fuck" on stage. Live.

The Romney crew did not call his bluff. The video went on as scheduled.

CHRISTIE THEN FIST-PUMPED his way onto the stage. His suit jacket flapped as he bounded toward the mic. His eyes were tight and his lips offered a faint, confident smirk. He looked as if he had been waiting to make this speech his whole life. The crowd was "showing me great respect and great enthusiasm and I was showing them the same thing back—that's called being polite, Jersey-style," he later said.

Enthusiasm indeed swept through the arena. Later, some reporters described the reaction to Christie as lukewarm, and claimed that Romney was shooting Christie death stares during the speech because he hated it so much. I didn't get that sense, but I knew as soon as I read an embargoed copy of the speech about an hour before go-time that there'd be problems. The speech simply had too much Chris Christie, and not enough Mitt Romney.

The self-love of the opening video probably set that impression. But mostly it was because Christie said the word "Romney" just *seven* times. In twenty-five hundred words. He said "I" thirty-seven times.

"We need politicians to care more about doing something and less about being something," Christie said in the speech. "And believe me, believe me, if we can do this in a blue state like New Jersey with a conservative Republican governor—Washington, D.C., is out of excuses. Leadership delivers, leadership counts, leadership matters." That leadership was exemplified by none other than Christie himself, he said: Taking on teachers' unions, reforming the pension system, lowering taxes. He even referenced a Bruce Springsteen song, and he told a story about his mother.

Eventually he moved on to Romney by saying that, like him, Romney knows how to tell "hard truths." He asked the crowd to stand for Romney. And twenty thousand faithful did just that. But he didn't get them revved up to storm the White House and take their country back. In fact, Christie never said the words "Barack Obama." He criticized the president, yes, but not as aggressively as one would expect from the blunt-talking Jersey guy.

Most surprising, the funny YouTube celebrity got just one real laugh line.

**THE PUNDITS' REVIEWS** were vicious. "It was one of the most off-key keynote speeches I ever heard," said Chris Wallace on FOX News. "A prime-time belly flop" is how *Politico* described it. Romney advisers were anonymously quoted with negative reviews.

"You guys had this speech for a week before it was given," Christie told one of Romney's advisers. "You did not ask me to make one change in the speech. Now you fucking guys are cutting my nuts off . . . I'm tired of it. I've worked hard for Governor Romney. I like him. And I see that you guys, for whatever reason, are playing this game."

He later got into an argument with a Romney aide in downtown Tampa: "You're a fucking liar! . . . I'm tired of you people!"

The speech would not prove fatal. In 1988, the governor of Arkansas made a speech at the Democratic convention that was so long and so boring that the words "in conclusion" garnered a sarcastic cheer from the crowd. And yet four years later, Bill Clinton was elected president.

# 9

# JERSEY STRONG

When thirty inches of snow dropped on New Jersey over Christmas 2010, state workers failed to clear major roads, particularly along the Jersey Shore. Hundreds of accidents ensued.

Christie was in short sleeves in Florida while this havoc was going down, vacationing at Disney World with his wife and kids. He said he had promised them a resort vacation on this, their first Christmas as New Jersey's First Family, and he wasn't about to try to book a flight back home. This was before he did most of his travel by private jet—and before he appreciated the significance of a chief executive's presence, or absence, as the case may be, during natural weather calamities.

The result was unflattering international news coverage about an absentee governor. Compounding the minicontroversy was the fact that Lieutenant Governor Kim Guadagno—the first lieutenant governor in the state history, a position created exactly for circumstances like this—was on a cruise in Mexico.

When he got back to New Jersey, Christie vehemently refused to acknowledge any mistake whatsoever. "I wouldn't change the decision even if I could do it right now," he said at a press conference. "I had a great five days with my children. I promised [them] that." He made fun of politicians who "hop on a plow" during snowstorms and pretend to be leaders. He said that the story got so much coverage because reporters needed "filler" during the slow holiday week.

When he left the press conference, he saw news photographers waiting for him in the snow. "You guys are out here just waiting for me to slip and fall, aren't you?"

. . .

CHRISTIE WOULD NOT put himself at risk of falling again.

When Hurricane Irene hit the East Coast the following August, the governor was not only in New Jersey, he was the face of the storm. Hours before landfall he delivered one of his most well-known sound bites, ever. He said he had just been watching TV and saw people still on the beach, tough guys braving the winds as the storm approached. It was standard prestorm TV fare, and Christie was sick of it.

"Get the hell off the beach in Asbury Park and get out. You're done. It's four-thirty. You've maximized your tan."

Here he was, like a guy at home on his couch screaming common sense into the TV: *"Get the hell off the beach!"* Keeping it real. Straight talk. Whatever you call, it was testosteroned and irreverent.

At one of his several press conferences during the storm he asked if there were more questions. Seeing none, he began to leave the lectern. That's when I remembered my question and finally blurted something out.

"Slow on the uptake today, Matt?"

"A little slow."

"Need some water? You comfortable?"

"I could use some water, yeah . . ."

That's when the governor of New Jersey *threw his water bottle at me.* The cabinet members sitting in front of me had to duck. I caught it with one hand.

"One hand," I said.

"Okay. What d'ya got?"

HURRICANE IRENE CUT power to 1.5 million people and closed scores of schools. Shelters were opened for the displaced and property damage totaled $1 billion, the most expensive natural disaster in state history.

A week after the storm made landfall President Obama visited New Jersey, taking Christie on his *Marine One* helicopter to visit damaged areas for four hours. The two politicians shared several laughs and talked about personal topics—like "the issues that fathers of teenage girls talk about."

Christie's unexpected chumminess with the president and tough-guy approach to storm leadership resulted in the highest approval ratings of his term to date—54 percent.

This was just a practice run, though, because Mother Nature was about to turn it up.

The Category 1 hurricane known as Sandy—it would be christened Superstorm Sandy—barreled in from the Atlantic Ocean in late October 2012. Christie was the most prominent national surrogate for the Republican presidential nominee Mitt Romney at the time, but Sandy would force Christie off the campaign trail and back home, where he took up position as New Jersey's protector—taking a proverbial stand on the Jersey Shore, arms crossed, eyes sharpened, staring down God's wrath. Flanked by the heavily uniformed adjutant general of the New Jersey National Guard at several press conferences before Sandy's arrival, Christie gave off a distinctly commander-in-chief vibe as he calmed New Jersey with confidence, emotion, and humor. His communications team live-tweeted his press conferences, word-for-word dispatches in rapid-fire bursts, and they emailed reporters YouTube clips of the best sound bites along with behind-the-scenes pictures from cabinet meetings in Christie's situation room. That projected the Christie image nationwide, dwarfing the profiles of New York City mayor Michael Bloomberg and New York governor Andrew Cuomo, who were managing their own storm responses.

On Saturday, October 27, Christie declared a state of emergency. Superstorm Sandy was forty-eight hours away. He made this announcement surrounded by emergency responders in North Middletown, and he wore a blue fleece emblazoned with his name as if you wouldn't know it: CHRIS CHRISTIE: GOVERNOR. It had been given to him by Steve Adubato, Sr., the North Jersey Democratic boss, on the day after he won reelection, and it was about to become the most famous garment in politics since Monica Lewinsky's blue dress.

"I know—I've lived here all my life, too—that everybody's saying, 'Crap, this isn't going to happen, the weathermen always get it wrong, and we'll just let it hang out and not pay attention to this,'" the governor said. "Please don't. We have to be prepared for the worst here . . . and as I'm sure you'll probably anticipate, I'll bring my subtle and understated style to the task."

At a second press conference that afternoon: "If you've got a transistor radio, put batteries in it. Because I know you don't want to go more than a day without hearing me. I know that."

The following day, Christie went before the media with a more urgent plea: "Don't be stupid. Get out . . . you have time to prepare yourselves.

If you're already prepared, go home and watch the Jets. Relax. Watch the Giants at four if that's your taste."

Christie then retreated deep inland up a hill in Ewing, near Trenton, to the New Jersey State Police Regional Operations Intelligence Center, a $24 million state police facility billed as "space-age" when it opened in 2007. They called it "the Rock." The walls are two feet thick, designed to withstand hurricanes and earthquakes.

Christie held one last press conference before everyone hunkered down for the storm. He asked to speak directly to the children of New Jersey: "Remain calm. The adults are taking care of business. Don't be scared."

SUPERSTORM SANDY MADE landfall in Atlantic City about 8:00 p.m. on October 29, bringing wind, rain, and a storm surge from the Atlantic Ocean up and down the Jersey Shore and around to its northern river and bay towns. Thirty-nine people died, including parents of two teenage children who were killed when a tree fell on their car in Christie's hometown of Mendham. Sandy damaged 325,000 housing units—a little more than 9 percent of the state's housing supply—causing $37.1 billion in damage. About 2.7 million residents and 91 percent of health care facilities lost power. Two dozen empty rail cars were carried by tidal surge onto an elevated part of the New Jersey Turnpike. In just the first few hours after landfall, fifty-five hundred people had checked into shelters.

Sandy battered Jersey all night long, terrifying the state with the noises of Mother Nature going to war with humanity. "The single defining moment of the governorship," as Christie would call it, came with the biggest storm in state history.

The morning after, Christie's team convened at the Rock in a room with TV monitors up and down the walls to look at the first aerial footage of houses sitting in the middle of highways and bobbing in water. The ocean had just run straight over the barrier islands into the bays, upending everything in its path.

"We're all sitting together and going, 'Oh, my God,' " Christie said.

Like a doctor in the waiting room telling relatives about the dire medical condition of a loved one, Christie described the condition of the state of New Jersey *to* the state of New Jersey, face to face. As the first witness to the full scope of the storm, he reported back with empathy, calm, and resolve.

He did five network interviews in the morning and then convened a press conference. Exhausted, his face puffy and his voice weighed down by the nasal hoarseness of a bad cold he'd been fighting, Christie began his press conference with this: "I know that many people in our state woke up today to absolute devastation.

"There are no words to describe what so many New Jerseyans experienced over the last twenty-four hours and what they will have to contend with over the coming days, weeks, and months. I'll first say to all of you, especially those out there who are facing loss, devastation, and the heartbreaking reality that your home may be gone: We are with you."

He went through the litany of damage: power outages, highway closures, railway damage. . . . He gave out some emergency information. Then he took questions.

Someone asked it. About the election for the president of the United States, exactly one week away. Christie had been full-time on the campaign trail for Romney. What would he do now? And how would Sandy affect the election?

"I will tell you this administration, at the moment, could give a damn less about Election Day. If you hear the things that I just talked about and the devastation that's been visited upon this state, I am sure that while the national election is obviously very important, that the people of New Jersey at this moment would really be unhappy with me if they thought for a *second* I would occupy *my time* thinking about how I was going to get people to vote a week from today."

And just in case you didn't get the message . . .

"So I don't give a damn about Election Day. It doesn't matter a lick to me."

Was this the true soul of the politician? Were we getting to the core of the man?

The people always thought so, one way or another.

CHRISTIE WAS UNEASY about whether he wanted to go on the ground to see the damage for himself. "Because do they want to see me? Do they *not* want to see me? Am I helping or am I not helping?"

Christie decided to reach out for some advice, to a colleague. He called Jeb Bush. The brother of the forty-third president, son of the forty-first, and future Christie rival to be forty-fifth was also the former two-term Florida governor who had led the state through plenty of storms.

"Should I go out there or shouldn't I?" Christie asked him.

"Go. You can't understand this right now, but they want to see you. People will feel comforted and calmed."

Christie told me: "It was great advice."

Against objections from the state police, who thought the trip was too soon, Christie called for his police helicopter and there he went, up the coast, landing in Belmar. Debris was strewn on every street. Guys in wetsuits were going in boats, saving people from their homes. Christie consoled the Democratic mayor, who was in tears.

The first Sandy victim he saw, a gray-haired woman, walked up to him. "It was the first moment I understood what Jeb was telling me," he said. "And she was sobbing. And she grabbed me and hugged me and said, 'Thank God you're here.' I just grabbed her and hugged her back and didn't know what to say.

"She was like, 'Governor, please, save us. Save us!' You're sitting there saying to yourself this has now gone to a totally different level of attachment, and need, for the people you're working for.

"And it would happen over and over and over and over."

Christie cried with lots of New Jerseyans that first day. Later, in Sayreville, a woman dragged him into her house to show him the easy chair, now ruined, that was the only memory she had of her deceased husband. "If I just sit here right now I can hear her voice: 'Everything's gone, I have nothing left of him now. I'm all alone.' People say that stuff to you, and if you have a beating heart, you're going to react."

After his first visit to see the devastation, Christie spoke to the press. It was the most emotional I had ever seen him. He was wearing that zip-up blue fleece, which made him look even larger than he already was—roomy in the sleeves and bunched at the shoulders. Couple that with the extra-large lectern that they used at the Rock, and Christie was enormously in charge.

"Let me start with: I just never thought I would see what I saw today. Ever," Christie said. "The boardwalk in Belmar—it's gone. It's not there. The boardwalk we walked on together this summer greeting residents, talking to those business owners, it's gone. And it's gone two or three blocks up off the beach down those side streets."

He sounded like a TV war reporter giving a scene-by-scene description of a bomb's aftermath. He began talking about the people he met out there, such as volunteers in wetsuits on jet skis who rescued a "petrified" eighty-five-year-old woman from her home. "I had three different older women come up to me and say 'I just wanted to be here to give you a hug and say thank you.' I said, 'I don't know what you're thanking me for, but I'll be happy to give you a hug.' "

Perhaps more than to any town on the Jersey Shore, Christie's connection to Seaside Heights ran the deepest. In the 1960s and seventies, the Christies vacationed there with cousins in a bungalow. They hung out on the beach, played mini-golf at Barnacle Bill's, and spun wheels at the boardwalk arcades to win prizes. Later, he partied there as a teenager and eventually took his own kids to cruise the boardwalk.

Now, he was flying overhead, and "the Jersey Shore of my youth, where we used to go all the time, to the boardwalk at Seaside Heights . . . it is gone."

Listening to him, it was as if he was transported back to it, as if he could hear the happy yells of little kids and the muffled yells of the carnival barkers; as if he could smell the Jersey Shore in summer—the mix of cotton candy and Coca-Cola, sunscreen and cigarette smoke. The promise of an endless summer was ending.

"The pier with the rides where I took my kids this August before the Republican convention—where I got in that famous yelling match with the guy with my ice cream cone—those rides are in the Atlantic Ocean. The log flume's in the Atlantic Ocean, the log flume that my two younger kids rode this summer, is in the Atlantic Ocean," he said.

He looked down, and went deep into his own head. "The stand in the middle of the boardwalk that sells sausage and peppers and lemonade is gone. Unlike the others where they're pushed farther back from the boardwalk, this one sat right in the middle of the boardwalk. It was unusual on that boardwalk. I remember it very well, and I looked for it today," he said. "And the entire structure is gone."

He went town by town, the way only a native could, explaining that Avalon got hit harder than Sea Isle City, that Brant Beach got it worse than anywhere else on Long Beach Island. Even the beach in front of his gubernatorial house at Island Beach State Park—gone.

"It was an overwhelming afternoon for me, emotionally, as a kid who was born and raised in this state, and who spent a lot of time over my life, both my childhood and adult life, at the Jersey Shore," he said.

"We'll rebuild it. No question in my mind we'll rebuild it. *But* for those of us who are my age, it will not be the same. It will be different. Because many of those iconic things that made it what it was are now gone and washed into the ocean."

Christie then looked down at the paper in front of him and went through the grim task of announcing the deaths related to the storm. This news was not being delivered to the public from a TV reporter reading a bureaucratic statement from the medical examiner's office. It was coming directly from the leader of their state.

Despite the dire circumstances, his personality couldn't be contained. When detailing the power failures at intersections, he said he was fascinated to learn that the state had 15,500 traffic signals. Then he stopped, looked up, and quizzed *Wall Street Journal* reporter Heather Haddon about what he had just said about the traffic signals.

"Fifteen thousand five hundred," she said.

"I knew I could count on the *Wall Street Journal* to get the numbers right," he said.

Christie refocused quickly, ending his press conference looking at the cameras. No notes.

"To the people of New Jersey: Hang in there. Tomorrow recovery begins. Today was a bit of a day of sorrow for a lot of people. And we need to feel that. It's appropriate to feel that. We need to feel it and take it in. There's nothing wrong with that. But as long as sorrow does not displace resilience, then we'll be just fine."

BEHIND THE SCENES at the Rock, Christie was the field general. "You can't conceive of it until it happens to you," he later said. "So every day I got the best information I could, and then just reacted and made decisions and moved."

That meant screaming and yelling at executives of at least one power company after days of delays in restoring power.

"We can't do this," the executives would say. "We can't do that."

"I don't want to hear that," Christie shot back. "You see the people I see every day?"

He told them to meet him in person. "Get your asses down here now," he said. And they came.

He called the governors of Alabama, Mississippi, and Florida for help. Rescue crews and utility workers by the truckload came from all over North America.

But one visit loomed larger than any other.

Dan Robles, Christie's "body guy"—the one who shadowed him everywhere, managing his schedule and holding the gubernatorial Sharpie for autographs with fans—got a call from Reggie Love, President Obama's body guy.

Robles handed Christie his phone. "Shhh," Dan told the rest of the staff in the conference room at the Rock. "He's on the phone with the president."

Christie didn't keep a journal during those days of Sandy—he wishes he had—but he vividly remembered his conversation with the president.

"Chris, it's Barack. How are you?"

"It's tough up here, Mr. President."

"How are Mary Pat and the kids?"

"We're all fine. They're at the governor's mansion. They're okay."

"Listen, I want to come tomorrow."

"Great."

"But is that going to put you in a tough position?"

After all, we were exactly a week away from Election Day. Christie would be welcoming someone to his state whom he had openly and aggressively campaigned against for almost a year. The president—and the governor—were well aware of the political implications of a trip like this.

"Tough position? You're the president of the United States, you tell me where and when, and I will be there."

"Great. I'll have our staffs work it out."

"I'll see you tomorrow."

"Now if you need anything, call any cabinet member. I've told all of them they have fifteen minutes to call you back. And if they break the fifteen-minute rule, you call me."

"I will, Mr. President. Thank you. See you tomorrow."


WHEN *AIR FORCE* One touched down at Atlantic City International Airport, the governor was in the same white Nikes, pin-stripe suit pants, and fleece embroidered with his name that he had worn all week. The president was in a blue windbreaker. They smiled, walked toward each other, shook hands—and then Barack Obama put his hand on Christie's shoulder and gave him a hug.

Except: It wasn't a hug at all. It was *maybe* a bro-hug, with double-handed physical contact, but the gubernatorial chest never touched the presidential chest. Conservatives, though, saw a hug—and they were furious. How could he hug the enemy? A huge Mitt Romney for President rally was planned in Pennsylvania, a key swing state, for Sunday. Christie was supposed to be there. He was supposed to be on TV every night, supposed to be trotting out his line about how Obama was searching for the "light switch of leadership." The presidential election was Tuesday!

And now, this? A hug?

Romney later said the alleged hug was irrelevant to the outcome of the election. Pollsters also found no evidence that it moved the needle in swing states.

"It was a handshake like you would shake hands with anyone," Christie recalled. "It was a perfectly natural, casual, normal type of greeting between two people. And, ya know, it's become legend."

Conservative bloggers were apoplectic. They theorized that Christie was just trying to get Romney to lose so he could run for president in an open field in 2016, or that Christie was acting out because he wasn't Romney's running mate.

Maybe, of course, Christie was just doing his job.

Nonetheless, by welcoming Obama to a disaster area Christie was certainly giving him the chance to be *presidential*—the very thing that Romney was trying to argue Obama was not.

It also made Christie look *gubernatorial*, signaling to the home state Democratic electorate that Christie was a reasonable, New Jersey kind of Republican.

Obama and Christie took off together to tour a shelter in nearby Brigantine, where they embraced victims and spoke to the press at a microphone with the presidential seal on it. "I can't thank the president enough for his personal concern and compassion for our state and the people of our state," Christie said.

Obama returned the favor: "He's put his heart and soul into making sure the people of New Jersey bounce back even stronger than before."

From *Marine One*, the president and the governor surveyed the coastline—from the intact glass towers of Atlantic City's casinos to the busted-up streetscape of Long Beach Island to the ripped-up decks and docks of Seaside Heights. Christie pointed out boardwalks that had been thrown blocks away.

Then they got to talking, about their daughters—and politics.

"You know you've been very decent through all of this and I really appreciate it," Obama said.

"No problem, sir. So have you."

In Christie's retelling, an awkward silence followed, which the governor broke by saying: "You know I'm not voting for you, right?"

Obama laughed. "I pretty much assumed that," he said.

"All right, good, I didn't want to leave a misimpression."

*MARINE ONE* LANDED and Christie got into his SUV to go back to the Rock. "This was as comfortable and relaxed an interaction as I've had with the president since I've known him," Christie told one of his aides.

Sure enough, at the next press conference Christie was more effusive about the president than he had been even the day before, saying that Obama "couldn't have been better today.

"For him to be able to see this stuff personally, for him to be able to hear from me directly about what the state was going through, and for him to be able to respond to me *strongly, directly* about what the citizens of the state need, was very gratifying," Christie said.

Christie was given a special number to reach Obama at the White House. In the first twenty-four hours after the storm, they spoke three times. Obama returned one of Christie's calls after midnight, waking him up. "Which is fine," Christie said, "he gets to."

Christie kept the Obama love in an interview on FOX News, the conservative agenda-setter. Christie was impressed that it had taken just two hours from the time he personally asked Obama for an emergency declaration to the time a FEMA official called to say it was done. "He has been very attentive, and anything I've asked for he's gotten to me," he said. "So I thank the president publicly, he has done, as far as I'm concerned, a great job for New Jersey."

The hosts pivoted to presidential politics. Christie's eyes narrowed, his head tilted downward, and he looked as if he was breathing heavily, like a bull. He was asked: "Is there any possibility that Governor Romney may go to New Jersey to tour some of the damage with you?"

"I have no idea nor am I the least bit concerned or interested. I've got a job to do here in New Jersey that's much bigger than presidential politics and I could care less about any of that stuff. I have a job to do. I've got 2.4 million people out of power. I've got devastation on the Shore. I've got floods on the northern part of my state. If you think right now I give a *damn* about presidential politics, then you don't know me."

Christie's big-time GOP political donors were watching TV. They started calling Christie's top people, complaining about all this Obama love.

"We're still pulling dead bodies out of buildings," Christie told one donor. "I don't give a shit. Have a nice day."

Several donors called Christie's chief fund-raiser, Bill Palatucci. "There were some *very* significant people," Palatucci said. "I can think of some very major players . . . who said, 'Don't ever call me, I never want to be with this guy or see this guy again.' " (They would eventually return to the fold, Palatucci said.)

Democrats and independents, in New Jersey and beyond, were thrilled rather than angered. They saw someone who put citizenship over partisanship. The liberal *Blue Jersey* blog posted a public letter of thanks. And I got an email at the newspaper from a reader named Ellis, who asked: "What's the dirty secret motive here that's going to snuff out this small ember of pride I feel for America?"

**A FEW HOURS** after the Obama meeting, I asked him what it was like.

"Can you talk about the unusual nature of today for you, that you're with a president of the other party six days before the election? . . . Were you at all pinching yourself? Did you talk to him about it at all?"

"I pinch myself every day, Matt. Every day I pinch myself, every day."

"That really wasn't what I was getting at."

There was some laughter. Christie said, "The president and I are big boys," both in "the business of politics." So of course they made the kind of small talk that professional rivals make with one another. He asked Obama, for example, where he'd be campaigning next.

"We're cognizant of the political side. But here's the bottom line of what the people of New Jersey know about me. When it comes to getting things done, I don't care about what party somebody's in. . . . Believe me, I'm aware of all the atmospherics. I'm not, ya know, I'm not in a coma. But the fact is I don't care. . . .

"You see the way people react when I come down the street. They want me to help them. And don't think that I don't go home at night and lay in bed and think about those people—think about how I'm laying in a bed that's dry and comfortable and those people are flooded out. And when you know you have responsibility for those folks, you could give a damn about the politics of things. I could care less today about it.

"And so the president of the United States came to offer help for the people I'm sworn to represent. And so I accept his help and I accept his goodwill and I accept his great efforts . . .

"There will be some folks who criticize me for complimenting him. Well, ya know what? I speak the truth."

But what about *Marine One*? Did he pinch himself?

"When I got on *Marine One*, I'm pinching myself. Sandy and Bill Christie's son on *Marine One* was not exactly what I thought was going to be happening with my life, ya know?"

SHORTLY AFTER THE storm hit, Christie looked around the Rock and saw that his chief of staff, Kevin O'Dowd, was like a "one-armed paper hanger" trying to get the state back up and running. "Why don't we have more talent around the table?" Christie asked. "Where's Regina Egea? Where's Michele Brown?"

"Well, I haven't called them in," O'Dowd said.

"Well, call them in."

Egea was a senior staffer overseeing local agencies at the time—she had nothing to do with schools. Whatever, Christie thought, "she's smart." He told her to find out why every school was closed—was it damage? power? something else?—and get them reopened ASAP so the state could get on the "path to normalcy."

Next, he told Brown: "You're in charge of getting the gas stations open."

"I don't know anything about gas stations," she said.

"Well, go learn."

Brown soon got back to the governor to tell him that many gas stations either had gas but no electricity, or electricity but no gas. Long lines were starting to build.

"Okay," Christie said, "let's get to the problem we can fix."

He called John Hess, CEO of the Hess Corporation, to try to get more gas out on the streets, but power at the refineries was down. So Christie contacted PSE&G, the state's largest utility, to make sure they prioritized returning power to the refineries.

Then he called the president. At ten or eleven at night, Christie used the direct number he had been given.

"Chris, it's Barack, what's up?"

"We need gas," Christie said. "We gotta return this place to normal. And people can't fuel their generators, and they can't travel around the state . . . I have lines, we're gonna have violence, and it's going to be mayhem. And I don't need that, Mr. President, I have a million other problems. I don't need mayhem on gas lines."

"Hold on one second, I'll get Leon on the phone," Obama said. And so the president put Secretary of Defense Leon Panetta on conference call, and asked him if he could get gas to New Jersey. Panetta said he could ship to McGuire Air Force Base in Burlington County the following day.

"Great," Christie said. He then called Pennsylvania governor Tom Corbett to ask for more tanker trucks from the Pennsylvania National Guard to move the gas off the planes, onto the trucks, and out to the stations.

"Then we just started moving," Christie remembered. "That was what it was like every hour of every day in the first, like, two to three weeks after Sandy. Just one problem after the other that you had to learn to fix on the fly. It was incredibly tiring. And I wasn't sleeping more than two or three hours a night, I was just so stressed out."

Turned out the gasoline issue wasn't solved as quickly as he thought. "Some genius from FEMA stopped the trucks without telling us because they wanted us to *charge* the gas stations for the gas," Christie said. So he called Obama again, told him what happened.

Obama was quiet for a few moments. "Give me five minutes," he said.

Five minutes later, Obama called back. "The gasoline is being delivered to your stations by order of the president of the United States."

"Thank you, Mr. President."

"Anything else tonight, Chris?"

"No, that will do it tonight, sir."

"Okay. Call me if you need anything."

Several days later, Christie went into a voting booth and pulled the lever for Mitt Romney.

But the Democratic president still called the Republican governor every day for those first ten days after the storm, just to check in.

ON DAY 2 I went onto the windy helicopter tarmac on the compound of the Rock and boarded a New Jersey National Guard helicopter. I put on a headset tapped into the in-flight communication system and flew low over the Garden State. Christie was beginning regular helicopter flights to damaged areas with a rotating pool of reporters. We trailed a state police helicopter carrying the governor and his senior staff up to Sayreville, a blue-collar town southwest of Staten Island surrounded on most sides by two rivers and the Raritan Bay, which leads out to the Atlantic Ocean. Storm surge had suffocated this town; nearly two hundred people were rescued, mostly by boat.

We landed in front of a school and were whisked in a police motorcade to a blacked-out blue-collar neighborhood off Bordentown Avenue where five feet of water had risen over front porches and into homes. Christie emerged from his SUV, greeting Democrats like Assemblyman John Wisniewski, who represented the neighborhood. Wisniewski would one day lead a multimillion-dollar legislative investigation into the governor. For today, he was part of the gubernatorial entourage.

Dazed, dirty, and damp, the storm's victims soon crowded around their governor.

"Please help us," said Theresa Mills.

"That's what I'm here to do," he responded.

Kim Bosso introduced the governor to her son, who had cystic fibrosis. He had been cut off from his breathing machines since the power went out, and the utility company told her she wasn't a priority case. Her insurance wouldn't cover the cost if she went to a hospital.

"This is my lawyer," Christie said, introducing her to Charles McKenna, his chief counsel. "He's going to take care of you."

McKenna took down her information.

In telling the governor about her situation, Deborah Decker said she didn't want to be too much of a pain. "Don't worry," Christie said. "I'm as big of a pain in the ass as anybody."

A ninety-five-year-old woman, rescued by a boat, told him she recently had heart surgery. "I want you to relax," he said. "You had all that work done on your ticker, I don't want you to get wound up."

A disabled great-grandmother, Dolores Beaton, sixty-two, asked Christie to go into her home. He took her hand and led her through a huge puddle up onto her porch. The four of us went inside—Dolores, Christie, the lieutenant governor, and myself. Furniture was toppled over and the house smelled like mildew. Bills were lying on a table, wet. She said the recliner that she slept on had been ruined.

"Everything's gone," she said. "I don't have anything to lose. I can't replace anything. I have no money."

Christie told her that he was going to make sure FEMA opened an office in Middlesex County so she could get the help she needed.

Patricia Smith showed the governor an outside door to her basement, where water had filled up like a pool.

"I'm devastated over this," she said. "I've been trying to keep it together, but it's very hard."

"Of course it is," Christie responded. "That's why I came."

Cody Buck had just put $8,000 into repairs to his basement after a tropical storm the previous year. Buck showed Christie how the back of the house just fell in. "It freakin' fell in, took the whole basement in," he said. "I think, Governor, we need to level the whole neighborhood, give everybody a check, and get out of here."

Christie would do just that, using FEMA funds to offer buyouts to property owners in this flood-prone area. But mostly, his visits weren't about policy specifics or long-term assistance. They were about now. And what was needed now were hugs.

Several women came up to Christie to cry in his arms. The governor put his hands on their shoulders, pulled them in close, and spoke softly in their ears, rubbing their backs with his palm again and again, as if these were his own children waking up from nightmares.

Two women began to break down as soon as he approached. When he grabbed their shoulders, they fell apart. "I don't know where to go," the older woman of the two said. "I don't know what to do."

Samantha Hartung, thirty-one, wept to Christie about her house, which she said had been destroyed beyond repair. She said she was hiding her pain from her children.

"Because that's what we do, right?" Christie said. He added: "It's not your fault. You were ready, but you can't be ready for that."

Christie told her that one of his sons had asked him if there was anything that was more powerful than water. And he said no, there wasn't.

THE FEDERAL DEPARTMENT of Transportation sent in hundreds of buses to help with transportation, given that the railroads were incapacitated. Police departments in eight states sent 280 cops to be temporarily sworn in as New Jersey state troopers. And although Christie now had gasoline, he had to figure out how to fuel generators for hundreds of blacked-out polling places before the election.

There was also the matter of Halloween, which fell forty-eight hours after the storm passed through. Trick-or-treating would be hazardous given the downed power lines strewn across the Garden State's sidewalks—but what can you do? It's not like you can *cancel* Halloween.

Yet Chris Christie did just that, suspending Halloween until the following week.

"DO HIS POWERS HAVE NO LIMIT?!" I tweeted after we found out his intention.

"I saw your interesting tweet last night," Christie said the next day. "Does his power know no bounds? And the answer is no, it doesn't, Matt."

THE NEXT TIME I hitched a helicopter ride we flew to the Port Monmouth Fire Company No. 1 firehouse in Middletown, where twenty-two firefighters who worked as rescue workers saw their homes damaged by Sandy.

By this point, five days after landfall, the water had receded and the damage was laid bare. Ruined contents of people's homes, lugged to the street; the comforts of life, right there in the gutter. Building foundations laid bare. There was looting now, too. I read a hand-painted sign on a house: "I assure you, we've got guns."

At the firehouse, Baptist volunteers from Oklahoma were helping the local firefighters distribute clothes, food, and beverages. "You're really an inspiration," Christie told them.

One woman said she evacuated because Christie told her to. When he hugged her, he closed his eyes. "Listen, I want you to know we're thinking about you, and we're here for you," he said. "We'll rebuild the rest of it. But we can't replace you."

An elderly handicapped woman had lost her home. But she somehow made her way to the firehouse, just to meet Christie.

"You inspire me," he told her.

"Do I?" she asked.

"You inspire me. Give me a hug."

Gail Doherty introduced her daughter, Ginjer, nine, who would likely never live in her home again. She was the same age as his youngest daughter. Christie put his hands on Ginjer's shoulders and bent down to look in her eyes. "It's bad stuff, but you know what? You have a bunch of adults here who are going to take care of you, so you're going to be just fine," Christie said. "What matters is that your mom, dad, and dog are just fine. It's a sad thing. I'm sad, too."

Afterward, Gail said: "That was so nice, wow. Amazing."

Christie's aide took Ginjer's cell phone number and the governor promised to call her in a day or two to see how she was doing. He did just that. In fact Ginjer became something of an icon of Sandy for Christie. He mentioned her later that day at a news conference: "I've hugged a lot of crying adults over the last week, and I'm okay with that. I have a harder time dealing with crying children and children who look scared."

Months later, he invited Ginjer to his State of the State Address in Trenton. He introduced her to the crowd, and told about how they met.

"I hugged her and told her not to cry anymore—that the adults are in charge now," he said. "In this year ahead, let us prove the truth of the words I spoke to Ginjer that day. Let us put aside destructive politics in an election year."

That charge would prove more than complicated. But for now, New Jersey, both blue and red, was behind its governor at a time of crisis. Christie handled this awesome responsibility by wrapping himself in the New Jersey flag. "America couldn't take New Jersey toughness before this?" he asked. "After this, we're going to be hell on wheels."

"You care only about New Jersey, and we appreciate it," one Sandy victim told him.

"You would beat Obama in a landslide!" said another.

Christie returned to his SUV and headed to Bolger Middle School in nearby Keansburg, where the darkened school cafeteria was a 24/7 relief center, serving meals to two thousand people. Christie went to the front of the room and told the crowd: "Your community has been hurt, but you've drawn together to each other. And I can tell you that traveling all over the state, this is an example of what's happening all over New Jersey. . . . People have lost a lot of things, but you haven't lost each other."

Christie said that none other than the king of Jordan had called him this week, and the prime minister of Great Britain had sent him an email. "They saw how tough New Jerseyans were on television," he said. "You're making people sit up and take notice of something we already knew: That the toughest, greatest people in America live right here in New Jersey."

Someone in the crowd yelled "Jersey strong!"—and Christie repeated the phrase to applause.

He told them he also didn't have electricity back home, in Mendham. And then he added: "I've been wearing the same pants for eight days!"

A man in the crowd responded: "Real guys use powder!"

CHRISTIE TOLD ME he cried a lot during those first few weeks after the storm. "Just every day, I didn't know how I was going to get up and go back, and I knew that every day I had to do it, *every day*," he said. When we spoke about this years later, it was as if he was transported back to the Jersey Shore, October 2012.

"It was just so incredibly exhausting to have people need you that much and express it to you that way. . . . And I realized that my role and position with people had changed probably forever. And I still feel it today. It's a different relationship. Been through a trauma together. And they think I did okay. They counted on me, and they feel like I came through for them. And that creates a bond between you and these folks that is much different than the normal politician."

IN THE COMING weeks Christie's polls in New Jersey skyrocketed, as did his national fame. Actor Bobby Moynihan donned a blue fleece on *Saturday Night Live* and did a Christie impersonation: "We don't get sad in New Jersey, we get even. *So sleep with one eye open, Sandy!*"

Two weeks later Christie himself made an appearance on the show's Weekend Update segment, where with skilled comedic timing he played up his angry Jersey guy shtick and yelled at host Seth Meyers. He also wore his fleece. "It's basically fused to my skin at this point . . . I'm gonna die in this fleece."

He closed by reciting the last verses to Bruce Springsteen's "Atlantic City": ". . . everything that dies, one day comes back . . ."

YOUNG CHRISTOPHER CHRISTIE was twelve years old when Springsteen's 1975 album, *Born to Run*, came "bursting into my summer vacation." The album "gave voice to the suburban kids like me who were filled with dreams and doubts."

It wasn't just the lyrics or the "exhilarating" music that Christie liked. "He was a star," said Christie, who was long fascinated with fame.

Christie started going to concerts, all the time. Several a year, through parenthood and politics. By his second gubernatorial term he had seen Springsteen north of 130 times. Christie's love of Springsteen is real American rock 'n' roll passion, not some greatest-hits fascination. All four of his children attended Springsteen shows in utero. He can recite the words to every Springsteen song ever released. "Thunder Road" is his favorite: "Well, now I'm no hero, that's understood. / All the redemption I can offer girl, is beneath this dirty hood."

Before he became U.S. Attorney, while in his late thirties working as a lawyer and lobbyist, Christie was an active member of a Springsteen email list called Luckytown Digest, named for the song "Lucky Town." Chris C. in Mendham was a loyal "LTDer" sitting down at his computer late at night after shows to post set lists and glowing concert reviews—"It was amazing," he wrote, "the master was at work tonight."

He volunteered for "trees," networks of people who record shows and then trade the tapes. "I would be interested in participating and since I do not yet have the requisite equipment, I would gladly trade with blanks?" Chris C. offered.

He bragged about winning a cancer charity auction for two front-row tickets that cost Todd, his brother, $11,750. "Despite the 'staggering' price, we had a night we will never forget. We wouldn't trade it for the world and it went to a wonderful cause," Christie wrote. He brought his son, Andrew, to the show, and when Springsteen noticed the six-year-old in the front row he tossed him a guitar pick.

Then there was that night in Minnesota in 1999, when he and Mary Pat entertained fifteen clients at a concert. The next morning they were board-ing their flight back to New Jersey when Christie recognized a voice down the aisle. "I knew immediately—it was Bruce!"

Christie loves meeting famous people, and the earnestness in which he described this encounter was palpable.

"I immediately go off the deep end," he told his fellow fans. Springsteen even signed autographs for his kids. "He was everything I hoped he would be if I ever got a chance to meet him—gracious and incredibly normal in a truly extraordinary way. That was my Christmas gift."

IN 2008 CHRISTIE was preparing to run for governor against incumbent Jon Corzine when both candidates attended a Springsteen benefit concert to raise money for the Count Basie Theater in Red Bank, the home of scores of Springsteen shows through the years. There were only fifteen hundred people in the audience, and The Boss played the album *Born to Run* from start to finish.

Christie was in the balcony; Corzine was in the front row. This was the best show that Christie had ever seen. But Corzine left during the encore.

"He just left," recalled Christie, still outraged. "You could see him look at his watch. He left during 'Raise Your Hand'—Bruce is on top of the piano screaming—and it just struck me that unless there's an emergency, which I found out later there wasn't, you don't leave. You just don't leave."

As governor he continued going to every possible Springsteen show, often with staff and cabinet members. When one tried to leave a concert early because she had to testify before the state Senate budget committee in the morning, Christie told her she was pulling the "Corzine Move."

To one show he brought writer Jeffrey Goldberg from the *Atlantic*, who watched Christie play air drums to "Badlands" and grab two of his cabinet members in bear hugs and headlocks while shouting the lyrics three inches from their faces: "Poor man wanna be rich, rich man wanna be king. / And a king ain't satisfied till he rules everything."

After the 2011 death of Clarence Clemons, the saxophonist and soul of Springsteen's E Street Band, Christie ordered New Jersey flags lowered to half staff and said he "felt like all the energy was drained out of my body. I just lay there silent on the bed, and [Mary Pat] said to me, 'I just want to understand what you're feeling,' and I said, 'My youth is over. He's dead and anything that is left of me being young is over.' "

If Christie communicates with something holy, if Christie connects with God, I believe it likely happens deep into the third hour of a Springsteen show.

In 2012 a photo surfaced in the *New York Post* depicting Christie sleeping at a Springsteen show at New York City's Madison Square Garden. I asked him if this was true. In response he called a staffer who had been with him at the show up to the microphone to vouch for him. He had closed his eyes during a "really spiritual song"—called "Rocky Ground"—but he never slept. "I have never fallen asleep during a Bruce Springsteen show," he said. "I will *never* fall asleep during a Bruce Springsteen show."

He added: "When I was like fist-pumping during 'Badlands,' I'm glad no one took pictures of that. When I was singing to 'Out in the Street,' thankfully no one took pictures of that. When I was contorting myself during 'Because the Night,' no one took pictures of that . . ."

CHRISTIE IGNORED SPRINGSTEEN'S long liberally tinged exhortations in the middle of concerts. "He's telling us that rich people like him are fucking over poor people like us in the audience, except that us in the audience aren't poor, because we can afford to pay ninety-eight bucks to him to see his show," he said.

This wasn't about politics for him. It was about life. He described the music as "aspirational to success, to fun, to being a better person, to figuring out how to make your life better."

Christie thought Republicanism should resonate with The Boss, who went from a working-class childhood to being one of the richest people in show business. "What's funny is that his progression is what Republicans believe can happen," Christie said.

But Springsteen, a New Jersey resident, apparently didn't think that Christie was digesting the true message of his music. So he penned a letter to the editor of his hometown newspaper, the *Asbury Park Press*, to respond to an article that reporter Michael Symons had just published about the effects of Christie's budget cuts:

> *The article is one of the few that highlights the contradictions between a policy of large tax cuts, on the one hand, and cuts in services to those in the most dire conditions, on the other . . . your article shows that the cuts are eating away at the lower edges of the middle class, not just those already classified as in poverty, and are likely to continue to get worse over the next few years. I'm always glad to see my hometown newspaper covering these issues.*
> Bruce Springsteen
> Colts Neck, NJ

In early 2012, I attended the opening of a new $2.5 billion casino in Atlantic City called Revel. Christie controversially chipped in $261 million in tax credits to finish the project after construction stalled for years, and when he showed up on this day the newly employed cocktail waitresses and blackjack dealers greeted him like a hero. Christie promised that the new casino would create fifty-five hundred jobs and boost the fortunes of the struggling resort town.

Afterward, I asked the governor an unrelated question. What did he think of Springsteen's new album, *Wrecking Ball*? The album's theme was the failure of governmental and financial institutions. It was particularly harsh on bankers—the same people who financed controversial projects like Revel.

"Bruce, if he's true to his lyrics, would love the fact that the state used taxpayer funds to invest in this place to create jobs for working men and women," he said. "Those are middle-class New Jerseyans who are looking for an opportunity to support their families, put a roof over their head, put food on the table. As I understand it, he's all for those folks. And so am I."

He then started spitballing, "making a direct plea to Bruce right now" that he should demonstrate his fealty to the working men and women of New Jersey by playing a concert at Revel the following Labor Day weekend. "To come down here on Labor Day weekend, and to perform at Revel, would be a real sign of support for those working men and women who have been put back to work," he said.

He cut a video of those remarks and created a hashtag to convince

Springsteen to play Revel. With an assist from my question, Christie had created a news moment to promote his message about heralding a New Jersey economic comeback.

He was also essentially trolling the only person in New Jersey more famous than he was.

The next night, at a show in nearby Philadelphia, Springsteen made a late addition to the set list and played "Atlantic City"—a more mellow and sadder version than normal. "Well, I got a job and tried to put my money away / But I got debts that no honest man can pay."

Officially, though, Springsteen never responded to the invitation to play Revel.

"We got nothing back from them," Christie later said. "Not even a 'fuck you.' "

Revel closed shortly thereafter. The casino's debts were too high to pay off.

**WITH THAT TORTURED** personal history as a backdrop, Sandy arrived several months later. Two nights after landfall, Springsteen took the stage in Rochester, New York, and dedicated "My City of Ruins" to New Jersey, to "all the people working down there: the police officers, the firemen, and also to the governor, who has done such a hard job this past week."

A few days after that, Christie and Springsteen ran into each other backstage at a telethon concert to raise money for Sandy victims.

"We hugged. He told me: 'It's official. We're friends,' " Christie later recounted, proudly.

The Monday after Sandy was the day before Election Day, and Springsteen was on the campaign trail with the president aboard *Air Force One*. Obama phoned Christie.

"You know, in a crisis like we're going through, you know the only thing that's better than one guy from Jersey?" Obama asked.

"No," Christie said.

"Two guys from Jersey."

Obama put the phone on speaker.

"Hey, man, ya know when the times get tough, they call the guys from Jersey," Springsteen said.

"How you doing, Bruce?"

"Good, Gov. You're doing a great job, baby. We meet in the wildest places, don't we?"

"Are you on *Air Force One*?"

"It is unbelievable. Yes, I'm on *Air Force One*."

Obama got back on the phone. "Anything else?"

"That's good enough for today, sir," Christie said.

ONCE THE FLOOD waters receded, once most of the electricity returned and the schools reopened, it was time for Christie and the other governors whose states were affected by Sandy to go to Congress for a $60.2 billion aid package.

Things moved slower than expected, and Christie began to get agitated. Weeks passed, then months. Christie didn't think the leader of the Republican Congress, Speaker of the House John Boehner, was understanding the need.

Christie knew many Republican members of Congress. He had campaigned for several. "So I had a lot of numbers," he told me. On New Year's Eve 2012 and New Year's Day 2013, Christie called as many as forty Republicans. He found an ally in Eric Cantor, the majority leader of the House of Representatives, and spoke to him five or six times in the days leading up to a scheduled congressional vote on the funds.

Christie had to woo members with Tea Party leanings from unaffected states who thought spending cuts should offset relief aid. And he also had to threaten: "You don't vote yes on this bill, next time you see me it will be with my arm around your primary opponent."

Christie was using the popularity he gained from his display of leadership after the storm. But the gambit didn't work. When Congress came back into session on January 1, Boehner canceled a vote on the relief money. Christie called Boehner four times. The speaker never called back.

At 1:00 a.m. on January 2, Christie called Congressman Peter King, a New York Republican who was also fighting for aid for his state.

"He was definitely charged up," King said. "Thank God he did what he had to do."

This is what Christie had to do: Hold a press conference the next day. Before he went out there, he wrote out his comments on a legal pad, which was unusual.

"Last night, politics was placed before our oaths to serve our citizens. For me it was disappointing and disgusting to watch," Christie said. He noted that it took ten days for aid to be approved after Hurricane Katrina but it was already sixty-six days and counting for Sandy. And he reiterated his threat to support challenges to these representatives' seats. "Primaries are an ugly thing," he said.

He called out Republicans for their "selfishness" and "duplicity," given that some had in the past voted on disaster relief for their own districts. He said these Republicans showed "callous indifference to the suffering of the people of my state," treating them like "second-class citizens."

Here he was, the Republican National Convention's keynote speaker, calling out the top elected Republican in the entire nation, a man who was third in line to the presidency. It was an exceptional encounter.

"Shame on you, shame on Congress," Christie said.

Christie's press conference excoriation dominated cable TV.

Minutes after he finished, the House Republicans made an announcement.

Votes on the Sandy aid package would be held within two weeks. Billions were on their way.

# 10

# FOUR MORE YEARS

Chris Christie was running for reelection as governor, and therefore he was headed to the diner.

New Jersey has more diners than any other state, and its north-south Route 130 is blessed with more diners than any road *in the world*. In recent years, diners have fallen victim to Starbucks coffee and foodie pretensions, but they remain as critical as ever in New Jersey politics. Diners are where politicians go to engage in bribery and campaign for elections.

As usual, on this day Christie was late. By the time his motorcade pulled up to the Edison Diner, Republican volunteers had been milling about for a couple of hours. Enthusiasm waned. So when the governor got out of his SUV, no one cheered. Then a woman yelled to him: "Thank you for having the balls to stand up!" And although no one knew what exactly she was referring to, everyone seemed to appreciate the sentiment. The crowd of supporters loosened up from there.

Christie stopped at each table to shake hands, pose for selfies, and demand Sharpies from Dan Robles, his body guy, to sign campaign signs. Then he got to Bert's table.

Bert Bueno, a retired elementary school teacher, was enjoying an 11:00 a.m. salad with a friend she had met a half century earlier at New Brunswick High School. Before the governor approached Bert's table, Bert stopped me. What about the gays, she asked. What does Christie think about the gays?

I told her that Christie had "conditionally vetoed" a gay marriage bill. That meant he rejected it and instead suggested that the legislature put a referendum on the ballot asking voters if there should be gay marriage.

But Democrats balked; they didn't think marriage rights should be a ballot question.

Bueno got that retired elementary school teacher gleam in her eye. I knew it well, because my mother is a retired elementary school teacher. I could tell Bueno was hearing something she did not approve of.

Christie got to Bueno's table. He took a picture with her friend and then leaned over and took Bert's hand.

"How are ya?"

"I'm great. What about gay rights?"

"What about them? What do you want to know?"

"I want to know how come you're in opposition. I'm a straight woman. I have children, grandchildren . . ."

His explanation for not supporting gay marriage was not that he thinks homosexuality is unnatural—in fact, he thinks gays are born that way. But he didn't believe legislatures should be in the business of changing two thousand years of marriage.

"My view is if you want to change it, put it on the ballot, let everybody decide. It shouldn't be decided by courts, it shouldn't be decided by politicians in Trenton, it should be decided by everybody. If the majority of people in New Jersey want same-sex marriage, I'll enforce the law."

"But how could you as the leader of the state speak and have such a point of view that is really in opposition to many many people in New Jersey, in the world?"

"Listen, whenever you have a point of view, it's in opposition to a lot of people."

"But this is different than gun control and taxes."

"I don't think it is different."

"It's a human rights issue."

"Says you."

"Well, it is."

Christie's position on gay rights was, in its way, nuanced. After a gay Rutgers University student leaped to his death from the George Washington Bridge following a bullying incident, Christie signed an antibullying bill that gay rights groups hailed as a national model. And in the middle of his reelection campaign he signed a bill making New Jersey only the second state in the country to ban what is known as gay conversion therapy for children, despite vehement opposition from social conservatives.

"Which was great," Bert said. "Which was great."

"So this is an issue where we have an honest difference of opinion. Okay, so put it on the ballot. I vote my way, you vote your way, and whoever gets the most votes wins . . . if you're waiting to find a candidate who you're going to agree with on everything, go home and look in the mirror."

"I agree, but for me, I pick a guy, a man or a woman, who is the most aligned with me on human rights. All the other stuff—like taxes and jobs and all that, which I am concerned about—all the other stuff is secondary to human rights."

"Listen, if we disagree, then you vote for the other person. If that's going to be your litmus test, I'm not going to sit here and convince you."

"I just have one more thing to ask you before you walk away. And I appreciate this interaction."

"Me, too."

"Oh, thank you. So here's the question: Would you ever be open to a conversation—not a political conversation, with cameras and all that stuff—a conversation with a whole group of gay and lesbian people to really see how this is affecting them?"

"I have relatives who are gay. I have friends who are gay. I think I have an understanding of it. That's not the point. We have a difference of opinion."

Christie's gay relatives, the ones he was referring to, were his brother-in-law Brian—one of Mary Pat's six brothers—and Brian's partner, Ernie. Christie told me that he and Brian talked about his gay marriage position. "Didn't affect our relationship at all," he said. "He would tell me that some of his friends in that community would say to him, like, 'What the hell, with your brother-in-law, why isn't he for it?' " Christie said Brian defended him, and understood. "Brian knows that Mary Pat and I have completely and totally accepted his sexuality and his partner Ernie—they've been together twenty-three, twenty-four years, he's Uncle Ernie to our kids, and we love him to death. It's great. To me it's a public policy position, and he knows that. It's not like about acceptance or equality. I love Brian and Ernie as much or more than I love any of my other in-laws."

Brian, a furniture maker, created the desk in Christie's home office, and he was an usher at the Christies' wedding. Whenever they see each other, Brian once said, Christie "gives me a big Italian kiss on the cheek."

Mary Pat agrees with her husband's position on gay marriage, but the governor's two oldest children don't, Christie told me. In a gubernatorial debate Christie was asked what he would do if one of his children told him he or she was gay. He was immediate in his answer: "I would grab them and hug them, and tell them I love them, just like I would do with any of my children who came to me with news that they thought was important enough to open themselves up to me in that way. But what I would also tell them is that Dad believes that marriage is between one man and one woman."

Christie generally didn't defend his socially conservative positions using religious arguments. In some ways that made his positions harder to explain, attracting doubters from both the right and the left who thought he was being inauthentic one way or the other. Mostly, he avoided talking about social issues at all.

I once asked him about "transvaginal ultrasounds," because Republicans in Virginia wanted to require such tests for pregnant women who sought abortions in an effort to discourage the procedure.

"I don't even know what the phrase means, I don't think I want to know what the phrase means, and you can be sure I'm not saying it from behind this podium," Christie said.

BACK AT THE Edison Diner, Christie's security detail was hustling me away from Bert. I heard her tell the governor how great he was after Hurricane Sandy. "I thought that was very courageous of you," she said.

The whole exchange seemed genuine. Even if they disagreed, it seemed as if he and Bert had come to an understanding, had made an actual connection at a Jersey diner amidst the ridiculous stage show of a modern campaign.

So after the governor left, I walked back to Bert's table. Are you going to vote for him now?

"Fuck no," she said.

THIS WOULDN'T BE the 2013 reelection campaign's only serving of real talk in a diner.

Hours before he left office, Governor Jon Corzine signed a medical marijuana law that Christie opposed. He said as a former federal law enforcement official he worried that medical marijuana would become a front for drug sales to the general public, as he said had happened with such operations in California and Colorado. He couldn't repeal the law but he did oversee the writing of regulations, from scratch, for the program. This took an unusually long time. Caregivers of ill patients who were waiting on marijuana said this delay was intentional. Christie said he was just being careful. In the end the program that the Christie administration created was small, with just three dispensaries statewide, and some of the most stringent restrictions in the country. Children with severe seizures, for example, were not allowed to be prescribed edible marijuana—even the kind that doesn't elicit a high.

At a campaign stop at the Highlander Restaurant diner in Scotch Plains, a local resident, Brian Wilson, stopped him. He asked the governor whether he was going to sign a bill on his desk to ease the regulations. Wilson's daughter, two, suffered from a potentially deadly form of epilepsy. Cameras crowded around the men as they squeezed in closer, at the center of a scrum, face to face.

"These are complicated issues," Christie said.

"Very simple issue," Wilson responded.

"Listen, I know you think it's simple. It's simple for you, it's not simple for me. . . . I wish the best for you, your daughter, and your family, and I'm going to do what I think is best for the people of the state, all the people of the state."

As Christie walked away, Wilson called out: "Please don't let my daughter die, Governor."

Christie ultimately agreed to part of the bill, which gave children access to medical marijuana, but with tougher regulations than any other program in the country.

MARIJUANA AND GAY marriage. Property taxes and education. Yes, these were issues in Christie's 2013 reelection campaign. But the only thing that really mattered was Sandy.

Gladys, an eighty-two-year-old woman from Newark who didn't vote for Christie in 2009, told him she planned to back him in 2013 solely because of Sandy. She told him she said this prayer before bed every night: "Dear Lord, please give our governor strength, because I don't know how much more shit this boy can take!"

The Gladys story became a favorite of Christie's. "These are my people! She was just a dignified woman, and then that comes out of her mouth. I said, 'Only in New Jersey.' She had absolutely no hesitation about telling the governor that in her prayer for him, she used the words *Lord* and *shit*. That's what it's like being governor of New Jersey!"

If not for Sandy, Gladys would not be praying for this governor. The storm changed everything.

Newark mayor Cory Booker, Senate president Stephen Sweeney, former governor Richard Codey, and Assemblyman John Wisniewski (the future lead legislative interrogator in Bridgegate) had all toyed with running against Christie. But their campaigns would have had to begin weeks after Sandy ended. Given Christie's Sandy popularity, they were scared off. Democratic operatives didn't think *anyone* could beat him now.

So in lieu of any man stepping to the plate, came a woman. From the back bench of the legislature, a pugnacious and affirmatively liberal longtime state legislator, lawyer, mother of four, and stepmother to two became the only Democratic candidate in the race. Like Christie, Barbara Buono was a New Jersey born and bred Italian American from Essex County who grew up in a household with lots of arguing. And like Christie, she still wore a chip on her shoulder.

But while Christie was a momma's boy, Buono was closest with her father, who died when she was nineteen. Shortly thereafter a fire in her first apartment left her with no place to live and forced her to make a call to the welfare office. She put herself through law school, then married and divorced. She was a single mother of four for a spell.

After getting her start in local town politics she moved up to the legislature where her poise, TV-ready looks, and work ethic helped her rise through the Democratic establishment—to majority leader in the state Senate, the number-two spot. But she was too liberal and not enough of a good ole boy. She opposed Senate president Stephen Sweeney and Democratic boss George Norcross in their deal with Christie on pension and benefits reform, which got her bounced from leadership.

In her YouTube announcement videos, she explicitly came out against "party bosses." Instead of sucking it up and pandering, she poked them in the eye.

Buono thought the fact that most of New Jersey agreed with her over Christie on the issues would mean that she'd at least get a fighting chance. Polls showed the state supported gay marriage and an increase in the minimum wage, just as she did, and they thought the governor had done a poor job handling property taxes, just as she did. If Christie made enough unforced errors, if his bullying tendencies were focused too pointedly at a female candidate, if Democratic donors from around the country saw a chance to knock off Christie before 2016, then perhaps she could attract enough attention to win.

She was really, really wrong.

Sandy rejiggered the political dynamics of the state. A poll taken a month after the storm found that 66 percent of women, 52 percent of public worker households, and 57 percent of Democrats (!) approved of the job Christie was doing. One poll in a ridiculous hypothetical gubernatorial matchup had him beating Bruce Springsteen.

Brewing controversies about the distribution of Sandy aid were in the newspapers, but New Jersey was not ready to hear anything bad about the general who had seen them through the war.

Christie sold a message of Sandy unity with a little help from his celebrity friends. He began his reelection year with an interview on *The Daily Show*, where Jon Stewart booked him for two segments, an honor normally bestowed on presidents. He hit a totally different demographic when he was interviewed on *Extra!* by actor Alec Baldwin's wife, Hilaria, who told him: "We love you." She called him "America's hero."

In January 2013 Christie was on the cover of *Time* magazine. In April 2013, he was named one of *Time*'s one hundred most influential people in the world. The blurb under his picture was written by Ginjer, the little girl he had met after Sandy.

At the annual governors' dinner at the White House that year he got the best seat available—next to First Lady Michelle Obama and, at one point, clinked his wine glass with hers.

Christie also went west for a fund-raiser, taking in a few hundred thousand dollars at the Palo Alto, California, home of Mark Zuckerberg. The Facebook founder had never before raised money for a candidate, but here he was, opening his home for the gov and inviting his friends. The CEO of LinkedIn came by, as did former secretary of state Condoleezza Rice.

When the weather warmed Christie presided over the first British royal visit to the Jersey Shore since 1939. Christie welcomed His Royal Highness Prince Harry, "the best way I know how, with his own royal fleece." Chris and Harry then toured heavily damaged Mantoloking before playing a boardwalk game with the Christie kids in Seaside Heights. Christie, as he always seemed to do, won.

The following week, Matt Lauer and the *Today* show cast showed up at the Shore for a special edition "cohosted" by Mr. and Mrs. Christie. That's where Christie ran into Snooki and the cast from MTV's reality show *Jersey Shore*. The two most famous New Jerseyans of 2013 finally had their summit after years of feuding with each other from afar. (Christie often said Snooki and friends should be sent back to New York, where they were actually from: "Take them out to Montauk, all the way out on the Point, and leave them there.") Now they were meeting on the Seaside Heights boardwalk—the place where the *Jersey Shore* cast partied and where Christie had so often vacationed. Snooki mostly complained to the governor about how he didn't like her; the governor kept his hands planted in his pockets, unable to say much more than "nice to meet you."

"Why are you standing so close to me?" Snooki asked Christie at one point.

THE GRANDEST MOMENT of Christie's celebrity-filled reelection year came the following week, when the governor hosted President Obama on the Jersey Shore. Christie "kicked the president's ass," as he described it, at a football toss boardwalk game in Point Pleasant Beach—"poor guy couldn't get it through the tire." The governor took the stuffed bear he won and handed it to the president.

The conservative *Daily Caller* griped: "Chris Christie wins a stuffed bear for Obama." But in blue New Jersey, Christie had demonstrated bipartisan adorability.

After they played their games the men went up the Shore to Asbury Park for the rarest of events: Leaders of two opposing political parties, delivering two inspirational postpartisan speeches at an event that felt like a campaign rally. The president encountered but barely spoke with Buono, in what was largely viewed as a snub.

"Our citizens' lives are more important than any kind of politics at all," Christie said against the grand backdrop of the classic Boardwalk Convention Hall, next to the Asbury Park beach, as a steady rain fell.

Obama praised Chris—he called him "Chris"—for doing a "great job." And he even paraphrased that statement Christie had made at a press conference hours after Sandy's landfall: We "cannot permit that sorrow to replace the resilience that I know all New Jerseyans have."

"I love you!" the crowd yelled at the president.

"I love you back!" he said.

This Obama visit came right before New Jersey's June primary elections. Christie went on to beat an unlikable, unknown, and underfunded Tea Party challenger in that Republican primary with 92 percent of the vote, and then a week after that he hightailed it to Chicago. He had a meeting with another Democratic president on the calendar.

CHRISTIE HAD MET Bill and Hillary Clinton in January 2005 at Donald Trump's wedding. "He had no idea who I was," Christie remembered. The then–U.S. Attorney introduced himself to the president while Clinton was working the cocktail hour "like he was running for something."

"He's the master," Christie said.

After that Christie and Clinton ended up sitting next to each other a few years in a row at Big East college basketball games. Some time after that Clinton invited Christie over to his office in Harlem to talk politics.

Now, Clinton had Christie onstage at the culminating session of one of the Clinton Foundation's Clinton Global Initiative conferences. Clinton looked absolutely giddy as he lobbed softballs at Christie for a Q&A about Sandy and leadership. They sat in large white armchairs. Christie was expansive in his answers; Bill wore a look of fascination. Two of the best American political craftsmen, cordial before the potential 2016 war.

BY JULY, CHRISTIE was stopping in towns hit hard by Sandy, media in tow, to personally check on things and announce governmental recovery funds of one sort or another. In Sayreville, Jon Bon Jovi's hometown, Christie toured with the rock star himself who, despite his Democratic tendencies, had become friends with the governor through a Sandy relief fund run by First Lady Mary Pat. The Christies and Bon Jovis would share dinners in Jersey and vacations in the Hamptons for years to come.

On that day I was one of three reporters shadowing the men as they walked through a quiet neighborhood where streets were named for military commanders and houses fetch a couple of hundred thousand dollars. Sayreville is "very blue-collar, middle-class America," as Bon Jovi told me. Sayreville is not near the actual Jersey Shore, but flood waters from the Raritan Bay, which hooks into New Jersey across from New York's Staten Island, rushed in and out during the storm, leaving tremendous damage.

No one knew beforehand that Bon Jovi and Christie were coming, so when residents opened their blinds and walked to the driveway to fetch their *Star-Ledger* that sleepy Monday morning they found a bunch of folks milling about and *oh, my God is that Governor Christie?* OH MY GOD IS THAT BON JOVI!

Bon Jovi and Christie walked through the street, arms on each other's shoulders, talking football and catching up on their kids before people started steadily descending from their stoops to say hi. The streets slowly lined with Sayreville's Sandy victims. The governor introduced himself as

"Chris." The older women told Mary Pat she was pretty. Bon Jovi reminisced about playing a dance in the neighborhood, and he kneeled to talk to a kid wearing a uniform from the Pop Warner football league he used to play in.

"What brings youse guys down the block?" one excited woman asked.

"Come to check everything out, see how everything's going," Christie said. "Jon's helping with things, so . . ."

"Thank you for all you do," said another. "You're my governor."

Near the end of the walk, Christie stopped to ask me about some tweets I had written the day before about Buono getting roughed up on MSNBC.

"Governor, she can't even get a break on MSNBC!" I told him. Buono's first two MSNBC appearances had been disastrous, with the hosts barely containing their low opinion of her candidacy.

"You gotta earn your breaks, Matthew, you gotta earn your breaks," Christie said. In other words: Famous Democratic rock stars only hang out with you after you save their state from a natural disaster.

Then Christie was gone, in an SUV with Bon Jovi and on the way to Sayreville Borough Hall, where a large crowd was gathering outside. Speakers were set up, and soon the crowd heard the recorded sounds of Bon Jovi's "Who Says You Can't Go Home." "There's only one place they call me one of their own, just a hometown boy, born a rolling stone. / Who says you can't go home?"

As the song ended the gov and the rock star walked out like the gov and the rock star they are, under a shining sun and before more than one hundred cheering residents.

Bon Jovi then announced that he was pledging $1 million to Sandy relief.

The crowd roared its approval.

CHRISTIE KEPT PULLING celebrities out of his pocket. He visited the Boys & Girls Club in Camden with New Jersey native Shaquille O'Neal, one of the most recognizable African American figures in the world. They were an odd-looking pair—Shaq is seven-foot-one; he made the governor look miniature—but they had become friends, bonding over the need to save New Jersey's inner cities.

"This is one of the few things I do as governor that make my kids think I'm actually cool," he told the crowd in Camden about his friendship with Shaq.

"Thank you, Governor," Shaq said. "I do think you're cool. Very cool." O'Neal later cut a reelection commercial for him.

Beyond the celebrities, Buono had to contend with Christie's political fame.

Christie got into a minor spat with future presidential rival Senator Rand Paul of Kentucky that ended up being the single biggest political story in the nation for a stretch of July and August. After Christie said he opposed Paul's libertarian belief in dismantling federal surveillance programs, Paul criticized Christie's push for federal Sandy aid as a "gimme, gimme, gimme" belief in government pork, like a "king of bacon." Christie then noted that New Jersey contributed more to the federal government than it received, especially as compared to Paul's own Kentucky.

To smooth things over, Paul asked for a beer summit that never happened. He ultimately sent Christie flowers. Really.

Buono was left out of the conversation. She tried to use Christie's national profile against him, saying that he'd "rather be campaigning in the cornfields of Iowa than creating jobs in New Jersey."

That may have been true, but New Jersey didn't care.

BUONO COULD ONLY afford two television ads in the pricey Philadelphia and New York markets. Christie, backed by rich Republicans from around the country and the Republican Governors Association, aired sixteen.

He ran a disciplined campaign, sticking with a few choice words about himself (*Sandy* and *bipartisan*) and one choice statistic about Buono (*154 votes in the legislature for tax and fee increases*).

But you can't win New Jersey without Democratic backers. That's why Christie was landing Democratic endorsement after Democratic endorsement.

Each endorsement didn't necessarily bring votes, but news about the endorsements—free media events surrounding the announcement events, plus campaign ads highlighting the endorsements in aggregate—was seeping into the collective New Jersey bloodstream and making the state realize that Christie wasn't any old Republican. He wasn't like Washington. In the end sixty elected Democrats endorsed Christie, and many other Democrats opted to sit out the race entirely.

Bipartisanship became his ticket to not only a landslide win in November but also, possibly, the White House. He would show America how to be a "principled conservative" and still win Democrats.

Buono, meanwhile, was blindsided by the extent of the Democratic opposition. "What is going on?" she'd ask. "This is an election, not a military junta." She said the ferocity of Democratic disloyalty "will make the history books."

CHRISTIE CALLED DEMOCRATS who crossed the aisle to support him "heroes."

The first endorsement came from the heart of Democratic Hudson County. "I'm a Democrat, I've been a Democrat all my life," Harrison mayor Raymond McDonough began by way of explanation. But Christie, he said, had shown interest in him—"me, a Hudson County Democrat, it's unheard of." For nineteen years McDonough had sought a train station from the Port Authority. Never got it. But with the powerful transit agency under Christie's control, the Harrison train station was approved for a $260 million overhaul.

Nearby, Union City held particular promise. About 85 percent of the city's population was Hispanic, and the city's mayor was an old-school pol who could turn out the vote en masse. Winning Mayor Brian Stack's endorsement meant Christie could land Democratic and Hispanic Union City, helping him boost his margins among both demographics statewide.

Stack had the whole town wired. He distributed twenty thousand turkeys to residents at Thanksgiving and commanded an army of ten thousand voters on Election Day. As with other new Democratic friends, as U.S. Attorney, Christie had investigated Stack. But relationships changed once Christie became governor. He refused to criticize Stack—even as Stack served simultaneously as mayor and state senator, which reform-minded Christie normally didn't like.

As Stack delivered Democratic votes that Christie needed in the legislature, the Christie administration fully funded all of Union City's $13 million request for aid. And when Christie came to Union City for a town hall meeting, Stack called him "the greatest governor the state's ever had."

All the way down in South Jersey, Burlington City mayor James Fazzone described himself as "further to the left" than anybody in South Jersey. But Fazzone told me that he liked that Christie gave local mayors attention with regular conference calls—and he liked how the Christie administration provided Burlington City with three transportation grants.

"Everybody wants to look behind the curtain and say, 'What's behind it?' And what's behind it is that I'm trying to get things done," Christie said of his odd bedfellows. "And I'm a Republican governor in a predominantly

Democratic state, so you can decide to do one of two things: Either hold your breath and wait for the state to become Republican and do nothing, or to work with like-minded, objective, fair Democrats."

Many of those fair-minded Democrats were minorities. When he collected endorsements from the Cuban-born Democratic mayor of the town of West New York, the mayor called Christie "the first Hispanic governor of New Jersey."

Christie took it as a point of pride that he actually went into black and Hispanic towns to deal with Democrats, and that he cultivated those relationships by inviting leaders to meet with him at the governor's mansion. During one such gathering with African American leaders Christie recounted how during college a black friend took him to visit the historically black Delaware State University. Christie said he stood out as a white man and was stared at. In this moment, Christie said, he experienced a small sense of what it was like for his friend back at the mostly white University of Delaware.

Michael Blunt, the black mayor of nearly all-black Chesilhurst, was moved by the story. He was also moved by a $200,000 special state aid package that the tiny borough received. When Blunt, a Democrat, was ready to endorse, Christie came to Chesilhurst for the announcement.

Buono tried to object. She noted that the U.S. Supreme Court had just rolled back federal voting protections for minorities, thanks to Christie's Republican Party. Six times over sixty-six days we asked Christie what he thought about the ruling. Christie dodged. Over and over again. The black Democrats who endorsed Christie didn't demand answers.

By the end of his first term, 56 percent of nonwhites in the state gave the Republican governor positive approval ratings.

CHRISTIE'S DESIRE TO win big became clear in the middle of the campaign when Senator Frank Lautenberg, an eighty-eight-year-old longtime Christie foe, died. Christie was empowered by the state constitution to appoint an interim senator until the next election. He chose his state attorney general and former chief counsel, Jeffrey Chiesa, a deeply loyal Christie guy who had worked with him going back to his days at the law firm.

But an important question arose: When should Chiesa's term expire? When would the special election be held for the seat?

What would have made the most sense, fiscally and logically, was to hold an election for the permanent Lautenberg replacement the following

November. There was already a scheduled election so this scenario would require no extra, costly special Election Day. And it would enfranchise the most people because turnout would be high.

That's exactly what the concern was. Newark mayor Cory Booker was expected to run and not only win Lautenberg's seat but perhaps draw loyal Democrats to the polls in high numbers, thereby adding votes to Buono's tally by default. Christie's game plan of pulling votes from Democrats, independents, and minorities to demonstrate national electability was in jeopardy.

Christie, a source told me, had this in mind when he instead ordered special elections—with a primary in *August,* an exceptionally unusual time to ask people to vote, and a general election in October, just a few weeks before the governor's election. Keeping the election in the same year as his own—but on a different date—would divert Democratic dollars from Buono. And turnout would be abysmal.

Liberals were furious, alleging that Christie was suppressing turnout just to boost his own reelection margins. Conservatives were upset because they wanted Christie to schedule the election the *following* November—that way they could keep Republican Chiesa in the seat for as long as possible.

But it was the cost—$12 million to print ballots and open polling places on each of the two new election days—that everyone criticized. "It's as if he gave the residents of this state the finger and that finger will cost $24 million," said State Senator Richard Codey.

Christie said he was letting voters decide their own senator as soon as possible, which is what Lautenberg would have wanted. "So for all of you who were bored with the governor's race, I have now solved your problem," he said.

Christie's deft political move was legally sound. There was a conflict in the law—one statute seemed to indicate the special election should be held in next year's November, the other said it had to be in the upcoming November. But both statutes agreed that the governor had the power to set another date—so that's what he did.

Booker easily won the Democratic U.S. Senate nomination. And then, even though he had actually endorsed Buono, he started quasi-campaigning with Christie. In a mutually beneficial moment for two politicians of different parties running in two elections three weeks apart, Booker and Christie joined together to cut the ribbon at a new Teachers Village in Newark featuring charter schools and homes for teachers. At a news conference, Booker referenced his "gov love."

"Gov love" were not the words that Buono wanted to hear from the most popular Democrat in the state less than three weeks before her election.

The day after he handily won his weird October Wednesday general election, Booker used the "gov love" line again as he embraced Christie at a groundbreaking for a ShopRite supermarket in Newark. He even likened the governor to none other than Ronald Reagan himself; in this scenario, Booker was Reagan's Democratic partner, House Speaker Tip O'Neill.

Christie's efforts to cultivate Democrats were paying off.

LABOR DAY, THE bona fide start of the campaign season, should have been Buono's chance to get New Jersey's attention.

The topic she chose for her first postsummer moment was the increasing cost of higher education in New Jersey. She announced it at a rally at Rutgers University's main campus, right across from the student center, first thing in the morning. The rally was horribly stage-managed, as traffic from a busy nearby street overpowered the voices of Buono and her running mate, Milly Silva. Students congregating nearby were loudly uninterested; this happened to be the first day of school, and they were excitedly reuniting with friends.

At the very same time, Christie was at a press conference in Newark taking some credit for the distribution of government money. Here, Christie was asked about a newly unearthed video showing Buono, several days earlier, making the following comment: "I don't know about you, but seeing Chris Christie frolicking on the beach is not going to drive me to go to the Jersey Shore." The context was how the Christie administration allegedly spent $2 million extra for post-Sandy Jersey Shore tourism ads featuring Christie and his family.

When asked about the comment, Christie proceeded to defend the everyday fat man from skinny elitists like Buono. "For me and for other folks across New Jersey," he began, "many folks are challenged by their weight. The fact that someone running for governor would make derisive comments about someone's physical appearance I think is really beneath the office that she's seeking. And I'm disappointed that she's done it."

So there I was, reading Christie's response on Twitter on my phone and standing at Rutgers in front of Buono while she talked about education. I took the bait. What was with your "frolicking" comment, Senator?

"I'm not going to even dignify that with a response," Buono said, flabbergasted.

Yet the news stories that came out of that first fall campaign day were about her weight joke—not her education plan.

FOR THE FIRST time in a quarter century of New Jersey politics, George Norcross didn't raise money for the Democratic gubernatorial candidate. Instead it was Christie who got the attention when Norcross hosted the governor at his Cooper University Hospital in October for an event marking the opening of a new cancer institute. As each took a turn at the podium they spoke of how they had attended Phillies-Mets games together in Norcross's luxury box. Phillies fan Norcross teased Mets fan Christie. Their relationship, partnership, and friendship was on full display; an election three weeks away be damned.

Norcross told a story that only he could have told, about seeing a man wearing a T-shirt that read: "Chris Christie: Too Big to Fail." That got a laugh, but then he turned to Christie and said this: "You're not too big to fail—you're too good and too important to fail us."

The Democrats had technically endorsed Buono. But their body language, particularly in the waning critical days of the campaign, said something entirely different. The top elected Democrat, Senate president Sweeney, rarely appeared in public with Buono. Sweeney told me he offered to campaign with her, but he acknowledged to me that they didn't get along. Instead, Sweeney kept popping up with Christie at manufactured media events that fit into Christie's reelection message of bipartisanship.

Christie populated his fall schedule with groundbreaking ceremonies for projects funded by a $750 million bond referendum for colleges and universities. Christie and the South Jersey Democrats shepherded the legislation that put this referendum through, and now they were ready to take a bow, just in time for their respective reelection campaigns.

Everyone benefited from the groundbreakings, not least of all Sweeney, who was up for reelection in a district where Christie was popular. At one event Sweeney thanked Christie four times in two minutes. At another Sweeney echoed Christie's talking points. "It's embarrassing what's going on in Washington now," Sweeney said.

At Rowan University's groundbreaking for a new academic building, a backhoe was brought in as a prop to sit behind the podium because construction there wasn't scheduled to begin for at least a year. And at Rutgers University's groundbreaking for a new nursing school in Camden, Christie and the Democrats scooped dirt with gleaming gold shovels even though Rutgers didn't even yet own the land where the school was supposed to go.

Buono could do little more than privately fume.

WITH CHRISTIE SPENDING so much time with South Jersey Democrats, Republicans whispered he was neglecting the GOPers who were running uphill campaigns to retake control of the state legislature. Here was a governor who had demanded that New Jersey give him a Republican legislature so he could fully implement his reforms, but he didn't appear to be fully committed to making that happen.

In Norcross's southern New Jersey territory, he wasn't campaigning for Republican legislative candidates at all.

That's because, a source told me, there was a deal.

They called it "the 195 Deal," for Route 195, the highway that forms the unofficial border between North and South Jersey. The terms of the deal were simple: Christie wouldn't campaign for Republican legislative candidates south of Route 195, in Norcross territory. In exchange, Norcross, Sweeney, and the South Jersey Democrats held their fire against him in the gubernatorial race.

Christie loyalists argued that the Republicans had no shot at winning enough of the South Jersey races to actually take control of the legislature anyway, so why bother fighting Norcross?

Evidence of the deal was all around. When Christie held a rousing reelection rally at Gloucester County GOP headquarters in the heart of South Jersey in an area where Sweeney was running for reelection, the governor didn't mention the local Republican candidates running for the legislature.

At one point Assemblyman Chris Brown, a Republican, went on a local radio station and referenced this deal between Norcross and Christie. "I had no meetings with George Norcross about politics," Christie said in response. "And two, if I did, I sure as hell wouldn't tell Chris Brown."

Late in the campaign Christie and Norcross were photographed together at an Eagles game by a Democratic activist and fund-raiser allied with both men. The activist then posted the picture to Twitter, setting Trenton tongues wagging. As Christie's Cowboys and Norcross's Eagles carried out a proxy war on the field like mercenaries, Norcross and Christie were above it all in a luxury box, breaking bread and doing politics.

Joe DiVincenzo of North Jersey, the third leg of the New Jersey political stool, confirmed that something like the 195 Deal existed. "There's no question there must have been deals that were done," he said. Not only wouldn't Christie campaign in South Jersey, Joe D. said, but Christie wouldn't raise money there, either.

The top Republican in the state Senate, Senator Tom Kean, Jr.—son of former governor (and Christie mentor) Tom Kean, Sr.—did not abide by the 195 Deal. He spent campaign funds trying to win Sweeney's seat.

The gambit didn't work, and shortly after the election Christie provoked a leadership fight in the state, encouraging a friend, State Senator Kevin O'Toole, to lead a coup to replace Kean as senate minority leader. Christie called two Republican senators into his office to twist arms. The move was largely seen as an attempt to punish Kean for not sticking with the deal.

The coup failed, and Christie eventually made peace with Kean.

But the Republican Party in New Jersey would never again be as unified under Christie.

UNLIKE NORCROSS AND Sweeney, DiVincenzo formally crossed party lines to give Christie an official, public endorsement. At the event the men were flanked by black elected Democrats along with Christian and Muslim religious leaders who were endorsing the governor.

And what did DiVincenzo get out of this? He was pretty blunt with me when I asked him at the time. If he stayed neutral in the governor's race and Christie won reelection, his Essex County would have had to "wait in the back of the line" for funding from the Christie administration. Unabashedly transactional, DiVincenzo said: "That's the way it should be."

"What am I supposed to do, die with the [Democratic] Party and screw eight hundred thousand of my constituents? No way."

At the beginning of their second gubernatorial debate Buono was asked about the defectors in her party. "Governor Christie represents the worst combination of bully and bossism, and that's what has motivated some of these Democrats to endorse him," she said. She slammed DiVincenzo as a corrupt political boss. "You're not interested in cleaning up the *Boardwalk Empire* of New Jersey bosses," she said to Christie, referencing the HBO show about Atlantic City organized crime, "you're just interested in getting their political endorsements, getting the backing of their political machine, and looking the other way."

Christie responded by defending Joe D. "Listen, let's be real direct about this. Joe DiVincenzo is sitting right there in the front row and I'm proud to have his endorsement and *you wish you did*," the governor said.

CHRISTIE'S OCTOBER SURPRISE came when he spoke to a Latino group and indicated he supported a measure providing in-state college tuition for immigrants living in the country without documentation. These were generally children brought to the U.S. at a young age who were allowed to attend free K–12 public schools but were then hit with out-of-state tuition—double the amount paid by their high school peers—if they went on to one of New Jersey's public colleges.

Christie's support of the so-called Dream Act was sudden. Just two years earlier he had said this about such tuition equality: "I can't favor that, because we need to have an immigration system where people follow the rules."

Now, Christie said times had changed, and after the election he fulfilled his promise and signed the bill (but vetoed a section that made such students eligible for additional financial aid).

Democrats accused him of pandering for last-minute Hispanic votes.

If that's what he was doing, it worked.

On the night before the election Christie held his last campaign rally in front of a raucous, largely Hispanic crowd of thousands outside City Hall in Union City, alongside his Democratic ally, Mayor Stack, and New Mexico governor Susana Martinez. A possible future running mate for Christie and hero for Latin American politicos, Martinez was the only outside surrogate whom Christie brought in during the entire campaign.

The rally had the feel of a successful coup, with huge posters of Mayor Stack's face and a banner the width of the street reading: "Union City Welcomes Governor Christie!"

"Union City, you have some of the most amazing diversity in the entire state. You care about each other," Christie said, jacketless in the early winter cold as Mary Pat and daughter Sarah huddled together in winter coats behind him. "You are an inspiration to me as governor, and I hope to inspire you for your votes tomorrow."

Christie had campaigned so much here that he once said: "There will be just one thing going through my mind when we win: 'Gracias, Union City.' "

In Union City, Christie would go from 20 percent of the vote in 2009 to 58 percent in 2013. And that helped him secure a majority of the Hispanic vote statewide—a major bragging point for his presidential campaign.

HUGE KLIEG SPOTLIGHTS visible from blocks around beckoned us into the historic Asbury Park Convention Hall, where Springsteen often performed. Tonight was Christie's victory party.

As the voting precincts closed, Christie sat down to a preparty dinner in a private room at an oceanfront Italian restaurant down the road from Convention Hall. The most important people in his political world were there—his innermost circle, his family, and his financiers (such as Ken Langone, founder of Home Depot, and Steve Cohen, whose hedge fund had pleaded guilty to insider trading a day earlier).

The election results came in—spectacular, really, with a win of 60.3 percent to Buono's 38.2 percent. He took nineteen of twenty-one counties. It was the strongest performance by a Republican in New Jersey since 1985. Exit polls showed that most women (57 percent), Hispanics (51 percent), and independent voters (66 percent) supported him. He won an impressive percentage of black voters (21 percent) and those ages eighteen to twenty-nine (49 percent). He seemed to have a Reaganesque appeal to the working class, winning 51 percent of the vote of those earning less than $50,000. Incredibly, he won 31 percent of liberals and 32 percent of Democrats.

Christie headed from dinner to Convention Hall, where he emerged onstage with his wife and kids as Stevie Wonder's "Signed, Sealed, Delivered I'm Yours" sounded overhead. There was an authentic energy from the crowd, as if this were a presidential campaign announcement, not just a gubernatorial victory party.

"How about this, New Jersey?" he yelled.

"You see, what people have never understood about us"—he pointed back and forth to the crowd—"is I didn't need an introduction to all of you. I know you, because I'm one of you."

He then went national. "If we can do this in Trenton, New Jersey, maybe the folks in Washington, D.C., should tune in their TVs right now!" Christie said. "I know that a dispirited America, angry with their dysfunctional government, looks to New Jersey to say: 'Is what I think really happening? Are people really coming together? Are we really—African Americans and

Hispanics, suburbanites and city dwellers, farmers and teachers—are we really all working together?' "

The rough-and-tumble politician was selling a message of harmony. He was a big guy who knew how to get people to sit down and shut up and compromise—just what Washington needed.

On Election Day my colleague interviewed a sixty-eight-year-old self-described left-wing liberal Democrat from South Jersey who voted for Christie because he worked with Democrats. "It's not like down in Washington," she said. "I think those people should be taken out and shot."

Those are the words of a Christie Democrat. Christie believed there were millions like her around America.

PART THREE

# THE BRIDGE

# 11

# "TIME FOR SOME TRAFFIC PROBLEMS IN FORT LEE"

R eelection won, the White House was next.

The first step was engineering a surprise coup to push away Louisiana governor Bobby Jindal and become chairman of the Republican Governors Association. The group acted as a pipeline, funneling millions of dollars from business and industry to establishment Republicans around the country. Without contributions from the RGA in his 2009 campaign, Christie believed he would never have been governor.

Now, he'd run the group as chairman for a year. The next twelve months were going to be critically important for Republicans, with thirty-six governors up for election. He would raise and dole out $130 million—winning friends and IOUs from the very people who finance and influence presidential campaigns. Plus, the gig came with perks (Christie likes perks)—free rides on private jets and meals with rich Republicans. What better way to spend the year before your presidential candidacy than by dining, gratis, with the very people who fund presidential candidacies? Christie would be in the right rooms with the right people who could help him when the time was right.

RGA Chairman Christie had broad discretion over staff, so his consultants back home who were running his New Jersey political operation got contracts with the group to help the governor maximize his new role.

In other words, the RGA helped Christie create a shadow presidential campaign. And no one complained. They were just happy that he'd be headlining their $5,000-a-plate fund-raisers in the coming year. Christie in November 2013 was the hottest draw in Republican politics.

Two weeks after winning reelection, Christie officially accepted the RGA chairmanship during a private meeting at a luxury resort in Arizona.

He had yet to be sworn in for a new gubernatorial term, but he just took another job.

A POLITICAL PROFESSIONAL named Bill Stepien roamed the gilded hallways at the resort that weekend. Stepien was an Alex P. Keaton wunderkind among New Jersey Republican operatives, known for winning, at barely the age of thirty, Christie's underdog 2009 gubernatorial campaign.

Now he had just been tapped as Christie's point man at the RGA—and the chairman of the New Jersey Republican Party. He'd be preparing the Christie presidential campaign while enforcing GOP obedience back home.

Small-statured and clean-cut, Stepien looked like a Republican. His ascension began at fifteen, when he worked at the Chimney Rock Ice Rink in Central Jersey and met a Rutgers kid named Mike DuHaime, who drove the Zamboni machine. Once Stepien got to Rutgers, DuHaime was his hockey coach. DuHaime went into politics and brought Stepien on as an intern for a state Senate campaign. Stepien then made his mark running a successful underdog campaign for Bill Baroni, a Republican assemblyman and state senator who would one day become deeply entangled in the Bridgegate affair.

Stepien and DuHaime were dubbed the "dynamic duo." They worked together on the 2008 presidential campaigns of New York City mayor Rudy Giuliani and then–Arizona senator John McCain. When they hooked up with the Christie for Governor campaign in 2009, DuHaime was the outside strategist while Stepien was the campaign manager on the inside. DuHaime's disposition was warm and welcoming; Stepien's was cold and cautious.

In the 2009 Christie campaign, Stepien was viewed as an elder statesman compared to the kids in their twenties with backward baseball caps who worked for him. He had an intensity—4:30 a.m. emails and doors shut on those who showed up at 8:31 a.m. for 8:30 a.m. meetings—that attracted a sort of respect beyond his years.

Sometimes, he just attracted resentment. In the waning weeks of the campaign Stepien called a meeting. "Nobody in this office is irreplaceable," he said, according to people in the room. "You're *all* replaceable. And there's a thousand other people who will step into your role for the last couple of weeks and do your job. So do your job."

This little chat dispirited the staff. "It was like a bomb went off," remembered one. "Nobody wanted to work. It was a hugely demotivational speech."

Stepien was described to me as a brilliant general and a loyal soldier. Once, a campaign worker committed a transgression. Years later that person remembered Stepien's reaction word for word: "Nobody's going to cause Chris Christie to lose what he's worked all his life for."

His nickname in the office was Smoke—now you see him, now you don't. His interactions with the press were limited to quietly standing on the sidelines at press conferences. When I ran into him at the 2012 Republican convention, we laughed about his unwillingness to talk to me, but even after a couple of beers I couldn't get him to tell me anything at all about the Christie political operation.

Clearly, Stepien had an innate understanding of the power levers of local politics. Sources told me he had the governor's trust, and his ear, known for being willing—and able—to voice dissent to the boss.

After the campaign Christie brought Stepien to the governor's office, where he named him deputy chief of staff. Briefly married and then divorced, he lived in an apartment attached to a mystery book store, close to the Statehouse, and by all indications worked constantly.

STEPIEN RAN THE governor's Legislative and Intergovernmental Affairs unit, known as IGA. Several former Christie campaign aides moved over to IGA, becoming the governor's political connections to the state.

In the opening days of the administration, regional directors within IGA contacted almost all of the state's 566 mayors and gave out their cell phone numbers. They did this for Democrats and Republicans. This was relationship building on a scale never before seen in the governor's office. They thought it was both good government and good politics.

So when a dam broke in a town at ten-thirty one night, an IGA staffer took that call from a mayor and deployed state government to help, immediately. And when veterans wanted the governor to issue an executive order to honor a New Jersey marine killed in action, IGA transmitted the message. During Sandy, Stepien created the "Sandy 5"—five regional IGA directors who worked with towns recovering from the storm.

Mayors weren't used to this kind of attention from Trenton.

All IGA wanted in exchange was support for Christie's policies. IGA was, in the words of one former staffer, "99 percent good government."

But the other 1 percent or so was politics.

Documents indicate that IGA employees did the kind of work that operatives do on political campaigns: identifying persuadable voters, seeking endorsements from elected officials, and analyzing election data. Much of this work was done during business hours, on the taxpayers' dime.

The IGA collected resumes from key political figures who sought gubernatorial appointments. With thousands of appointments at the governor's discretion Christie could secure support by making a simple nomination.

IGA maintained briefing books filled with election data and political strategy. The most important document, IGA's most confidential creation, was just a list. They called it the T100. At WNYC, we sued to get a copy of the T100. The judge ordered that it be turned over.

But Christie appealed, effectively delaying its release for years. That's how badly he wanted it kept secret. Sources told me that Stepien devised the list using a formula to determine the biggest increases in Republican votes from the 2005 gubernatorial race to Christie's 2009 gubernatorial race—the very towns where the vote margins had made Christie governor, made up of the very voters the governor needed to win reelection.

The T100 list was therefore used as a guide for selecting locations for Christie town hall meetings. To get the word out about the meetings, IGA officials made personal phone calls to invite key individuals, "on behalf of the governor." To find those people they consulted other lists, like the TK1 List of the one thousand most important people in those one hundred towns—local politicians, priests, high school football coaches, and the guy who owned the shoe store on Main Street for the last forty years. These were connectors, people who could vouch for the governor in their communities.

Once the invited guests arrived at the town hall meetings they were corralled backstage, behind the curtains, for meet-and-greet photo ops with the governor. Here Christie collected the kind of constituent complaints—*that field up the street? the one you passed on the way in? it really needs to be fixed, Gov*—that could create supporters on Election Day.

Stepien's IGA gave advance notice about the town hall meetings to local Republican groups, which kept the audiences extra friendly. The meetings were held during the week and during the day, which skewed the crowd older, more conservative, and teacher-free.

They packed in 300, 400, 500 New Jerseyans—once, more than 1,000 showed up—in school gymnasiums, church chapels, YMCAs, and senior citizen centers. Town halls were held at a shopping mall, inside a military aviation museum, and in the sunny atrium of an office building for an insurance company. Some were so crowded that spectators peeked through open windows.

At first Christie stood on a stage at the front of the room. It didn't work. Maria Comella, the communications chief, thought it looked as if Christie was looking down on the people. "I think you are going to have to take some chances," she advised him.

Christie moved to a theater-in-the-round format. From the rafters hung massive American and New Jersey flags alongside banners with aspirational messages like "THE JERSEY COMEBACK HAS BEGUN." Several hundred folding chairs encircled a single music stand, which served as a lectern holding a few sheets of notes.

Attendees showed up more than two hours before start time and signed in, providing important data to Team Christie. IGA operatives then fanned out to identify assorted VIPs, like military veterans, to sit in the front two rows.

And then Jim or Joe or Wells, one of the guys from the advance team, went in front of the curtain and grabbed the microphone. They welcomed everyone to the event. They pointed to the fire exits. And then they used the same line, every time.

"Does anybody have any questions?"

Silence.

"Nobody ever does."

Laughter.

Cue the music—Springsteen or Bon Jovi, obviously—and the wrestling match–style announcement: "Ladies and gentlemen, please welcome the governor of the great state of New Jersey, Chris Christie!"

Christie took a few deep breaths behind the curtain before revealing himself. "All right, all right!" he'd say. "Thank you!"

He often began with a personal story, about picking up his dry cleaning on Saturdays—yes, he still does that, but now three state troopers and two black Chevy Suburbans accompany him. He moved on to sell whatever policy he was pushing. And he just annihilated random Democrats along the way.

After twenty or thirty minutes or so, "the fun part"—the question-and-answer period—began with a recitation of "The Rules." That spiel, four and a half minutes long, included: Don't yell out questions. ("And it's not because I'm governor! It's because I'm a father! And that means I am highly trained at ignoring people who are yelling at me.")

Then Christie ripped off his suit jacket—they loved this part—and tossed it to an aide, who suddenly appeared fifteen feet away to catch it.

"All right, it's time to work, it's time to work," he'd say, opening the first of two water bottles, tearing off the cap. "For those of you who have seen some of my appearances on YouTube—this is when it normally happens. This could happen right here, ladies and gentlemen! . . . Get ready! If you have your own cameras, start rolling!"

Yet confrontations during the Q&A sessions didn't happen that often. Most town halls were Christie love fests. "Gov, you're doing a great job," they'd say, or "I want to take this moment to say two words to you, and that is 'thank you.' "

The governor waxed nostalgic about the halcyon days when middle-class families could have enough to spend a week down the Jersey Shore *and* save for retirement. "We talk about these problems in our house," he said. He spoke, dreadfully, about becoming an "airplane grandparent."

"You want to be able to get in your car and drive to the Little League or the spring concert or the one-year-old birthday party around the kitchen table," he said. "Those are the events that make life meaningful."

BY THE BEGINNING of his fourth year in office more than thirty thousand voters had attended town hall meetings and heard these stories, with eleven hundred people asking questions, yielding 168 YouTube videos of Christie's best bits, which in turn built bigger crowds. Each town hall came with suspense, because you never knew when a YouTube moment could happen.

In the beginning, Christie's staffers shot video of the meetings on flip cameras so Christie could watch them later and see how he did. Then, after posting a video of the governor fighting with an art teacher, Team Christie realized the power of posting video. Christie hired an extensive team to staff town halls, including videographers and a guy with a stage management degree to set up professional lighting that made him look approachable but in charge.

At a town hall meeting in Hopatcong, a woman stood up and told the governor that because of his policies, she thought he was "hot and sexy."

"Comments like those after twenty-five years will keep [Mary Pat] on her toes!" Christie quipped.

Afterwards, I asked the woman, a lawyer, what she liked about the governor. "I was amazed by how quick he is on responses and how engaging and funny he is," she told me. "I just see a guy that's smart and not afraid to stand for what he believes in. That's so refreshing with politicians."

Christie won supporters every time he stepped out in front of a town hall crowd.

IGA then had to turn that support into a reelection win.

> *CODE OF CONDUCT FOR EMPLOYEES OF*
> *THE OFFICE OF THE GOVERNOR*
> *(H) CAMPAIGN WORK*
> *(1) An employee shall not engage in campaign work on State time. "Campaign work" is work that both:*
> *(a) does not reasonably and primarily fulfill the employee's official duties; and*
> *(b) materially contributes to a person's chance of election or reelection to public office or the prospects of a candidate.*

When an IGA staffer raised concerns about whether it was legal for tax-funded IGA workers to work on Christie's reelection, Stepien brought the issue to the attention of Christie's deputy chief counsel. It was decided that IGA staffers could work on the campaign and seek endorsements, but only after work hours.

And yet during regular business hours and using government resources, IGA staffers identified elected officials who would work "for us"—for the governor's reelection campaign.

One young IGA staffer, Matt Mowers, was Christie's point person for 183 municipalities and as many as six counties. He had a clean reputation and an easygoing charm that belied an aggressive style that would one day land him a plum gig running Christie's New Hampshire presidential campaign operation.

A disciple of Stepien's who worked for Kelly, Mowers wrote official governmental memos with sections entitled "Political Narrative." Here, he downloaded the political intel that he picked up from working the phones and attending political dinners. He found out who was running in the next elections, who was on Christie's side, and whether the local GOP was unified or "scattershot." He carried the message that a Republican Party boss wanted to talk about an appointment on the county tax board and he noted that the Hudson County Republican chairman was quitting smoking.

Information was political power, which led to Christie's reelection, which led to the White House. The IGA took the long view.

Twenty months before Christie's reelection, Mowers delivered the good news that a congressional candidate in Bayonne "will likely enable us to keep the volunteer infrastructure intact for the reelection campaign."

Democratic endorsements were particularly coveted, because they would help Christie win over voters in this overly blue state—and create a bipartisan sheen going into the 2016 presidential race.

After efforts by the IGA failed to secure the endorsement of Democratic Hoboken mayor Dawn Zimmer, Stepien bemoaned having been "kissing her ass" for nothing. And so the message came down through IGA: "Do not bend over backward for the mayor, and do not rush to return phone calls."

ONE WAY OF kissing ass was to provide artifacts from the place where 2,753 Americans died on September 11, 2001: Ground Zero in Lower Manhattan.

Through Christie political appointees at the Port Authority, the IGA collected shards of steel that had burned when the World Trade Center's twin towers exploded into fire. They also gathered American flags that had flown over Ground Zero during a ceremony for the tenth anniversary of the attacks.

The steel and flags were then distributed to New Jersey mayors. Like Trojan Horses, they provided a way in. After Mowers dropped off a flag with Mayor Peter Massa of North Arlington, the men took a walk through the tiny borough's downtown. Massa showed Mowers the Catholic school he had attended. Then the conversation turned political. Mowers reported back to Trenton what he learned about the target: "While he is older now, and seemingly less political, I think there may be a chance we can win his endorsement next year . . . ."

This was no casual operation. More than fifty World Trade Center flags were distributed. All came with letters from the governor. According to IGA memos the head of the Garfield Veterans of Foreign Wars group was "very excited that they could receive such a rare gift," unaware that the gift was not rare at all. The Teaneck mayor had a picture taken of the flag presentation in order "to improve his image as someone with connections through the state," Mowers told his bosses. In Bergen County, "County Executive Donovan was thrilled (literally gasped when she saw it) to be presented with the flag," while the mayor of Fair Lawn "could hardly contain herself with excitement . . . she will be sure to make a big issue out of it at the next council meeting, noting that the governor has shown continued care and commitment to Fair Lawn and that this is just the latest example."

Mowers later explained that the flags were given out, as far as he understood, "to municipalities that had an undue, a large loss of life." But I read the grim list of hometowns of victims of the September 11 attacks and I found that even towns with as few as one death received a flag.

The flags may have been meaningful, but they were also a way for Christie operatives to get into towns and do some old-fashioned politicking.

In a similar vein Christie's appointees at the Port Authority opened Ground Zero for private tours for political allies like mayors and administrative officials. One source at the Port Authority acknowledged to me: "They leveraged 9/11 to the max."

BUT CHRISTIE OFFICIALS didn't just offer carrots. They maintained a constantly changing list of hands-off mayors. "No need to call to check in" on that mayor, they'd write. Messages were being sent. And even the IGA staffers didn't always know why.

Christie didn't invent this move, one longtime operative explained to me, he just perfected it.

Months into his term, the Republican mayor of the eighty-nine-hundred-person town of North Haledon had the gall to tell a weekly newspaper reporter that Christie should "calm down a bit" with all of his budget cutting. The mayor's IGA contact immediately called to tell him that going to the papers with complaints is not proper protocol; instead, if you have an issue, contact your rep at IGA. "No one tells the governor to calm down," the IGA rep told the mayor. "Be a team player."

Hardly an elected New Jersey Republican spoke a negative on-the-record word about the governor for his entire first term. Legislators felt IGA operatives breathing behind them on the Senate and Assembly floors as they voted on bills. The IGA was allowed into lawmakers' caucus rooms to monitor who was saying what about whatever piece of legislation. Transgressions were aggressively handled. "This guy doesn't forget," they whispered about Christie.

One assemblyman told me that a lawyer from the governor's office, backed by a Republican senator, threatened to take away Christie's support in his next election if he didn't change his vote on an amendment. It didn't matter that the amendment had failed and the vote was inconsequential. Any hint of deviation from the governor had to be squashed.

This was no longer the Republican Party; this was the Christie Party.

"He came in and people thought he was going to be the leader of the party," one GOP politician griped to me. "But it's been about him since Day One."

With governmental functions closely integrated with political objectives, Christie ran a quasi-campaign throughout his time as governor. Reform Jersey Now, a group headed by Christie's allies and backed by construction companies, engineers, and law firms that had contracts with the state, aired pro-Christie radio ads five months into his term. Later his college buddies, through the Committee for Our Children's Future, put up TV ads praising his bipartisanship.

IN EARLY 2013, just after Christie announced his reelection, it was time to cash in and get some Democrats to commit to endorsing. Stepien wrote, with a flourish: "Let's go fishing and see what we get."

One of the towns where an endorsement was sought was a place in northern New Jersey called Fort Lee, a 2.8-square-mile borough best known as the town that straddles the New Jersey entrance to the George Washington Bridge, and less known as the site of an encampment during the Revolutionary War named for General Charles Lee, a rival to George Washington and a traitor who leaked military information to the British.

Fort Lee was number forty-five on the T100 list, but its importance was even more pronounced because its population was more than a third of Asian ethnicity—and Asian Americans were a demographic Team Christie targeted for votes. So, in Christie's first term, Democratic Fort Lee mayor Mark Sokolich got the IGA treatment.

IGA invited Sokolich to two holiday parties at Drumthwacket, plus a private lunch (beef tenderloin in cream sauce was served) to discuss capping property taxes. "It's not often you have a captive audience with the governor," Sokolich later remembered. "I was impressed. He was very focused."

Sokolich was also aggressively courted by the IGA's associates at the Port Authority, which ran the bridge that loomed in town. The Port Authority repaired Fort Lee potholes for the mayor and provided emergency radios to the local police. And a mysterious Christie appointee at the Port Authority named David Wildstein gave Sokolich and his cousins from Croatia a personal tour of the 9/11 Memorial Plaza at Ground Zero before it was open to the public.

"I was told to be nice to you," Wildstein told him at the time, over and over again.

Fort Lee received eleven Ground Zero artifacts, more than any other town in New Jersey. "You have no idea how much these kinds of things mean to us," Sokolich told his contact at IGA.

After Christie personally signed off on a $162,000 shuttle service to take Fort Lee residents to the Hudson River ferries in Edgewater, Stepien wanted to make sure Christie got credit from Sokolich. "We approved this months ago," he wrote to Mowers, who was in charge of Sokolich's endorsement. "Hope he remembers."

"I'll be sure to remind him when we speak later," Mowers replied.

When it came time to finally nailing down Sokolich's endorsements, Mowers visited Fort Lee. Saying most of the conversation with the mayor was about state business, he billed the travel to New Jersey—it was $9.40. But he filed an official government report about the endorsement "target," writing of "next steps": *Continue developing the relationship as we have and reapproach at a later date.*

That he did. At least three times Mowers brought up the endorsement with Sokolich, mentioning other Democrats who had joined the team, and asking, "What do you think?"

But the mayor wouldn't agree to sign the endorsement form. And by March of 2013, Mowers thought the mayor was a lost cause. "It's a shame, too—I really like the guy," Mowers wrote to a colleague.

One reason Sokolich was reluctant to endorse? The governor hadn't shown up to a recent groundbreaking ceremony for a redevelopment project in town.

After all they had given Sokolich. After more attention than just about any other mayor in the whole state of New Jersey. But it wasn't enough.

On the day of that Fort Lee groundbreaking Christie was in Wisconsin, campaigning for the Republican governor there. If only he had been home that day, if only he hadn't been preoccupied with his post–New Jersey political career, if only he had given Sokolich a little more attention . . .

BRIDGET ANNE KELLY came up in New Jersey Republican politics. She worked for local legislators and ran phone banks for Christie's 2009 campaign, becoming a key hire for Christie as his legislative director in the IGA, handling all contact with Assembly members and senators.

Kelly presented well in dealing with bosses and Democrats. Assembly Speaker Sheila Oliver, a Democrat, called her "a breath of fresh air." When her coworkers wrote down a list of her positive attributes for a team-building exercise, Kelly was described as a "creative problem solver" and "always willing to jump into a burning issue." She was a "very reliable" and "hard-working" manager with "great political relationships" who "knows how to laugh and not freak out when things go wrong." She was called "ultra-dedicated and loyal," and "the truest team player."

"Always asks the tough questions and keeps out of trouble," the memo said.

But at least some of her employees saw a different side. As a manager she was concerned about being outshined by those below her, and she could get angry without warning. "You never knew who you were going to get with her," said one former employee. She was accused of playing favorites, with a crew of loyal young staffers who wore bow ties on Fridays that matched the preppiness of her smart suits and pearls.

Kelly had a toughness that helped her fit in with Team Christie. During intense legislative votes, Kelly was seen on the floor of the legislature, keeping score on her BlackBerry. She coordinated which VIPs could sit in the governor's box at sporting events, and she stored in her office the flags from Ground Zero that would later be used as political gifts.

But Kelly was not a part of the epicenter of power. She was a degree separated, seen as more of a Stepien protégée.

Kelly was going through a divorce during the first term. As a single mother with four kids, commuting ninety minutes each way to the State-house became a strain, and Stepien allowed Kelly to spend time out of the office tending to family matters.

After Stepien left IGA in early 2013 to run the reelection campaign, she was promoted to his position—deputy chief of staff overseeing IGA. It was about this time that Kelly and Stepien are believed to have started dating.

The details of their personal relationship were as secret as their T100 list, but coworkers noticed the flirtation for some time. He was her boss, but he gave her more leeway than others, and they *looked* like a couple— a handsome pair of blond Republicans out of central casting.

They worked long hours together, communicating constantly via BlackBerry Messenger. At the daily 9:00 a.m. IGA meetings they seemed to be most sympatico, professionally and personally. Colleagues thought Kelly viewed Stepien as a political god, "falling in line with whatever he wanted without question," while Stepien empowered Kelly beyond her station.

Kelly confided to a colleague that they spent a few weekends together that spring.

**THE GOVERNOR'S LAWYERS** later claimed the relationship ended in August 2013, just before a fateful phone call was made.

On August 12, 2013, Mowers was at a coffee shop across from Jersey City's City Hall. He had recently joined the reelection campaign, and he was spending the afternoon courting a Democratic city council member's endorsement when his old boss back at the Statehouse, Kelly, called. She had a question.

"Is Mayor Sokolich endorsing?"

"No," Mowers said, "he's not."

"He's definitely not endorsing, right? Not going to happen?"

"No, not going to happen. From everything I know, the door's shut; like, not going to happen."

"Okay. That's all I need to know."

*Click.*

**THE NEXT DAY** at 7:34 a.m., Kelly sent the following email to David Wildstein, that mysterious appointee at the Port Authority who had once given Mayor Sokolich's family a tour of Ground Zero:

*Time for some traffic problems in Fort Lee.*

One minute later, Wildstein wrote back to Kelly:

*Got it.*

# 12

# A BRIDGEGATE TIMELINE

H ere's how the 123 days that changed Chris Christie's life unfolded.

### FRIDAY, SEPTEMBER 6, 2013

Happy fifty-first birthday, Gov.

To mark this occasion Christie's communications staff releases a video that compiles clips of his most famous put-downs (three *idiots*, five *stupids*, one *dope*) and his best out-of-context sound bites from the podium ("I look like Tony Soprano, for godsakes"). This happy birthday ditty to the governor, built to go viral, is another chance for his tax-funded staff to show off his gubernatorial personality two months before Election Day. Just *Christie being Christie*.

As that YouTube video flickers on screens in the Garden State and beyond, at the headquarters of the Port Authority, an official named David Wildstein is cooking something up.

Wildstein landed a $150,000-a-year Port Authority job as director of capital projects without submitting a resume. He didn't have to—he went to high school with the governor and he built close friendships with Christie advisor Bill Stepien and Port Authority executive Bill Baroni from his years as a Republican operative and anonymous blogger at a New Jersey political news site he created, PoliticsNJ.com.

Wildstein brings his encyclopedic knowledge of New Jersey politics and his knack for the political dark arts to the Port Authority. He has helped Christie secure key reelection endorsements from the Port Authority unions, distribute flags to allied mayors, and organize Ground Zero tours for Christie endorsement targets. Wildstein acts as Christie's eyes and ears at agency headquarters, arriving at 6:30 a.m. each day and giving the impression to other employees that he is spying on them.

On this day, Wildstein is on the phone with Bob Durando, the manager of the George Washington Bridge. Durando has been at the Port Authority, which runs the busiest bridge in the world, for thirty-five years. But he has never gotten a call like this.

Those three local access lanes from Fort Lee, Wildstein orders Durando, reduce them to one lane, effective 6:00 a.m. Monday. All traffic from Fort Lee, everything coming from Martha Washington Way and Bruce Reynolds Boulevard, must be funneled into a single-file line to Toll Lane #24 and onto the bridge. The lane will accept both cash and E-ZPass. Most important, Wildstein tells Durando, do not notify officials in Fort Lee about this. This is for a traffic study.

Durando—once described as "loving that bridge as if it were his baby"—finds this request peculiar. Traffic studies require months of planning and approvals. There are official Port Authority traffic study procedures, and they don't allow for unannounced, intentional disruptions on the roadways. Traffic studies do not involve moving cones and changing the flow of traffic. Instead, workers count cars, cameras capture traffic patterns, and helicopters observe from above.

If cones are moved on the roadway it's because of construction, probably, not a traffic study. And the lead time for such a project is *years*. Not a weekend.

Durando warns Wildstein of "severe traffic consequences." But Wildstein is a big muckety-muck at the Port Authority—he is known to have regular and direct contact with the governor's office—so Durando does as he's told.

Durando calls for an emergency briefing. He directs the maintenance guys to go out and cover the traffic signs in Fort Lee that point to the lanes before the Monday-morning rush hour. He calls in an additional toll booth operator on overtime in case the lone operator at the local lane needs to go to the bathroom. And he tells a Port Authority Police Department commander to bring on extra officers to handle the inevitable traffic.

Is this a permanent change?

Durando has no answers to that or any questions about why, exactly, this is happening.

Last week Wildstein had told the traffic engineers to work up some scenarios for a study on reducing traffic at the bridge. They took it seriously, compiling hour-by-hour data and presenting four different options. Now, word comes down that Wildstein is choosing the most radical of the four: reducing three lanes to one. The plan is a go for Monday.

Mark Muriello, the assistant director of the Tunnels, Bridges, and Terminals Department, alerts his staff in a group email.

Everyone is very confused.

"There are likely to be increased delays and queuing on the local approach," Muriello writes. For extra guidance he adds Gerald Quelch from planning and operations on the email, even though Quelch is vacationing in Florida. "Jerry—I bet Florida is looking a whole lot better now!"

"What is driving this?" wonders one staffer.

"That is my question as well," responds Jerry. "A single toll operation invites potential disaster." He adds: "It seems like we are punishing all for the sake of a few. Very confused."

At the Port Authority Police Department, Deputy Inspector Darcy Licorish agrees. He memorializes the bizarre traffic order in an email to top police brass:

> *On this date the undersigned was informed by the general manager Robert Durando that he was instructed by Wildstein to change the traffic pattern entering upper toll plaza specifically involving toll lanes 20, 22 and 24. . . . This measure could impact the volume of traffic from the local streets.*

The bridge was birthed by an early-twentieth-century traffic study. New Jersey governor George Sebastian Silzer needed to sell his bridge idea to the Port Authority, which at the time was only in the business of railways. To make his case Silzer enlisted a Swiss engineer, O. H. Ammann, to study how a grand span across the Hudson River from the borough of Fort Lee to 178th Street in Upper Manhattan might work. He wrote a report that looked at engineering, financing, and, yes, traffic patterns. The concept won an important victory with an endorsement from the Bergen *Record*, and in 1925 the Port Authority commissioned Ammann to build the bridge.

Named for the Revolutionary War hero who spent more time in New Jersey than any other state, the George Washington Bridge was built mostly by Mohawk Indians who earned a whopping eight dollars an hour. It comprises thirty-five hundred feet of concrete and enough steel wire to wrap around the world four times. Viewed from Manhattan, the bridge's twin 604-foot towers dramatically jut into the skyline.

On October 25, 1931, at 5:00 a.m., the George Washington Bridge opened eight months ahead of schedule and $1 million under budget. It was the rare public works project that at the time of its grand opening actually exceeded the already lofty promises from politicians. On that first day, fifty thousand vehicles and one guy on a horse crossed from the borough of Fort Lee to Upper Manhattan, six hundred feet over the choppy Hudson River.

In 1962, a week before Christie was born, a second level was added to the bridge, and by the turn of the next century about 50 million vehicles would traverse it annually.

CEDRICK FULTON, THE director of the Tunnels, Bridges, and Terminals Department at the Port Authority, is on his way to work when Wildstein calls him on his cell and tells him the plan: We're closing the lanes on Monday.

Fulton had heard Wildstein talk about this lane issue before. Wildstein was always asking: "What about the three lanes? How long have the three lanes been in effect?"

Always, Fulton would say. He'd been there twenty years. As long as he had ever known.

If you're going to mess with this, Fulton tells Wildstein, notify the media relations team. And definitely give a heads-up to the town of Fort Lee. "Typically we notify our hosts—neighbors—when we are doing something different," he says.

"We will take care of it," Wildstein replies.

Fulton asks if Patrick Foye, the executive director of the Port Authority— the top guy at the agency—is aware of this.

"Don't worry about that," Wildstein says. "We will take care of it." This is a New Jersey issue, Wildstein explains. Foye may be the executive director, but he is an appointee of the New York governor, and the Christie guys don't answer to him.

Wildstein tells colleagues he has a "constituency of one"—the governor. The leadership of the bi-state agency is split between representatives of New York and New Jersey, and Wildstein revels in the rivalry. No one trusts anyone.

When he founded PoliticsNJ.com, he trafficked in political gossip, and

Wildstein still loves to dish. He once contacted a Christie staffer who was on maternity leave to tell her about "fireworks" between New York and New Jersey—he just wanted someone "to appreciate the drama."

Publicly, though, Wildstein is quiet about his activities. "I don't do anything publicly," he once told a reporter. At PoliticsNJ.com, Wildstein was so anonymous his own employees didn't know his name. He communicated with sources almost entirely through AOL Instant Messenger instead of by phone, so even his best sources never knew who he really was.

He took a nom de guerre for his byline—Wally Edge. That was the name of an Atlantic City newspaper publisher who dominated New Jersey politics in the early twentieth century, serving as governor (two terms, twenty-five years apart), U.S. senator, and ambassador to France.

Edge also played a critical role in creating the Port Authority.

Now, a different Edge seeks to have a similar impact.

**AFTER FULTON GETS** off the phone with Wildstein, he still feels uneasy. So he calls back to ask more about the plan. Fulton repeats: Foye should be notified.

Wildstein is through. "Go silent on Fort Lee," he instructs.

"This will not end well," Fulton responds.


### SEPTEMBER 7, SATURDAY

Wildstein vows to keep Bridget Anne Kelly over at the governor's office in the loop about the operation. They had first gotten to know each other when Wildstein was still Wally Edge and Kelly was a young operative in Bergen County.

"I will call you Monday a.m. to let you know how Fort Lee goes," he emails her.

"Great," she responds.


### SEPTEMBER 8, SUNDAY

Tonight the Dallas Cowboys are hosting the New York Giants, and the governor of New Jersey is there to cheer on the team from Texas rather than the one that plays in his home state. Christie walks into the $1.3 billion AT&T Stadium—the largest domed stadium in the world—and he experiences a moment that young Christie could have never dreamed of. Here he is, accompanied by big-shot Texas Republican Ray Washburne, who would one day be the finance chairman of his presidential campaign; Reince Priebus, the chairman of the Republican National Committee; Roger Goodell, the commissioner of the National Football League; and—and!—the famous owner of his favorite team, Jerry Jones. Rocking a blue shirt and a sport jacket with a red, white, and blue pin shaped like New Jersey, Christie sits right next to Jones himself.

The Cowboys go on to beat a turnover-prone Giants team 36–31 after quarterback Tony Romo heroically returns to the field despite a shot to the ribs. It's the Cowboys' first win against the Giants in their new stadium.

Does being governor get any better than this?

The next day Christie will headline three fund-raisers in three Texas cities, including one at a Houston mansion owned by a Texas oilman who last year gave presidential nominee Mitt Romney $1 million. Christie is being a good soldier in raising some cash for the national Republican Party, but he's also using these events to make connections for his inevitable 2016 presidential run.

There's a reelection campaign to be run at home, sure, and local New Jersey Republicans are desperate for cash and attention from their governor. There's a state government that needs attention, of course, and a Sandy storm recovery to oversee. But that can wait. He'll be back soon enough.

Years later, one could look at this trip to Texas as a big-shot American Republican—free Cowboys games and fancy meals and private jets—and see it as the moment when hubris takes over and New Jersey is forsaken for ambition.

Perhaps the governor just isn't paying as much attention as he once did. Because, back in New Jersey, Wildstein is setting a fuse that will soon light Christie's political career on fire.

### SEPTEMBER 9, DAY 1 OF THE LANE CLOSURES

The Monday morning roll call begins for the Port Authority police officers who handle traffic at the George Washington Bridge.

There is a new traffic pattern, the commanding officer says, for some sort of a traffic study.

That means a few things, he says. The officer at Post #10—which monitors Fort Lee's three access lanes—is reassigned to regulating traffic. And, everyone, regardless of what happens, listen: "Do not move the cones."

OFFICER JIM CRONIN, a fourteen-year veteran of the Port Authority police, walks out to the bridge and immediately realizes that this is not going to be a normal rush hour. Cones along the southernmost approach to the bridge are effectively diverting two toll booths away from the Fort Lee entrance. Cronin also notices something weird—the cones are jammed together, touching one another, when normally they are a few feet apart.

Whoever wants these lanes closed wants them *very* closed.

With the new cones in place, at 6:00 a.m. sharp, the traffic study begins.

THERE ARE TWENTY-NINE lanes on both levels of the George Washington Bridge. It's $14 to New York—$11 with an E-ZPass tag. Truckers can pay as much as $102, depending on the number of axles on their vehicles.

The GWB is a vital thoroughfare not just to New York but also to the entire northeastern corridor of the country. A nexus of New Jersey highways converges at the bridge, but commuters also come via local Fort Lee roads—as many as sixteen thousand vehicles clogging Palisade Avenue and ten thousand others on Center Avenue each morning. Their cars carry residents from not just Fort Lee but also Edgewater, Cliffside Park, and Leonia.

Bridge commuters often paralyze the town. Frustrated by the traffic coming from other towns to use the bridge lanes, Fort Lee mayor Mark Sokolich once tried to close the municipal borders by shutting down parts of Fort Lee Road. The town of Leonia successfully filed suit over that plan.

So, early in Christie's term Sokolich wrote to Bill Baroni, Christie's top staffer at the Port Authority, begging him to address the "unbearable" traffic that is "holding our residents hostage" and causing an imminent "state of emergency." He said at one point, in twenty out of the previous forty days, the borough had experienced "complete gridlock"—it took an hour to go from one end of the 2.54-square-mile town to the other. Sokolich said when he takes his kids to Fort Lee High School, he is immobilized at Lemoine Avenue and Bridge Plaza South for a full thirty minutes.

Sokolich even threatened to shut off access to the bridge if Christie's people at the Port Authority didn't help him with this: "This is an action that

I would rather not take; however, we find ourselves with no other alternative."

In issuing that threat, Sokolich revealed that his greatest vulnerability as mayor was traffic.

This fact would not be forgotten.

ACROSS FORT LEE, four thousand schoolchildren zip up brand-new backpacks. Moms and dads wet their fingers to push down cowlicks and they wipe Cheerioed milk off lips before hustling the kids off to carpools and bus stops.

It is the first Monday after Labor Day. The first day of school.

Some five-year-olds have talked all summer about this moment, happily steeling themselves for their inaugural voyages on big yellow buses that will deliver them to kindergarten. By 7:00 a.m. those buses are on their routes in Fort Lee.

But this is not the same first day of school that everyone else in New Jersey is having.

The buses get stuck in gridlock amid stopped Hondas and Chevys carrying moms and dads to cubicle farms across North Jersey and Manhattan. Those brand-new kindergarteners are on the big yellow machines for what feels to them like an eternity. Students all the way up to Fort Lee High School are in the same jam—at this rate, they won't get to school until third period. Teachers districtwide are late to work.

The 911 call center gets a hint that this is no normal morning at 7:29 a.m., less than ninety minutes after the traffic study order is executed. An elderly woman at a nursing home has fallen, cutting her face. Someone from the nursing home had called 911 more than an hour earlier, but an ambulance hadn't shown up.

"Have the medics been notified?" asks the desperate caller.

Yes. But the ambulances are in traffic, just like everyone else.

EVERY SINGLE ONE of the arteries in Fort Lee is now clogged. A police supervisor orders twenty traffic cones to close off a road that leads to the bridge entrance. There's just too much gridlock.

Police officers are reassigned from their normal posts to traffic duty. The officers farther away from the bridge keep alerting those cops near the lanes that they need "a pull"—code for pulling vehicles through an intersection to avoid blocking the box.

"Can I get a pull on BRB?" one officer asks, referring to Bruce Reynolds Boulevard. "I got people here that been twenty minutes that haven't moved."

"We'd pull 'em but we got nowhere to pull 'em to," an officer responds.

**"FORT LEE TRAFFIC** is a nightmare!" a first responder says on his radio.

"Ten-four," the dispatcher responds. "We're getting calls from irate motorists."

A dispatcher then gives a police officer two explanations for what's happening. "They're testing a new pattern, traffic, from Martha Washington. It's down to one lane now," the dispatcher says. "And sun glare, also."

On this perfect seventy-degree fall day, sun glare is seen as an obvious culprit. What else but an act of God could cause this much widespread mayhem?

**ABOUT 8:00 A.M.,** Florence Genova goes to the bathroom before breakfast. She has lived in her modest brick home at 800 Harvard Place in Fort Lee for fifty years, since emigrating from Italy. She is ninety-one now—although she has kept her age a secret from everyone, even her family.

Her daughter, Vilma Oleri, arrives at the house. But Genova is still in the bathroom. Something is wrong. Oleri calls 911.

Seven minutes later, an EMS crew arrives to find Genova has suffered cardiac arrest. She can't be revived. Paramedics, better equipped to handle such a situation, are on their way from Englewood Hospital but they are stuck in traffic on Fort Lee Road. So the EMTs load Genova onto an ambulance and they meet up with the paramedics en route to the hospital.

Genova dies. Oleri says the emergency response time—it took three minutes longer than it would have under normal traffic conditions—is not to blame.

"I honestly believe it was just her time," Oleri says.

**AT 8:42 A.M.,** an EMS crew is dispatched to Brinkerhoff Avenue and Juanita Place for a car accident with injuries. But the emergency crew is back at Linwood Plaza, on the *other* side of the entrance to the George Washington Bridge. It can't get through. EMS coordinator Paul Favia steers an ambulance over a curb to avoid Fletcher Avenue. Four people with injuries need transport to hospitals.

At 8:49 a.m., a call comes into 911 from 2143 Hudson Terrace. A forty-five-year-old man is complaining of chest pains. "We'll do our best," says the dispatcher. As the man sits on his couch, waiting, an emergency crew sits in traffic at Bridge Plaza South, waiting.

At 9:44 a.m., a dispatcher gives an address to an EMS driver for another emergency. "You are aware that the town is in total gridlock, correct?" the driver asks.

Back-up emergency crews from the nearby towns can't help. There's no way to even get into Fort Lee.

WILDSTEIN IS AT the Port Authority's communications desk for a while, checking on the feeds from the cameras that look over the roadways to see how things are going. But that's not enough—he wants a closer view. He grabs Chip, and they go for a ride.

Port Authority police lieutenant Thomas "Chip" Michaels found out about the lane closures the day before and was concerned enough to email his boss: "Will this affect our normal rush hour operations?"

Yes, the police supervisor responded. We complained, but there is nothing we can do.

Like Wildstein and Christie, Chip is from Livingston. Growing up, Chip was friends with the Christies and is now awed by the governor's rise to fame. "We break his chops a little bit, just saying, 'You're the governor?' It's crazy," he once told the *Star-Ledger*.

Chip follows the chain of command and doesn't push back anymore on the lane closures. Wildstein, after all, is an emissary to the gov. Instead Chip acts as Wildstein's personal cop, taking Wildstein on a ride to see how the traffic looks at the bridge. They meet up with Licorish, the top bridge police commander, who says the traffic is "horrendous" and "tremendously backed up."

"Don't look too bad," Wildstein replies.

Wildstein and Michaels go to a diner to talk politics. Thousands of commuters are having their lives temporarily halted, but here the number-three official at the agency responsible is sitting at a diner with a ranking officer in the bridge's police force talking about . . . Chris Christie's prospects as a presidential candidate.

Wildstein looks beyond New Jersey and Christie's inevitable reelection victory in two months. He envisions working on a Christie campaign, possibly in the early primary state of New Hampshire.

After breakfast, Michaels continues to send Wildstein periodic status updates on the traffic. At one point, he sums it up like this: "Fort Lee traffic disaster."

AT 9:20 A.M., a Port Authority official contacts Baroni, the top New Jersey guy at the agency. The subject line says it all: *phone call: Mayor Sokolich . . . re: urgent matter of public safety in Fort Lee.*

Baroni doesn't respond. Instead, he forwards the email to Wildstein, who instructs, simply: "radio silence."

AT 9:51 A.M., a commanding police officer asks a patrolman: "How's the traffic condition right now?"

"Complete disaster, sir," comes the response.

AT 11:24 A.M., Baroni gets an email. The Fort Lee borough administrator is concerned about the traffic because the borough's cops and EMS had trouble responding to calls about a missing child and a case of cardiac arrest. We had no advance notice about the change in traffic, the borough administrator says.

Baroni does not respond.

Radio silence.

TRAFFIC SEEMS TO break up, finally, about 11:30 a.m., five and a half hours after the cones were moved. Durando, the bridge's general manager, views the whole thing as a sham. He tells his staff he just had a tense conversation with the chief of the Fort Lee police about the traffic study, or "test." "Their characterization was that the 'test' was a monumental failure," Durando emails his colleagues. "Fort Lee is not happy."

Port Authority staffers want the test, whatever it is, shut down. They tell Wildstein, but Wildstein isn't budging. So Durando asks him: How long is this going to last?

"One day does not make a test," Wildstein says. "People make adjustments." He wants to continue the study—he won't say for how long—"to see if people's travel patterns change."

BUT HOW MANY travel options do commuters have in the most congested few square miles in the nation? This gridlock means a Fort Lee councilwoman can't get to New York to be at her husband's side while he gets a stem cell transplant, and it means that it takes the superintendent of Fort Lee schools forty-five minutes to drive the last 1.5 miles to his office.

Boredom sets in. And thirst. They flip radio stations. Make cell phone calls. Stare at the people in the cars all around. Worry about running out of gas, about getting to the drugstore to pick up prescriptions, about getting home to walk the dog. Everyone is late, and many people have to go to the bathroom.

The life disruptions are innumerable. There's James from Manhattan doing elder care for a parent in Fort Lee, restaurant shift workers who must arrive on time to avoid termination, taxi drivers who can't make a day's wages sitting in traffic.

And what about the ambulances?

These concerns swirl as Durando, increasingly desperate to protect the bridge he is in charge of, tries an act of subterfuge. He asks the Fort Lee police chief, Keith Bendul, to meet him in the parking lot of the Port Authority building at the bridge—but don't tell anyone and don't come inside the building under any circumstances. If you tell anyone we met, Durando says, I'll deny it.

Chief Bendul thinks this is bizarre, but they rendezvous anyway.

At the meeting Durando advises Bendul that in order to get the lanes reopened, he should instruct Mayor Sokolich to complain to the top New Jersey official at the agency, Bill Baroni.

Bendul does as advised. He meets with Sokolich and passes along the advice. He also tells Sokolich about the rumors that the lane closures are punitive, related to a beef between the mayor and the governor.

Sokolich doesn't quite understand what's happening.

**COMMUTERS ARE STANDING** outside their cars on the local lanes, furiously watching the other side of the cones as their commuting brethren fly down the main lanes, right over the glorious George Washington Bridge. The stuck commuters flag down Port Authority cops: What the hell is going on?

Complain to the mayor, the cops say.

And they do.

Complaints are also flowing into the Port Authority, where one woman accuses the agency of "playing God with people's jobs." Her husband, who has been out of work for a year, was forty minutes late today to a brand-new job that he finally landed.

·        ·        ·

**AT 1:30 P.M.**, seven and a half hours after the operation began, the traffic flow is back to normal. At the governor's office, a low-level IGA operative, Evan Ridley, gets an email from Bridget Anne Kelly. This is unusual. Kelly is two steps above him on the organizational chart.

"Have you spoken to the Fort Lee mayor?" Kelly asks.

"No, not in a while," Ridley responds.

**THAT NIGHT, 8:46.** Wildstein is worried: "911," he types to Baroni. "Call me."

Baroni has spent the day in Sea Girt, representing the Port Authority at a ceremony honoring victims of the September 11 attacks. The agency provided burned steel from the World Trade Center, which Sea Girt affixed to a memorial stone.

The day goes long. After getting Wildstein's "911" text, Baroni calls the chairman of the board of the Port Authority, David Samson, a fatherlike figure to Christie. Samson, in turn, is in contact with both Wildstein and Regina Egea, Christie's soon-to-be chief-of-staff.

There is evident concern, about something. But traffic problems in Fort Lee will nonetheless continue in the morning.

### SEPTEMBER 10, DAY 2 OF THE LANE CLOSURES

Officer Ray Rodriguez, working overtime after his overnight shift to deal with the situation, spots a frustrated driver jump a traffic island. He writes the driver a ticket.

At the 911 call center, a distraught woman keeps begging for help. Three times she calls.

"Where are they?" she asks on the phone at 7:20 a.m. "It's, you know, an emergency here and they are not still here!"

A few minutes later, she calls back, yelling: "Where are they!"

**MAYOR SOKOLICH TEXTS** Baroni, as he was advised. Baroni is Sokolich's point man at the Port Authority and his fixer for all things Fort Lee: "Presently we have four very busy traffic lanes merging into only one toll booth. . . . The bigger problem is getting kids to school. Help please. It's maddening."

Baroni copies the "maddening" text and passes it along to Wildstein, who immediately forwards it to Kelly. Everyone is now in the loop, aware of the mayor's outrage.

"Is it wrong that I'm smiling?" Kelly asks.

"No," Wildstein responds.

"I feel badly about the kids." She waits a minute. "I guess."

Wildstein references Barbara Buono, the Democratic candidate now running against Christie for governor. "They are the children of Buono voters," he writes.

Wildstein is pleased, because Sokolich is not yet alleging that public safety is endangered. That would take things to a different level.

A half hour later, Wildstein reports to Kelly that the main approach to the bridge has a better flow of traffic than normal, given its two extra lanes. That means this "study" is having some kind of positive impact.

"That is good, no?" Kelly asks Wildstein.

"Very good."

"Small favors."

SOKOLICH KEEPS CALLING and texting Baroni, who continues to ignore him. The mayor is increasingly desperate—and confused. He genuinely thought he and Baroni were friends. Baroni used to tell him all the time: "You got a problem, call us. We're your guys."

With Baroni icing him out, Sokolich calls Tina Lado, another contact at the Port Authority. He tells her he's trying to "keep a lid on this," to protect everyone politically, but there's a "life-safety" issue here. Yesterday, Sokolich says, an ambulance driver had to abandon his vehicle in traffic and respond on foot! Please, have Baroni call me.

By the end of the week, Sokolich will make thirteen separate pleas to the Christie administration.

PORT AUTHORITY POLICE officer Steve Pisciotta, who has been working the bridge for five of his twelve years with the force, is one of the first to arrive for his 6:00 a.m. shift every day. He is stationed right at the heart of where the lanes normally funnel into the bridge, at Bruce Reynolds Boulevard and Martha Washington Way, and he sees, for the second day in a row, the gridlock nightmare the lane closures caused. He gets on his police radio and reports that traffic is creating dangerous conditions. He asks: Can the cones be removed, and the lanes reopened?

"Shut up," responds his boss, a Port Authority deputy. There will be no further talk about lane closures over the airwaves.

Later, two supervisors stop by Pisciotta's post. Your radio communication, Michaels says, was inappropriate.

CHRISTIE HEADS TO Camden, his little urban miracle, for a media event at a school. There's no announcement of new funding or a new program; just a chance to crow about the change he has made there. Plus, there's a *CBS Sunday Morning* crew shadowing him around today for a ten-minute profile entitled, "Chris Christie, a Fighter from Jersey."

Christie and the CBS crew also go to Newark, to the very vacant lot where his childhood apartment building once stood. Reporter Tracy Smith asks him about his mother.

"Coming back to places like this, you know, with you is, you know, makes me feel her presence," he says, clearing the lump in his throat, "even more, even more."

Smith asks Christie about his personality. " 'Idiot,' 'stupid,' 'crazy'— these are all words that you've used to describe people. Are these words that a person in your position, a leadership position, should be using?"

"Sure."

"You think so?"

"Sure. Someone's an idiot they're an idiot."

"Are you a bully?"

"No. I'm not a bully. But what I am is a fighter."

"What is the difference?"

"Well, I think a bully is abusive. And a fighter is willing to mix it up to defend his or her point of view."

### SEPTEMBER 11, 2013, DAY 3 OF THE LANE CLOSURES

The eleventh day of September is still, twelve years later, solemn in New York and New Jersey, where a new war on terrorism began. The day is particularly mournful for the employees and police officers of the Port Authority, the agency that created and operated the World Trade Center.

The Port Authority was headquartered in a dozen floors at 1 World Trade Center when terrorists flew planes into the building. Eighty-four employees, including the executive director, were killed. Thirty-seven were officers of the Port Authority Police Department, including first responders who rushed into the burning buildings to save colleagues and strangers. The attacks marked the largest loss of law enforcement personnel in one agency in American history.

Within the Port Authority, September 11 is sacred.

Christie begins the twelfth anniversary commemorative ceremonies at Liberty State Park on the Hudson River in Jersey City, where a new memorial offers an unadulterated view of Downtown Manhattan. Called "Empty Sky," and built with funds from the Port Authority after the usual political wrangling, it pulls your vision right across the river into Ground Zero.

Christie solemnly stands beside the memorial's two 208-foot-long stainless steel walls etched with 746 New Jersey names. A mourner walks over. She tapes a red flower to a name.

ISLAMIC TERRORISTS SCHEMED to blow up the George Washington Bridge in the early 1990s. The Fort Lee police and Port Authority know the bridge could be a target again, and they have a twenty-page plan for dealing with such an attack.

But it is not consulted before lanes are closed on the twelfth anniversary of 9/11.

Over in Fort Lee, the morning commute is shaping up to be a mess, once again. There's a fender bender between a Ford Explorer and a school bus. No one is hurt; a police report is taken.

Many stuck in the gridlock have September 11, 2001, weighing on their hearts. With added security at the bridge and other landmarks, machine-gun–wielding National Guard members remind everyone that it could all happen again.

AT 8:00 A.M., Christie, First Lady Mary Pat Christie, and the families of victims board a ferry to New York—the same kind of ferry that took Mary Pat from Manhattan back home to New Jersey on September 11, 2001. The New Jersey State Police gubernatorial security detail is already there in Manhattan. Officers drive the Christies to the appointed site at hallowed Ground Zero, which is still owned and operated by the Port Authority, for the annual World Trade Center Remembrance Ceremony. As they do every year, Christie and New York governor Andrew Cuomo will enter the ceremony together.

While Christie waits for Cuomo, Wildstein and Baroni walk over to their governor. The three men share a laugh as an official photographer from the Port Authority snaps photos that will one day become the center of national intrigue.

Wildstein checks his phone. Then David Samson, chairman of the Port Authority board of commissioners, arrives in a police motorcade of his own. Christie wraps his right hand around Samson's shoulders. The men embrace; their cheeks press together.

They're all chatting now—Wildstein, Christie, Baroni, Samson. And smiling. Wildstein will later remember talking to the governor at this moment about traffic in Fort Lee; Christie will not recollect this.

A couple of the other Port Authority commissioners come by, as does a Port Authority police officer who gets a picture with Christie and Samson. Then Christie, blue memorial ribbon affixed to his lapel, meets up with Cuomo and walks in, greeting first responders and families of victims.

At the memorial, where victims' names are etched, Christie sticks a little American flag in a crevice and touches the name of a neighbor from Morris County.

Family members from podiums read the names of each and every victim, slowly and sadly. The politicians listen, occasionally whispering to one another in that subtle way one does at church.

### SEPTEMBER 12, DAY 4 OF THE LANE CLOSURES

Some adapt. Parents wake up earlier just to get their kids to school on time.

Others complain. One Fort Lee resident calls the Port Authority with threats to alert the White House about how it's taking an hour and forty-five minutes to travel six miles to work.

Traffic continues, on this day, right on through the afternoon rush hour. Mayor Sokolich finishes off a formal letter, complete with the Fort Lee borough seal at the top, and his aide emails it to Baroni, who then forwards the email to Wildstein, who then sends it to Kelly and Bill Stepien, Christie's campaign manager.

For the first time, Sokolich is formally suggesting this lane thing was an act of political revenge:

> *Having received absolutely no notice of this decision, not having obtained any response to our multiple inquiries concerning same, and try as we may to understand its rationale without the benefit of a response from the Port Authority, we are reaching the conclusion*

*that there are punitive overtones associated with this initiative. What other conclusion could we possibly reach?*

"Please call me as soon as possible," he writes.
But no one calls Sokolich.

LOCAL MEDIA GET a whiff of something.

The publisher of the *Record* of Bergen County, Fort Lee's hometown paper, hears about a major traffic jam at the George Washington Bridge. The tip makes its way to John Cichowski, aka "The Road Warrior," who writes about all things transportation for the paper.

At 1:17 p.m. Cichowski emails the spokesperson at the Port Authority to ask what happened with the elimination of two toll lanes from Fort Lee. He includes an email he got from a local resident who said it took two hours and fifteen minutes for a thirty-minute commute into Manhattan. This is the first official media inquiry into the lane closures.

From his Gmail account, Wildstein drafts the first public comment about the unfolding situation at the toll lanes:

*The Port Authority is reviewing traffic safety patterns at the George Washington Bridge to ensure proper placement of toll lanes. The PAPD has been in contact with Fort Lee police throughout this transition.*

Both of those statements are lies. Wildstein sends the sentences to Kelly and Michael Drewniak, the governor's spokesman. The statement is approved to be sent to Cichowski.

Later, the Port Authority communications team issues its nightly memo, "Port Authority Nightly Media Activity Report," to several top employees:

*We told a reporter that the Port Authority is reviewing traffic safety patterns and that the PAPD has been in contact with the Fort Lee PD throughout the transition.*

The New York appointees at the Port Authority see this memo flash across their BlackBerries. This doesn't seem right to them. What traffic safety patterns? And what is the PAPD doing, exactly?

Port Authority commissioner Scott Rechler tells Port Authority executive director Patrick Foye, "We need to get to the bottom of this."

"Agree," Foye replies, "very troubling."

THE *RECORD* BEGINS to learn that there may be something nefarious, such as political retribution, going on with this traffic jam. The paper's editor, Marty Gottlieb, walks over to his reporter who covers the Port Authority, Shawn Boburg.

"Is there anything to this?" Gottlieb asks. "Do you really think anybody would be so petulant as to close lanes for political purposes?"

"Actually," says Boburg, "yes."

Boburg immediately thinks of David Wildstein, whom he had profiled two years earlier. Boburg had revealed that Wildstein had a reputation at the Port Authority for making enemies and spying on employees. Boburg thinks that this has Wildstein written all over it.

THE "TRAFFIC STUDY" is getting more scrutiny, sooner than anticipated.

So, a traffic study—an actual traffic study—has to be written.

Durando collects data, as he's instructed. He calculates the cost for permanently shutting down Fort Lee's two local lanes: $600,000 a year. At least.

A PowerPoint presentation, "Reallocation of Toll Lanes at the GWB," is produced. It highlights how eliminating the lanes led to queues of six hundred vehicles over four hours. That's a whopping 2,800 hours of delays, which equals 116 days of traffic.

The good news is that the other lanes headed directly to the bridge were moving faster than ever, but overall, the lane closures caused more delays and cost more money for the Port Authority.

No final conclusions are made, though. The study would have to continue.

SOKOLICH IS FED up. He calls the governor's office—but he uses a new phone. Not his cell. Not his office number. Not his number at his real estate office.

With a new number, Evan Ridley in IGA actually picks up the phone.

Sokolich is pissed. And he communicates that to Ridley, the same aide whom Kelly had emailed days earlier to see if he had spoken to Sokolich.

Ridley immediately relays the conversation to his boss, Christina

Renna, who takes out a piece of paper, writes "Fort Lee" at the top, and scribbles some notes about Sokolich's complaints:

- *Lanes were reduced from 3 to 1*
- *Traffic is backed up*
- *He has no idea why*
- *But there's a punitive undertone to the whole thing, like it could be retribution for something*
- *The council members, Democrats, are considering a press conference/picket at the foot of the bridge*
- *This is an extreme emergency*
- *He feels like a fucking idiot*
- *He's about to lose control of the situation*

Renna ends the note: *Evan told the fine mayor that he was unaware that the toll lanes were closed, but he would see what he could find out.*

She sends the note to Kelly, who responds with one word.

"Good," Kelly writes, forwarding the whole exchange to Wildstein.

Wildstein responds to Kelly: "Call me when you have a moment."

But Kelly is already on her way to Seaside Park. Another crisis is developing.

**SEASIDE PARK AND** Seaside Heights sit next to each other on the ocean, linked by an iconic boardwalk where Christie vacationed as a kid and yelled at a heckler (ice cream cone in hand) as a governor. When Sandy washed away the boardwalk, Christie vowed to rebuild, and that's exactly what he did.

But this afternoon, underneath the boardwalk's Kohr's Frozen Custard stand, near some wiring exposed to sand and saltwater during the storm surge, a fire is raging.

The flames build and move into the custard stand before extending all the way to Funhouse Pier, with all of its amusement games, now collapsing.

Around 3:00 p.m. Christie is notified about the blaze. "I feel like I want to throw up," he says.

At 4:00 p.m. it is a six-alarm fire, capturing full blocks on the boardwalk. Christie rushes to Seaside. Kelly, his liaison to local officials, goes with him. For Sandy victims, this moment feels all too familiar. There he is, back on the Shore, holding a press conference and hugging strangers and telling everyone that everything is going to be okay.

It's a ten-alarm fire now. Twenty-nine fire companies and four hundred firefighters are on the scene. As pressure in the fire hydrants fades, firefighters pull water from the bay to finally extinguish the flames.

Fifty businesses in two towns burn. No one dies, but twelve firefighters suffer from smoke inhalation. Christie declares a state of emergency and redirects $15 million in federal Sandy aid for the affected area.

That evening, eerily buzzing on television ads through New Jersey, is Christie's brand-new reelection ad. In the final frame the camera closes in on a shot of Christie heroically gazing at Funtown Pier, still standing after Sandy. "When tragedy struck," the voiceover says, "he was there every step of the way."

But now, Funtown Pier is burning.

IN FORT LEE, Christie is not there every step of the way. No state of emergency is being declared, no press conference is being held, and no one knows how long this traffic jam is going to keep going.

Sokolich cannot figure out why his town is under siege, and why no one seems to care. He texts Baroni, again: *My frustration is now trying to figure out who is mad at me.*

Baroni passes along the message to Wildstein, again. But this time he uses a code name for Sokolich. They call him "Serbia."

He is actually Croatian.

## SEPTEMBER 13, DAY 5 OF THE LANE CLOSURES

The Road Warrior column in the *Record* publishes. Columnist Cichowski details the mysterious lane closures and the disgruntled commuters caught up in the fiasco. And he quotes Sokolich: "I'm beginning to wonder if there's something I did wrong. Am I being sent some sort of message?"

PATRICK FOYE, NEW York governor Andrew Cuomo's top official at the authority, doesn't need a newspaper column to realize how shady all of this is. He emails Durando, a lifer at the agency, at 6:01 a.m. They get on that phone at this ungodly hour because Foye has a very specific question. Foye asks: Were you told not to tell anyone about the lane closures?

That's correct, Durando replies.

An hour later, at 7:44 a.m., five days and seventy-four minutes after the operation began, Foye sends top Port Authority officials an email marked with "high" importance. He is reopening the lanes and ending this non-sense.

> After reading last night's media pendings, I made inquiries and received calls on this matter which is very troubling. Here is what I learned: reversing over 25 years of PA GWB operations, the three lanes in Fort Lee eastbound to the GWB were reduced to one lane on Monday of this week without notifying Fort Lee, the commuting public we serve, [me,] or Media. . . .
>
> I am appalled by the lack of process, failure to inform our custom-ers and Fort Lee and most of all by the dangers created to the public interest, so I am reversing this decision now. . . .
>
> I pray that no life has been lost or trip of a hospital- or hospice-bound patient delayed.
>
> This hasty and ill-advised decision has undoubtedly had an adverse effect on economic activity in both states. . . .
>
> I will not allow this hasty and ill-advised decision to delay the travels of those observing Yom Kippur tonight or the holidays to follow.

Baroni immediately emails Samson, using the nickname derived from his brief stint as state attorney general: "General, can I call you on this now?"

But it's too late for Baroni or even Samson to stop Foye from reopening the lanes.

At 8:04 a.m. Durando confirms to Foye that the cones have been moved back to their normal positions. "We have restored the 3 toll lanes to Ft. Lee," he writes.

**BARONI'S CONCERN NOW** shifts to how this is going to play out in the public. The lid had to remain on. He writes to Foye: "Pat, we need to discuss prior to any communications."

Foye responds: "Bill, we are going to fix this fiasco."

Not good enough for Baroni. "I am on way to office to discuss. There can be no public discourse."

"Bill, that's precisely the problem: There has been no public discourse on this."

They meet in Foye's office. Foye brings an assistant in, as a witness.

This traffic study was "something Trenton wanted," Baroni tells him.

"Trenton" means the governor's office. Baroni demands that Foye immediately reinstate the lane reductions.

Foye refuses.

So Wildstein messages Kelly: "New York gave Fort Lee back all three lanes. We are appropriately going nuts. Samson helping us to retaliate."

Samson, from his weekend home in Connecticut, then gets on the phone with Christie's top deputies in Trenton.

Everyone realizes this situation could soon spiral out of control.

### SEPTEMBER 14

The Road Warrior is up with another column, trying to suss out from government officials what happened with this so-called traffic study.

> *Answers to basic follow-up questions: What was the goal? Who authorized this plan? And why didn't the Port Authority publicly warn motorists about it?—were met with stone-cold silence.*

He writes that Sokolich needs to be careful.

> *You never know when the next "study" might fall on you like a huge net and imprison everybody around you for miles.*

### SEPTEMBER 17

"The last four reporters that contacted me suggest that the people they are speaking with absolutely believe it to be punishment," Sokolich writes to Baroni. He wants a face-to-face. "Perhaps someone can enlighten me as to the errors of my ways. Let me know if you'll give me ten minutes."

Baroni feels squeezed from all sides. Wildstein tries to console him over text. "Right now you are taking punches," he writes.

"That's not helpful," Baroni responds.

"I don't know what to tell you," Wildstein says. He tries to get Kelly on the phone to talk over what's happening. "Have not heard back fr Bridget," he writes, using texting shorthand.

"Fck," Baroni responds. "We could sched a meeting to stave off reporters then pull a faps."

"Pull a faps": This is code for sending a message by scheduling a meeting with the intention of canceling it. That's what Wildstein and Baroni had recently done to a Port Authority tenant, a company named FAPS, where Mayor Steve Fulop of Jersey City worked as a consultant. Like Sokolich, Fulop is a Democrat who didn't endorse Christie.

Wildstein suggests pulling a faps on Monday.

"Too cute," Baroni decides. "Tuesday or later next week."

**JUST AFTER 2:00** p.m., a *Wall Street Journal* reporter calls Wildstein, which freaks out Baroni.

"Jesus," Baroni tells Wildstein, "call Drewniak."

Michael Drewniak is the governor's chief spokesman. One day, when wounds scab over, "Jesus, call Drewniak" will be used as shorthand within the administration whenever things go wrong.

Drewniak and Wildstein got to know each other during the Christie years, and have dinner every few months. Wildstein explains to Drewniak that the lane realignment was done for a study on how to ease congestion. "We conducted a traffic study—no big deal," Wildstein tells him. "It's our prerogative." The study was kept secret from even local officials, he adds, because "informing people of it beforehand would skew the results."

That sounds right to Drewniak. He works on a response, runs it by Wildstein, and sends it to the *Wall Street Journal*. It drips with quintessential Christie press office condescension:

> Pardon? It's an independent agency, and I'll refer you to the Port Authority. Traffic studies or pilots are done all the time. They're temporary, and if they're not done, how can the effectiveness of a new approach be tested?

At 11:12 p.m., *Wall Street Journal* reporters Ted Mann and Heather Haddon post their story, "Bridge Jam's Cause a Mystery." The story says the lanes were reopened after five days out of fear that the "abrupt shift in traffic patterns caused a threat to public safety." And it drops this bombshell: Elected officials in Fort Lee, local police officers, and even some top Port Authority executives hadn't been given a heads-up about this major operation.

This isn't just an issue for the local papers anymore. The *Wall Street Journal* is the biggest newspaper in the country, read by the billionaires who are supposed to fund a Christie presidential campaign.

### SEPTEMBER 18

Wildstein is up early reading the *Wall Street Journal*. At 4:54 a.m., he forwards the article to Bill Stepien, Christie's campaign manager.

"It's fine," Stepien writes. Then Stepien calls Sokolich an "idiot" and delivers the most famous autocorrect in the entire Bridgegate affair: "When some, lose some."

But despite Stepien's assuredness, Wildstein thinks he's on the verge of getting fired over what happened. "I had empty boxes ready to take to work today, just in case," he writes. And he blames the mayor for not keeping his mouth shut. He vows to Stepien: "It will be a tough November for this little Serbian."

It is already a tough September for Sokolich. What could Wildstein have in mind for November?

**THAT NIGHT, DAVID** Samson, the chairman of the Port Authority board of commissioners—the elder statesman looking over Baroni and Wildstein—fires back at Foye, the executive director of the Port Authority from New York.

In the complicated power-sharing arrangement at the Port Authority, the chairman of the board of commissioners is chosen by the New Jersey governor while the executive director, essentially the top staff person there, is chosen by the New York governor.

New Jersey's Chairman Samson and New York's Executive Director Foye despise each other, as per tradition. And while their benefactors, Christie and Cuomo, have forged a personal friendship and political nonproliferation pact, there is vicious infighting among their staffers that is now threatening the balance of power at the Port Authority.

Samson believes Foye leaked to the *Wall Street Journal* the news that top Port Authority officials didn't know about the traffic change. Samson says this is "very unfortunate for NY/NJ relations." He writes to a colleague: "More evidence of reckless, counter-productive behavior."

Samson issues a veiled threat to Foye. "He's playing in traffic," Samson writes, "big mistake."

## OCTOBER 1

The reporters at the *Wall Street Journal* now have a copy of the email that Foye sent to Port Authority officials after finding out about the lane closures. "I pray that no life has been lost or trip of a hospital- or hospice-bound patient delayed," Foye had written in the message.

Drewniak, the spokesman, goes downstairs at the Statehouse to see his boss, Maria Comella, the communications director. He's all worked up, she will later remember, about the incoming press calls on this strange matter.

Officially, the governor's office washes its hands of anything untoward that may have gone down. Stay out of it, Comella instructs Drewniak. This is a Port Authority issue. The governor does not want on the eve of his reelection to be pulled into something that he has nothing to do with.

But will he have that option for much longer? Because late that night the *Wall Street Journal* publishes a story refuting the existence of a traffic study, and therefore the whole alibi for the operation. An anonymous quotation is tantalizingly attributed to someone familiar with the matter: "There was no study."

WILDSTEIN AND STEPIEN blame Foye for these leaks.

"Holy shit, who does he think he is, Capt. America?" Stepien asks.

"Bad guy," Wildstein replies. "Welcome to our world."

## OCTOBER 2

Stepien doesn't seem as concerned as he was yesterday. "Ultimately, not an awful story," he tells Wildstein. "Whatever."

But Wildstein wants to take action. "We need to address leaks from Foye and his messing with us five weeks before election . . . I feel terrible that I'm causing you so much stress this close to November."

Stepien offers some consolation: "For what it's worth, I like you more on October 2, 2013, than I did on October 2, 2009."

Stepien likes having Wildstein on his side. Four years earlier, during the initial gubernatorial run, Wildstein was a reporter covering the campaign for PoliticsNJ.com. He was on the outside; now he's on their team.

Wildstein responds with a paraphrase of a seventeen-hundred-year-old Jewish adage. "In the land of the blind," Wildstein says, "the one-eyed man is king."

Is Foye ruling a land of Port Authority idiots? Or is Wildstein the one-eyed king?

**OTHER REPORTERS START** paying attention and questioning Drewniak about what happened.

So Drewniak asks Kelly what she knows.

Kelly rolls her eyes. Just something about traffic, she says.

### OCTOBER 7

State Senator Loretta Weinberg is the self-described feisty Jewish grand-mother of the New Jersey legislature. Pushing eighty, and yet still one of the hardest-working legislators under the golden dome of the Statehouse, Weinberg is tough, liberal, and skilled at the political arts. She didn't run for office until her fifties, but she's now the highest-ranking female Democrat in the state Senate—the majority leader.

Her constituency is Bergen County, where the George Washington Bridge sits, and her bugaboo is transparency. The Port Authority does what it wants when it comes to releasing documents because it doesn't see itself as subject to either New York or New Jersey laws. To Weinberg, whose daughter told me her mother was exceptional at sussing out lies when she was a kid, the secrecy is suspicious.

And so that's why Weinberg is in Jersey City today, addressing the Port Authority's Ethics and Governance Committee. She tells the commissioners that she's "looking for answers to unilateral actions taken to reduce access to the George Washington Bridge."

Afterward she talks to the media and describes Christie's reelection campaign team as "a whole bunch of frat-boy types sitting in their office one night having a beer and a pizza" and plotting revenge on enemies.

### EARLY OCTOBER

For the first known time Christie is involved in discussions about what to do about the escalating controversy over the lane closures. He meets with his two top deputies—Chief Counsel Charlie McKenna and Chief of Staff Kevin O'Dowd. At one time, these three men were all federal prosecutors. They are skilled at seeking out the truth.

They determine that a real traffic study was conducted, even if mistakes were made in how the notifications of the lane closures were handled.

McKenna will later not recollect this meeting. Christie wasn't sure who was there. Only O'Dowd would one day report that they determined Foye was leaking documents and blowing things out of proportion.

### OCTOBER 15

Christie shows up at Montclair State University for the second of two gubernatorial debates against Barbara Buono, the Democratic candidate. And for the second time, Buono makes a passing reference to the George Washington Bridge.

Asked about the lack of support she has from Democrats in the state—about why some fifty Democrats endorsed the Republican incumbent—Buono insinuates that Christie bullied them into it. "Witness the unexplained closure of two lanes starting in Fort Lee going over the GW Bridge," she says. "We have no idea why they closed, but it caused a traffic snarl-up in Fort Lee and there's an investigation. Well, lo and behold! The mayor of Fort Lee is a Democrat and he has *not* endorsed the governor."

Buono then pivots to slamming Joe D., the North Jersey Democratic boss who endorsed Christie. Christie responds by defending Joe D. Christie doesn't mention the bridge, and he won't publicly be asked about it again for seven weeks.

### OCTOBER 16

Senator Weinberg goes to yet another Port Authority meeting looking for answers about the bridge.

The Christie rep at the meeting—Regina Egea, soon to be Christie's chief of staff—reports back to her staff about how it went. "Questions ensued on ft lee," Egea writes, "but holding to script of 'all under review.' "

### OCTOBER 17

Mann, from the *Wall Street Journal*, finds out from sources that Wildstein was actually in Fort Lee directing the lane closures on the morning of September 9.

Wildstein defends himself to Drewniak. Foye is the leak and "a piece of crap," Wildstein writes.

But Drewniak is concerned. He texts O'Dowd: "A new high level of shit is hitting the fan tonight on the Ft Lee/GWB issue. Maybe you should know about it."

**WILDSTEIN FEELS ISOLATED**, realizing he's becoming the fall guy.

So he begins telling Drewniak that both Kelly and her onetime paramour, campaign manager Stepien, knew about the traffic study, too.

"Look," Wildstein tells Drewniak, "this is not something I did without letting people know."

But what exactly about the traffic study did they know?

Christie's team makes little effort to find out.

### OCTOBER 28

Reporter Steve Strunsky from the *Star-Ledger* is on the story. He asks Drewniak if there were any political motivations to closing the lanes, and whether the governor was involved.

Drewniak is defiant and dismissive. "No, for goodness sake," he writes. "The governor of the state of New Jersey does not involve himself in traffic studies."

Drewniak is a former *Star-Ledger* reporter who apparently hasn't lost the reporter's fondness for the f-word—because he then calls Strunsky "a fucking mutt" in an email to Wildstein.

### NOVEMBER 5, TUESDAY

Governor Christie wins reelection and delivers a speech at the Asbury Park Convention Hall about leadership.

"The biggest thing I've learned over the last four years about leadership is that leadership is much less about talking than it is about listening, about bringing people around the table listening to each other, showing them respect, doing what needed to be done to be able to bring people together and to achieve what we needed to achieve to move our state forward," he says.

## NOVEMBER 21

Reelection behind him, Christie is in the lobby of a five-star resort in Scottsdale, Arizona, on the way to a dinner in which he'll be feted as the newly selected chairman of the powerful Republican Governors Association. He is trailed by a TV reporter from a local Phoenix station who asks the same question the governor has been asked over and over again this week.

*Are you running for president?*

"For godsakes," Christie tells the reporter.

I grab my recorder and (literally) run over. I've been stationed all day in the lobby, waiting for a chance to see the man of the moment. The place was crawling with reporters earlier but at this point most have gone to the bar. I would be there, too, but this is just my second week on the job for WNYC and I have yet to get an interview with the man I had come to see.

Christie jokes with me about getting another one of these "are you running for president" questions. Then, feeling generous and seemingly at ease to see a face from home, he says: "You came a long way. What do you need?"

I ask him what he's been doing all week. He acknowledges that he's there meeting with corporate lobbyists and billionaire political donors.

At this moment, Christie is the center of the American political universe. He just won reelection by dramatic margins and he is now at the top of all polls of potential Republican presidential candidates for 2016. So I do not ask him about the bridge. The thought doesn't even cross my mind.

Back home, though, the bridge is about to become something that cannot be ignored.

## NOVEMBER 25

Bill Baroni, Port Authority deputy executive director, is involved in top-level meetings about preventing further fallout. The message from the governor's office is simple: Issue a written statement. Apologize for a vague communications failure. Say little else. Kill this thing, stat.

But then the New Jersey Assembly Transportation Committee calls Baroni to testify about this very issue at a public hearing at the Statehouse in Trenton. This would be voluntary, and not under oath. If he doesn't show up, though, the Democrats can subpoena him.

This testimony offers the Christie administration its last chance to try to keep the bridge issue from becoming Bridge*gate*. Fortunately for him,

Baroni has some experience handling Democratic legislators in such settings. If Christie could have anyone up at the plate in this situation, it'd be Baroni.

That's because back in 2012, Baroni, in his same role as the top New Jersey staffer at the Port Authority, was called to testify before a U.S. Senate hearing. Democratic New Jersey senator Frank Lautenberg, Christie's nemesis, wanted to grill Baroni about the quick, secretive nature of the Port Authority's approval of massive toll increases at the bridge and tunnels.

At the hearing, Baroni flipped the tables.

"Senator, respectfully, I understand the concerns that people have about paying tolls across the Hudson," Baroni said. "It is something that commuters, as you mentioned, Senator, pay each and every day. But respectfully, Senator, you only started paying tolls recently. For years, senator, as a former commissioner of my agency, you received free E-ZPass. In fact, I have a copy of your free E-ZPass."

Baroni raised Lautenberg's E-ZPass and waved it in the air.

Lautenberg was floored. A legendary Jersey political street fighter, he had been duly provoked, as planned. The rest went like this:

"I'm not going to permit you to continue with this silliness," Lautenberg said.

"Well, senator, you took 284 trips for free in the last two years you had a pass."

"I want you to answer this question!"

"Sure."

"Is this fair? Is this toll increase fair to the public at large?"

"I think, senator . . . it is impossible to argue fairness in tolls if you don't pay them."

Then everything went off the rails. Lautenberg wanted to try to prove that Christie and Baroni conspired to secretly hike the tolls. Baroni kept dodging the question.

"Are you running a *protection agency* there?!" Lautenberg asked.

This exchange went on for some time, and about an hour after it began, while Baroni was midsentence, Lautenberg abruptly adjourned the hearing. He shuffled some papers in front of him and got up to leave.

Baroni had won. But in an indication that his bark was worse than his bite—and an affirmation of his nickname in some corners, "Phony Baroni"—Baroni sent a message through an intermediary back to Lautenberg: *Trenton put me up to it. Hope there are no hard feelings.*

The next day, Christie called Lautenberg "an embarrassment to the United States Senate" who "got caught with his hand in the cookie jar."

WOULD BARONI PULL such a maneuver in his upcoming testimony about the lane closures? Thing was, up until this whole bridge thing, even though Baroni was seen as a quintessential politician, too slick by half, he was well liked on both sides of the aisle. A lobbyist and lawyer specializing in election matters, Baroni knocked on 10,809 doors to win his first Assembly seat in a campaign run by future Christie campaign manager Stepien. He became the youngest member of the legislature at the age of thirty-one and a "folk hero among Republicans," according to the *New York Times*. A few years after that he formally presented New Jersey's delegates on the floor of the 2008 Republican convention.

Baroni made a name for himself as a rising political star willing to buck Republican ideology to support same-sex marriage, a higher minimum wage, and medical marijuana. He backed anticorruption legislation and taught classes on ethics at Seton Hall Law School, where he was adored by his students. Baroni told the *Washington Post* that New Jersey's "political culture of corruption" was a "pox on both political parties."

On the day Christie's gubernatorial campaign began, Stepien gave Baroni's contact information to reporters who needed a quote praising Christie. His rhetorical skills were so good that he played Democrat Jon Corzine in debate prep for Christie. "Every answer he gave, he found a way to work George W. Bush in, in a way that only Baroni could, and try to get under my skin, and work it in, and work it in," Christie later said.

Once Christie got into office, Baroni proved adept as the new governor's muscle. He reportedly delivered a message from the governor to a firefighters' union official, who had criticized him: "Go fuck yourself."

"The governor told me to make sure you don't get this message mixed up; say these exact words," Baroni told the official.

Christie and Baroni were about a decade apart, but they had a lot in common. Both had preternatural political skills. Both began volunteering for New Jersey Republican campaigns at the age of fourteen. And both waged public battles with weight.

Baroni remembers being the fattest kid in third grade and then struggling with weight right up to college. His first job was as the driver for a Republican running against Lautenberg. There's a lot of eating on campaigns, and Baroni attended so many events with food that he typically ate two or three breakfasts, two or three lunches, and then two or three dinners in a single day. Late night, Baroni and the candidate, Chuck Haytaian, went to Hackettstown Diner to prepare for the following day. Baroni would order the roast turkey with gravy. After Baroni dropped off Haytaian at home that night, the young aide then hit the drive-thrus—first McDonald's, for extra-large fries and a Coke, and then Burger King, for the fried chicken sandwiches or a bacon double cheeseburger.

Baroni brought that food home and ate. He went to sleep and did it all over again in the morning. He was getting heavier and heavier. He couldn't climb a flight of stairs without losing his breath. One day Baroni was at a campaign event at a racetrack when he was struck by chest pains. He looked in the mirror. *This is what dying feels like,* he thought.

Baroni checked himself into Duke University Diet & Fitness Center. He weighed 312 pounds. He was twenty-two years old.

Baroni lost 130 pounds in a matter of months. He told his story in a book that he wrote, *Fat Kid Got Fit and So Can You!* He had a new life in front of him. By the time the book came out, Baroni was at the Port Authority, having been appointed by new Governor Christie to be the $291,100 deputy executive director.

BARONI'S BIGGEST MOMENT as a Christie foot soldier comes today, before the Assembly Transportation Committee. Democrats had watched Baroni's Washington victory over Lautenberg, so they are bracing for his counter-attack.

Baroni arrives for his interrogation at a long table in a Statehouse hearing room before a half circle of legislators. He is armed with props. Ninety seconds into the opening statement Baroni stands, opens a red marker, and walks over to an easel holding an aerial picture of the lanes in question. He draws a long curved line along where traffic cones normally designate Fort Lee's "special" and "segregated" lanes.

This issue, Baroni says, is about fairness. Why do special lanes enable Fort Lee residents to "skip the general traffic at the George Washington Bridge"? On the surface, he makes a convincing case: 4.5 percent of those driving onto the bridge use 25 percent of the lanes on the upper level.

But the stat is a half-truth—the 4.5 percent he's referring to is just Fort Lee residents. Many residents from towns surrounding Fort Lee also use these lanes. In fact seventy-five thousand motorists use these Fort Lee lanes every day—representing 25 percent of the total traffic using 25 percent of the lanes.

In fact, there is no fairness issue.

Baroni correctly notes that during the lane closures most drivers experienced a better commute. But he insinuates that the Port Authority police signed off on the operation, which isn't true.

Then Baroni offers the requisite apology, saying that the Port Authority didn't "provide timely notice of the lane closures . . . nor secure the complete buy-in from the entire agency before proceeding." He attributes this to "communications breakdowns."

"We must—and we will—do better," Baroni says.

He repeats, again and again, the statistics on the drivers' use of the lanes.

"I got that part," says Assemblyman John Wisniewski, Baroni's lead interrogator.

Wisniewski, again: "I got that. And you said that already."

And again: "I know you made the point."

Baroni tries to pull a Lautenberg, redirecting the interrogation onto Wisniewski. Wildstein had collected E-ZPass data on the travel patterns of bridge commuters, broken down by each legislator's hometown, and provided that to Baroni. "Your hometown—forty-two of your neighbors in Sayreville—are in the pool that's waiting in longer lines," Baroni says to Wisniewski. "Maybe that's okay. Lemme tell you, when I was in the Senate I wouldn't have gone back to my constituents and said, 'That's fair.' "

"Bill, Bill," Wisniewski says, dispensing with the formalities for his old colleague. "I understand your point." But, he asks, who made the decision to close the lanes?

Baroni tries another redirect. "The policy question behind whether or not—*question*—behind whether or not one community should have three lanes—when I see my former colleague Assemblyman Romano, who represents the western part of Bergen County, where—"

Wisniewski turns off his mic. Baroni becomes inaudible.

"What are the steps that he or anybody else that occupies that office has to take to actually have some police officer physically go out and move those cones?" Wisniewski asks. "Can you answer that question?"

Baroni says some people from various Port Authority departments did the actual closing of the lanes. He does not name names.

"I am just a little mystified as to why you couldn't have said any of this at the Port Authority meeting last week," Wisniewski says.

"The opportunity to spend time with you, Chairman, at your committee was too wonderful to pass up," Baroni says. He smiles an open-mouth smile. He facetiously offers to take Wisniewski on a "field trip" to examine the bridge situation more closely.

"A field trip with you?" Wisniewski asks.

"Come on. I'll even pack your lunch."

"I'll want to get it tested first," Wisniewski says.

(Do other states' legislatures feature cracks about poisoning deaths, or is that just New Jersey?)

Democratic assemblywoman Linda Stender then cuts through the noise and accuses Baroni of a cover-up. "There is no email trail, not a *single* email that explains how this was done! That defies all logic, and *nobody* in this room believes that," she says.

Baroni sticks to the game plan. He extends his finger and points at the assemblywoman. "What you will not answer to are the 585 people in *your* district who sit in *more* traffic because of the special lanes. What do you say to *them*? What do you say to them!"

"You are a masterful dancer," Stender says, "and we appreciate your dancing skills."

CHRISTIE OFFICIALS ARE cringing. Baroni is not sticking to the script.

The highest-ranking advisers to the governor prepared Baroni's opening statement to the committee. The statement was so important it was Top Secret—with drafts having been passed around via hard copy only. At one point a Port Authority official in a Port Authority car drove the statement from the agency's Park Avenue South headquarters in New York City to the Trenton Statehouse, ninety minutes away. There was great concern that if the statement was sent electronically, it could leak.

Baroni went rogue and did his own work on a statement, including his own research. But he didn't know the most rudimentary facts about the bridge—he had to text Wildstein to find out the number of lanes on the upper level. (Wildstein didn't know, either.)

Christie's advisers told Baroni to stick to the basics in his hearing—*This was a legitimate traffic study that was communicated poorly, and we're sorry for that.* Instead, Baroni attacked.

"Trenton feedback?" Baroni asks Wildstein after the hearing, referring to the governor's office.

"Good."

"Just good?" Baroni says. "Shit."

### NOVEMBER 26

In the morning Baroni gets a nod of approval from Christie's top political adviser. "Hey, great job yesterday," Stepien says. "I know it's not a fun topic, and not nearly as fun as beating up on Frank Lautenberg, but you did great, and I wanted to thank you."

Democrats "will keep their nonsense," Baroni says, "but at least we have explained the counter-narrative."

### NOVEMBER 27

The *Star-Ledger* doesn't buy the counter-narrative. An editorial writer is calling for subpoenas to be issued, so he asks for comment from the Port Authority, which dutifully forwards the request to Drewniak, Christie's spokesman.

"Fuck him and the S-L," Drewniak responds.

### DECEMBER 2

Christie is having a press conference to announce top-level staff changes going into the second term. Communications chief Maria Comella preps him on possible questions about the bridge.

Reporters assemble in the ornate outer room of the governor's office. I raise my hand.

"Governor," I ask, "did you have anything to do with these lane closures in September outside the GW Bridge?"

Eighty days after the lanes reopened, Christie is being asked about the lane closures for the first time. His answer is instantly infamous.

"I worked the cones actually, Matt. Unbeknownst to everybody I was actually the guy out there. I was in overalls *and a hat*. But I was actually the guy working the cones out there. You *really* are not serious with that question."

I ignore the taunt and try to press on. "What happened?" I ask. "Have you spoken to David Wildstein about what happened?"

"No I haven't," he says. He goes on to call his Democratic interrogators, Weinberg and Wisniewski, "obsessed"—"it just shows you they really have nothing to do." But because he's sat in traffic at the George Washington Bridge he now plans to instruct the Port Authority to review the "dedicated lanes" for Fort Lee. "The fact that one town has three lanes dedicated to it?" he says. "That kind of gets me sauced."

And then he brings it all around. "I don't get involved in lane closures. I didn't work the cones, just so we're clear on that, that was sarcastic," he says. But "three lanes for one town? I don't quite get it."

"The idea that this was about no endorsement from the mayor—they just made [it] up, out of thin air?" I ask.

"To the best of my knowledge, I don't know if I've ever met the mayor of Fort Lee. I may have met him once. So the fact that he didn't endorse me came as no, you know, wild shock to me."

In Fort Lee, Mayor Sokolich is teed off when he hears this. He and the governor had certainly met before.

But, the governor meets a lot of people and has a lot of conversations. He doesn't remember everyone.

### DECEMBER 4

A man named Paul Nunziato is Baroni's last hope. Nunziato is the slick-haired, hard-nosed head of the Port Authority police union, and suddenly he claims he's the one who came up with the lane closure idea. In fact, he says, it was actually *his* idea.

As long as the traffic study idea came from the cops, then it could be seen as legit.

Nunziato was close with Christie's people at the Port Authority. His union broke ranks with all other cops in New Jersey to endorse Christie's reelection. Under Christie the Port Authority force had grown by a third, overtime had exponentially increased, and instead of replacing Port Authority police with the New York Police Department at Ground Zero, as had been the plan, Christie supported their current assignment. "I know that I don't have to worry when Chris Christie says he has our back; he has been there every time," Nunziato said when endorsing Christie.

The Nunziato endorsement was secured through Wildstein. The men met almost weekly, over breakfasts at New Jersey diners and at bars in Manhattan. Now, Nunziato is defending the bridge incident. He says no ambulances were delayed due to the traffic, which isn't true. And he says it's normal to not warn Fort Lee officials about bridge operations, which is likewise not true. As for why the Port Authority traffic engineers weren't informed about the study? "They fuck up everything," Nunziato tells reporters. "Do I know more than a traffic engineer? Do my guys know more? Yeah, probably, because we stand out there all day."

He adds: If you think this action was politically motivated, then you might as well be investigating where former mobster Jimmy Hoffa is buried.

This is just about New York trying to embarrass New Jersey, he says, as part of the states' long-running feud over the agency.

WILDSTEIN WANTS TO have dinner with Drewniak. He makes it seem "ominous," as Drewniak describes it.

Drewniak and Wildstein initially got to know each other when Drewniak was a spokesman for Christie at the U.S. Attorney's Office and Wildstein was Wally Edge. Edge had paid particular attention to chronicling Christie's rise, beginning with a 2002 scoop that a major corruption bust was coming from his U.S. Attorney's office. The scoop helped put PoliticsNJ.com on the map, which in turn boosted Christie's notoriety and crime-fighting image. When Edge wrote a post about how Christie liked Bruce Springsteen, the U.S. Attorney himself responded with a long ode to Springsteen that he unspooled into a political speech about the First Amendment.

Christie must've reminded Wildstein of the real Edge—both men had a flair for the dramatic in their corruption busting but at the same time they cozied up to political bosses, when necessary. Once Christie became governor Edge outed himself as Wildstein, but Christie would continue to call him "Wally."

Wildstein had called Drewniak to reveal himself. "I'm Wally Edge," he said. "My real name is David Wildstein." Then Wildstein asked Drewniak to dinner.

"I was just fascinated at meeting this character who had written all that stuff, all those years," Drewniak later recalled. "And to be honest with you, when he walked in the door at the Clinton House restaurant, you know when you see somebody you go, *really*?"

Wildstein isn't what anyone expects.

Once Wildstein began working at the Port Authority, he and Drewniak began getting together to gossip about politics, as longtime political insiders like the two of them are wont to do. Wildstein took Drewniak's family on a behind-the-scenes tour of the Freedom Tower construction at Ground Zero. He called Drewniak often to complain about the New York side of the Port Authority. Drewniak was a sympathetic ear, once calling Wildstein's nemesis—New York's Patrick Foye, the executive director of the Port Authority—a "piece of excrement."

Tonight, when Drewniak shows up at Steakhouse 85 in New Brunswick, he already knows that Wildstein is going to be forced to resign. Wildstein hasn't heard the news yet; he thinks he can talk his way into keeping his job.

Wildstein brings to dinner a large Redwell—one of those accordion folders for papers. "Let's talk, and at the end of the dinner I want to show you this," Wildstein says.

Drewniak doesn't ask what the folder is. The men talk about politics and family. Drewniak orders a steak.

Wildstein pulls out the folder. Wildstein seems anxious; Drewniak grows uncomfortable.

"This is the traffic study," Wildstein says.

Drewniak asks what the hell happened at the bridge that day. He asks why he had to do a traffic study in the first place.

Wildstein apologizes, says he knows it wasn't handled well. He digs through his folder. He says he had wanted to do a traffic study for years—the main lanes are just way too backed up, and getting rid of the lanes will benefit North Jersey commuters.

Wildstein assures Drewniak that he is a team player and will fall on the sword if necessary. Maybe that would help him stay in Christie World, maybe get a job on a future campaign, if this goes presidential?

Wildstein talks about his accomplishments at the Port Authority, and his contributions. He doesn't want to go out like this; he doesn't want his career to end like this.

Then Wildstein starts dropping bombs. Kelly and Stepien knew about this traffic study, too, he says.

And: So did the governor. Wildstein tells Drewniak he told Christie about it during that last September 11 ceremony at Ground Zero.

The meal ends. Wildstein picks up the tab.

## DECEMBER 5

Kevin O'Dowd, Christie's chief of staff, is Christie's pick for attorney general as part of a staff reshuffling for the second term. Drewniak stops by O'Dowd's office to congratulate him.

O'Dowd's office is next door to the governor's. Christie, as he often does, walks in and sees Drewniak. What's up?

"You're not going to believe this," Drewniak says. "He's now thrown you in, too." Drewniak tells Christie about Wildstein's new allegation that he talked to the governor about the lane closures on September 11, Day 3 of the operation.

Christie says he doesn't remember this at all. "He tells me at a September 11 event, some fly-by or drive-by remark about—something about traffic. And I'm supposed to understand what he's talking about?"

There's more, Drewniak tells the governor. Wildstein says that Kelly and Stepien knew about it beforehand.

Christie wonders aloud if Stepien, one of his most trusted advisers, is telling everything he knows.


## DECEMBER 6

The governor's chief counsel, McKenna, informs Wildstein he has until 2:00 p.m. that day to resign. Or he'll be fired.

Drewniak goes to work on a resignation statement for the governor to issue. He sends a draft up the chain. Christie himself edits it to make it more laudatory:

> *Mr. Wildstein has been a tireless advocate for New Jersey's interests at the Port Authority. We are grateful for his commitment and dedication to the important work of the Port Authority and thank him for his service to the people of New Jersey and the region.*

Drewniak sends the statement to Wildstein—who asks that it be even more effusive.

They're getting "itchy" to get this over with, Drewniak tells Wildstein.

Wildstein relents. The statement is sent out. His last day will be December 31.

### DECEMBER 8

Drewniak texts Wildstein: "Hey. How you doing?"

Wildstein: "Doing fine. A little bummed out, a small amount of growing anger. My father thinks it's the end of the world. But in the village having dinner and nothing a little Valium won't fix. Thanks for checking in and being a great friend."

Drewniak: "You are a great friend and this too shall pass."

### DECEMBER 9

A second day of hearings by the Assembly Transportation Committee begins. Bob Durando, the general manager of the George Washington Bridge, is up to testify. Assemblyman Wisniewski is trying to figure out why lifelong bureaucrats felt that they had no choice but to carry out a political appointee's shady orders.

"So a man with whom you have very little interaction comes to you and says, 'This bridge that you're in charge of—change these lanes.' And you said, 'Yes, sir'?"

"Mr. Chairman, it is a well-known fact that Mr. Wildstein is one of the ranking New Jersey officials in the Port Authority. I followed my chain of command after being given a directive by the second person in New Jersey in charge of my agency."

"Did you for a moment think that his direction was wrong?"

"It was odd."

"Did you think it was wrong, yes or no?"

"Yes."

"And notwithstanding that, you went ahead and implemented it."

"Yes, sir."

"And you're responsible for the safety of the passage of vehicles across that bridge?"

"I am."

Wisniewski asks Durando whether Wildstein instilled fear in him.

"I was concerned about what Mr. Wildstein's reaction would be if I did not follow his directive."

"Does Mr. Wildstein have the ability to terminate your employment?"

"I suspect he does."

"So would it be fair to say that you did have a concern about your continued employment if you went outside of his direction?"

"I honestly don't know how to answer you."

"Well, either you did or you didn't."

"Well, I was not fearful that I was going to get fired."

"So then why didn't you—"

"Because I didn't want to tempt fate."

ALL OF THAT is just the amuse-bouche for the real meat that's about to be served from none other than Port Authority executive director Foye, whose angry email, later leaked, cracked the scandal open. Foye sits down before the committee.

The New Jersey side of the Port Authority has long despised Foye. New Jersey officials complained that he leaked internal business to favored reporters to gain leverage, and that he delayed the authorization of money for Garden State projects. Wildstein fought with him the most—one eyewitness called it a "holy war." At one point Foye hired outside counsel to investigate Wildstein for allegedly harassing an employee.

Now here he is at the hearing. Under oath. Bitter that New Jersey has seized control of the Port Authority police and the bridge. And ready to tell all. Assemblyman Gordon Johnson, a Democrat, does the questioning.

"Was there a traffic study?"

"I'm not aware of any."

"We were told . . . there was a traffic study by Mr. Baroni. You're not aware of any traffic study?"

"I'm not aware of a traffic study. No, sir."

Christie is listening to the day's hearings—and this bombshell refuting a traffic study—on his computer. He texts back and forth with Regina Egea, the governor's office liaison to the Port Authority, and also his incoming chief of staff. They exchange a dozen texts in all, talking at least in part about the hearings.

Neither Christie nor Egea later remember exactly what their text conversation was about. They delete the messages.

But after the hearing Christie makes his feelings known. He gets on the phone with his ally, Democratic New York governor Andrew Cuomo, who appointed Foye to the Port Authority. Christie recounts the conversation to his staff: "I told Cuomo to tell Pat Foye to fuck off."

### DECEMBER 12

Stepien went on a much-needed vacation after quarterbacking the big Christie reelection win. He is back now, ready to get back to work preparing for a Christie presidential campaign.

But first he is summoned to Drumthwacket, the ornate governor's mansion in Princeton. The governor has something he wants to talk about. Stepien likely realizes that. He talked to his longtime compatriot, DuHaime, on the way to Drumthwacket.

After a breakfast meeting with union leaders in the music room at Drumthwacket, Christie and Stepien retire to the dining room. The governor has questions: Do you have any emails linking you to this? What did you know, when? How are you vulnerable in this? Wildstein is telling people you knew about it—what's going on?

Stepien says he had nothing to do with the lane closures—although he did, technically, know about them. Wildstein would have fifty crazy ideas a month, Stepien tells Christie. When he brought up the traffic study idea, Stepien says, he told him to just run it by Trenton. After all, Stepien was on the campaign at this point and no longer a government official in Trenton.

And what about the Sokolich endorsement? Christie asks.

Stepien says that yes, last spring, Sokolich was approached for his endorsement. But Sokolich said no. So the campaign let him be.

O'DOWD, THE OUTGOING Christie chief of staff now being nominated as state attorney general, has an 11:00 a.m. meeting with the governor at Drumthwacket. On the way there he runs into Stepien and Christie huddled in the dining room.

Christie brings O'Dowd into the conversation. He wants him to check up on Bridget Anne Kelly. "Kevin, this bridge issue is still out there, all the noise about politics, local retribution—this is a major distraction," Christie says. "I need you to talk to Bridget and ask her whether or not she had anything to do with closing the lanes at the bridge."

BACK AT THE Statehouse, O'Dowd stops by Kelly's office.

She's out. Her daughter is having surgery.

O'Dowd reaches her on the cell. O'Dowd thought highly of Kelly—she was a team player and a hard worker. He asks about her daughter's surgery.

He tells her about his recent vacation to Florida. There's an assemblyman who has a request about something—what do you think about that?

Then he brings up the real reason for the call. "Bridget," he says. "I need to ask you about the lane closures." So he asks her directly if she had anything to do with this.

"Absolutely not," she says. "Why are you asking me that?"

"Well, I was at Drumthwacket today with the governor and he asked me to ask you that. So I am."

"Does he think I did?"

"He just told me to ask you that question directly, so I'm asking you directly: Did you have anything to do with closing the lanes at the bridge? Check your emails, check your texts. Make sure nobody sent you anything on this, and let me know if you find anything or if anything jogs your memory. Call me or see me tomorrow."

**LEADERS IN THE** Statehouse are now getting official word that subpoenas from Democratic legislators have been issued to seven Port Authority officials. This time, Wisniewski wants documents.

Kelly starts to cover her tracks. Because she has an email out there that she knows doesn't bode well.

On Day 4 of the lane closures, Sokolich finally got IGA aide Evan Ridley on the phone to express concerns about the traffic nightmare. Those concerns were then summarized in an email written by Ridley's boss, Christina Renna—"He feels like a fucking idiot," she wrote of Sokolich, and "he's about to lose control of the situation." Renna wrote that Sokolich believed there was "a feeling in town that it is government retribution for something."

Kelly responded to that email with one word: "Good."

Kelly now realizes this is a problem, a potential vulnerability. So she calls Renna.

"I didn't know anything about this—the lane closures," Kelly says.

"Well, yes you did, because Mayor Sokolich called Evan, and I emailed you about it."

Kelly's demeanor changes; it grows nervous and exasperated.

"Oh, are you talking about the email I responded to with, 'Good'?"

"Yes."

"Well, 'good' can mean a bunch of different things. You can read that a bunch of different ways. Ya know, just do me a favor and get rid of it."

"You want me to delete the email?"

"Yes. Listen, I'm getting a lot of questions, and I'm just really nervous. And, you know, I can't take getting grilled about this over and over again."

Then the call dropped.

BIG MEETINGS HAPPEN in person. No phones. No confusion. O'Dowd drives more than an hour to the governor's satellite office in a Newark office tower. With McKenna in the room, O'Dowd instructs Baroni to resign immediately. By order of the governor, who appreciates your service.

"I know that you know that you're not likely to be here for a second term, and you may or may not know who your replacement is," O'Dowd tells Baroni. "What I don't think you do know is that tomorrow is your last day."

Baroni apologizes to O'Dowd. He insists that everything he testified to was truthful—"I'm a former state senator, I'm a former constitutional law professor, I'm a member of the bar," he says. He stands by his story that there was a traffic study hampered by notification problems.

At this point neither O'Dowd nor McKenna, two former federal prosecutors who are the top aides to the gubernatorial throne, asks for a copy of the traffic study. They do not ask who authorized the traffic study, nor if anyone in the governor's office knew about it.

Instead, they listen to Baroni's requests. Severance? Continuance of benefits? A new gig, maybe?

Baroni is told to call Christie political strategist Mike DuHaime; he'd find him a soft landing somewhere.

Next up is Wildstein. McKenna meets with him alone. Wildstein had actually resigned the previous week, effective December 31, but now McKenna tells Wildstein that his last day is tomorrow.

Wildstein's position would never again exist. Deputy chief of staff Deborah Gramiccioni, praised in her role leading the governor's Authorities Unit, will replace Baroni in the second term.

Days earlier, Baroni told Gramiccioni that he thinks there are emails indicating Kelly knew about the lane closures; Gramiccioni promptly ran this information up to the top three aides to Christie: Comella, O'Dowd, and McKenna.

Tonight, Gramiccioni reiterates this allegation to Christie himself. There's a "hum" out there that Kelly is on the emails, she says.

The governor seems upset.

### DECEMBER 13

At 5:00 a.m., the governor is working. He calls Gramiccioni: "I'm announcing you as the next deputy executive director of the Port Authority at a press conference today."

She knew this was coming. But she never expected to be taking this position so soon. She had last spoken to the governor eleven hours ago, and he hadn't told her.

CHRISTIE CALLS A meeting around the conference table in his office. O'Dowd and McKenna, the chief counsel and chief of staff, sit in their typical positions on either side of the governor. Kelly is there, as are the other senior staffers.

Christie enters. He slams the door. He is evidently furious.

This is not a normal meeting. Gramiccioni will remember that Christie was angrier than she had ever seen him. Drewniak later said that "everybody in the room was absolutely riveted because we had never heard him talk to us this way."

Christie has a lot to get off his chest. He begins ticking off what he is angry about, from the bad publicity around a recently failed coup to oust Senator Tom Kean, Jr., as Republican minority leader to a *Wall Street Journal* scoop about a private conversation he had with New York governor Andrew Cuomo. Christie accuses his staff of suffering from senioritis since the big reelection win, just as they are under more national scrutiny than ever.

"This is no time for you to screw up," he says. "The spotlight can turn into a searchlight if I can't trust all of you. And I've trusted all of you. Many of you have been with me for years. And if you want to continue to have a good and viable government I must have your attention, and you must always tell me the truth."

Then, the bridge. He says he thought he had put the issue to bed at his last press conference when he sarcastically dismissed the accusations. But now he has to deal with it again. "This is a mess," he says, "and now I have to clean it up.

"We don't have scandals," Christie declares. "This is not us."

He wants to know everything, to make sure he has this crisis under complete control at this moment. If you were involved in this, Christie says, or had knowledge of it, you have until my 11:00 a.m. press conference to go to O'Dowd or McKenna and talk.

"The confessionals are open," he says.

After this, the governor says he will tell the media that no one was involved. "I will cut your balls off in front of the press unless you tell me the truth," he says.

"Do not make a liar out of me."

The governor walks away from the conference table and over to his desk. Everyone walks out, silently.

O'DOWD HEADS TO Kelly's office; rumors about her involvement need to be addressed.

Stepien, her former boss and ex-boyfriend, is also there, standing with O'Dowd. She's sitting, and she looks upset. "Baroni says there's emails or an email that indicate you knew something about this," O'Dowd says. "Do you have any idea what he is talking about?"

Kelly says no. But she does reveal a printout of the email from her aide, Renna, summarizing a phone call with Sokolich during the lane closures. Sokolich "feels like a fucking idiot," Renna wrote, because no one would tell him what was happening with the bridge. Kelly shows this email to O'Dowd.

Kelly does not reveal her reply to the email, which was "Good."

And fortunately for Kelly, O'Dowd doesn't go to the other person on the email, Renna, to ask if this version is the whole story. If he had, maybe he would have found out that Kelly instructed her to delete that "Good" part of the message. Destroying government correspondence, they all know, is illegal.

Instead, O'Dowd, a former federal prosecutor, trusts his employee. Maybe the volume of crises that the administration has dealt with over four years is dulling the team's senses. Maybe top staffers have been going ninety miles per hour for too long, and should've been swapped out midway through the first term. Maybe everyone is just ready for Christmas break already. But if O'Dowd had done more—if he had just looked at the other names on the email chain—then O'Dowd might have uncovered the whole scheme. From there O'Dowd might have been able to squeeze Kelly for more information about why these lanes closed—and who issued the orders.

But O'Dowd doesn't do that. Instead O'Dowd takes this email and brings it to the governor. Christie and O'Dowd decide it is consistent with Kelly's assertion that she didn't know about the lane closures *before* they happened. And they believe that is what Baroni and Wildstein must've been referring to when they alleged Kelly *knew* about the lane closures.

But don't they have questions about the implication of that email—that the mayor of Fort Lee is intentionally being ignored? Could that have something to do with why he faced a five-day traffic jam?

Don't Christie and O'Dowd wonder about this?

O'Dowd, who is on the verge of being nominated as New Jersey attorney general, simply tells Kelly to go back and look in her deleted email files for anything else about the lane closures. He does no further investigation.

**A PRESS AIDE** circulates a list of "Questions for 12/13/13 Press Conference." There are twenty-three Bridgegate-related questions.

Christie steps to the podium and fields no fewer than thirty-seven questions on this topic for more than an hour. This is a growing media storm, but the governor is not defensive. He barely gets testy with reporters. He is careful and calm. He can't afford to be anything else right now.

Angie Della Santi of the Associated Press asks him directly: "Can you say with certainty that someone else didn't, on your staff or in your administration, act on your behalf for the lane closures for political retribution?"

The governor responds that he has "absolutely no reason to believe that."

His campaign manager, Stepien, doesn't know anything about this either, Christie adds. Stepien is in the room, watching the press conference. Christie has demanded he be there, to see what the governor is now going through.

"I've made it very clear to everybody on my senior staff that if anyone had any knowledge about this that they needed to come forward to me and tell me about it, and they've all assured me they don't," Christie says.

Christie does not mention that his deputy chief of staff was aware on Day 4 of the lane closures that the mayor of Fort Lee was extremely upset and concerned that this was about "retribution." Likewise Christie fails to tell us about why the day after that email, the lane closures continued unabated, despite suspicion of something untoward and possibly illegal.

Christie also doesn't reveal that Baroni has been forced to resign immediately in an emergency decision that had apparently come just hours before. Instead he praises Baroni for his service, saying, "This was a change I was going to make anyway."

The governor doesn't provide Wildstein the same cover. Asked if he is satisfied with the explanation from Baroni and Wildstein, the governor skips over Wildstein in his answer and defends Baroni as a "truth teller" and a "good friend."

In contrast to the riot act he has just read his staff, Christie downplays everything before the press. The matter is "sensationalized" and "a whole lot of hullabaloo." The fact that the lane closures happened shortly after Sokolich's nonendorsement was "a coincidence of timing." And despite his staffers later describing him as the angriest they had ever seen him that morning, the governor claims to me that he wasn't angry at all. "I wouldn't characterize myself as angry, Matt," he says. "I think 'anger' would probably be a little bit too strong a word. 'Bothered' probably would be the better word, you know?"

As for the traffic study? I point out to Christie that the top guy at the Port Authority has testified under oath that there was no such traffic study.

"Matt, you really think that I want to, like, go now and say show me the traffic study so I can read it? The fact is Bill Baroni, *Senator* Bill Baroni, is a friend of mine, has been I think an outstanding public servant both in his time in the legislature and his time at the Port Authority," he says. "And I have no reason not to believe him, and I don't interpret Mr. Foye's testimony in the same way you do. He didn't say there wasn't one. I think what he said was he wasn't *aware* of one. That's very careful wording."

None of this interests him any longer, he declares, and he is not "curious" what the traffic study entailed. "Believe me, I've heard more about this than I ever wanted to hear," he says.

He tries to keep things light. At one point he winks at me, saying: "Now that I'm governor there's less of a concern about the traffic for me." That's because he gets police escorts everywhere.

I ask if he is ultimately responsible as the head of the government, even if he wasn't personally involved. "I'm ultimately responsible for every person that I put in this government and the actions they take," he says. A video of that answer would soon be emailed to reporters as an example of his straight-talk approach.

Christie declares this whole thing over. "The chief of staff and the chief counsel assure me that they feel comfortable that they have all the information we need to have, so . . . you know, we're going to turn the page now," he says.

There are so many more pages to turn, though. And Wildstein is holding the only copy of the book.

Kelly is in the room for the press conference, nervously watching. She texts O'Dowd, who is standing about fifteen feet away, to ask him if she should speak with the governor.

O'Dowd doesn't respond.

GRAMICCIONI WALKS BY Kelly's desk. It looks as though she's been crying, so Gramiccioni steps inside and sits down. What's wrong?

Kelly says she's been going through her emails all morning for O'Dowd, but can't find anything about the lane closures. She explains that she deletes most of her emails so her kids don't read her correspondence with her ex-husband.

Gramiccioni thinks this is an odd thing to say. She tells Kelly that it's best to be the one to come forward first with information that someone else might have.

Kelly just stares at her.

Just talk to O'Dowd again, Gramiccioni advises.

KELLY GOES TO O'Dowd's office. She shows him yet another email. This one is a letter that Senator Weinberg had originally sent to a Port Authority commissioner, complaining about the lack of answers over the lane closures. The email had been forwarded to Kelly.

O'Dowd is angry. He has instructed her to go through her emails and texts the night before, and yet she is only now coming up with this?

But the substance of the email—since it came after the lane closures—does not get Kelly in trouble.

Even as Baroni and Wildstein are hustling out of the Port Authority with boxes, hiring criminal defense lawyers, Kelly remains in her job.

## DECEMBER 19

At the next Christie press conference, the third time in a row that Christie is being asked about this, the governor changes his approach. He goes aggressive, responding to a question from a reporter at the *Wall Street Journal*, which has led the bridge coverage to this point, with this: "At the end of this, you know, you and your paper will owe an apology to Senator Baroni and Mr. Wildstein."

Christie is the front-runner for the Republican presidential nomination. This is why the scandal is getting so much attention, he says.

"It's not that big a deal," he says, "just because the press runs around and writes about it both here and nationally."

DECEMBER 22

Wildstein hires a criminal defense lawyer, Alan Zegas, who calls Christie's lawyer, McKenna, to talk about the subpoena from the Democrats in the legislature.

McKenna tells Zegas to hand over whatever documents he is required to.

Zegas replies to McKenna that there could be some embarrassing information in those documents.

Like what?

Zegas doesn't say.

McKenna asks Zegas to send him a copy of any documents that he sends to the Democrats.

Zegas never does that, and Team Christie will be in the dark for two more weeks about what exactly Wildstein is turning over.

DECEMBER 23

At home in Sayreville in Central Jersey, Wisniewski is waiting on documents.

Wisniewski is a third-generation resident of Sayreville, a state assemblyman and onetime chairman of the state Democratic Party with gubernatorial ambitions. His region of the state currently lacks a Democratic Party boss with clout, which means he has cultivated an independent streak that seems to come natural to him.

A tall, thin lawyer with blue eyes that sharply contrast with his otherwise perpetual paleness, Wisniewski has coarse, graying hair that gives him a vaguely Founding Father look. Wisniewski was classmates with Christie at Seton Hall Law School, but the governor doesn't think much of him, consistently mispronouncing his last name—Wiz-NOOS-kee instead of Wiz-NES-kee. He is the tenacious underdog foil to the powerful governor, which has, until now, been as quixotic as it sounds. After all, Wiz, through his Assembly Transportation Committee, has had subpoena power over the Port Authority for nearly two years now—seeking documents on the agency's quick toll increases, hiring of political cronies, and skyrocketing use of overtime—but none of it has turned up anything significant. That subpoena power expires in a few weeks, on January 14.

At first when news surfaced about days of traffic jams on the George Washington Bridge, Wiz didn't think much of it. But he grew suspicious when people he described as "well-placed Democratic intermediaries"—those establishment Democrats connected with the governor's office—began calling him about the traffic situation. "You're not getting involved in that, are you?" they asked him. "This is foolish, you don't want to be involved in this."

Then Wiz definitely wanted to be involved in this. So in a last-ditch effort, Wiz subpoenaed the agency and Wildstein for documents related to the lane closures. If this didn't turn up anything, it was thought, the Democratic leadership in the state allied with Christie would surely quash his subpoena power.

So now here he is, just a guy in Central Jersey trying to get paperwork from the office before Christmas break. The documents are due at 5:00 p.m. today.

They don't arrive. Wiz is not surprised that the Port Authority isn't cooperating.

Yet it's just an email glitch. At 8:30 p.m., the documents land in an inbox at the state's Office of Legislative Services. From there a PDF file with nine hundred pages is emailed to Wiz.

He sees the email, but it's getting late. And besides, his previous subpoenas to the Port Authority had yielded tens of thousands of pages of nothing. Wouldn't this be more of the same? He goes to bed.


### DECEMBER 24–26

The next day is Christmas Eve, and even a political geek like Wiz doesn't slog through government emails on Christmas Eve. He goes to dinner with his family, his wife and three daughters, and then celebrates Christmas Day at his mother-in-law's house.

Finally, on the day after Christmas, late that night, when his wife and daughters are off watching TV or reading or sleeping, Wisniewski sits down at his iMac. Not a soul is stirring. Except for Wiz.

**HIS HOME IS** McMansion-y and classy, with an open layout that extends from the kitchen into a carpeted living room lined with a fireplace and a bookshelf containing an extensive Harry Potter collection and two books on Thomas Jefferson—John Meacham's *Art of Power* and Stephen Ambrose's

*Undaunted Courage*. Since it's Christmas time, Sirius Radio Channel 151 is playing holiday music as Wiz sits down in a nook between the kitchen and living room, in front of his computer screen and a piping hot cup of Earl Grey.

Scrolling through, hundreds of pages in, the clock hits 9:00 p.m., then ten. Wiz spots an email from David Wildstein saying that the "gov" had personally approved $60,000 for a "traffic study" in Springfield. He emails his aide, Aaron. *That kind of caught my attention,* he says.

About page 800, he sees something else. On August 13, 2013, at 7:34 a.m., Bridget Anne Kelly wrote: "Time for some traffic problems in Fort Lee."

Wow.

First thing Wiz notices: This is from a personal email account. *Why isn't this a government email?*

Next he tries to think of anyone else in Trenton named Bridget Anne Kelly. *Could this really be the Bridget Anne Kelly in the governor's office?*

He asks Aaron: *Is this the same Bridget Anne Kelly who is deputy chief of staff to the governor? This goes all the way to the governor's office?*

Wiz thought he was investigating corruption at the Port Authority, where some good ole boys loosely connected to the governor were performing antics at the public's expense. This email raises a whole new specter of what the governor knew, and when.

Wiz circulates the email to a few staffers to figure out what to do next.

They cannot believe how obvious this email is. If there were such transgressions going on, he wonders, why didn't they just use the phone so there'd be no public record? What kind of cavalier attitude had they taken to abuse of power?

### DECEMBER 31

Wisniewski issues a rare New Year's Eve press release to announce that he is subpoenaing Wildstein to testify before his committee, to provide "insight into this decision that put public safety at risk."

Media interest mounts. Public records requests pour in looking for correspondence between the governor's office and the Port Authority.

But Team Christie goes on as if the world isn't about to fall apart. His communications staff spends the day self-publishing a compilation of Christie GIFs to *BuzzFeed*: Christie taking selfies, throwing his sport jacket to an aide, and hanging out with Bon Jovi, Shaquille O'Neal, and Barack Obama.

### JANUARY 7, 2014

Christie is in Union City, the town that put him over the 50 percent mark in the Hispanic vote for reelection. He signs the Dream Act, which allows immigrant children brought to the country illegally to qualify for in-state college tuition. This marks a reversal of his previous opposition to such a proposal and is an indication that he is preparing to run as a Big Tent Republican, a conservative who's able to break party orthodoxy and attract new voters to the Republican side. He is a governor prepared to govern all of America, not a Republican trying to shift the country to the right. That will be the message.

More good news: Christie makes it official that Stepien has a new job running the New Jersey Republican Party. The appointment had been postponed while they weathered this scandal. With that behind them, Stepien takes the job. Christie calls him "the best Republican operative in the country."

Kelly, too, thinks the worst may have passed. She tells an underling: "I've been hiding under my desk nervous anytime someone walked in here with questions about Fort Lee, and I'm just happy it's dying down."

# 13

# NO SURRENDER

At 8:00 a.m. on January 8, 2014, I went to a coffee shop in Philadelphia. I was working on an NPR story about an escalating traffic-jam scandal that I was scheduled to record in a couple of hours at the nearby studios for WHYY public radio. I ordered hot coffee and *shakshuka*—poached eggs, tomato sauce, chili peppers, and onions all mushed around into deliciousness.

I still think about that meal. Because I never ate a bite.

As I sat down in front of my laptop a story flashed across my screen. Shawn Boburg of the *Record* in Bergen County had just dropped the scoop of his life.

> *Governor Christie's deputy chief of staff told one of his top Port Authority executives that it was "time for some traffic problems in Fort Lee" several weeks before controversial lane closures took place at the George Washington Bridge, according to sources.*

BOBURG BECAME INTERESTED in journalism after reading Robert A. Caro's masterpiece, *The Power Broker*, about Robert Moses, the behind-the-scenes political player who was more influential than anyone in shaping the tristate area in the first part of the twentieth century. Moses used deft political maneuvering to create public infrastructure, from parks to bridges to highways. Moses's political rivals ran the Port Authority, and in 1955 they worked out an arrangement that resulted in construction of a second deck to the George Washington Bridge, increasing use of the bridge 75 percent. Caro writes that this deal "sealed, perhaps for centuries, the future of New York and its suburbs."

Boburg began covering the Port Authority a half century later, finding an agency still run by the same cohort of rich, politically connected white men engaged in closed-door deal-making. "I was really impressed—and not in a positive way—about how opaque the Port Authority was," Boburg told me. It took Boburg more than six months just to get the agency's payroll. And when he got it, it turned out the list was incomplete and incorrect. The Port Authority was "a can that was calling to be opened."

The Port Authority had a lot of secrets, and few reporters were ferreting them out. He'd see only one or two other reporters at Port Authority meetings; I'd seen the same number at school board meetings in small New Jersey towns. The difference was Boburg was reporting on a government agency that had a budget the size of Chicago's.

About a week before January 8, Boburg was tipped off to the existence of the email reading "time for some traffic problems in Fort Lee." Boburg knew that it was written by a woman from the governor's office, but he didn't know her name. Was it Lieutenant Governor Kim Guadagno? Was it communications chief Maria Comella?

Then he asked his source: "Wouldn't it be weird if it was a person who had the word 'bridge' in her name?"

The source laughed. Bingo. It was Bridget Anne Kelly.

Soon enough Boburg got a copy of the actual email, which had Kelly's name right on it. Then he got the green light to go ahead with the story.

Boburg sat at his computer at home in Newark and started typing the article on the night of January 7, 2014. At three or four a.m., after finishing working through the story with his editors, Boburg sent an email to the newspaper's chief lawyer, Jennifer Borg, a scion of the family that owned the newspaper. He wanted to let her know what was coming.

About 8:00 a.m., Boburg called Kelly on her cell phone. Kelly was on a conference call for work but she picked up, thinking the call might be about one of her four children. Kelly didn't recognize the voice. She had never before spoken to Boburg. He introduced himself.

"I've got an email from you to David Wildstein, and it says, 'Time for some traffic problems in Fort Lee,'" Boburg said. "I'm writing a story about it. Do you want to comment?"

There was silence. Then stammering. This was the very call that Kelly had feared for four months. "I'm literally in the middle of a conference call," she told Boburg. "I can't do this right now. I'm going to have to call you right back." Kelly hung up on him.

Boburg's next call was to Michael Drewniak, the governor's spokesman. Boburg told Drewniak that the paper had also obtained emails between him and Wildstein.

Drewniak cautioned Boburg to be careful with the story. "This is explosive stuff," he said.

At 9:13 a.m., Boburg posted his story online. A few minutes later, Democratic staffers from the state legislature began sending reporters the "time for some traffic problems" email and a trove of other documents that Wildstein had supplied in response to his subpoena.

KELLY GOT OFF the phone with Boburg and called Drewniak. He didn't answer. So she called Comella.

Comella was at her apartment in New York City on a work call when Kelly's name kept popping up on caller ID. She finally picked up. Kelly was freaking out, saying she had just gotten a call from this reporter at the *Record*, she didn't know his name, and he was writing a story about one of her emails. "I don't know what to do," Kelly told Comella. "He said it was going to be a big story. And he wanted me to comment."

"Who's his source?" Comella asked.

"I don't know. I'm sorry. I'm so sorry, Maria."

"Stay where you are. I'll call you back."

Comella was the calm in any storm; only her occasional nail-biting, standing on the side of the room scanning the scene during press conferences, betrayed the stress of managing a larger-than-life political force every day. As the final gatekeeper between Christie and the rest of the world, she was his most important governmental aide. And so it fell to her to make the call.

Christie had just finished a morning workout at home with his trainer. He got out of the shower and picked up his cell.

It's bad, Comella told him.

The governor pulled out his iPad, and together they read Boburg's story online.

The governor remembers feeling sick to his stomach.

"What should I do?" Christie asked Comella.

They made a plan to meet him at Drumthwacket.

MINUTES LATER I was on the air with Brian Lehrer, the host of our morning program at WNYC. Lehrer started off his show with the latest developments.

"We begin with some breaking news about GW Bridgegate, the closing of local access lanes in Fort Lee to the bridge for commuters for a few days in September. The question has been: Was it political payback against the Democratic mayor of Fort Lee for not supporting Christie for reelection, right? So the *Record* newspaper of Northern New Jersey has just broken some new details, and New Jersey Public Radio reporter Matt Katz, who covers the Christie administration, has been checking them out. Hi, Matt, good morning, what's new?"

"Good morning, Brian. I just got those same emails and they're pretty explosive, to be honest with you. We thought—the governor had told us—that nobody on his senior staff—that he talked to everybody on his whole senior staff—and nobody knew about these lane closures in September. And these emails indicate otherwise. . . . [Kelly] wrote an email to Christie's contact at the Port Authority, Christie's appointee at the Port Authority, David Wildstein, and she wrote: 'Time for some traffic problems in Fort Lee.' "

"No!" Lehrer said. "It's as specific and direct as that? 'Time for some traffic problems in Fort Lee'?"

"That's correct."

**THE NEWS SPREAD.** Top Christie staffers were throughout the state when they heard—at home, in Trenton, at a New Jersey Transit board meeting in Newark. Via BlackBerries, the revealing emails were passed around, each PDF presenting a new wallop of shock.

Because it wasn't just the "time for some traffic problems in Fort Lee" email. There were all kinds of emails between Wildstein and Kelly, including this email—"Is it wrong that I'm smiling?"—that Kelly sent after finding out that school buses were stuck in traffic.

"They are the children of Buono voters," Wildstein had responded.

In those few emails, it was clear that a) Fort Lee was being punished, and b) the reason was ugly politics. The question then became: So who else knew?

**"MEETING WITH TRUMP** today," Mike DuHaime told his old buddy David Wildstein when he called him first thing that morning. Not too long ago, back in the nineties, DuHaime and Wildstein were running local state Assembly races. Now here DuHaime was, on the verge of helping to guide Christie's presidential campaign—and meeting with Donald Trump about the billionaire's possible run for governor of New York.

DuHaime first met Christie in 1997 and began working for him in 2009 under the title "chief strategist." The son of a former New Jersey mayor, DuHaime had run New York City mayor Rudy Giuliani's presidential campaign. That's where he met Comella, whom he recruited to the Christie campaign. Like a general manager for a baseball club, DuHaime started building the Christie Team, bringing on his old friend Bill Stepien as campaign manager. Together they would formulate the path to 2016.

After his call with Wildstein, DuHaime stopped at the Clifton Diner, where he was scheduled to have breakfast with Alfred Doblin, the *Record*'s editorial page editor. He walked into the diner blissfully unaware—until Doblin handed over his phone so he could read the breaking news on the *Record*'s website.

DuHaime read the story. Then the governor called. DuHaime went outside to talk.

Come to Drumthwacket, Christie told him.

DUHAIME, COMELLA, AND Kevin O'Dowd were all at Drumthwacket—a mansion that had been owned by the real Wally Edge before he bequeathed it to the state for a governor's residence. O'Dowd had put the call out to get everyone in the inner circle over there—Port Authority chairman David Samson, brother Todd Christie, and adviser Bill Palatucci. They started arriving around noon, seated around a large table on the second floor, poring over documents from the fake Wally Edge. They'd all be there until dark.

The room hung heavy in shock. "I don't understand," someone would say. "I don't get it," muttered another.

As those in the room would retell it, Christie didn't know, for sure, whom to trust nor whom to blame. That made him nervous, and emotional. He cried, and asked *again* if anyone had anything to do with this.

They denied it. Each and every one.

So then they began looking outward from that room.

Michael Drewniak, who had been Christie's chief spokesman since his U.S. Attorney days, was summoned. For two and a half hours, Drewniak was interrogated by colleagues-turned-investigators: Christie attorney Paul Matey, a former federal prosecutor who had worked with Christie at the U.S. Attorney's Office, and Chris Porrino, who was in his first day as Christie's chief counsel. Porrino was supposed to start the following week, but the governor needed immediate legal help. He was a former criminal defense attorney who had represented Solomon Dwek, the con man who cooperated with Christie's U.S. Attorney's Office to bring down all of those local politicians in the middle of the 2009 gubernatorial election.

Matey and Porrino took Drewniak into a private room where he was questioned about his role in the whole affair—about his frequent interaction with Wildstein, including the steak dinner right before he was forced to resign. He was asked about emails showing him cursing out reporters and Patrick Foye, the top official at the Port Authority.

Drewniak was not at ease. He asked if he was going to be fired. He showed Porrino and Matey about a dozen documents, with handwritten notations, to prove his innocence.

After the questioning, Porrino and Matey had Drewniak wait in the room for fifteen long minutes while they went over their findings with Christie.

Christie came into the room, and said he had reached a verdict. "I've talked this through fully, and they've reported back to me," Christie told Drewniak. "I'm comfortable with, at this point, that you had no involvement in this. You're good." Christie enveloped Drewniak in a warm hug. He told him: "You're okay. I love you."

Drewniak then went to the table in Wally Edge's old dining room, joining the rest of the group at the big table.

UNLIKE THE DECISION to retain Drewniak, firing Kelly required little discussion. Comella told Christie she had to go; so did O'Dowd, Kelly's formerly supportive boss. They considered talking to her about everything first, to get some more information, but the lawyers in the room saw a potential land mine. They didn't want charges of interference. Perhaps they didn't want to know anything else, given the legal scrutiny.

The job of firing Kelly fell to Porrino, a man whom Kelly had never before worked with, with an assist from Matey.

Kelly waited at home before finding out her fate. At nine the next morning, the men called to fire her.

She asked that her personal items not be sent to her house—there were too many news trucks gathered outside. A feeding frenzy on everything Kelly-related had commenced. Soon enough, reporters found a picture on Kelly's Twitter feed of her celebrating her fortieth birthday party with the governor himself.

Back in Kelly's old office in Trenton, the IGA employees were told by Christie's top lawyers: DO NOT DELETE ANYTHING.

A lot of tears were shed in that office that day.

OVER AT DRUMTHWACKET, DuHaime might have been the most uncomfortable. He was friends with just about everyone involved.

The numbers inherent in modern politics animate DuHaime in conversation—polls, voting trends, results of elections past. But it's relationships that DuHaime excels at. Over the past several weeks he had become a sounding board for several players entangled in the escalating scandal, particularly Wildstein. DuHaime was also an unofficial liaison to the governor for those who sought to get messages to him.

Perhaps DuHaime's closest friend in Christie's world was Stepien, whom he had met back at that ice rink in Central Jersey when Stepien was just a teenager. Just two months earlier Stepien and DuHaime had navigated Christie to a massive reelection win and then, victorious and inseparable, they took a victory lap at a hotel in Arizona where Christie was anointed chairman of the Republican Governors Association. Together, DuHaime and Stepien were supposed to lead Christie's presidential campaign.

But now here DuHaime was at Drumthwacket, but not Stepien. This critical member of the inner circle—said to be like a son to the governor—was under suspicion because of his emails with Wildstein.

Christie dispatched DuHaime to go meet with Stepien, suss out what he knew. DuHaime left Drumthwacket for the thankless mission.

At the Corner Bakery restaurant on Route 1 near Drumthwacket, DuHaime advised his friend Stepien to hire an attorney because the Democrats were going to subpoena him. Stepien said he wasn't involved in this scandal one bit—and he was outraged that he couldn't talk to the governor to make his case. Remarkably private, even to his friends, Stepien acknowledged a relationship with Kelly, but he characterized it as a summer fling and said it had ended before the lanes closed.

DuHaime asked if he thought Kelly was lying when she had told them that she wasn't involved in this.

Yes, Stepien said.

DuHaime told Stepien that there was talk of his being forced out of the Christie operation. The tone of the emails made the governor question whether he could trust him anymore.

Stepien noted that nothing linked him to the planning, execution, or cover-up of the lane closures. Stepien's explanation was that he was trying to comfort Wildstein by sympathetically attacking Sokolich—after all, his traffic study idea had just blown up in his face. Would this governor—who, by the way, has the pottiest of potty mouths—really nail him on calling the mayor an "idiot"?

Stepien's behavior did beg questions about whether he knew that something was amiss sooner than he had let on and, if so, why he hadn't done anything about it. Why hadn't he just told Wildstein *no* when he first brought up this meshuga idea? Why didn't he foil this rogue plot?

These questions were now swarming around Stepien. He was deemed politically toxic.

After their meeting DuHaime returned to Drumthwacket, where he argued to keep Stepien in the fold. He said that Stepien had done nothing related to the lane closures.

Others were spared, after all. Port Authority chairman Samson, for example, was implicated in one email as perhaps retaliating against New York officials after the lanes were reopened. And he was keeping his job.

Stepien became the closest casualty to the governor. Worst of all for Stepien was that Christie didn't fire him in person. Instead his friend DuHaime did the dirty work. This was not Abraham at the mount sacrificing his son; this was Abraham passing the job off to Ishmael.

The execution came by cell phone. DuHaime texted Stepien to get off a phone call with the Republican Governors Association so he could give him a buzz.

Stepien told DuHaime he'd agree to step down from his new role as the chairman of the New Jersey Republican Party.

But DuHaime said that his new high-paid consultancy with the Republican Governors Association would also be canceled.

Being cut off from both gigs meant Stepien was gone from Christie's universe. He would not run the presidential campaign. Suddenly, it was all very much over.

Stepien complained that he had worked harder than anyone for the governor, and now he was being put in the same category as Kelly.

DuHaime repeatedly apologized.

Afterward he called the governor and told him it had been taken care of. He said Stepien was pissed.

Stepien called DuHaime again. He again tried to get DuHaime to push the governor to change his mind.

DuHaime transmitted that message to Christie. The governor wasn't swayed.

**WILDSTEIN EMAILED DREWNIAK** late that night. The subject line was "Serbian." He asked Drewniak about Sokolich's appearance that day on CNN: "Did you see that bastard hamming it up on Wolf Blitzer?"

Drewniak couldn't believe it. He thought it was some kind of trap. Was Wildstein trying to make it seem as if Drewniak was involved if and when these messages were subpoenaed? Or was he really expecting Drewniak to be sympathetic?

Drewniak sent the email to the lawyers in Christie's office. He was furious at Wildstein, for everything, and wrote this to his twin sister that night about Wildstein: "I could claw his eyes out, pour gasoline in the sockets, and light him up."

**THE HEADLINES THAT** Christie woke up to the next day were brutal.

"Christie stuck in jam over GWB lane closings," read the *Record*, with a lede that said the "vindictive lane closures" "plunged the administration into a deep crisis on Wednesday, threatening Christie's national profile as a straight-talker and feeding criticism that his administration has used its power to bully political enemies." The article went on to quote Barbara Buono, the Democrat whom Christie had so easily beaten for reelection, calling Christie's staffers "terrible people."

The *New York Times* used four of its six columns at the top of the front page with a bolded, italicized headline: "*CHRISTIE FACES SCANDAL ON TRAFFIC JAM.*" The headline was attached to a picture of a grim-faced Christie, an infographic laying out the gory details, and a sidebar, "Carefully Tended No-Nonsense Image in Peril."

Even Republicans were ready to indict him, with talk show host Rush Limbaugh saying: "The point of the story is that Christie will do payback. If you don't give him what he wants, he'll pay you back."

**AFTER KELLY GOT** the official call firing her that morning, she contacted her former underling and confidante, Christina Renna. Kelly was hysterical, to the point where she couldn't get the words out. Renna was crying, too.

"I don't know what I'm going to do," Kelly said. She talked about how a reporter had chased her seventeen-year-old daughter at school.

"Did you talk to the governor?" Renna asked.

"He won't talk to me."

Kelly just apologized, over and over again. And then she said something cryptic: "You can't trust anyone, Christina."

After they got off the phone, Kelly texted Renna.

"I'm sorry to tarnish IGA," she wrote.

"We did amazing things to be proud of for 4 years in IGA. Never forget that," Renna responded.

"Hard to remember right now. I was the luckiest girl in the world with an amazing group of people."

"Hang in there, BK."

CHRISTIE WOULD HAVE a press conference to lay it all out there. Comella wrote talking points for an opening statement that would be followed by questions until there weren't any questions left to ask.

I arrived forty-five minutes early and the hallways in front of the governor's office were already jammed with famous national TV faces and bulky cameras. I thought I might not even get in, but Christie's communications team corralled the local reporters and let us cut the line. Given the circumstances, this was a nice gesture.

Would Christie actually apologize? One person who knows him well told me he was "constitutionally unable to say he's wrong" about anything. He had publicly apologized only once in his years as governor, and that was after a statement he made about gay marriage that was deemed offensive to 1960s civil rights activists. He had never apologized for an action of his government.

Christie emerged in a pin-stripe suit, red tie, and white shirt. He looked gray. He looked exhausted. He looked depressed.

The first thing he did was, indeed, apologize: "I come out here today to apologize to the people of New Jersey. I apologize to the people of Fort Lee and I apologize to the members of the state legislature. I am embarrassed and humiliated by the conduct and behavior of some of the people on my team."

He said he fired Kelly "because she lied to me." He said he was "heartbroken" that he was "betrayed."

Then he grew angry, referencing his answer to my question about wearing overalls and a hat. "I would never have come out here four or five weeks ago and made a joke about these lane closures if I had ever had an inkling that anyone on my staff would have been so stupid to be involved and then so deceitful as to just—just to not disclose the information of their involvement," he said.

But no, he said, this was not evidence that he was a "bully."

"Politics ain't beanbag, okay?" he said. "And everybody in the country who engages in politics knows that. On the other hand, that's very, very different than saying that, you know, someone's a bully."

He took more questions. And more questions. He delivered an epic performance. Modern politics had never seen such a thing. He revealed vulnerability, explaining in depth about how he was second-guessing himself over the last twenty-four hours or so. But he appeared much more upset with the lies than the crime itself. "There's a lot of soul-searching that goes around with this," he said. "I'm sick over this. I've worked for the last twelve years in public life developing a reputation for honesty and directness and blunt talk, one that I think is well-deserved."

Even though Sokolich had been so heavily courted for his endorsement, even though they had dined together, Christie said he couldn't "pick him out of a lineup." Christie even seemed to have trouble, at one point, pronouncing his name. "I never even knew that we were pursuing his endorsement," he said.

Christie also aggressively distanced himself from Wildstein, downplaying how much they had hung out both in high school and government. Yes, they went to high school together, but they were not friends—"not even acquaintances." He said: "You know, I was the class president and an athlete. I don't know what David was doing during that period of time." (In fact, while Christie played high school baseball, Wildstein was a statistician on the team.)

The press conference kept going. This would become, as far as anyone knew, the longest political press conference in modern American history.

He was humbled as I had never imagined he could be. He was uncharacteristically patient with reporters, allowing follow-ups and gently explaining that calling out questions was against the rules. "I didn't quite understand your question," he politely said to one reporter. "I had trouble hearing you, too."

And when someone asked a question I had just asked, he calmly repeated the answer instead of castigating the journalist for not paying attention.

Who *was* this guy? One thing was familiar—his eyes. I hadn't seen his eyes that heavy since Superstorm Sandy.

Nearly ninety-four minutes in, he got his most emotional. His voice was raw now. His left arm was on the lectern, he was leaning into the mic. "I am a very sad person today," he said. "That's the emotion I feel . . . I'm a sad guy standing here today."

And yet this was still Chris Christie. He was able to draw a laugh, when asked if he still thought there should be a traffic study of the local Fort Lee lanes. "You think I'm suggesting any traffic studies anytime soon? Ya gotta be kidding me! I don't want a traffic study in front of my house, Marcia," he said. "I think I'm out of the traffic study business for certain."

Only after leaving the room did he realize the press conference had lasted twelve minutes shy of two hours.

AS THE GOVERNOR'S press conference was taking place a related drama was under way on the other side of the Statehouse. Wildstein was scheduled to appear before the Assembly Transportation Committee to testify under oath.

In fact, that hearing was already supposed to have started, but Christie's press conference kept going and going, keeping Democrats on the legislative side of the Statehouse glued to two TV screens. They couldn't step away, so they delayed the hearing. These Democrats, having seen the losing side of so many wars against Christie, having thought they had him dead to rights so many times only to see him resurrect himself and emerge stronger, thought this was it, here he was, *finally* getting his. And it was all because of a traffic jam. God bless New Jersey.

Earlier that morning Wildstein's lawyer had gone to Mercer County Superior Court across the street to try to wiggle Wildstein out of this subpoena for testimony. He had already provided the legislature 907 pages of documents, but the Democrats wanted actual testimony to help them connect some dots. A judge denied Wildstein's request to reject the subpoena. So he went to the Statehouse to testify.

Alan Zegas, Wildstein's attorney, was an old Christie nemesis who represented two high-profile defendants indicted by U.S. Attorney Christie. Zegas publicly accused Christie of politicizing his prosecutions, and after Christie was elected governor, Zegas took to writing op-eds accusing Christie of tampering with the state's justice system and running a tyranny like King George III.

Zegas would soon have his shot at Christie again. For now, he had to get through these Democrats.

Wildstein was bespectacled, chubby-faced, and stoic. Assemblyman John Wisniewski swore Wildstein in under oath and then asked him to spell his name. He asked him what town he lived in. And he asked him whether he was currently employed.

"No," Wildstein responded.

Then Wildstein stopped talking entirely. "On the advice of my counsel, I respectfully assert my right to remain silent under the United States and New Jersey constitutions," he said. Even though he had answered one part of the subpoena (providing documents), when it came to the testimony part Wildstein would exercise his Fifth Amendment right not to incriminate himself.

Just when the Democrats thought they had somebody singing, he shut his mouth. Wildstein wasn't just a wild card to be played against Christie; he was the wild card in this whole scandal.

The hearing was jam-packed with reporters, lobbyists, government staffers, and assorted politicos. A low murmur peaked into a loud murmur when Wildstein first said he was pleading the Fifth.

Wiz, though, wasn't going to let Wildstein out of his grasp that easily. He referred Wildstein to page 706 of the subpoenaed documents.

"This is an email communication, is it not?" Wisniewski asked.

"On the advice of counsel, I assert my right to remain silent, chair," Wildstein said.

"Okay, you can't tell me whether it's an email or a text message?"

"Same answer."

"Okay. That's an email between Bridget Kelly, the governor's deputy chief of staff, and yourself?"

"Same answer."

"And that email says, 'It's time for traffic problems in Fort Lee.'"

"Same answer."

"And you responded to that email?"

"Same answer, sir."

Finally, Wiz turned to Wildstein's lawyer: "Mr. Zegas, I'm coming to the conclusion that I'm wasting my time in asking these questions."

"Yes, sir," Zegas responded.

The committee unanimously voted to hold Wildstein in contempt for not answering questions.

Then Zegas tipped his hand—not to Wiz, necessarily. But to the feds. "If the attorneys general for New Jersey, New York, and the United States were all to agree to clothe Mr. Wildstein with an immunity, I think that you'd find yourselves in a far different position with respect to the information he could provide," Zegas said.

Zegas wanted a guarantee that Wildstein would never see a day behind bars. Then he'd talk.

With that, the hearing ended, and amid a mob of reporters throwing microphones in his face and yelling questions, Wildstein left. He made a right out of the hearing room, then another right, fleeing the cameras and going . . . somewhere. Soon enough he and Zegas realized they were at a dead end, and they had to circle back around toward the elevators—returning to a sea of hungry reporters.

The man who knew every detail of New Jersey politics—the man who now had the power to alter the course of New Jersey politics—didn't know his way around the Statehouse.

IN THE MIDDLE of Christie's epic press conference, he announced he would go to Fort Lee to apologize to the mayor personally.

That message had already gotten to Fort Lee, where Mayor Sokolich was holding his own press conference and saying he wasn't ready to see the governor. He called such a trip "premature." I read this quote on Twitter, and then immediately asked Christie about it.

His response was that he was going to come anyway, even if the mayor wouldn't see him. That message was then tweeted and transmitted to Fort Lee, where a reporter then read Christie's answer to Sokolich.

"Send back the message to Trenton: I've reconsidered. Come on up," Sokolich said.

The governor took a helicopter to North Jersey. He walked up the stairs of Fort Lee Borough Hall and into Sokolich's office, which was decorated with three pictures of the George Washington Bridge. Sokolich's wife, the police chief, the town attorney, and the town administrator were all there, ready to greet the governor.

Christie delivered his apology. Sokolich accepted. At one point, Sokolich made a joke about Christie having said that Sokolich wasn't on his radar screen.

"Governor, am I on your radar?" Sokolich asked.

"We now have our own screen," Christie said.

They sure did. The cable networks covered the official delivery of the apology live. Dozens of Fort Lee residents showed up at the scene, with some thanking Christie for apologizing and others making their grievances known.

While Sokolich forgave the governor ("I'm a forgiving guy," he said), that didn't change what had happened. "When you read about yourself being called an 'idiot,' when you read about yourself being called a 'little Serb,' ya know, it hurts," he said. "It does, it hurts. We didn't sign up for this. We signed up to build Little League fields and lower taxes here. That was our job. We're local government."

Sokolich also questioned the governor's assertion that his leadership style wasn't at issue. "It appears that the great latitude that the governor provides his inner circle, apparently they've taken it to a level they shouldn't have taken it—to venomous, petty, political politics," he said.

Yet the situation inside Christie's orbit was nuanced; there was more humanity within than perceived. That night, IGA staffer Christina Renna messaged Stepien, her old boss. "Thinking of you, Bill," she wrote. "I am extraordinarily proud and fortunate to have worked for you and to have learned from you for the past four years."

"Thanks a lot, CG," Stepien responded. "Your kind words mean a great deal, and I can't thank you enough for thinking of me. Keep making me proud!"

LATE THAT NIGHT Drewniak, Christie's spared spokesman and Wildstein's former friend, wrote a colleague an email ruminating on Wildstein.

"He was always mysterious, intense, but a nebbish nonetheless, who blew you away with his knowledge of politics and political history and his sense of loyalty," Drewniak wrote.

"How he ended up fucking up so many people's lives I'll never understand."

# 14

# THE CRISIS

In January 2013 one of Christie's staffers—he wouldn't tell me who—bet him dinner that he'd reach the 60 percent mark for his reelection that November.

"You don't understand New Jersey, you're crazy, that will never happen," Christie responded. He didn't even crack the 50 percent mark in the three-way 2009 race.

Christie took the bet anyway. Eleven months later, on election night, campaign manager Bill Stepien walked into the room. "You'll be over 60 percent," he told the governor.

First Lady Mary Pat was smiling. But her husband wasn't. And it wasn't just because he'd have to pay up on that debt. "Sixty percent in a blue state? Someone they think is going to run for president?" Christie asked. "They're coming. I don't know when, or how. But they're coming."

Two months later, his premonition proved accurate, as far as he could tell. His enemies were coming for him. And now he had to brace for war.

ALL EYES TURNED to 970 Broad Street, Newark, the same building where Christie made his name as U.S. Attorney of New Jersey. Immediately after his epic Bridgegate press conference, federal prosecutors sent a message to the governor's office that a criminal investigation into the lane closures had begun.

Investigators contacted Bridget Anne Kelly's relatives, and FBI agents showed up at Stepien's apartment, where they questioned his landlord about his marital status and whether he paid his rent on time.

New Jersey U.S. Attorney Paul Fishman, Christie's successor and a President Obama appointee, was running the probe. Christie and Fishman ran in the same prosecutorial circles, and Fishman had represented one of the hip-and-knee-device companies that Christie had prosecuted. Their relationship was described to me as either friendly-competitive or openly disdainful. Regardless, Fishman was now the biggest potential obstacle between Governor Christie and President Christie.

There were few similarities, stylistically or substantially, between these men. Fishman was small and short, reportedly nicknamed "Napoleon" by Christie. As U.S. Attorney, Fishman focused less on corruption and clamped down on U.S. Attorney Christie's use of high-cost Deferred Prosecution Agreements, which Fishman believed gave too much power to prosecutors to cut deals with companies. The powers, he thought, were especially risky in the hands of a U.S. Attorney looking to use such agreements to give government contracts to friends and allies.

Two months before the investigation began, Fishman and Christie teased each other from the stage in front of a room of lawyers during a ceremony honoring a judge. Christie tweaked Fishman for his verbosity: "If each and every one of you . . . were given the time to come up here and speak, you all would have spoken less than Paul Fishman."

THE U.S. GOVERNMENT'S investigation was one of several. The Manhattan district attorney and a U.S. Senate committee had related probes. And Senator Weinberg and Assemblyman Wisniewski were starting up a new Bridgegate committee, appointing members and dropping subpoenas. Democratic groups were spending serious money on oppo research, flooding government agencies with requests for scandal-related documents. More than a dozen reporters were covering Bridgegate full-time, from MSNBC to the Los Angeles Times. With little else going on politically at the time, the governor was the top political story in the country for weeks.

Christie could do nothing more than hunker down and wait for the bombardment to ease. The inner circle called it "The Crisis."

Christie had survived crises before. And he had done so by doing what he did on January 9—long press conferences in which he answered every question in the room. When his brother's legal problems started to dog his campaign in 2009, he held a press conference in which he exhausted all reporters' questions and then went looking for more ("C'mon, I drove all the way to Trenton!").

But Christie's offering to the media of 108 minutes of his political heart and mortal soul did little to quell the interest. Reporters were calling

Democratic elected officials throughout the state who had once allied with Christie to suss out if they, too, were victims of his administration's bullying tactics. We peppered his press office with so many questions that veteran political hands on his team said it reminded them of the height of a presidential campaign.

Christie's problems were a publicity boon to local reporters like myself, much to his frustration. Covering the guy in the midst of the top political scandal in the country means your parents suddenly have a reason to learn how to use their DVR. At one point I was on the phone with an MSNBC producer who was trying to book me on a show when I got a call from *another* MSNBC producer trying to book me on another show.

We had plenty of time to pontificate on the air about Christie's political problems because the governor himself wasn't saying anything. He canceled all press conferences for the near future. When he traveled to Camden for a school visit, he made perfunctory remarks about education before fleeing to shouted questions from TV reporters.

My sources in Christie World were still talking, but more carefully. No more texts and emails, given that subpoenas were flying. Phone calls only.

FOUR YEARS EARLIER, in Christie's first year in office, the NFL announced that New Jersey would host the Super Bowl. That's how long the governor, a sports freak, had been looking forward to hosting the big game.

Then David Wildstein stole his moment.

The Super Bowl was played three weeks after Bridgegate broke, right in the middle of The Crisis. On the Friday afternoon before the game, the *New York Times* sent out a breaking news alert to phones and inboxes across the land:

*Christie Knew About Lane Closings.*

The story said that Wildstein now alleged "that the governor knew about the lane closings when they were happening, and that he had evidence to prove it." Wildstein's revelation was a new bombshell. Christie could no longer enjoy his moment in the spotlight as the unofficial face of the New Jersey Super Bowl. He was toxic.

The *Drudge Report* ran with a big headline—"He Knew?"—and the news spread rapidly . . . for about ninety minutes. Turned out the story wasn't true, in that no such allegation was actually being made. Wildstein had *not* said that Christie knew about the lane closings. Rather, in a letter that Zegas had sent to the Port Authority seeking payment of Wildstein's legal fees, the lawyer wrote: "Evidence exists as well tying Mr. Christie to having knowledge of the lane closures, during the period when the lanes were closed."

*Evidence exists.* But Wildstein wasn't saying he had that evidence.

Less than two hours after the story posted online, the *Times* changed its lede, but the damage was already done. Reporters eagerly reported the *Times's* scoop. Whatever media magic dust Christie had used during his first four years in office seemed to have been wiped away.

The next day Christie's people tried to push back, sending an email to allies entitled, "5 Things You Should Know About the Bombshell That's Not a Bombshell." The memo delved unusually far into Wildstein's past—into his childhood—to cast doubt on his credibility: "He was publicly accused by his high school social studies teacher of deceptive behavior."

That was true. At Livingston High, Wildstein tried to run for the school board even though he wasn't yet eighteen; then his social studies teacher accused him of unethically securing his endorsement. (Later, Wildstein would be elected to the Livingston Township Council and serve two tumultuous years as mayor; another former mayor said he "frightened people.")

Christie's anti-Wildstein memo only invited scorn from the political press on Twitter.

Later that day, at a Super Bowl ceremony in the middle of Times Square in Manhattan, Christie was lustily booed by the crowd. "We hate traffic!" someone yelled. *Booo* was a sound the governor rarely heard. Making matters even more awkward was the fact that Christie sat on a stage alongside New York governor Andrew Cuomo and right across from a huge ABC News ticker with the message: *Christie aide says Christie knew about bridge closures.*

"I said to Cuomo, 'Can't you get that turned off? Kill the power or something?' " Christie remembered.

"It was a bad day, bad day, at a very inopportune time. We had worked hard to get the Super Bowl on my watch," Christie told me. "And for this stuff to happen right on the eve of the Super Bowl? Bad timing. But, ya know, it's just a game."

The Patriots beat the Seahawks, 28–24. Afterward, while fans were waiting in long lines trying to get onto New Jersey Transit, a chant emanated from the human traffic: "Blame Christie! Blame Christie!"

**IN THE FIRST** week after Bridgegate broke, Christie's idol, Bruce Springsteen, whom he had won over after Superstorm Sandy, teamed up with late-night TV host Jimmy Fallon, whom Christie had cultivated as a celebrity friend, to sing the most hilarious Bridgegate takedown imaginable: a duet, "Governor Chris Christie's Fort Lee, New Jersey Traffic Jam," to the tune of "Born to Run." Dressed like 1980s-era Springsteen—with a red bandana and sleeveless jean jacket—Fallon began:

> *In the day we sweat it out on the streets, stuck in traffic on*
> *  the GWB.*
> *They shut down the tollbooths of glory, 'cause we didn't endorse*
> *  Christie.*
> *Sprung from cages on Highway 9 we got three lanes closed, so Jersey*
> *  get your ass in line.*
> *Whoah, maybe this Bridgegate was just payback, it's a bitchslap to*
> *  the state Democrats.*
> *We gotta get out but we can't!*
> *We're stuck in Governor Chris Christie's Fort Lee, New Jersey, traffic*
> *  jaaaaam.*

Then Springsteen himself walked onto the stage:

> *Someday, Governor, I don't know when, this will all end.*
> *But till then you're killing the working man,*
> *who's stuck in the Governor Chris Christie Fort Lee, New Jersey,*
> *  traffic jaaaaam.*

The traffic jam had now been labeled "Governor Chris Christie's." He had been described by the king of the working man as "killing the working man." Six million sets of YouTube eyeballs watched that video—several million more views than anything on the governor's own YouTube channel.

Christie's son told him about the video, but Dad couldn't handle watching it. Months later, Springsteen and Christie ran into each other at the United Airlines VIP lounge at Newark Liberty International Airport. Springsteen and his wife "were great with the kids," Christie remembered, and no one talked about the Fallon video.

"I let him know we were fine," Christie told me. "We never talked about it directly, but we left the meeting with the understanding that he and I are just fine."

BRIDGEGATE HAD ENTERED the national consciousness. Announcers at an NCAA basketball game showed an image of the George Washington Bridge and made fun of Christie. *Family Guy* sent a flier seeking votes for an Emmy nomination that read: "Vote for us, or it's time for some traffic problems in Brentwood." Traffic engineers complained to the *New York Times* that Christie had maligned their craft.

Christie and his scandal became a late-night TV one-liner—"traffic study" became a shorthand, like "Monica's dress."

"The Seahawks beat the Broncos, 43–8," David Letterman deadpanned. "The Broncos are blaming it on a traffic study."

In a rare public appearance during The Crisis, Christie went to a roast for former New Jersey governor Brendan Byrne and had to listen to this from comedian Joy Behar: "When I first heard that he was accused of blocking off three lanes on the bridge, I said, 'What the hell is he doing, standing in the middle of the bridge?' "

"This is a Byrne roast!" Christie said, interrupting her, standing up.

"Stop bullying me!" she responded.

Behar said she wasn't sure he should seek the presidency. "Let me put it to you this way, in a way you'd appreciate: 'You're toast,' " she said.

THIS WAS NOT how Christie had envisioned it. His fame was supposed to improve New Jersey's image, not destroy it. He often spoke of how New Jersey was "a punch line rather than a place of pride" until he came into office and turned the state into a national model for well-run government. "The New Jersey comeback has begun, and you are a part of it," he said to a crowd in Atlantic City. New Jersey was no longer "just the butt of late-night talk show hosts, we are the focus of the evening news and Sunday morning talk shows, because we work together."

Christie's pep talk was more aspirational than reality at first, but sure enough, polls in his first term indicated a spike in New Jerseyans' approval of their state.

Bridgegate killed that progress. New Jerseyans' satisfaction with their state dropped, and a poll taken in the scandal's wake showed New Jersey as the only state in the country that Americans as a whole have a negative opinion about. In other words, New Jersey under Christie was the most disliked place in America.

Quinnipiac University pollsters once asked New Jerseyans to choose a word to describe their governor, and "bully" won in a landslide. "Asshole" was further down the list. But in between were words like "tough" and "strong" and "determined" and "bold"—voters liked that he was shaking things up. And they appreciated that he said difficult things. Like when he appointed a Muslim to be a county court judge, and conservatives accused the judge of practicing Islamic Shariah law, Christie called the accusation "BS" and said he was "tired of dealing with the crazies."

But Bridgegate turned "tough" into "tough guy" for too many New Jerseyans. His approval ratings would halve in eighteen months.

Bridgegate began to define Christie because it fit the shtick; the guy who goes after a heckler on the Jersey Shore with an ice cream cone in his hand could certainly have closed lanes to go after a mayor, the thinking went. Certain threads from the Bridgegate story seemed so *Christie*: the vindictiveness, the gruff language, the guts to do the unprecedented. Just as he was decrying the stereotypical Jersey thing, he was somehow embodying it. The *Courier-Post* newspaper concluded: He "represents our state just as poorly as the buffoons on the trashy reality TV shows filmed in the Garden State."

This may have been his greatest personal failure as a political figure.

"I will not let this scandal define the state of New Jersey," said a Christie impersonator, Bobby Moynihan, in a *Saturday Night Live* skit right after The Crisis hit. "Instead New Jersey will continue to be defined by organized crime, pizza, no-show jobs, a vague chemical smell, and *fuggedaboutit*."

Christie attended the first White House Correspondents Dinner after Bridgegate. President Obama joked: "Gridlock has gotten so bad in this town, we have to wonder: 'What did we do to piss off Chris Christie so bad?' "

The dinner's host, actor Joel McHale, just used the bridge to tell fat jokes. Christie, the guy lampooned as a bully, had to sit there on national TV and pretend to be perfectly okay with this. On the way out Christie told a reporter: "Listen, baby, it's better to be relevant than ignored." He hung out at the after-party till 3:00 a.m., and took a bunch of pictures play-fighting with McHale.

·           ·           ·

**ONE DAY IN** the midst of The Crisis I was hustling through the Statehouse to do a live MSNBC interview on the building's front lawn, where the satellite trucks were camped out. On my way I passed by the governor's office, and as I always did, I peeked through the glass doors. For the first time since I had been covering him, Christie was standing right there in the hallway. With a hand motion, I asked him if I could come in. He waved me through.

He didn't want to talk about the scandal. He wanted to talk about Bob Czech, a cabinet member who chaired his Civil Service Commission, which oversees the state workforce.

Czech was a healthy man when Christie appointed him to his cabinet at the beginning of his term. But he developed ALS, or Lou Gehrig's Disease, and his bodily functions severely deteriorated. Then, on the day the "time for some traffic problems in Fort Lee" email was revealed, Czech's wife— a registered nurse, and Czech's caregiver—got into a fatal car accident in Central Jersey. When we spoke Christie had just returned from the funeral, and Christie was shaken by how Czech's wheelchair was too wide to get into a pew, so Czech couldn't sit with his own children at their mother's funeral. Czech also couldn't lift his own hands, so his children kept getting up from their seats to walk over to him and wipe the tears off his face as he cried. Christie was contemplative and emotional as he recounted this to me. He seemed depressed, but at peace with life's unexpected travails.

Nearly a year later, I asked Christie to explain what was going through his mind that afternoon. He said he was thinking about how even as Czech's health worsened he continued to come to work every day, running Civil Service meetings by writing his agendas using eye movements and an iPad, letter by letter. "You realize things could be worse," Christie told me. "And that you have to remember things you're blessed with—your own health, your family's health. You don't feel bad for yourself at that moment."

Despite this "perspective," Christie said, The Crisis was "the most awful professional experience" of his life.

"You hug your children. You love your wife. You just *live*. You appreciate your friends," he said. "And you realize that the only thing that moves stuff along is time. And so you just keep going, ya know? Some people quit, some people keep going. I keep going."

**BEFORE JOINT SESSIONS** of the legislature, the scene is festive. The New Jersey nexus of politicians, businesspeople and journalists, friends and enemies

and colleagues, all here reuniting, gossiping, and dealing. But today's gubernatorial State of the State Address was coming just five days after Bridgegate
broke, so everyone was talking about just one thing.

Christie walked out of his office and made a right and a left toward the
grand, impressive Assembly chambers. Inside, the clerk called us to order,
and Senate president Stephen Sweeney announced the arrival of "the hon-
orable Chris Christie."

They rose to their feet and turned toward the door, dramatically
opened by guards. In he walked, led by six handpicked legislators, two huge
uniformed state troopers, and a guy in a suit from his security detail. The
governor needed a haircut.

Christie began his traditional zigzag down the aisle toward the lectern,
shaking hands and kissing cheeks and whispering with legislators on both
sides. The ceremony has a nice cadence to it, a reminder that partisanship
and corruption do not have to undermine democratic respect for the office.

In fact the first hand that Christie shook when he entered the chambers
was that of Assemblyman Wisniewski, the Democrat leading the committee
that had uncovered the smoking-gun Bridgegate email. Christie had never
before shaken the assemblyman's hand during these things, just pirouetted
right past him. But now, amid the cacophony of the standing ovation, they
leaned in close.

"Happy new year, John," Christie said.

"Governor," Wisniewski said, "this is not about you, this is not about
me, this is about getting at the truth."

"Happy new year, John."

Debbie Wisniewski, the assemblyman's wife, was standing next to them
during this exchange. She looked right at Christie's intense, angry eyes. And
she was scared. "That's a reason to lose sleep at night," she thought.

She turned to her husband. "What are you in the middle of? Are you
serious? Are you kidding me? We are in the middle of this with this guy, *did
you see the look he just gave you?*

"If looks could kill," she said, "you'd be on the ground."

**AFTER THE SPEECH** Christie gathered staff, guests, and family in the outer
office of the governor's suite. He leaned on the podium he uses for press
conferences. "There's been no day when you all have given me more strength
than today," he began.

"We're used to over the last four years having the whole country watching us. We're not used to it in the current context. That sucks. But on the other hand, it's temporary. I guarantee you it's temporary." He paused.

"I can't tell you how temporary it's going to be." They laughed. He joked that no one should read newspapers, watch TV, or look at the Internet "until further notice."

And then he told these soldiers of the Christie Army that what he had done earlier, when he shook Wisniewski's hand, was deliberate. "That is the example I expect you to follow. This is not a funeral procession into that chamber today. By any means. What this is is the next step on the journey we're going to have together."

He told them of going to Czech's wife's funeral the day before, and watching Czech's children wipe tears from their father's face because he couldn't wipe his own. "We don't have problems," he said. "We have challenges that we will overcome. Yesterday? That was a problem."

Challenges—"some self-created, some foisted upon us by others"—are what we have, he said. "No great accomplishment has ever come without great challenges."

He thanked them for their calls and emails and texts. It meant so much, he said, "just the fact that you showed me you still had confidence in me."

"This was not one of our choosing," he said. "But we will choose how it ends . . . I don't want to see any hanging heads. I don't want to see closed doors and muttered conversations and peering over our shoulders, all the rest of that. That's not what you're here for. . . . We got a government to run. We got work to do."

He got emotional. "There's not a person in this room I don't have love and respect for, and that—*that*—is what really matters in life," he said. "The rest of this shit we'll shoulder through."

BUT IT GOT worse for Christie before it got better. Next came the spate of news stories that, for a time, made this Fort Lee situation look less like an aberration and more like Christie administration policy.

It started with Steve Fulop, who had been elected mayor of Jersey City, the second-biggest city in the state, the previous June. He was a fresh face on the political scene—a former Wall Street investment banker who joined the Marines after September 11, fought in Iraq, and returned to win a seat on the city council. Fulop seemed like an independent-minded Democrat, and Christie had designs on his endorsement. So Christie's political and governmental apparatus went to work—Christie spoke at his inauguration, and Fulop was given extraordinary access to Christie cabinet members. Fulop's point person at the governor's office was Bridget Anne Kelly, who talked to him at his inauguration about endorsing the governor and then scheduled what she called a "Mayor's Day" so five cabinet members—plus Bill Baroni, deputy executive director of the Port Authority—could trek to Jersey City for hour-long meetings with the new mayor in a single day.

Word was Fulop was on board with an endorsement, although nothing was official. Mayor's Day was set for July 23.

Then Fulop decided not to endorse. Suddenly, all the meetings with top Christie officials were canceled. As if to make sure the message was clear, four meetings were canceled within a single hour. All cited "scheduling conflicts." No alternative dates were offered.

Fulop repeatedly tried to reschedule his meeting with Baroni. "I am not sure if it is a coincidence that your office canceled a meeting . . . that seemed to be simultaneous to other political conversations elsewhere that were happening," Fulop wrote to Baroni.

Buried in the newly released Bridgegate emails was evidence that the meeting cancellations were retaliatory. While the lanes in Fort Lee were closed Wildstein had written an email to Kelly about Mayor Sokolich: "His name comes right after Mayor Fulop."

This added a Jersey City storyline to The Crisis, and another question for reporters to pursue: How deep did this pattern of retaliation in the Christie administration go?

Christie later acknowledged to federal investigators that he was aware that the meetings were being canceled. But he said it was done not to punish Sokolich but to preserve his relationship with Senate president Steve Sweeney, a Fulop rival.

"It's a dick move," Fulop said, "but it is what it is."

THEN BRIDGEGATE TEMPORARILY ensnared Christie's official number two, the lieutenant governor.

Kim Guadagno was a town commissioner in little Monmouth Beach (population thirty-two hundred) for just two years before being elected sheriff of Monmouth County—a position she also held for about two years before Christie tapped her as his running mate and lieutenant governor. Sheriffs have an array of responsibilities—serving warrants, enforcing foreclosures, and running jails—not necessarily the experience one would expect for a lieutenant governor. But Guadagno had something else: a pedigree as a prosecutor, both state and federal, which was a world that Christie knew and loved.

After Christie won the nomination he invited the Guadagnos, virtual strangers, to hang out in his backyard one Saturday, with Mary Pat cooking and the three Guadagno kids and the four Christie kids, all seven of them, in the pool till past ten-thirty at night.

Back home the next morning, Guadagno was out picking up Sunday morning coffee when her cell rang. It was Chris. "How would you like to be New Jersey's first lieutenant governor?"

"Honey," she said to her husband when she got home. "The good news is here's your coffee. The bad news is that I'm not going to be able to get you coffee anymore."

Guadagno headed straight to North Jersey, where she was informed she needed to immediately shoot an introductory YouTube video for the campaign. Guadagno went back to Christie's house, where she borrowed the future First Lady's blouse and jewelry. In their master bathroom, Kim put on the gubernatorial spouse's makeup while Christie shaved. There was little pretense to this guy; he got comfortable quick.

Statewide candidacy was not something Guadagno had sought for herself, but with a quick smile and charm, she was pretty good at it. Not so good at it as to overshadow her boss, of course, but good enough not to cause him much trouble. She was there only because of him—that was something he could remind her of as the years went on.

Guadagno was deployed to tasks and events and people that the governor didn't have either the time or desire for. She also became his official liaison to corporations, small and large, known for giving out her cell phone number from podiums at business luncheons. She did events that the governor may have considered below his station, such as a ribbon cutting for a new IHOP on Route 36 in Keyport, and so she had far more public events than Christie—about one thousand in the first term.

But Guadagno was not inner circle. She was not involved in sensitive decision-making; she'd be informed when she needed to know. She met with local politicians only if okayed by the front office, and she was never allowed to sit down for a full-bore newspaper profile. She stood behind Christie at press conferences on an $X$ marked with masking tape on the floor, and rarely was she allowed to have a press conference of her own.

I was fascinated by the muzzle Christie kept on her, and I reported about it regularly. As a panelist on a televised gubernatorial debate in 2013, I used one of my questions to ask Christie about this. If you run for president and leave office, Guadagno would be in charge. Shouldn't we have a chance to get to know who she is?

"Matt, let me tell ya, I'm really proud of the lieutenant governor," Christie said. "She appears publicly all the time, and if you in the press would show up, she answers questions from you all the time. My understanding is you guys just never show up to see her."

But I asked for interviews with her all the time; the governor's office strung me along and then stopped responding. During the Legislative Correspondents Club dinner one year, Guadagno and Christie did a spoof video in which Christie pretended to be Guadagno's assistant, carrying her hand sanitizer and briefcase.

GUADAGNO: What do we have on the schedule today, Chris?

CHRISTIE: Matt Katz wants five minutes.

*They both laugh.*

GUADAGNO: Okay, what else?

Once, I ambushed her at a dairy farm that she was visiting as part of the governor's outreach to farmers.

"Matt has a crush on me," she said to an aide as soon as she saw me standing there, microphone in hand.

I asked if she'd sit down with me for a few minutes.

"You don't want to sit down with the secretary of agriculture?"

Nope.

Guadagno clearly wanted to talk. She could handle herself. But this was the Christie administration. And that meant, singularly, Christie.

That's why it was so odd when Guadagno, a second-tier figure in the administration, suddenly became the center of the Bridgegate storm. On a Saturday morning nine days after Christie's Bridgegate press conference, still in the thick of The Crisis, the mayor of Hoboken went on MSNBC to level a startling allegation: Guadagno, acting as an emissary of the governor's, tried to shake her down. The scene Hoboken mayor Dawn Zimmer described confirmed what many were now beginning to believe about Christie: He was not a straight-talker; he was a thug. The narrative was changing suddenly, almost overnight.

Zimmer alleged that the previous year, in a private conversation during the grand opening of a ShopRite in Hoboken, Guadagno had threatened to take Sandy aid away from Hoboken unless Zimmer did the big guy a favor. Christie wanted to fast-track a development project from a politically juiced company, the Rockefeller Group, which had just bought about $100 million worth of property in an industrial area on the north side of town. The company needed Zimmer to take care of some zoning and tax issues to pave the way for what it planned to put there: a $1 billion office complex with sweeping views of Manhattan.

What could Christie send Zimmer in return for this favor? Millions of dollars in Superstorm Sandy relief funds to help protect Hoboken from the kind of cataclysmic floods it had just been subjected to during the 2012 storm. About 80 percent of the city was flooded, up to three feet of sewage-tainted water, inundating homes, fire stations, and hospitals. Sandy was Christie's lever—if Zimmer didn't comply with Christie's demands for Rockefeller, he could withhold federal antiflood funds until she did.

This, at least, was how Zimmer alleged on national television that it went down. "The fact is," Zimmer alleged, "that the lieutenant governor came to Hoboken, she pulled me aside in the parking lot, and she said, 'I know it's not right. I know these things should not be connected, but they are, and if you tell anyone, I'll deny it.'"

Zimmer told a compelling story—with lots of intriguing similarities to the lane closures. As with Bridgegate, the Port Authority was deeply involved in these allegations. Rockefeller's lobbyist was Port Authority chairman David Samson, a close friend of the governor's, and the Port Authority inexplicably paid for a feasibility study that Rockefeller used to justify the project.

As with Bridgegate, there were whiffs of retaliation. An aide to Guadagno remembered that after the lieutenant governor got back into her SUV following the ShopRite meeting she said something about Zimmer not "playing ball."

In the end, Zimmer failed to push the Rockefeller project. And sure enough, when she requested $100 million in Sandy flood aid, she got only $142,000. Zimmer claimed that she was so upset by this shakedown attempt that she wrote about the incident in her journal. Pictures of the passage in her journal were put up on TV. The handwriting looked as if Zimmer could have written this in the back of the SUV on the way to the MSNBC studios, but a public official couldn't possibly make something like this up, could she?

Zimmer also alleged that yet another Christie cabinet member, Community Affairs Commissioner Richard Constable, threatened her on the same issue. She put that incident in her diary, too, quoting Constable as saying: "If you move that [development] forward, the [Sandy] money would start flowing to you."

Zimmer wrote about how upset she was: "My beloved governor who wants to run for president, I cannot understand it . . . I cannot figure it out, but I have no option but to stand up to him."

Zimmer went on a media assault, and soon her story got grander. The day after the MSNBC interview she said that a third top Christie official had pressured her—Marc Ferzan, Christie's czar for Sandy recovery. Zimmer said when she asked him about Sandy funding, he replied: "Well, Mayor, you need to let me know how much development you're willing to do."

The feds took the case.

Guadagno, Ferzan, Constable, and Christie vehemently denied that Sandy aid was used as a cudgel. Christie's media team cited positive tweets that Zimmer had written just months earlier, such as: "I am very glad Governor Christie has been our governor." Privately, Christie allies whispered that Zimmer was simply out of her mind—that she either made this up or misinterpreted an innocuous conversation about the limited amount of Sandy aid available.

But then my WNYC colleague Scott Gurian found out that Hoboken *did* get ripped off when it came to Sandy aid. Just as Zimmer had suspected. Gurian looked at the Christie administration's formula for doling out money from the Sandy fund that Zimmer had complained about—a $25 million program intended to help towns keep the power on during floods. After Sandy, 85 percent of Hoboken lost electricity—from firehouses to senior citizen apartment buildings. The city had to post handwritten disaster recovery messages on bulletin boards throughout town. So Hoboken seemed like an ideal candidate for this program, and based on the state's own rules the Christie administration should have provided $700,000 to Hoboken for back-up generators instead of the $142,080 it actually received.

This wasn't an isolated error. Some towns received hundreds of thousands of dollars more than the state criteria called for them to receive while others got hundreds of thousands less. Officials were forced to finally acknowledge, and correct, hundreds of problems in the distribution of aid. They attributed the mistakes, simply, to data entry error.

These were not criminal errors, it turned out. More than fifteen months after the investigation into Zimmer's Sandy shakedown began, the U.S.

Attorney's Office sent out this statement: "The investigation of those allegations has been closed."

I tweeted the news. Zimmer immediately responded, both to me and to Guadagno: "Not criminally charged does not mean acted properly. New Jersey deserves better."

**IN THE EARLY** twentieth century, New Jersey's Wally Edge championed the creation of a bi-state agency to manage the joint economic and political interests of two states on one river. Nothing like it had ever existed in the United States. The Port Authority became a model for the Progressive Era's efforts to professionalize government and get rid of graft. Over the next several decades the agency aggressively reshaped the region through transportation and real estate projects; by the time Christie got into office it had an operating budget larger than that of nine states. The Port Authority ran four bridges, two tunnels, four airports, a commuter rail, and a smattering of industrial parks, overseeing the transport of millions of people and endless goods across twelve thousand acres.

The Port Authority's twelve-member politically connected board of commissioners was led by a chairperson, an appointee of the New Jersey governor. In exchange, New York got the top staff position—the executive director. Later, New Jersey was given the deputy executive director position. This situation was awkward and dysfunctional, but it was an imperfect way of easing rivalries that existed as far back as 1927, when New Jersey governor A. Harry Moore demanded that steel from the Roebling Co. in Trenton be used to build the George Washington Bridge.

Likewise, Christie sought to leave a New Jersey imprint on the agency, installing at least fifty of his own people in Port Authority jobs, such as an $85,000 gourmet food broker hired as a financial analyst and a state senator, Bill Baroni, brought on for $290,000 a year. Baroni in turn hired a friend, a part-time soap opera actor who cowrote his book, *Fat Kid Got Fit*, to edit Port Authority publications.

The Port Authority had traditionally spent money without anyone knowing, because it adhered to neither New York nor New Jersey transparency laws. But now, thanks to Bridgegate, legislative subpoenas were like explosives destroying the locked vault of the Port Authority. All kinds of secrets were being revealed.

**IN 2010, CHRISTIE'S** recently ousted education commissioner was testifying before a legislative panel about the loss of federal education dollars when reporters were suddenly called into the governor's office for an unrelated surprise announcement.

Christie announced that he was killing, unilaterally, the largest public works project in the nation.

The Access to the Region's Core, known as the ARC Tunnel, was a decades-old plan to add a tunnel under the Hudson River to double the number of rush-hour train passengers between New Jersey and New York. More than a half billion dollars had already been put toward the project. The existing century-old tunnels were in a constant state of disrepair, causing delays for Manhattan commuters and rail passengers through the Northeast corridor. With demand for mass transit expected to increase 38 percent over the next twenty years, the need for a new tunnel was immediate.

ARC would not only address this need but also create 6,000 short-term construction jobs and 40,000 long-term jobs. Home values within two miles of train stations were estimated to increase $18 billion, and tax revenue was expected to go up $1.5 billion. Proponents said the tunnel would mean 22,000 cars off the road every day, forty-five-minute reductions in daily train commutes, and 70,000 fewer tons of greenhouse gases in the atmosphere every year.

Ground had already been broken on the project, and $3 billion in federal funds had already been committed. Reaching such a deal—between two states and multiple transit bureaucracies—was like seeing a comet. It might be decades before such an opportunity came along again.

And yet, ARC was dead, with no chance of resurrection. "This decision is final," Christie said. "There is no opportunity for reconsideration of this decision on my part. I am done. We are moving on."

Christie called ARC a "worthwhile project" that "we simply cannot afford."

"I do this with no sense of happiness at all," he said.

Christie had once supported the tunnel, but he said he had learned new, more detailed information about how New Jersey taxpayers would end up shouldering the bulk of cost overruns. He said the $8.7 billion cost could reach $14 billion. He backed up his position with a press release headlined: "Christie Administration Enforces Budget Discipline and Protects New Jersey Taxpayer Dollars."

Some liberals would forever believe this was the worst decision of his governorship. The *New York Times* editorial board, no doubt made up of some New Jersey–dwelling commuters, was particularly indignant: "If you find yourself in a stopped train in a Hudson River tunnel, or in a vehicle on a choked highway, in coming years, at least you will know why. In his drive to become the darling of the cut-costs-at-all-costs Republican crowd, Governor Chris Christie of New Jersey ignored real economic analysis and relied on exaggerated worst-case scenarios to kill the largest public transit project in the nation."

As always Christie had an effective rhetorical way of dismissing the project—"the train to Macy's basement." He said the tunnel would have terminated not at Penn Station, the critical transportation hub with lots of subway access, but underneath Macy's department store about a block away. And ARC also wouldn't go to the east side of Manhattan, to Grand Central Station, as had been originally conceived. It was, even backers admitted, an imperfect project.

But they were blindsided by Christie's decision to kill it rather than alter it. New Jersey senator Frank Lautenberg, Christie's Democratic nemesis, called it "the biggest public policy blunder in New Jersey's history."

Meanwhile, President Obama's transportation secretary, Ray LaHood, rushed to Trenton to try to get Christie to change his mind. On the way there LaHood and his team scribbled on the back of an envelope some ideas to sway the governor, such as a plan for private entities to finance the cost overruns and $358 million in new federal funds. "We're going to find a way to fix this," LaHood said.

Christie told LaHood he'd think about it—and then he said no. He had yet to be governor for a full year, and he was already pulling a power move against the feds.

Conservatives were thrilled. The decision helped to turn Christie into a Republican rookie of the year. Shortly thereafter he was campaigning for Republicans around the country and he found himself at a roundtable for GOP contributors in Portland, Oregon, when one donor turned to Christie and said: "Your rejection of the ARC tunnel tells me all I need to know about you. Because I'm a westerner, and for somebody to tell Washington to take their money and stick it because of the strings attached is what real leadership is all about."

Over on *60 Minutes*, Christie gave the national Sunday night audience his brand of straight talk: "Gotta cancel it. I mean, listen, the bottom line is, *I don't have the money.* And ya know what? I can't pay people for those jobs if I don't have the money to pay them. Where am I getting the money? . . . The day of reckoning has arrived."

More than a year later the federal Government Accountability Office determined that the cost overruns actually would have been lower than Christie's estimates and New Jersey would really only be responsible for 14 percent of it, anyway. Meanwhile the need for new tunnels was later made clear by Superstorm Sandy, which filled the existing tunnels halfway with seawater, causing corrosion. The head of Amtrak warned that the current tunnels would fail and be forced out of service in as little as seven years.

Whatever. Christie boasted to Republican audiences of having the guts to kill the big tunnel. "When they want to build a tunnel to the basement of Macy's, and stick the New Jersey taxpayers with a bill of $3 to $5 billion over, no matter how much the administration yells and screams you have to say no!" he said. "You have to look them right in the eye, no matter how much they try to vilify you for it, and you have to say no."

Beyond the adoration from the growing Tea Party movement within the Republican Party, Christie got something else out of the ARC's cancellation: a whole lot of money. Several billion dollars allocated for the tunnel was now available for New Jersey's taking. Sure enough, sources told my WNYC colleague Andrea Bernstein that as soon as Wildstein got to the Port Authority, he began asking about using the ARC money for road projects in New Jersey.

The state's infrastructure was in disrepair, with one out of every three bridges considered decrepit and residents paying, on average, more for roadway-related automobile repairs than drivers in any other state. Improvements to these bridges and roads were supposed to be paid for through the state Transportation Trust Fund, which is bankrolled by a tax on gasoline. But the Trust Fund was nearly empty. Christie had been moving money out of there to backfill the general fund in the state budget. And he balked at increasing the gas tax to replenish the fund, even though the tax was the third lowest in the country and hadn't gone up in two decades. A penny increase would cost just $60 a year for most drivers—cheaper than the $600 a year spent, on average, to fix pothole-damaged cars. But future presidential candidate Christie couldn't, or wouldn't, commit such a political sin as to raise a tax. He needed another way.

Enter ARC. Wildstein, the link to Christie operatives in the IGA and governor's office, helped to move $1.8 billion from the Port Authority's share of the tunnel to New Jersey roadway repairs so taxes wouldn't have to be raised. Contrary to Christie's characterization that he barely knew Wildstein, Andrea and I found that in fact over the course of the first term Wildstein met at least twice with Christie in the governor's office, joined the governor at seven public events, and had regular contact with his closest confidants.

During one of those meetings Christie brought Wildstein up to the third floor of the rotunda of the Statehouse to show the fake Wally Edge a painting of the real Governor Wally Edge. Christie tried to take the portrait down off the wall right then and there—he wanted it for his office. But a security system held it firm. Later, Christie had it removed and hung in his office hallway, replacing a portrait of the man Christie defeated for the job, Jon Corzine.

While Edge looked over the governor's office, Wildstein looked over the Port Authority. Wildstein's job was simple: Squeeze as much out of the Port Authority for New Jersey as possible.

THE ONLY REASON we know about the lane closures at all is the Port Authority's most controversial move: its 2011 toll increase on the George Washington Bridge and the Hudson River tunnels. This was what prompted New Jersey Democrats to seek subpoena power in the first place.

The Port Authority needed money for critical projects that were actually related to the mission of the agency—such as rehabilitation of the decrepit Port Authority bus terminal in Manhattan—since billions were now tied up in New Jersey road projects and New York's World Trade Center construction. Fortunately, unlike a gas tax, tolls could be raised to secure funds without violating Republican orthodoxy. So on the fifteenth floor of the Port Authority headquarters in Manhattan, a door with a sign that read "Do Not Enter" led to a conference room dubbed "The War Room." Here, officials and outside political consultants went to work on selling this toll hike.

A list was kept of who knew about the plan. A subordinate was told he couldn't tell his boss what he was working on, and a janitor feared being fired after he was caught trying to get into the War Room to fix a broken pipe.

The increase would be quick and dirty—a midsummer cash grab before commuters could realize what had happened. Because they weren't looking for just a couple of bucks. The Port Authority would propose a nine-dollar phased-in increase, which would make it seventeen dollars to cross the Hudson River from New Jersey to New York. *Seventeen dollars.*

On a Friday evening in August the toll hikes were announced. The governors released a joint statement shortly thereafter saying they were dismayed by the decision.

"I said, 'You're kidding, right?' " Christie later said, recounting when he was told about the increase. "And they said 'no.' "

Did the governor really not know about such a significant policy decision? Was he really not in a position to dial it back before it was publicly announced? Had Christie's top political guys at his most important government agency suddenly gone rogue?

The top three New Jersey Port Authority officials—Samson, Baroni, and Wildstein—had all recently met with Christie, according to the governor's calendar. Christie spoke to Samson more than almost anyone, and the *New York Times* reported that Christie personally instructed Samson, Wildstein, and Baroni to raise tolls $6.00 for cars by 2014—not $4.00 as planned—during a Statehouse meeting. This would protect him politically, because he would criticize the plan and force, so to speak, the agency to lower the tolls.

That's basically what happened. Christie and New York governor Cuomo came out against these new tolls. So a new proposal was issued: Tolls would go up $4.50 for cars by 2015.

When that plan was announced, the War Room generated thirty-six supportive press releases, comments were posted on online news stories, and eight public hearings were scheduled. All of those hearings were held in a single day, with a political operative from the local laborers' union helping to pack the room with union workers wearing bright prison-orange T-shirts that read: "Port Authority = Jobs." The laborers wanted the toll hikes because it meant construction work for their members; they took up half the seats at one toll-hike public hearing on Staten Island. Held in what was described as a "tricky-to-find" building, the meeting featured testimony from union guys who appeared to be speaking from scripts.

The commissioners of the Port Authority didn't attend a single hearing. Later, anonymous officials at the Port Authority told the newspapers that the meetings were "all bullshit" and a "farce" intended to "set the governors up to look like heroes."

The *Star-Ledger* called it "Hollywood on the Hudson."

Christie dismissed this allegation as a "conspiracy theory." But the toll hikes not only helped his state finances but also had a big political payoff—

the following year, the laborers' union gave Christie the first endorsement of his reelection. That's twenty thousand members, thrilled by the jobs created through the toll-funded construction projects. The union leader was a Port Authority commissioner who had endorsed Corzine in 2009.

"This campaign has just started," Christie told the raucous crowd of laborers at the endorsement event, "but I doubt that I'll have many better days than the day I was endorsed by the Laborers International Union of North America."

ALL OF THE Port Authority mini-controversies from the first term got new scrutiny in the wake of Bridgegate. But it wasn't until reporters started digging into David Samson, the top guy at the agency and one of Christie's closest friends, that The Crisis reached new heights.

The greater New York region first learned about this dapper young lawyer from Newark in the early 1990s, when he became the other man in one of the most notorious political sex scandals in New York history. The chief judge of New York, an expected future gubernatorial candidate named Sol Wachtler, stalked and harassed Samson when Samson began dating the judge's ex-girlfriend, Joy Silverman. Wachtler demanded $20,000 to turn over tapes he supposedly had of Silverman and Samson having sex.

Wachtler's political career imploded in full view of the New York tabloid-reading public. For decades, Wachtler would represent one of the most epic political flameouts in history.

Years later, Samson was named New Jersey attorney general under Governor Jim McGreevey, who would be forced to resign amid his own sex-fueled epic political flameout.

Samson was not unfamiliar with scandal.

In December 2001, when McGreevey introduced Samson as his nominee for attorney general, Christie put on a suit and drove fifteen minutes to McGreevey's announcement. He hadn't been invited, but he had just been nominated U.S. Attorney, so he wanted to introduce himself to Samson. The new attorney general was immediately impressed that the new U.S. Attorney went out of his way to pay his respects.

As New Jersey's top two law enforcement officials, Christie and Samson worked together on investigations and ended up getting joint death threats from the Latin Kings street gang—"which brought us closer together," Christie said. They were both provided security, 24/7.

Samson left the Attorney General's Office after about a year and turned into a power Republican lawyer-lobbyist and perennial top ten on the annual list of the most influential unelected people on Wildstein's *PoliticsNJ* *.com* (later renamed *PolitickerNJ.com*). Samson and Christie kept in touch, having lunch every month or two and making annual dinner bets about the Mets and Yankees. Christie's U.S. Attorney's Office gave Samson a $10 million contract to be a compliance monitor for a company facing criminal charges, and Samson began helping Christie with his fledgling return to politics.

When Christie ran for governor, Samson was the campaign lawyer, with the conference room at Samson's law office used for debate prep and for big meetings. On the day after he won election, Christie's first meeting was with Samson. Later that morning the first personnel announcement Christie made as governor-elect was to name Samson as chairman of the transition team that would determine the focus of the future governor's office. At the inaugural, Samson served as the master of ceremonies.

"David's a really wise guy and a really good person," Christie told me. "I sought advice from him on everything from legal decisions I had to make, to situations with my children, to situations with friends. Really smart, wise person. And always was incredibly generous with his time and advice." Samson was twenty-three years older—"it's a father-son age difference type, so it's that kind of interesting relationship."

Samson was known as fun to be around, entertaining with a good story, and he accompanied Christie on political trips around the country. Christie called him "General" because of his stint as attorney general, but Samson was really the general of Christie's Army, in charge of shaping the policies and personnel of the new administration. "We serve one client," Samson was known to say. "Chris Christie."

Among Samson's chief recommendations was that the Port Authority's billions be used to backfill New Jersey state budgets. "The Port Authority of New York and New Jersey is an underutilized asset," read Samson's transition report to the newly elected governor. Money from the Port Authority, including the ARC tunnel, should be used for New Jersey projects to save the state money.

Before Christie was inaugurated Samson was also negotiating with Governor Jon Corzine to make sure the outgoing governor didn't make last-minute reappointments to the Port Authority board of commissioners and instead let Christie put his own people at the agency.

Once in office, Christie of course appointed Samson board chairman.

But his role was covert. After the Democratic Senate approved Samson's nomination, a reporter asked Christie if he had given Samson a list of priorities for what he wanted him to do at the Port Authority.

"That's between me and Mr. Samson," Christie said.

**ON JANUARY 8,** when The Crisis broke, there was disagreement at Drumthwacket about whether Samson should keep his job.

Unlike Stepien, whom Christie fired for poor judgment, Samson seemed to actually know something about the lane closures from at least right after they happened. He was portrayed in the emails by Baroni as plotting revenge against New York Port Authority executive director Foye for reopening the lanes. If guilt could be assessed by just that first batch of emails, Samson seemed more at risk than Stepien.

Sources familiar with what went on in the room say a few of Christie's advisers looked the governor in the eye and told him Samson was a problem that needed to be eliminated. He should be forced to resign, they said.

The governor talked to Samson for two full hours on that day. Just the General and the Governor. The gov's verdict? Not guilty. He trusted Samson more than almost anyone else in the world. "I'm confident that he had no knowledge of this," Christie said.

Yet keeping Samson around after Bridgegate proved to be a problematic move, politically, because it made Christie more vulnerable to continued scrutiny. He was still working for the governor, in charge of the region's infrastructure, showing up to public meetings. So reporters continued to examine his role at the Port Authority, and what they uncovered was shocking.

Because of Bridgegate, reporters now had access to thousands of Port Authority documents that the Democrats had subpoenaed. Suddenly, inside sources—bitter about how their bosses had led the agency—were talking. And it turned out that Samson didn't just help New Jersey seize money from the ARC tunnel and toll hikes, he also appeared to have been helping himself, too. Much of the negative coverage that Christie sustained in the months ahead was about Samson and his own pocketbook. Or as one of Samson's former political allies described his actions to me: a "piggish" approach to public service.

**WE BEGIN IN** Harrison, where the Port Authority announced a new $256 million train station nine months before the mayor there became the first Democratic mayor to endorse Christie's reelection. This seemed like the normal course of local politics until it was revealed that a builder represented by Samson's law firm proposed building luxury apartments near the train station. Samson, as Port Authority chairman, voted in favor of the project, which would undoubtedly benefit the builder.

In Atlantic City, the Port Authority proposed taking over the airport even though it was two hours outside the Port Authority's official district. Samson's firm was bond counsel for the financially struggling entity that ran the airport, the South Jersey Transportation Authority. The deal had political benefits for Christie, because South Jersey Democrats supported the takeover, but it also had potential benefits for Samson, given that it could aid his client and, therefore, himself. Samson didn't vote on the deal. Instead, he spoke up in favor of it at a Port Authority meeting.

And then there was North Bergen. Samson came up with an idea to privatize train station parking lots owned by NJ Transit, the commuter railroad. Shortly thereafter Samson's law firm was hand-picked by NJ Transit for what would become a $1.5 million contract to do the legal work for privatization. Then, it turned out, one of those NJ Transit parking lots, in North Bergen, was actually owned by the Port Authority. So as chairman of the Port Authority, Samson voted to transfer the North Bergen parking lot to NJ Transit for just one dollar annually for forty-nine years—far less than the $900,000 annual rent it had been paying. To recap: NJ Transit paid Samson's private firm, and he then voted in his public position to reduce the amount of money NJ Transit had to pay every year.

This could seem like a conflict of interest. But lawyers figured it all out. The Port Authority determined that Samson actually "intended to recuse himself" on that vote and the fact that he cast a vote was nothing more than a "clerical inadvertence." The "yes" vote was officially changed to a recusal. An unprecedented do-over vote was scheduled.

Wherever reporters looked, they found potential conflicts of interest with Samson. My WNYC reporting partner Andrea Bernstein began digging into Samson just as Bridgegate broke, finding that once his friend became governor his firm's New Jersey lobbying business ballooned—going from $42,000 to more than $1 million a year. Everyone with deep pockets knew: He had a direct connection to the governor's office.

And that was just the lobbying wing. The firm's lawyers now represented a half dozen agencies in Christie's government, earning more than $12 million.

Samson, through lawyers and spokespeople, maintained all along that none of this was done for personal gain and all was pursued for the betterment of New Jersey. If that was the case, this veteran government lawyer wasn't very careful about making that clear to the public. At one point Samson didn't recuse himself even as the board voted to award $2.8 billion in contracts to three companies with financial ties to his firm. He called the votes "joyous and happy." The story about that vote ran on the front page of the *New York Times*. Samson and Christie, the story said, "operate in a state with a long history of cozy, back-scratching relationships among politicians, lawyers and businesses tied to real estate and construction."

What was now being documented as fact by reporters was sharply disconnected from the shtick that Christie had pushed for his entire career. He was supposed to clean it all up, not appear complicit in it. This scandal now seemed to call into question everything Christie had told us about his leadership. As Christie impotently watched, the hard-fought narrative he had written for himself collapsed under the weight of that damn bridge.

**PATRICK FOYE**, the executive director of the Port Authority, publicly declared that Samson lacked the moral authority to continue as chairman. Samson finally resigned, seventy-nine bloody days after "time for some traffic problems in Fort Lee."

Samson hired a lawyer, Michael Chertoff, the former U.S. director of Homeland Security whom two decades earlier prosecuted Wachtler, Samson's former stalker, when he was U.S. Attorney for New Jersey. Chertoff's father was the rabbi who Bar Mitzvahed—and later presided over the wedding of—David Samson, a source close to the family told me.

More recently, Chertoff's security-consulting group had entered into a $300,000 no-bid contract with Samson's Port Authority that ballooned to $1.5 million.

I thought Nick Acocella explained all of this well. He is something of the political poet laureate of the state of New Jersey—a chronicler of the smoky back rooms who writes *Politifax*, a weekly newsletter about state politics. "All we've seen is confirmation, as if that was necessary, that everyone in New Jersey knows everyone else, everyone has multiple roles, and everyone scratches everyone else's back," he wrote. "It may not be right. It may not be pretty. But it pretty much defines this thing of ours."

·          ·          ·

**AND THEN SOMETHING** happened that even New Jersey had never seen before. This was perhaps the most outrageous alleged act of corruption since the bridge lanes were closed—an act brazen and infuriating to every American flying coach.

The *Record* revealed a federal investigation into whether United Airlines created a flight to Columbia Metropolitan Airport in South Carolina from the Port Authority–owned Newark Liberty International Airport to accommodate Samson, who had a weekend home less than an hour's drive away in the horse country of Aiken, South Carolina.

The century-old $1.7 million Samson home nestled behind a brick wall was known as "Rest Period," which is what they call halftime in the game of polo. It was described as "captivatingly elegant" in a long feature about the property in *Augusta* magazine. There are statues in the house dating back two thousand years to the Han Dynasty. But getting to this gem of a weekend pad was a bit difficult for Samson. He had no problem at Newark Airport—Port Authority executives had special escorts to cut through security lines. But the closest airport to the house itself was in Charlotte, North Carolina, a nearly three-hour drive away.

Samson himself brought up his predicament about the weekend home while dining with United Airlines' chief executive at a pricey Italian restaurant in New York. He noted that United used to fly to Columbia; maybe that route could be reopened?

United had a lot of business before Samson at the Port Authority, and therefore reason to stay on his good side. The airline was negotiating a $150 million airport lease, deciding whether to start flying out of the newly acquired Atlantic City Airport and hoping to get a $600 million train extension to Newark Airport. Meanwhile, thirteen United executives from around the country were donating to Christie's reelection campaign. This was the largest pool of donations Christie received from a publicly traded company.

Perhaps United didn't react quickly enough to Samson's hint about the flight. Because *Bloomberg News* revealed that Samson then threatened to block United's agenda at the Port Authority. Samson's lawyer denied the claims, but what happened next is indisputable: United added a flight to South Carolina. It left Thursday nights and returned Monday mornings—a perfect schedule for someone looking to have long three-day weekends. It had fewer passengers than almost any other flight out of Newark.

Chairman Samson called the flight the Chairman's Flight, reports said.

Four days after Chairman Samson resigned, the flight route was canceled.

The following year, amidst a federal investigation into the flight, the United Airlines CEO resigned.

TYPICALLY A "NEWS dump" hits on a Friday afternoon—a press release announcing something unpopular that a politician wants to hide in the mix of weekend plans. Christie's most notorious dumps were when he vetoed gun control bills, released Bridgegate legal bills, and announced Wildstein's resignation.

This, though, was other level. At 6:15 p.m. on the Saturday before Christmas and New Year's Eve 2014, the governors of New York and New Jersey dropped an epic news dump. Christie and Cuomo announced they were vetoing legislation that had unanimously passed both houses in the New York legislature *and* both houses in the New Jersey legislature. All four chambers had recently agreed to Bridgegate-inspired reforms of the Port Authority—a range of comprehensive steps to return the agency to its core mission of transportation, making it less political and more professional. Only a freak incident, the closing of lanes to the world's busiest bridge, could inspire such a freak moment of bipartisan, bi-state consensus.

Now, those reforms were dead, killed in secret less than a year after Bridgegate broke.

Christie and Cuomo met a few days before the decision, at an Italian restaurant in Carlstadt, New Jersey, not far from the New York border. They were friends, veterans of the art of transactional politics who never aired their dirty laundry in public. Cuomo hadn't criticized Christie about Bridgegate, and Christie, as head of the Republican Governors Association, hadn't financed Cuomo's Republican gubernatorial opponent. When Cuomo faced an ethics scandal, Christie was mum.

The bills they vetoed would have created a Port Authority inspector general's office, a whistleblower protection program, and annual independent audits. Commissioners would have been required to take an oath of fiduciary responsibility and testify before the legislatures.

No, thanks, Christie and Cuomo said. After jointly vetoing the bills, they released a ninety-nine-page report with their own ideas for fixing the Port Authority—ideas that preserved and perhaps increased gubernatorial power over the agency.

The New York Democrat who sponsored the original reform bill, Assemblyman Jim Brennan, said that the New York governor's office told him that killing the proposal was Cuomo's favor to Christie.

"I'm sure it has to do with a desire to keep a lot of the operations there secret," Brennan said, "because they benefit from that."

# 15

# THE INVESTIGATIONS

**"I**'m not talking about it," Christie says to me.

We are sitting down for our second interview for this book in a conference room within a suite of offices that the government of New Jersey maintains for the governor near the train station in downtown Newark.

"I choose not to talk about it," he says. "It's a choice."

I am asking about Bridgegate.

"This is going to be a very quick part of this," he warns me.

I risk a general question. I ask if there's a different perspective to look at what went down in the very beginning, when the lanes closed and Fort Lee mayor Mark Sokolich could not get an answer—any kind of answer—from the Christie administration about what in the world was happening. "Sokolich is freaking out about public safety," I remind Christie. "And everyone is ignoring his calls and emails and texts. Is there another way to view that other than a coordinated nonresponse?"

"I have nothing to say about that," he says to me flatly. He is unhappy with where this is going, so I make the miscalculation of trying to break the ice with a joke. A Bridgegate joke.

"This is like the David Wildstein testimony in front of Wisniewski," I say. In that legislative testimony, of course, Wildstein pleaded the Fifth and didn't answer Assemblyman John Wisniewski's questions.

"Well, that was insulting," Christie says to me. "I'm not going to fucking kick you out after saying something like that. But you're coming close."

I've never been in a more uncomfortable room.

"Listen, let's make this really easy, okay? I have no interest in discussing this," he says.

"I know."

"You can continue to ask, feel free to, but—"

"Will you ever discuss it?"

"I don't know . . . I'm just not going to get into remembering, reinterpreting, relitigating, reliving this. So I've already said everything I'm going to say about this."

I tell him that I think there are still open questions, certain things that contradict the way he described things.

"You are using post–January 8 knowledge to impute pre–January 8 knowledge," he says. "And it's wrong. You guys have consistently done it in the media. And you don't care to be careful or discerning about it. So I'm not going to sit here and give you a lesson on how to be careful or discerning."

This is the argument his allies have made since the "time for some traffic problems in Fort Lee" email was released on January 8. They hadn't known about that email before that moment, so they thought the lane closures and related controversy was logically explained by a traffic study.

But I cannot unsee that "time for some traffic problems" email. "It's hard to put myself in your shoes," I tell him.

"But you have to. I know it's sexier or easier to not do it. It's not impossible . . . There's pre–January 8 knowledge, attitude, and outlook and post–January 8 knowledge, attitude, and outlook, and they're completely different worlds. And if you guys don't understand it by this time after all that's happened, then you just don't want to understand it."

I should stop asking questions right there. He isn't going to say anything else. But I can't walk out of this room without trying to get a few more hints about what caused the greatest traffic jam New Jersey had ever known. There may never be another opportunity for a reporter to get into the weeds with him on this issue.

So I keep asking, and the governor keeps blowing me off, growing increasingly steamed.

"Next . . . *next* . . . NEXT," he says.

The governor begins to answer one question, but stops. "First of all," he says, before stopping himself. "No. Next."

I ask whether he had set a tone in his office that allowed something like Bridgegate to happen, whether any of this could have been because of the leadership he set, the people he chose, the environment he created.

"Ya know, Matt, grow up," he says. "And look at what happens in every administration. There are going to be people who decide to do things that they believe are appropriate responses to things that are being battled about. And no, there's no tone set at the top. The tone I set at the top is we work with everybody, which we have. And that's why we've been able to accomplish the things we've been able to the last five years with hostile, overwhelming majorities by Democrats in the legislature, and accomplishing things that no one else around the country in similar circumstances is accomplishing. If there is a hostile, vengeful mood at the top, you don't get those things done. So no. The answer is no."

I ask about the Intergovernmental Affairs unit in his office, the IGA, which appeared to be doling out punishments and rewards to local politicians depending on whether they politically supported the governor or not.

"We worked with everybody," he says. "And that's what this administration is all about. And you guys just want to write about this stuff."

The conversation goes on for twenty-eight minutes. The rest of the interview, and maybe our working relationship, never fully recovered.

ON THE LAST miserable snowy weekend of a miserably snowy January 2014, Bridget Anne Kelly pulled up to her driveway in a tony North Jersey suburb called Ramsey. She was in the passenger seat of her attorney's Mercedes S550, and raw footage from an NBC camera captured the bizarre moments that followed.

For three weeks, ever since her email was released, local cops had kept TV cameras away from Kelly's property. But suddenly paparazzi on the curb in front of her driveway got their glimpse. "That's her! That's her!" a videographer screamed. Kelly and her lawyer, a New Jersey legal legend named Michael Critchley, got out of the car. Critchley's high-profile career included keeping twenty alleged mobsters out of prison, winning millions of dollars for a child nearly starved to death by his foster parents, and defending Rielle Hunter, the woman who helped to bring down former presidential candidate John Edwards's political career.

This was not Critchley's first brush with disgrace. He knew the made-for-TV routine. And so he made a deal with the photographers to walk Kelly toward the cameras if they agreed to stop staking out her house.

"Hi, Miss Kelly, how you doing?" one of the photographers called out.

She slung a pink backpack over her shoulder and followed Critchley through falling snowflakes toward the paparazzi. "Just walk, just walk," Critchley instructed Kelly. Then they stopped, for a split second, in front of the cameras. "Okay, now we just go back."

They turned, and shuffled toward the house.

The photographers weren't satisfied. Critchley negotiated a do-over. Critchley and Kelly got back into the Mercedes. They sat in the plush leather interior for exactly fifteen seconds before emerging. Again, he led her to the videographers.

"Walk with me, Bridget," Critchley said.

This time, she went a bit closer to the paparazzi. They zoomed in on her face, revealing stress lines in her forehead and eyes so big, pretty, and heartbreaking, they could be innocent. Snowflakes settled on her blonde hair. The cameras clicked and video rolled.

"Thank you *so* much," said a voice from the other side of the lenses.

"Okay, that's it, guys, right?" Critchley said, like a carnival barker with his star attraction. "That's it now, right? Okay, we're done."

Kelly's brown boots kicked the snow as she walked up her stoop. She gave a long glance at Critchley, and together they went inside.

THE LEGISLATURE NOW had a joint Select Committee on Investigation into Bridgegate—led by Assemblyman John "Wiz" Wisniewski and Senator Loretta Weinberg, the two Democrats who had pushed for the damning documents that we now had. I called them Wizberg. Their committee, made up of some loyal Christie Republicans but mostly Democrats, convened and immediately issued thirty-eight subpoenas to Port Authority and Christie officials for correspondence and other documents. Thirty-six of thirty-eight people who were subpoenaed complied.

Unfortunately the two people who refused—Kelly and Bill Stepien—held the documents the legislators were most eager to see.

Kelly and Stepien went to court to get out of the subpoena. It was early March, on the first warm day of 2014, Mercer County Courthouse, downtown Trenton. Reid Schar, the legislature's lawyer, argued that if Kelly and Stepien refused to comply with the subpoenas, that could set a precedent in which government officials flatly oppose all subpoenas, even in situations involving attacks against the country.

The lawyers for Kelly and Stepien countered that the subpoena violated their clients' Fifth Amendment right under the Constitution to not incriminate themselves. They argued self-incrimination applies not just to courtroom testimony but also to the production of documents. "Don't blame me," said Critchley, with the line of the day, "blame James Madison."

Then he went outside to talk to the media. Kelly stood next to him, instructed not to speak. "She is a forty-two-year-old single mom with four children, trying to make do through a difficult time," he said. And she was out of work. "If anyone needs someone to work with, give me a call. I have an excellent employee."

News coverage showed empathy for Kelly. But reporters also reminded New Jersey of what she had allegedly said when those Fort Lee students were stuck in epic traffic jams. "I feel badly about the kids," she had written. "I guess."

Six weeks after their hearing, a judge ruled that Kelly and Stepien did not have to respond to the subpoenas because they were "overly broad" and they could indeed incriminate themselves.

If only Wildstein had objected to his own subpoena! The legal challenge would have likely resulted in the same outcome. *Time for some traffic problems* would not have been released. Democrats' subpoena power would have expired shortly thereafter, shutting down the investigation before it started. Stepien—perhaps Wildstein, Kelly, and Baroni—would have all ended up working for the Chris Christie presidential campaign. And no one may ever know why those lanes closed at the George Washington Bridge.

**DEBRA WONG YANG** was U.S. Attorney in Los Angeles when Christie was U.S. Attorney in New Jersey. They were colleagues who became friends, once vacationing together at a game ranch in Texas. They brought their families, and together they chased wild pigs after midnight and tried not to answer their BlackBerries.

After Yang went into private practice, Christie gave her a contract to serve as a Department of Justice monitor in an orthopedic equipment manufacturer case. Later she was impressed by the kind of governor he became. She described him as a blunt everyman—"talking the same way we talk when we're sitting around our kitchen table." As she told an important Chinese American group in New York City once, Christie was a man of "unwavering ethos" who went to Trenton, looked at problems in jobs, taxes, and education, and "decided to fix all of them at once." Her daughter became an intern in his office.

On January 7, 2014, Yang donated $500 to Christie's inaugural celebration after his reelection. Then Bridgegate broke, and Yang's high-profile law firm, Gibson Dunn, was hired by the governor's office to conduct an internal investigation into the lane closures. Yang suddenly became one of the lead lawyers responsible for concluding the governor's guilt or innocence.

But she did not cut personal ties with her friend Chris. A few days after the firm was hired she traveled from California and got a ticketed seat to attend Christie's inauguration.

And then she billed the rest of the day to taxpayers as she conducted interviews for the Bridgegate investigation.

Nearly three months after that internal investigation began, Yang joined the lead attorney of the investigation, Randy Mastro, at Gibson Dunn's palatial Midtown offices with panoramic views of Manhattan. With help from Christie's advance team and press office, Mastro was holding a press conference to publicly release what would become known as the Mastro Report. Mastro was a storied trial attorney who had been a mob prosecutor and deputy mayor under New York City's Rudy Giuliani, a Christie ally. Dealing with Mastro was like "wrestling an alligator," according to his own website. Now he had to grapple with an aggressive press corps.

These weren't forced lane closures, Mastro concluded, but were instead a "lane realignment decision." After Christie found out about it, "he took appropriate action," in part by ordering this investigation, or a "search for the truth." The so-called Mastro Report that the Gibson Dunn attorneys wrote had concluded that Christie was innocent, Wildstein and Kelly were at fault, and the three people closest to Christie—Samson, Stepien, and Baroni—had nothing to do with anything.

Yet the Gibson Dunn lawyers never interviewed Wildstein, Kelly, Samson, Stepien, or Baroni—or anyone at all from the Port Authority, the agency that ran the bridge in question. The most important potential witnesses wouldn't sit down for questions.

So reporters were deeply skeptical about the legitimacy of the Mastro Report and Gibson Dunn's methods. Mastro's press conference got contentious. Reporters were yelling questions at him, and he lost control of the room.

Then he started talking about sex.

WE HAD ALL heard about the relationship. That was the word back in January, that Stepien and Kelly had been dating. But none of us reported it. We didn't see how it connected to the Fort Lee fiasco.

The relationship, though, was central to Christie's lawyers' version of what happened, even though the information came from just two of the seventy-five people they interviewed, and not from the two people involved. Gibson Dunn lawyers publicly released the details of when the relationship began and ended, who ended it, and how Kelly felt after it was over. The way Mastro described it: The relationship started only *after* Stepien left the governor's office, where he had been Kelly's supervisor, and ended *before* the "time for some traffic problems in Fort Lee" email. And, besides, Stepien dumped her—so maybe that's why she lost her mind and decided to cause a traffic jam on the busiest bridge in the world? Under this scenario Stepien—and by extension, the reelection campaign for Christie that Stepien was running—had nothing to do with the lane closures. If Stepien wasn't involved, the logic went that Christie wasn't, either.

"We found that whatever relationship, brief, that Stepien and Kelly had," Mastro said at the press conference, "had ended in the first week of August 2013, and they largely stopped speaking, and so I don't expect—"

"How do you know that?" a female reporter yelled from the back of the room.

"We know that from our witness interviews, and it was confirmed by multiple interviews."

"Who told you that?"

"Let me just finish, let me just finish, let me just finish. We shouldn't be yelling out."

Instead of delving into Samson, Christie's confidant and the top figure at the Port Authority, the report delivered what became known as the "slut-shaming of Bridget Anne Kelly." The report used the word "emotional" to describe Kelly after Stepien broke things off. There were multiple anecdotes of her in tears, and hearsay about her desperate need for affirmation: She was "habitually concerned about how she was perceived by the governor." The report put Kelly on the couch, concluding: "Events in her personal life may have had some bearing on her subjective motivations and state of mind."

As Jon Stewart quipped on *The Daily Show*, the Mastro Report could've been titled: "Bitches be crazy, right?"

At the *New York Post*, this was the lede: *Two Chris Christie aides embroiled in Bridgegate had a hot and heavy romance before the scandal exploded, it was revealed yesterday . . .*

"I WILL GO on the air now!"

Hours after the report's release, Stepien's attorney was furious. And he wanted to go on our station, WNYC, to complain about it.

Kevin Marino is one of the brand names in New Jersey criminal defense, a foul-mouthed and fast-talking attorney who once defended a client with a three-hour closing courtroom argument, his voice "thundering" and the veins in his neck "bulging," as the *Philadelphia Inquirer* described it.

Marino was now heated over Stepien's treatment. He thought his client's sex life was being used to distract from the real scandal at hand. "It's completely irrelevant," he told me. "From the tabloids on up, that's how to get a headline."

But Marino didn't disagree with the nature of the relationship. He told me Stepien and Kelly dated just three or four times.

Likewise, Kelly's lawyer, Michael Critchley, called it "short-lived and no big deal." "Didn't go on vacation," he said. "Didn't meet each other's relatives." But contrary to Mastro's characterization of a weepy Bridget, Critchley said the relationship ended peacefully. "The report's venomous, gratuitous, and inappropriate sexist remarks concerning Ms. Kelly have no place in what is alleged to be a professional and independent report," Critchley said.

No one suffered more aggressive treatment in the Mastro Report than Wildstein, who was depicted as a madman who came up with the idea to shut down the lanes—an idea "like so many other 'crazy' ones he'd had before." He "seemed to have all sorts of bizarre personal and political animus toward a variety of people," Mastro said, and therefore his motives may have had nothing to do with the governor but instead everything to do with Wildstein's own feuds, real or imagined.

A Wildstein lost in his own delusions, sick with power, was deemed ultimately responsible for the five days of traffic jams.

Most of the Mastro Report actually deals not with the lane closures but with the allegations from Hoboken mayor Dawn Zimmer that Christie officials tried to shake her down. To dismantle one of Zimmer's claims that she was threatened during the filming of a local TV special, Mastro included eleven blurry still shots from the video to prove, using a layman's analysis of body language, that nothing inappropriate was discussed. The video showed Zimmer "yawning about midway through, and then smiling at the end—hardly the demeanor one would expect of someone who had just been threatened," the report said.

Such a keen eye was not used to scrutinize photos in the other matter at hand, Bridgegate. These photos depicted Wildstein and Christie talking during a Ground Zero ceremony on September 11, 2013, at the very moment when the lanes were closed. Body language was not analyzed to determine why, in fact, Christie was laughing.

Weeks later Mastro released a 437-page "Interview Memoranda"—nonverbatim summaries of interviews that witnesses did with the lawyers. Some of these summaries would later be called inaccurate by those interviewed.

Christie himself was interviewed three times with three lawyers in the room, including his friend, Yang, and Mastro. Seventeen times in Christie's interview memo the phrase "not recall" is used. Most notably, he doesn't remember a conversation with his chief spokesman, Michael Drewniak, in which Drewniak informs the governor of Wildstein's claims that Kelly and Stepien knew about the lane closures.

Gibson Dunn would charge taxpayers a reduced fee of $350 an hour per lawyer for this investigation and for fighting document requests in federal court. That added up to about $10 million.

To put it another way, if four lawyers did six hours of interviews with one witness, that was $8,400—the amount it costs to educate some children in New Jersey for a full year.

ONE OF THE Mastro Report's primary findings was that Christie didn't engage in "partisan retaliation," noting that staffers said they had never been asked their party affiliations. But that wasn't the point—the real question about Christie's reign wasn't *partisan* retaliation, but rather *political* retaliation, regardless of party. Fear of retaliation was part of the reason why he had been an effective governor up to that point—and it was why reporters entertained the possibility that he had ordered a traffic jam to punish a defiant mayor.

There was the time a Democratic senator who had once served as governor, Dick Codey, was supposedly blocking a Christie nomination using his power as a senator. Christie's allies said the nomination was for education commissioner; Codey said it was just a part-time appointment to a sewerage commission.

Whatever the reason for the dispute, it was clear that Codey was going to be a problem for the new governor. So Codey soon got a call from the state police superintendent, who informed him that the occasional security detail he had been afforded as a former governor was over, effective immediately. That same day, Codey's friend was fired from a top job at the Division of Community Affairs, his cousin was replaced as the top lawyer at the Port Authority, and his ally was booted from the New Jersey Sports Exposition Authority.

Bill Palatucci, Christie's longtime adviser, told me that this was just how a new governor let a former governor know that power had shifted. After all, Christie was now allied with North Jersey Democratic boss Joe DiVincenzo, a Codey rival. "That's just showing Joe D. how deep our relationship is going to be: '[Codey's] your mortal enemy, then fine, I'm on your side,'" Palatucci told me. "Had Dick been more respectful of [Christie] in the office, maybe there was a chance of building a relationship there."

Christie wouldn't acknowledge any connection to politics. "There's lots of examples of how I will send messages to people," Christie said, "but that just wasn't one of them."

One way Christie sent messages was with judicial nominations. A feud between Christie and Democrats over nominees for various state government positions led the governor to simply stop nominating judges in Democratic Essex County, even as judges retired and left seats open.

A judicial crisis ensued, with twenty-two vacancies on the Essex County Superior Court, nearly half of the allotted judgeships in the busiest court in the state. This impasse led to years-long delays in trials and a temporary freeze of matrimonial matters—it was impossible to get divorced in Essex County for part of 2011 and 2012. The New Jersey Supreme Court had to send ten judges from other vicinages to temporarily fill the seats.

Christie and the Democrats eventually agreed on a new slate of judicial nominees. But that deal was almost scuttled when Democrats called one of the nominees to testify before the legislature. Testimony hadn't been part of the agreement with the governor, so Christie temporarily pulled all eight nominees.

"You have to show your seriousness of purpose when you're governor," Christie said later on. "You have certain authority that you can utilize to bring people to their senses."

Christie insisted he plays nice more than he plays rough. But the strong exercise of gubernatorial authority is "one of the clubs you have in the bag."

"I have no hesitation in using it," he said. "You gotta use it."

DIANE SAWYER BROUGHT her ABC News crew up the hill in Mendham, Morris County, to the tastefully palatial Christie spread. He loved that house so much he stayed there instead of moving to Drumthwacket after he was elected.

Few reporters are given the honor of being allowed into the home. But the setting was an ace in the hole for the governor's media team. With six weeks left in his first gubernatorial race Christie invited a *New York Times* reporter to the house for an interview about his love of Bruce Springsteen. The story ran on the front page alongside a photo of Christie at his kitchen table, an old box of Springsteen ticket stubs laid out before him, one of his kids doing a cartwheel in the background, and just off to the side, Mary Pat, hands in her jeans pockets, ski jacket on, a suburban mom passing through on the way to pick up another kid at whatever practice. Thousands of New Jerseyans looked at that picture and saw a mirror.

Now, Sawyer was sitting him down, gently prodding about whether he created the climate that allowed Bridgegate to happen.

"I spent a lot of time in the last eleven weeks thinking about what did I do, if anything, to contribute to this," he said. "I don't believe I did. But I certainly am disappointed in myself that I wasn't able to pick up these traits in these people. That I didn't look closer. That I trusted too much."

"You don't think there's a single possibility that in your rough-and-tumble style that they thought this would please you?" she asked.

His eyes were as soft as I'd ever seen them. He said "no" immediately.

Christie revealed that he had been sleeping and eating less over the "struggle" of the scandal, and even his own son had asked if he indeed closed the lanes. "It was a tough question that your son would ask you, and I said, 'No, I didn't,' and he said, 'Good, I'm glad.' "

He hinted that he still might run for president, saying the scandal had, in fact, made him a "better leader."

And following the script of every scandal-tinged politician, he said he was now closer to his family, that he was spending more time at home than before. "My responsibilities here"—in the house in Mendham—"are important, too," he said.

The next day Christie took his carefully stagecrafted comeback message to the conservative masses on FOX News in a more official setting, the Statehouse. Interviewer Megyn Kelly never asked, directly, about Bridgegate, but instead looked forward, referencing an upcoming speech he was scheduled to give in Las Vegas. "You're headed to Vegas. Do you feel like your luck is changing?" Kelly asked.

"I feel like tomorrow will be better than yesterday. And that's all you can hope for in this life," he said. "That tomorrow will be better than yesterday."

ACTUALLY, YESTERDAY WAS better. The sit-downs with the selected TV stars proved far more congenial than the press conference with the New Jersey and New York media that followed the next day. The same man who chatted with Diane and Megyn did not show up for this press conference. Gone was the patient, contrite, down-on-his-luck pol. Back were the cockiness, the Jersey swagger, the abrasiveness. Christie began by reminding us that the Gibson Dunn firm pored through 250,000 documents, including his own emails and texts, to "find the truth, no matter where it led."

"Questions?"

A reporter asked why all those former federal prosecutors working in the governor's office didn't realize something bad happened at that bridge, especially after concerns were raised about public safety and laws being broken.

Good question, but the reporter delivered it with a long preamble, which the governor hates. "Why don't you just cut the commentary and get to the question?" he demanded. "Can you *get to it already*?"

Asked by another reporter why the state attorney general wasn't involved in the investigation and was instead sitting there "like furniture," Christie went off: "To characterize the attorney general as a piece of furniture is really beneath what you guys should be doing."

On the appropriateness of his joking about closing the lanes back in December: "Stop! You have to get the facts right if you're going to ask me a question. . . . The premise of the question is so *infirm* that I'm not answering it."

On not wanting to know if Kelly was complicit: "I don't know whether you can't take notes or you're not listening, but for you to characterize my last answer . . . as 'I didn't want to know' is so awful that it's beneath the job you hold."

After eleven weeks of controversy and distraction, after eleven weeks of a paused pre-presidential campaign, after eleven weeks of a flock of reporters picking apart his political soul, Christie was venting. "Everybody is now looking through the retrospectroscope," Christie said, employing a rare word that means to look back into time. "You're always smarter, you always know more, when you have that."

He refused to look down the retrospectroscope and instead insisted that a traffic study, however flawed, was actually conducted.

"It's such an extraordinary joy and relief for me to be able to come back and interact with you in the kind and gentle way that we always have," Christie said as he folded his notes to leave.

"I'd love to say I missed you," he paused, "but I didn't."

**RANDY MASTRO CALLS** me at 11:00 p.m. I pick up and begin to say, "Hi, Randy," but he starts talking before I can get the words out.

I realize Christie's chief lawyer thinks I'm someone else.

"So I got back to Matt Katz, I don't know if he's still doing a story, but he was saying that they got *no* documents from the governor! And I said, 'Duh! Duh! Of course not! Because he didn't know!' Ha! . . ."

Hours earlier, I had called Mastro to find out why, after the release of 4,612 pages of documents as part of the investigation, just one came from the governor himself. Christie had made a big deal about how his electronic devices and email passwords were turned over to investigators, and yet the only thing the public had seen with Christie's fingerprints on it was a resignation statement for Wildstein that he edited to make stronger.

It was curious. Christie didn't send an email or a text after learning that Patrick Foye, the top New York guy at the Port Authority, was alleging that Christie officials may have broken state and federal laws? And where were the phone logs between Christie and his mentor Samson? Didn't they talk all the time?

When I first called Mastro about this, he insisted that a few other documents from the governor hadn't been released yet, and that he did a complete job collecting all materials relevant to the inquiry. A few hours after that was when he accidentally called me back instead of someone in the governor's office.

"Randy," I interjected. "Randy, Randy, *Randy*! . . . As much as I want to hear what you have to say about me, I wanted to do the right thing and stop you. This is Matt Katz."

"Matt! So like I was saying. . . . Uh, I was calling my contact, my media contact, I was going to report back to them. I thought—"

"No problem, Randy. Tell the governor I said hi."

"Ha! I don't call the governor, no, no. My contact that I have to report back to is . . . I respect you, Matt! Call me *any time*. I'll talk to you *any time*."

**ANY GOOD INTERNAL** investigation includes recommendations for ethics reforms. So Mastro made several suggestions: Ban the use of personal email accounts for official state business. The "time for some traffic problems in Fort Lee" email was sent from a Gmail account to a Yahoo account, which was a common Christie administration maneuver that bypassed government channels. And the one email released from Christie came from the governor's personal Yahoo account. "That practice has to end," the Mastro Report declared.

It didn't. A year later, I found that state employees were still using personal accounts—email, phone, and instant message—for government business. Because in that full year since the Mastro Report, Christie hadn't followed through on his pledge to implement the report's recommendation to strengthen the state's official email policy. Even though the governor was going around saying things like this—"Since the incidents of 2014, we have required as a policy in the governor's office that everyone maintain business on a state email account"—that wasn't true. There was no new policy.

The Mastro Report also warned that texting poses "a host of legal and practical challenges," including security vulnerabilities and the circumvention of open record laws. And yet Christie himself was still sending texts to his cabinet members in the aftermath of Bridgegate.

Thing is, since his freeholder days, Christie had talked big about ethics reforms and come through with something less. He ran on ethics in his first race—but in the process he incorrectly disparaged his opponent for being unethical, which got him sued and eventually voted out of office. Years later as governor he signed an executive order establishing an ethics panel, which ended up not meeting very often, if at all. The panel didn't produce a single public piece of paper, and it didn't conduct any sort of examination over Bridgegate. Nonetheless one of its members, John Degnan, would soon get a new, bigger job—as chairman of the Port Authority, replacing Samson.

Christie did create a new ethics position in the aftermath of Bridgegate—an "ombudsman." Even though the Mastro Report said the ombudsman should be independent of the governor, Christie chose an ally for this job who had served on his transition team. Paid $75,600 annually, ombudsman Patrick Hobbs worked part-time, didn't have an office in the Statehouse, and never updated the governor's communications policy, as he was supposed to do. Hobbs did not issue periodic public reports, as called for in the Mastro Report.

To take the new job Hobbs had to step down from another position with yet another entity that was supposed to be watchdogging against New Jersey government corruption—the State Commission of Investigation. To replace Hobbs on this commission Christie chose his former office manager. She would make $35,000 a year on this commission working about ten hours a month investigating various aspects of state government—including political corruption.

**THE DEMOCRATS IN** the legislature spent the remainder of 2014 keeping the Bridgegate story alive with a series of dramatic Statehouse hearings.

The Democrats' joint legislative committee first subpoenaed Christina Renna, the former aide to Kelly in the IGA.

Reporters from New York and Washington returned to Trenton for the event. In the same room where David Wildstein had repeatedly pleaded the Fifth Amendment, Renna was now giving what sounded like an open portrayal of what she knew as a midlevel administration official.

Renna testified that Kelly was erratic, insecure, and prone to anger without cause. She said Kelly was "instrumental" in the scheme to close the lanes, but was not the "architect" of the plan. While Renna wouldn't speculate about who that architect was, she did say that Kelly "relied heavily on other people, I think, to make decisions for her . . . she wouldn't challenge really anyone, even at her level or above her at all."

This characterization of Kelly reflected the culture of the governor's office. Militarylike in its deference to superiors, all in service of the boss man himself, the governor's office ran on loyalty with a dose of fear.

"We have a government that is run by intimidation," Wisniewski concluded after listening to Renna.

But Renna also spoke to the team-driven, all-for-a-greater-good idealism of the IGA. She refuted the notion that IGA was a political weapon, saying that despite documents targeting Democrats for endorsements, her staff reached out to politicians regardless of party. The IGA was 99 percent good government, she said.

Democrats were more curious about the other 1 percent.

Democratic assemblyman Paul Moriarty pressed Renna about why she wasn't more suspicious as tidbits about Bridgegate began to break, and why she didn't ask Kelly more questions about her potential involvement.

"I understand, again, in retrospect how that looks," she said. "But the work environment was enormously fast-paced; it was round the clock at this point. And this was—you know, no one, I think, I can say that *everyone* just didn't think this was as severe of an issue until it was . . . the governor is asked about a zillion things in the news all the time. And it was just a part of a fast-paced work environment. I mean, I know in retrospect it sounds crazy, but that really is the answer."

"Do you regret not doing something?" Moriarty asked.

"I—yes."

**A FEW WEEKS** later, the next testimony was about to begin before the Bridgegate committee. I walked over to the day's witness. I told him he looked nice in his tailored dark suit, crisp white shirt, and red tie with blue diagonal stripes.

"Thank you," he responded. "You've got schmutz on your face." The witness then wiped leftover flakes from my breakfast croissant off my cheek.

Weeks earlier, the witness, Christie chief spokesman Michael Drewniak, had yelled at me in a Statehouse stairwell about something I had written. Weeks later, he would yell at me on the phone about something else entirely. But the flack-hack relationship is generally more complicated than the mere sum of its incidents of mutual disgust. As Christie used to say, it's "harder to hate up close," and Drewniak was up close as the primary conduit for reporters to interact with the governor's office. He was incredibly kind to me after he learned that my sister had suddenly died, but familiarity didn't always breed respect—while one veteran political reporter called Drewniak "one of the most combative and aggressive press secretaries I've ever encountered," another declared that she "loved" him.

Drewniak is tall and bald. That's the first thing you notice about him. If you look at him long enough, if you see him standing on the sidelines of a press conference year after year, you will notice more: that 10 percent of his face is smirking, always, and that he hunches his shoulders just a bit so his head juts out in what comes across as a constant state of near excitement.

He could pass for a midlevel villain in a comic book—perfect for a larger-than-life politician to use as his first line of defense against the press. For Christie's entire career as U.S. Attorney and governor, Drewniak was Christie's go-between to the media, eventually coming to echo his boss's tongue in sound bites, sarcastic quips, and infuriated ALL CAPS emails to reporters. Drewniak didn't speak for his boss; he spoke *as* his boss. He was the most colorful quote in Trenton, with barbs that dripped with dismissiveness: "If you want to cherry-pick this particular utterance, be my guest," and "Is it possible to quote me looking disinterested?"

Drewniak had some juice. He dined with top politicos and spoke to legislators of both parties. The chief justice of the Supreme Court presided over his wedding, which was attended by both Christie and David Wildstein. I heard it was quite the party.

Drewniak also was the last known Christie official to dine with Wildstein just as Bridgegate was breaking. And that's why he was here to testify. He seemed to be the last direct connection between the man who allegedly did all of this, Wildstein, and the governor himself.

AFTER WIPING MY face that May morning, Drewniak sat down for seven hours of testimony that focused not on who closed the lanes but on who had covered up the lane closures. Democrats were testing a theory that Christie, aware that his people were involved, intentionally ignored alarm bells about Bridgegate in the four months between the lane closures and the day "time for some traffic problems in Fort Lee" was released.

Drewniak had a unique perspective on the situation. He knew about all of the initial press inquiries and was concerned enough to alert Christie's chief counsel, chief of staff, and even the governor himself about allegations that were bubbling up.

Drewniak had also become something of a minor celebrity in the whole Bridgegate affair because of well-publicized emails featuring him cursing out a range of people, like *Star-Ledger* traffic columnist Steve Strunsky ("Such a fucking mutt").

During his testimony, though, Drewniak kept his cool. He did not raise his voice. Despite a pounding headache that he was treating with allergy pills, Drewniak kept visions of his upcoming fly-fishing trip in his head and soldiered through, looking calm. He addressed legislators as "sir" and "ma'am."

He said he was uninvolved in "this strange, unnecessary, and idiotic episode that brings us here today." He described the lane closures as reckless. "The conduct, callousness, and cavalier attitude expressed in them was like nothing I've witnessed in my entire working lifetime—and certainly not in this administration," Drewniak said.

He explained that he had no reason *not* to believe the traffic study story, given the fact that the governor's adversaries in the controversy were highly partisan Democrats and rival Port Authority officials from New York. There was a belief that this story was "being ginned up," Drewniak said, "by two of the most partisan members of the legislature."

Meaning, of course, Weinberg (who had run for lieutenant governor against Christie's ticket) and Wisniewski (who was a former chairman of the state Democrats).

"No offense, please," Drewniak said.

"I understand," Weinberg said.

Later, Assemblyman Moriarty asked Drewniak—who worked at the U.S. Attorney's Office on September 11—if he had ever asked why the Port Authority decided to do a traffic study on "the highest terrorist watch day."

He had not.

"At one point in time you had been a reporter. Your reporter instincts didn't kick in and say, 'This makes no sense?' " Wisniewski asked.

"I really don't have any response to that, sir," Drewniak responded.

Weinberg and Wisniewski said they were perplexed by the "curious lack of curiosity" displayed by Drewniak and just about everyone else in the administration.

THE DEMOCRATS ON the legislative committee would never get the scalp some of them sought from the beginning.

But, eventually, they got close.

Regina Egea's job in the governor's office was to oversee the Port Authority. She had seen Foye's whistleblowing email when it was sent on the fifth day of the lane closures, and she later helped prepare Baroni's explanation that this was all just a traffic study.

On December 9, 2013, as three Port Authority officials testified that the traffic study may have never existed, Egea and Christie started texting each other, which was unusual. What about? What were two tax-funded government officials saying to each other about these new allegations?

Christie said he didn't remember what the text exchange was about. "I have no recollection of it at all," he said. "It obviously was something of no moment or no import." He deleted the texts.

In testimony before the Democrats, Egea acknowledged at least one text message to Christie about Bridgegate, but the message was just meant to praise an official for being "balanced and professional" in his testimony. She, too, deleted the texts.

My colleague Andrea Bernstein found phone logs indicating a dozen texts were sent back and forth between Egea and Christie during the six hours of Port Authority officials' testimony. Andrea lined up the logs with the testimony and determined that around the time the messages were sent some of the harshest revelations about the traffic-study cover story were coming out.

**MAY 1, 2015.** Two years after Mayor Sokolich decided not to endorse Christie and nearly sixteen months after the investigation began, a Bridgegate decision was handed down from U.S. Attorney Paul Fishman.

Kelly, Wildstein, and Baroni: guilty, guilty, and guilty.

Wildstein pleaded guilty and agreed to testify against the other two in exchange for a chance at a shorter prison sentence. Kelly and Baroni pleaded not guilty on nine federal counts—including misapplying Port Authority property, conspiring to "oppress the residents of Fort Lee," and taking away residents' civil rights to "localized travel on public roadways free from restrictions unrelated to legitimate government objectives."

If convicted, Kelly, age forty-two, and Baroni, age forty-three, were looking at four years apiece in prison.

"They callously victimized the people of Fort Lee who were just trying to get to school, go to work, or travel wherever else they needed to go," Fishman said at a news conference in Newark. "The laws of the United States do not permit this kind of behavior. And the public has a right to expect better."

First Wildstein showed up to federal court in Newark to enter a plea. He had a beard, and he was ninety-one pounds lighter than the last time the world saw him. He looked healthier and older.

Inside the courtroom, Wildstein, fifty-three, pleaded guilty to two counts of conspiracy.

"Did you agree with others, including Mr. Baroni and Ms. Kelly, to punish Mayor Sokolich for not endorsing Governor Christie by deliberately causing significant traffic problems in Fort Lee?" the judge asked.

"Yes," Wildstein answered.

He answered forty-two other questions just like that. And he was released on $100,000 bond.

After the Wildstein plea, Kelly read a statement to reporters at her attorney's office. Short in stature, she stood on a purple Fisher-Price step-stool to see over the bank of microphones at the podium.

"For over a year I have remained quiet while many of the people who I believed in, trusted, and respected have attempted to publicly discredit and even humiliate me," Kelly said with confidence and certainty. "I am here today to say that I will no longer allow the lies that have been said about me or my role in the George Washington Bridge issue to go unchallenged."

She teed off on the Mastro Report. "Contrary to the way that I have been described by some of my former colleagues, I am not stupid, I am not weepy, insecure, unqualified, or overwhelmed," she said. She insisted she had not conspired with Wildstein on a scheme of retribution. "Let me also say this. I am not a liar. And I never lied to anyone about the George Washington Bridge issue." Wildstein, she said, is the liar.

But Kelly acknowledged that she was embarrassed by emails she had sent, and she attributed some of her comments simply to poor attempts at sarcastic humor.

A legal defense fund was set up in her name. And her lawyer, Critchley, made the pitch: "Some of her friends have abandoned her, powerful people are trying to destroy her, she's attempted to get a job but everybody says she's too toxic, and she may lose her home. Other than that, things are peachy in the Kelly household."

Three days later Baroni and Kelly came to court to enter their not guilty pleas. They greeted each other in the courtroom, with Baroni touching his heart and then clasping her hands. She smiled. They had barely known each other when they worked for the governor. Now, they would be forever linked in a criminal case, *United States of America* v. *William Baroni, Jr., and Bridget Anne Kelly*. Each was released on $150,000 bond.

Baroni's indictment was a surprise, in that previously released documents didn't indicate he planned the operation. But Fishman said Baroni pushed for the lanes to be closed in September, when school started, "to further ratchet up the injury to Fort Lee's residents." When the lanes reopened five days later, Baroni even tried to close them again, Fishman said.

After he walked out of court Baroni made a ninety-five-second statement in which he talked about votes he had taken as a Republican legislator—favoring gay marriage, medical marijuana, and paid family leave—that defied GOP doctrine. "Those are the things you risk your career over," he said. "I would never risk my career, my job, my reputation, for something like this. I am an innocent man."

**WITHIN ALL OF** this was good news for Christie. Fishman said he had no evidence, currently, to charge him with a crime.

But a trial was coming—in the middle of a presidential campaign. The governor himself could get called to testify. And Christie never got the full exoneration he could have used. Asked if Christie was "in the clear," Fishman said: "I'm not sure what that means, so I can't really answer that question . . . I'm not going to comment on whether anybody is going to be further investigated."

He added, tantalizingly: "It's like the end of *Downton Abbey*, and you've got to wait for a whole other season."

So it would fall on Christie's shoulders to spin these indictments as best as he could.

Shortly thereafter Christie was in New Hampshire, holding one in a series of town hall meetings as he flirted with a presidential campaign. For ninety minutes Christie won the crowd over as he fielded softballs, praised Ronald Reagan, and slammed Obamacare.

The final question went to a woman in the back row. "How about a slightly tougher question from an old Jersey girl?" asked Eileen Sahagian, originally of Teaneck, New Jersey, a town right near the George Washington Bridge.

Have at me, the governor said.

"When I heard about the bridge scandal, I was beyond horrified," she said. "I'm worried about having a president who has people around him who think that's okay. I feel like the people of Fort Lee were the sacrificial lambs. It reminds me of feudal times—I'm furious—feudal times when the king would say, 'Who cares about the peasants?' "

In one soliloquy Sahagian got to the heart of the scandal.

Christie's answer went on for several minutes. It was at times passionate and at times defensive; the most he had publicly spoken about Bridgegate in more than a year.

He began by saying that the scheme was too dumb to be directed by someone like him. "People can think a lot of different things about me, people have called me a lot of different things over time—stupid has never been one of them," he said.

Then he papered over some details, saying the Mastro Report, legislative investigation, and U.S. Attorney indictments had come to the "same" conclusions. In fact Mastro described the lane closures as a rogue operation conceived by a crazy person and a woman upset over a broken relationship, while Fishman said they were a political revenge scheme orchestrated by three Christie loyalists. Mastro and Fishman didn't even agree on who was primarily responsible.

No matter. Christie was defiant. "It has been a painful process. Painful," he said. "I'm not proud or happy of what happened, but I'm going to stop apologizing for it, too."

# 16

# CHRISTIE LOSES HIS FLEECE

M SNBC *Morning Joe* host Joe Scarborough was the governor's biggest TV booster over the first term. But on this day, Scarborough is brutally depicting the new political reality.

> It's been called the greatest collapse in modern American history. Of course we can only be talking about one man, Governor Chris Christie, a man who had the Midas touch. Poll numbers are plummeting, just an absolute collapse.

Scarborough actually said this in 2013, *before* Bridgegate, at the apex of the Christie popular phenomenon, as part of a spoof video that Christie produced. Scarborough was reading a script put together by Christie's own Maria Comella, the communications director who harbored a quiet interest in (and talent for) screenwriting. The bit was just another of Christie's jokey videos unveiled annually at the Trenton Legislative Correspondents' Club Show and released to the masses via YouTube.

*That* is how far-fetched the idea of a Christie collapse seemed—Comella created an elaborate joke around the idea, and a morning news host joined in the gag.

The video showed the governor with all of his celebrity friends. The plot involved Christie's search for his famous Sandy fleece, which was apparently stolen by Hillary Clinton or Alec Baldwin's wife. Christie's advisers warn him that without his fleece, his national political career is in trouble. He thinks that's ridiculous. He has *Morning Joe* in his pocket, he says. That show's a "love fest." And he's besties with Bruce Springsteen and Jon Bon Jovi—"Stop worrying so much," Christie tells his staff.

But Bon Jovi warns: "He ain't nothin' without his fleece."

**ABOUT A YEAR** after that video was released, in 2014, life imitated art. Scarborough turned on Christie, marking a sea change in Christie's relationship with the media and, in effect, the American people.

No single news show did more than *Morning Joe* to make Christie seem likable and lovable, ballsy and bipartisan, Just three months into Christie's first term Scarborough's cohost, Mika Brzezinski, declared: "I love him." Seven months later, Scarborough added: "How many times can we tell Chris Christie we love him?" They talked up his presidential chances ("he is the one") and referenced the text messages they exchanged with him.

During a 2011 appearance, Scarborough cited Christie's "courage" and asked him: "What makes you so great?"

Then, Bridgegate. At first they defended him. Then they gradually grew skeptical. Covering Bridgegate one morning they put an altered logo from the movie *The Godfather* on the screen—it read "The Govfather."

The relationship soured. Then came the *sit down and shut up* incident.

**ON THE SECOND** anniversary of Sandy, in October 2014, a man stood up while the governor was speaking to a crowd at the Jersey Shore. He said that he had volunteered helping Sandy victims, and he wanted to meet with Christie to tell him what more needed to be done. He kept talking and talking over the governor.

"Do your job," the man said.

"Well, you do yours, too, buddy," the governor shot back.

The man kept talking.

"Now listen," Christie began, revving his engine. "I'd be more than happy to have a debate with you, guy, because someone like you who doesn't know a *damn thing about what you're talking* except to stand up and show off when the cameras are here. I've been here when the cameras aren't here, buddy, and done the work! . . . So turn around, get your fifteen minutes of fame, and then maybe *take your jacket off roll up your sleeves and do something for the people of this state!*"

Now Christie was yelling over the man. I had never heard him scream like this. "All you've been doing is flapping your mouth and not doing anything! So listen, you want to have the conversation later I'm happy to have it, buddy, but until that time *sit down and shut up!*"

The governor never took kindly to being challenged. And once he got going, his staffers knew, he didn't always know when to stop.

A crowd had gathered for the press conference—gritty residents of this town of Belmar who had survived the storm and were now repaving roads and rebuilding small businesses and trying to recapture a little of the glory. They loved Christie, he was still their conquering hero, critics be damned. He had been good to Belmar. So they clapped and cheered as he said those words—*sit down and shut up*. The Belmar mayor, a Democrat, was standing right there behind him at the podium as Christie went off, and he applauded, too. The First Lady of the state of New Jersey was at the podium, her smile juxtaposed with her husband's growl throughout.

The protester kept going, undaunted. But the crowd couldn't hear him; Christie was the one with the mic, coming through loud and clear as he seemed to accept a request to duel. "Any time you like, buddy, *any* time you like!" he said.

When the video rolled on *Morning Joe* the next morning, Scarborough was incredulous. He kept asking: "Why? . . . Why? . . . Why?" He said Christie needed to see "an anger management professional."

"What's going on with him?" he added. "He went over the line there. That may work in Jersey—I don't even know if that works in Jersey. It's not going to work in New Hampshire. It's not going to work in Iowa. It's not going to work in South Carolina. It's not going to work in the early primary states."

Former Democratic presidential candidate Howard Dean—whose own political obituary was written after he did something nicknamed "The Scream"—declared on MSNBC that Christie's political career was over. "This guy is never going to be president," he said, "*ever*."

**THE *SIT DOWN*** and shut up video highlighted a problem potentially more nagging than Bridgegate: Sandy, once his greatest strength, was now turning into something else entirely.

By the end of 2013, at the one-year anniversary of the storm, a senior state official told the *Wall Street Journal* that the Sandy recovery had started to look like a "disaster." Plywood windows were still common on vacant homes throughout the blue-collar neighborhoods that felt the brunt of the storm's wrath. People were still living in trailers on their front lawns and in houseboats moored in their backyards. Motels were still doing brisk business housing victims, while other victims were still bouncing from couch to couch. Marriages broke up over the stress.

Other realms of the storm recovery fared better. The state dispersed hundreds of millions of dollars for rental aid to those waiting on their homes to be rebuilt. Christie officials approved cash buyouts of properties in flood-prone neighborhoods. And in relatively quick order, more than $1 billion was allocated to fix infrastructure—roads, marinas, government buildings, and the boardwalks that attracted tourists. First Lady Mary Pat Christie lent her star power, too, creating a nonprofit that raised more than $37 million for one hundred nonprofits.

But as time went on, more and more questions were being raised about how the governor was spending federal Sandy aid.

The first major cleanup contract went to a company called AshBritt. Christie found out about AshBritt from its lobbyist, former Mississippi governor Haley Barbour, who as chairman of the Republican Governors Association sent over millions in contributions to help Christie win the governor's seat. Christie gave Barbour more credit for his victory than anyone.

Barbour's AshBritt landed Christie's Sandy contract without a competitive bid. At the same time, he was helping with Christie's next election— Barbour's business partner held a fund-raiser for Christie in Virginia.

Christie said he didn't have time to bid out the contract, worth up to $100 million, given the emergency. There was debris everywhere and the governor wanted to clean it up fast. But AshBritt proved to be pricey—with some subcontractors routinely overbilling for mileage hauling storm debris.

"I don't care who they paid and who their lobbyist was," Christie later told me. "Because guess what? Every one of them has a lobbyist and someone's going to get paid. That's the nature of this business, so I don't give a damn who it is. I didn't hire 'em because of Haley Barbour and I wouldn't *not* hire them because of Haley Barbour."

He added: "If you worry about how that looks and put it ahead of getting the job done, then you're a schmuck. And I'm not a schmuck."

AshBritt was just the beginning of Christie's Sandy contractor problems. Wary of increasing the government work force and anxious to get money out the door as quickly as possible, Christie relied on contractors to handle the distribution of funds—but those overseeing the operation for the government lacked experience in contracting and construction, sources told me.

Some months later I broke the news that the Christie administration had secretly fired a company in charge of distributing $1 billion to Sandy victims. Officials concealed the firing from the public. Christie's top Sandy guy had just testified to the legislature without mentioning the termination. Even after I reported the story Christie officials refused to tell me why Hammerman and Gainer, known as HGI, was gone two years before the contract expired.

HGI was supposed to give out grants of up to $150,000 to fix some of the 350,000 housing units damaged or destroyed by the storm. But that program was barely off the ground. Applicants complained of long wait-lists and lost paperwork. About twenty thousand applicant documents went missing, applications were rejected for the wrong reasons, and some people were given grants twice. Nearly three years after the storm just a quarter of the eight thousand homeowners in the rebuilding program had finished reconstruction.

Christie blamed the slow distribution of Sandy aid on onerous federal regulations to prevent fraud that were put into place after Hurricane Katrina. But if his officials were preoccupied with following regulations, they didn't do a very good job of it—a federal audit later concluded that New Jersey failed to abide by federal contracting requirements in giving out Sandy work.

At least ten companies hired by the Christie administration for Sandy relief donated to the Republican Governors Association, which funded both of Christie's gubernatorial runs. Their cumulative donations, which would have been forbidden by law if given to the governor directly, amounted to $300,000. Several Sandy contractors later purchased tickets to attend the RGA confab in Arizona, where Christie was crowned chairman of the group.

Democratic criticism of this system was muted. Companies like Ash-Britt also hired Democratic lobbyists. Even President Obama's secretary of housing, Shawn Donovan, came to the Jersey Shore to praise Christie as just a "Jersey guy, an American who was going to stand up and fight to get this state back as quickly as possible, and who was going to do the right thing no matter what anyone says."

*What anyone says.* I was one of those anyones. I asked Donovan whether New Jersey needed to be concerned about yet another politically connected contractor, CDM Smith, which was hired by New Jersey despite a questionable track record doing the same job after Hurricane Ike in Galveston, Texas.

Christie took the mic. "Many people in the press think their job is to go back and Monday morning quarterback every decision that gets made," he said. (He was right. I did see that as my role.) "If in fact you're going to exclude every company who ever has had a disgruntled customer, then basically *Matt Katz* would be doing all of the work here on behalf of rebuilding the state," he added, as the crowd of local residents at the press conference laughed at me. "I'm sure even at a place as great as Bain's across the street, I'm sure every once in a while they have a crazy customer who comes in there and gives poor Mr. Bain hell," he said. "Doesn't mean you shouldn't go in there and shop at Bain's Hardware."

The crowd, including Mr. Bain himself, nodded in agreement.

CHRISTIE'S SANDY LEADERSHIP looked stronger immediately after the storm than it did over the long term. Three hundred and forty-two pieces of train equipment for NJ Transit were damaged—a quarter of the fleet for the second-largest commuter rail in the country, costing $120 million. Before Sandy, NJ Transit had parked its trains in low-lying lots next to wetlands, and they were subsequently engulfed by the storm surge. Months of train delays ensued, even as New York City's public transit system was back up and running. Why?

An investigation by WNYC and the *Record* found that while the New York Metropolitan Transit Authority's plan for severe storms was contained in five four-inch-thick binders, NJ Transit's hurricane plan was three and a half pages, the contents of which were blacked out to the public because, the agency said, it could aid "an al-Qaeda-led terrorist plot targeting rail service."

Unlike the MTA, NJ Transit did not appear to take into account global warming and sea level rise in preparing for the storm. Asked about whether climate change may have worsened Sandy's wrath, Christie repeatedly refused to answer. "I'm not a climatologist," he said. That's a "distraction" and "over my head" and an "esoteric question" that only "liberal public radio" would ask, he declared. And, besides, victims of the storm "don't give a damn."

Probably true. They were more concerned about what they were seeing on TV.

The Christie administration was running $25 million federally funded tourism ads that looked like Christie reelection commercials. Images of the

Jersey Shore were set to an exceedingly catchy if not annoying jingle that sounded like a bad summer anthem:

*It's in our blood, our DNA.*
*It's who we are, we're here to stay.*
*Because we're stronger than the storm. Oh, oh, ohhhh, oh!*

Then came the commercial's finale—Christie and his family, hanging out at the beach.

"The Jersey Shore is open!" Mary Pat says.

"The word is spreading!" chimes in Andrew, the oldest Christie son.

"Because we're stronger than the storm!" the governor says.

The ad ran in 2013 during Christie's reelection bid and was sometimes described as his most effective campaign ad, reminding voters of Christie's Sandy triumphs while also tapping into New Jersey pride and family values. Plus, as a tourism commercial it aired far beyond New Jersey, a nice setup introduction to a national audience for a presidential campaign.

Best yet, it didn't cost Christie a dime.

The *Asbury Park Press* revealed that the ad could have been done $2 million cheaper. A Christie administration selection committee chose a politically connected advertising agency at a higher cost. One major difference between the proposals? The selected agency planned to include Christie and his family in the ads.

The governor's office defended the decision, saying the proposal from the selected agency was the most comprehensive. And besides, defenders said, Christie was the strongest voice to represent the state after the storm.

But news stories about money going to the wrong places continued unabated. The *Star-Ledger* reported that $6 million funded the construction of a senior housing project in an inland town barely affected by the storm (but with a Democratic mayor who endorsed the governor's reelection shortly after the money was announced).

In the beginning Christie spent at least half of every working week on Sandy recovery. Now, he was spending half of many weeks traveling the country doing politics. A poll showed 64 percent of those who applied for home rebuilding aid were dissatisfied with the experience; 74 percent said they thought they were forgotten in the recovery.

The *Atlantic City Press* concluded: "The entire Sandy recovery effort—

a key part of the Christie myth—has been marked by endless bluster, self-promotion, obfuscation, and stonewalling."

Christie defended his Sandy record when we talked about it. He insisted that the recovery had gone better than in New York, and far more swiftly than in Louisiana after Hurricane Katrina. "I don't think I've done anything particularly wrong," he said. "I guess if I went back to look at every decision there's probably decisions I could have made differently. But I haven't spent a lot of time thinking about that because there are so many decisions that have to be made, I kept plowing ahead."

**THE YEAR 2014** was not working out as planned. Bridgegate. Questions about his Sandy leadership. And bad economic news everywhere.

The New Jersey unemployment rate was far lower than when Christie got in, but still higher than the national average. Even though the state had added about two hundred thousand private-sector jobs by his sixth year, the rate of job growth during Christie's first six years ranked forty-fourth in the country. While the country as a whole had regained more jobs than it lost during the recession, New Jersey was still struggling to come close to pre-recession employment numbers.

Meanwhile, three separate credit agencies had downgraded New Jersey's bond rating three times apiece under Christie's watch. New Jersey now had the second-worst credit ratings in the country. The downgrades increased borrowing costs and perpetuated the perception that this supposedly fiscally conservative governor wasn't much of a fiscal conservative.

Invariably the rating agencies cited the poor condition of the employee pension system—the very thing that was supposed to be his greatest success!—for the downgrade. The system was the most underfunded of any in the United States, with a larger unfunded liability than when he got into office.

Christie's historic pension reform measure wasn't working as well as expected because the governor wasn't exactly following the law. His famed pen-ben law called for annual increases in pension payments from the state budget. Christie had said he was obliged to pay into the system because it was a "contractual right" that was "codified" into law. So he wouldn't skip pension payments, as his predecessors had. But Christie had banked on a robust economic recovery to bring enough tax dollars to make the payments, and the economy didn't recover as he expected. The only way he could make full pension payments was by doing what the Democrats wanted—passing hefty tax increases on the wealthy and corporations.

But Christie couldn't raise taxes because he'd be running for president as a no-tax Republican. In 2014 a judge gave him a pass, allowing him to pay less than half of a $1.58 billion pension bill. The following year he allocated just $900 million on $2.25 billion due. The year after that: $1.3 billion out of $3.1 billion. The unions representing public employees and pensioners kept filing suit, but in court Christie's lawyers made the unusual argument that the governor's very own pension reform law was unconstitutional. The state Supreme Court ultimately agreed. The part of the law mandating state payments was ruled invalid. That was the good news.

The bad news was brutal headlines like this in the *New York Times*: "Christie Broke Law With Pension Move, New Jersey Judge Says."

*Christie broke law.* It was enough to make Bridgegate-weary potential presidential campaign contributors shake their heads in regret and turn the page.

Of course it sounded worse than it was. The law he broke was about appropriations, and laws about appropriations are broken every single year in Trenton. Christie tried to explain that he had actually contributed more to the pension fund than any other governor in New Jersey history and his reforms had unquestionably *helped* the problem, even if they didn't go far enough.

Then again, this *was* the pension system that he had boasted he "saved" on national television as keynote speaker at the 2012 Republican convention.

**THE NIGHT BEFORE** his annual budget address in February 2015, Christie sent out a press release reading: "Governor Christie Brings Pension & Health Benefit Challenge Full Circle, Working With NJEA on Groundbreaking Changes to Bring Fairness to Taxpayers and Fix the Problem Once and For All."

Christie was trying again to fix the problem. Or so he said. When officials at the NJEA—the teachers' union—read that they had agreed to "groundbreaking changes" with Christie on the pension problem, they were flabbergasted. Yes, the union had signed a "roadmap for reform." The governor even released a copy of everyone's signatures.

But Christie had duped the NJEA, which thought it signed a two-

and-a-half-page memo outlining options for reforms—such as a consti-tutional amendment mandating full payments into the system. The union didn't realize that Christie was going to use the document to make it seem that a deal had been agreed to.

Christie's plan was for employees to give up more benefits, just as they had the last time. His proposal involved freezing the retirement system and moving toward 401(k)-type plans—plus a similar revamping of the health benefits system to force more employee contributions.

Other public worker unions were furious with the NJEA for apparently giving so much away in an agreement that, in reality, didn't exist. Furious and having lost face, the teachers tweeted at the governor during his budget speech: "Hold your horses." Then they walked away from the negotiating table. Likewise, the proposal was dead on arrival in the legislature.

Christie wanted to show progress. But he had no progress to show.

Sounded a whole lot like Atlantic City.

ATLANTIC CITY WAS a beach getaway for Philadelphians in the mid-nineteenth century that turned into a swinging resort town with fancy Vic-torian hotels in the early twentieth century. During Prohibition, the city was a playpen of alcohol, entertainment, and gambling. By the 1960s com-petition from newer vacation destinations stole AC's luster, leading to hotel closures and skyrocketing unemployment. Atlantic City's first revitalization scheme came in the 1970s, when—as a means of "urban redevelopment"—it became the first place in America outside of Nevada to open legal casinos.

Boom times came with the casinos, but after thirty years gambling had cropped up everywhere, at newer, more conveniently located casinos in adjacent states. From 2006 to 2010, Atlantic City casinos saw a 31 percent decline in revenues. That meant less tax revenue for schools and city ser-vices. The city was in crisis.

In swept Christie. Urban revitalization, done his way.

Among Christie's first moves was a takeover. He created the Atlantic City Tourism District, carved out as a separate state-run entity patrolled by the state police to ensure a "clean and safe" place for visitors. The black Atlantic City mayor likened this special state-run area—which he said separated poor black residents in the residential neighborhoods from the mostly nonblack tourists—to "apartheid."

But Christie plowed ahead. The takeover came with $30 million for a national marketing campaign to turn Atlantic City into "Last Vegas East."

Atlantic City's marketing campaign featured car magnets, billboards, and a hashtag: #DoAC. Christie offered a pitch like a salesman: "Nobody wants to be in Las Vegas in the middle of the summer, ya been there? Nobody wants to be there. . . . But would you want to be on the most beautiful beaches on the East Coast?"

Christie was applauded by hundreds of construction workers on a freezing February day in 2011 as he announced a new plan for finishing the development of the city's latest casino. Revel Casino & Hotel was under construction when its banker, early in Christie's first term, pulled out of the project. That left a half-built glass tower on Atlantic City's coast. Another $1 billion was needed to finish the project.

Inside the skeletal beginnings of Revel, Christie told the construction workers that the company had secured new financing. The state would throw in on the deal—an extraordinary $261 million in tax breaks for Revel once it became profitable. "The taxpayers are putting forward this investment, and they deserve the opportunity to share in its success," Christie said.

The potential of Revel was evident as you drove toward Absecon Island, on which Atlantic City sits. The casino's fifty-seven floors of blue glass were an exclamation point to the casinos that spread south down the skyline. Built to look like a wave, Revel incorporated the Atlantic Ocean into its design, with pools, outdoor decks, and foodie restaurants that had spectacular ocean views. Revel was about "bringing this city back to a place where it feels once again like the preeminent entertainment resort on the East Coast," he said.

But Revel was too fancy for this AC market (there was no buffet, and casino visitors love their buffets). Smoking, a habit linked with gambling since the dawn of sin, was prohibited everywhere (to get outside you had to take a massively long escalator before trying to light a smoke against wind from the Atlantic Ocean). And the building was said to have $150 million in design flaws, including difficulties visitors had in just figuring out how to get into the gaming area.

Revel, after all that potential, after all those jobs, after all that hope, was a bad bet. Revenue did not cover the debt incurred from construction, and Revel filed for bankruptcy in 2013, eleven months after it opened. Another bankruptcy followed, as did scuttled sales attempts, and the casino closed indefinitely in September 2014. There it sat as Christie's second term stumbled on, a 6.3-million-square-foot abandoned building and a multibillion-dollar symbol of lost opportunity. The Associated Press called the closure "the most spectacular and costly failure in Atlantic City's thirty-six-year history."

Within three weeks of the Revel's closure two other AC casinos closed. In all, four of the city's twelve casinos closed in 2014, leaving large dead spots on the city's iconic beachfront boardwalk. Almost at once eight thousand people lost their jobs, mostly low- and middle-income earners who now couldn't pay their mortgages. No surprise, then, that less than a year later Atlantic City had the highest foreclosure rate of any metropolitan area in the country.

Christie tried to breathe life into the city by signing a bill allowing sports betting at casinos, which would have attracted visitors, but the law was opposed by the federal government (and the sports leagues) and tied up in the courts. He approved casino-sponsored online gaming so New Jerseyans could play cards on their computers from their living rooms, but the games failed to generate nearly the kind of revenue anticipated.

And then, in the ultimate embarrassment for Christie, Atlantic City itself nearly went bankrupt. The governor brought in two consultants—including one who had just managed the bankruptcy of Detroit—to right the city's ship. They had more power than the mayor, answered only to Trenton, and collected nearly $2 million in consulting fees in six months. Early indications were that they knew what they were doing, but perhaps they were just delaying the inevitable for a city tied to a fundamentally broken business model.

The $30 million #DoAC campaign, car magnets and all, was put on ice before Christie's "Las Vegas East" was realized. The money was needed as a tourniquet to the city budget.

AFTER BRIDGEGATE, CHRISTIE couldn't do press conferences or one-on-one interviews without Bridgegate dominating the conversation. As a consequence, Christie, who talked his way to American prominence, was now nearly mute.

Nearly.

Christie had one bullet left in the chamber. The town hall meeting.

Christie first started the town hall meetings in May of his first year in office in order to push his property tax cap proposal. He knew that he had to sell his positions, campaign-style, to have any hope of getting them through a majority Democratic legislature. Holding town halls was "a way to force the press to write a little bit about what I actually wanted to talk about."

Months after Bridgegate, Christie began holding town hall meetings again. But these events, once passionately pro-Christie with nary a Democratic agitator in sight, now had protesters outside—teachers, Sandy victims, and assorted liberals—holding posters with messages like, "Hey Gov: Bruce Springsteen Hates You." Inside, college students snuck into several events and simultaneously stood up to yell about the cost for Bridgegate lawyers and the slow pace of Sandy recovery. Their governor taunted them as they were escorted out by police.

The state police set up metal detectors, wanding everyone who walked in. They confiscated posters and photographed hecklers. Once, a cop took away my coffee, explaining that there was concern that hot liquid could be thrown at the governor.

The protesters reflected this reality: By 2015, Christie's approval ratings in New Jersey had dropped to an abysmal 30 percent. New Jersey was losing its faith in him.

The first town hall meeting after Bridgegate was at a VFW Hall in Port Monmouth, where a pigtailed three-year-old Sandy victim named Nicole Mariano, who had been living in a trailer, asked: "When will you fix my house? It's still broken."

He knelt on one knee. He said his people would talk to her parents. "We're going to try to see if we can get your home fixed, okay?" he said. Then he gave her a high-five.

The crowd applauded.

"I'm just Debbie from Brick and I just wanna go home," said one woman from the town of Brick who was waitlisted for grants to rebuild her home.

"And Debbie, I'm Chris the governor and I want you to go home," he responded, eyes locked, not even blinking. "But the fact is if the checkbook was purely at my disposal and I could review your papers personally, and not have the federal government involved, you probably would be home already."

A woman told the governor that she had lost her home and, last weekend, her mother. "She's not even buried yet," the woman told Christie. "And she really liked you. We both did."

"I suspect if she were here, she would say to me, 'Take care of my daughter,' " Christie said. "So that's what we're going to try to do."

Christie was having his YouTube moments again.

But there was someone else here that day, too: Little Ginjer, the girl he had hugged after Sandy, the one who sat in the audience during his State of the State speech. Via YouTube, Ginjer had become the personification of how Christie soothed New Jersey's soul after the storm.

But Ginjer's family still didn't have their home back, and after the town hall meeting her mother vented to the *New York Times*.

"He's full of it," she said. "I don't think he's kept his word."

**IN LAW SCHOOL**, Christie remembered, "if you find a few people to cling on to, and you share the same worries and the same pressures, you create friendships for life." Christie came of age with a small group of friends from Seton Hall Law School. They vacationed together as singles, as married couples, and then, as families. Every year.

One particular guy, whom he doesn't name when telling this story, was the smartest and best looking in his crew. He was associate editor of the law journal, and then he landed the best GPA and biggest job as a multimillion-dollar rainmaker for a major firm. He married a doctor—who became Christie's doctor. He had three daughters.

When the man hurt his back, he was prescribed painkillers. He grew addicted. Christie started getting calls from his friend's law partners, saying he was showing up late to work, leaving early, not functioning the way he used to. Christie and his buddies did an intervention and got him into treatment. He went to twelve different treatment facilities over eight years.

Nothing worked. He lost his job and his home. He was divorced by his wife and had no contact with his daughters. "No matter how many ways we tried to help him, *desperately* tried to help him, and have hope, he continued to lose this struggle against this awful disease," Christie remembered in a speech in 2014, shortly after the man, fifty-two, was found dead in a motel room alongside bottles of vodka and painkillers. "You live with the absolute certainty and incredible hope that you don't get a phone call, telling you they've finally lost that fight. Well, two months ago on a Sunday morning, I got that phone call."

Drug addiction had long been a top concern for Christie. Before he became governor he served on the board of an adolescent drug rehabilitation facility in his town, Daytop Village. "I watched kids, teenagers, come into that place addicted to heroin, to PCP, to cocaine, had been arrested numbers of times, and they looked as if they were completely hopeless," Christie said. But treatment turned them around. He met a sixteen-year-old recovering crack addict there. He later gave that boy an internship at the a Republican, could be a launching pad for Christie's inevitable presidential candidacy.

Christie spoke of his drug treatment agenda in the language of the Christian right. "It's great to be prolife," he said. "But you need to be prolife after you get out of the womb, too. We have to be prolife all the way along." And that means taking care of addicts, even when they "make mistakes," even when they "anger us."

Later, during Christie's presidential campaign, a speech that he gave with this message went viral, becoming one of his biggest YouTube hits ever.

Still, drug reform advocates didn't completely back Christie. He pushed for treatment, but there weren't enough treatment beds in New Jersey to handle the need. Advocates sought more state funding. And his stance on the continued criminalization of marijuana use, a major driver of drug arrests, was seen as conflicting with his push to end the war on drugs. Christie had never smoked marijuana; he saw reefer as a gateway drug, and thought that the federal government should crack down on states that legalize its recreational use.

Christie could seem cold when challenged by parents of sick children who wanted him to ease access to medical marijuana. But to mothers of heroin addicts, Christie was warm and empathetic. Victims of the disease of addiction shouldn't be in prison, he'd say, they should be getting long-term care.

"People don't really understand," one mother told the governor.

"I do understand," he responded.

Declaring that the war on drugs had "failed," Christie took significant steps to change drug policy. He created a $2.5 million program requiring nonviolent drug offenders to go to drug court instead of criminal court, redirecting them to treatment programs instead of jail. Drug courts expanded to all twenty-one New Jersey counties on his watch.

Christie also signed a bill providing legal protection to those who attempt to help an overdose victim, and he authorized police officers to administer a drug, naloxone, that counteracts heroin overdoses. In short order, naloxone saved hundreds of lives.

Christie even agreed to allow those who had completed drug treatment programs to collect welfare benefits and rental assistance once they got out, helping them integrate back into society.

Christie's biggest move to disengage from the war on drugs came with a comprehensive proposal to reform the state's criminal justice system. One

U.S. Attorney's Office. When the boy grew up to become a lawyer, he credited Christie with helping to get his life on track.

As governor, Christie pushed treatment rather than incarceration. His time as U.S. Attorney gave him legitimacy on this front. "I feel like it's incumbent on me to do this because I've been a prosecutor, no one is going to say with any credibility that I'm soft on crime," he said.

In 2012 Whitney Houston, the sensationally talented singer and a resident of Christie's town of Mendham, died of a drug overdose. Christie ordered state flags lowered in her honor, triggering a brief national controversy. Opponents thought it was inappropriate to honor someone who overdosed. In Michigan, the father of an American soldier killed in Iraq bought a New Jersey flag and burned it on his outdoor grill in protest.

But Christie, who had issued forty-two executive orders to fly flags at half-staff at that point in his tenure, mostly for military service members, aggressively defended his decision, saying he was offended by those who emailed him calling Houston a "crack ho."

"We need to start dealing with the underlying disease and stop calling people names," he said. "That's not what's going to make them better."

When Christie attended Houston's funeral at New Hope Baptist Church in Newark, he got a standing ovation.

Christie took up the drug policy fight in earnest in his second term, when he had lost so much political capital due to scandal that there were few other issues he could address. The economic comeback he promised had not happened. Sandy was becoming more of a political vulnerability than a strength. And Bridgegate had dreadfully damaged his reputation.

This issue, though, fit with the story of personal political redemption that he was now selling. He gave a speech to doctors asking them to submit patient names to a state prescription database to prevent addicts from "doctor shopping" for painkillers. He met with injured high school athletes who got hooked on prescribed medication, and he went to treatment centers to talk with addicted mothers.

Christie also unveiled an eight-minute video featuring recovering addicts telling their stories and the governor himself talking about his friend who died from an overdose. In conjunction with the release of the video he did his first national interview blitz after Bridgegate (CNN, FOX, CBS, *Yahoo*, and *Politico*), with the reporters instructed to ask about his efforts on drug policy. This yielded stories about how this cause, unusual for element was tough on criminals: Christie demanded the legislature put a constitutional amendment on the ballot to allow voters to decide whether judges should be able to deny bail to those accused of violent crimes. Christie told horrifying stories of violent criminals released on bail, only to return to the streets of New Jersey cities and wreak more violent havoc. The other element of his proposal was to allow judges to impose nonmonetary bail for nonviolent drug criminals. When impoverished defendants can't post bail, he said, jails turn into de facto warehouses for poor, nonviolent drug offenders. The plan was to allow these drug addicts to get treatment outside of prison.

Facing resistance from the Democratic Assembly, he called legislators back from vacation in August 2014 and delivered twenty minutes of remarks that Bergen *Record* columnist Alfred Doblin described as "one of the finest speeches of his career." "The compassionate Republicanism of the first President George Bush from the mouth of General George Patton," Doblin wrote. "This was the master politician at his best."

"To me, every day that someone fears for their life on our streets is a crisis," Christie told the legislature. "To me, every day that someone is deprived of their liberty in a jail for no reason is a crisis."

The following week the legislature approved his proposals. At a subsequent press conference Christie was joined in support by representatives from the NAACP and the American Civil Liberties Union—advocacy groups that were longtime Christie nemeses. Christie also surprised these advocates by using the occasion to sign a bill to "ban the box"—forbidding employers from asking about job applicants' criminal histories.

"Here in New Jersey, we are continuing to show that we can do things differently," Christie said.

Christie was in political recovery, working to get a second chance.

# REBORN TO RUN

C hristie began his stint as chairman of the Republican Governors Association just as Bridgegate broke, which darkened the beginning of a year-long tenure that was intended to set up a presidential campaign.

In some GOP circles, he was suddenly toxic. He went to Illinois to raise money and three of the four Republicans running in the gubernatorial primary found reasons not to appear publicly with him.

So at first, Christie took a more subtle role, eschewing attention from the press. But he finally broke out two months after Bridgegate at CPAC, the conservative conference.

He showed that he could still be Republicans' seething attack dog, biting Obama: "What the hell are we paying you for?!" He belittled the media, defended the conservative financier Koch brothers, and reminded everyone that he is prolife by repeating the refuted applause line that Democrats have never allowed a prolife speaker at their national convention (they have).

Christie went on the road, visiting thirty-five states in his year at the helm of the organization and raising a record $100 million–plus. He spent all or part of 137 days in 2014 out of state.

But it was months before he took questions from the press on these trips. When he finally did, in Maine, the encounter with reporters was uneventful. Afterward the governor got back into his SUV with Bill Palatucci, his longtime political consigliere, who turned to him and asked: "That went so well, why aren't we doing more of these?"

Christie loosened up from there and began doing retail stops, campaigning with candidates and talking to local reporters. Shaking hands at a restaurant in Nashville with Tennessee governor Bill Haslam, Christie ran into a bachelorette party where the inebriated women, decked out in white cowboy hats and tank tops reading "One Last Rodeo," were thrilled to take selfies with a jovial Christie.

Christie then gave the biggest speech of his life to a southern audience—seventeen hundred people at the Tennessee GOP's annual Statesmen's Dinner—offering a vision of a moderate Republican candidate in the 2016 race. He unabashedly endorsed practical, centrist, anti–Tea Party Republicanism, re-staking his claim as the leader of the establishment wing of the Republican Party.

"I don't know when it became wrong to go to talk to people on the other side, to respect them, and to become their friends," Christie said, referencing his own bromance with Democratic Senate president Stephen Sweeney. Backing an establishment Tennessee Republican against a Tea Party upstart in that state's governor's race, Christie warned against sending more "divisiveness" to Washington, D.C.: "Let's not start getting dumb."

The Tea Party challenger, Joe Carr, responded by calling Christie "a fixture of controversy and scandal."

Whatever. Winning elections, Christie emphasized, was the point. And accomplishing things done once elected was the goal. "Compromise," he said, was not "capitulation."

Christie's political redemption tour was funded through RGA's checkbook. Christie had broad discretion in how the RGA could spend the money he was raising from titans of industry, and his ability to bestow millions on selected candidates seemed to gradually thaw relations with many Republicans.

Plus, Christie hustled. He worked his butt off for candidates who had a chance, attending ninety campaign and fund-raising events in the two months before the November 2014 gubernatorial elections. He'd travel via RGA-funded jet with his taxpayer-funded security detail and a rotating cast of insiders from his political, governmental, and familial worlds.

Christie seemed to love each of the 106,000 miles he logged as RGA chairman. "If I'm having a one-on-one meetings where I'm making $250,000 or $500,000 asks of people, and they say yes, it's pretty exhilarating," he said. "It's a good day." He'd be briefed beforehand on what this particular potential donor cared about—education reform, regulatory issues that affected their businesses, taxes—and then talk about how that related to what so-and-so candidate was running on. He didn't meet with anyone if the pitch was for anything less than $100,000. At most of his meetings he asked for at least $250,000. "It's always somewhat awkward to ask people for their money—at least for me," he said. "But I'm good at it. And I've gotten better over time."

Entities that did business in New Jersey, including the company Christie hired to privatize the state lottery and the law firm that investigated Bridgegate, donated to the RGA. Even Donald Trump, future GOP rival, gave Christie's RGA $250,000.

At the end of many fund-raising and campaign trips, on the way back to New Jersey, he flipped on a Bluetooth speaker, pulled up his twenty-five-hundred-song iPhone playlist, and turned it up—Motown, Bob Seger, sometimes Springsteen.

He was indefatigable in this role, culminating with a final swing before the election in which he visited nineteen states in five days. For this trip he brought along his oldest son, Andrew, who between stops dozed off. Christie nudged him. "Why are you sleeping?"

"You are a machine," Andrew said, "I am not."

A machine fueled, often, by public attention. "I draw energy from this stuff," he said. "I really do. I draw energy from crowds."

When Christie campaigns, he is all physical. Christie gives you the most complete handshake you've ever had. He hugs you and slaps your back and grabs both of your arms. He wraps his arms around teen girls in bikinis and bros in beaters and ninety-year-old women in wheelchairs, bending down to look them right in the eyes.

And he remembers faces—from the last campaign stop or that other time down at the Jersey Shore. In 2013, he recognized a guy who had asked him for his autograph about a decade earlier at Penn Station in Manhattan. That was the first autograph he had ever given out.

"You never forget your first, Matt, you never forget your first," Christie explained to me.

Eventually Christie took so many selfies that his staff compiled a video of him taking selfies and posted it to Facebook.

"Selfie? Absolutely," he would say.

And afterward: "Perfect, perfect! I can't wait to see that on Facebook."

On the road with the RGA, Christie routinely stayed for selfies and handshakes long after the candidate whom he was ostensibly campaigning for had left the premises. In Charleston, South Carolina, Christie and Governor Nikki Haley cruised through a burrito joint, talked to the press, and then walked out together to waiting SUVs, which were to whisk them off to a fund-raiser. But before he got into his SUV, Christie stopped at a hat shop next door. The shopkeeper asked him to try on a hat and take some pictures. And then the owner of an eyeglass shop next door invited him to come by to check out sunglasses. "I'm gonna go back and see those sunglasses, what the heck," he said to his aides. "I got a little time, don't I?"

No, an aide responded, Haley was waiting in the car.

Christie was already out the door for more selfies, more friends, and more promises to return.

IN NEW HAMPSHIRE, after a rally for the gubernatorial candidate, a middle-aged independent voter named Joyce Lai came running up to him in the parking lot of a diner.

"I love the way you talk to some of the reporters," she offered.

"Like him especially?" Christie said, pointing to me. "He's a real pain in the neck, this one."

"I think somebody needs to say that to them!" Lai said.

"If they ask stupid questions you have to tell them it's stupid. And if they're good, they're good. If they're not, they're not."

"That's right!"

"See? That's the way they all feel about you, Matt, I'm telling you. That's the way they all feel about you!"

Christie fans love the way he takes down reporters and hecklers alike. A Republican at that same rally told me he fell for the governor after binge-watching two hours of Christie YouTube videos.

Campaigning for Iowa governor Terry Branstad, Republicans told him he had the right tough-guy mentality to win the presidency, and that he reminded them of Ronald Reagan. Invariably, they cited style over substance. Showing more than a passing familiarity with the fame derived from his YouTube videos, seventy-two-year-old Joyce Dierks told me: "I like the way he goes after people."

In some corners Bridgegate was even seen as a credit to his character. "They tried to get you early," a seventy-nine-year-old named Bob Kazimour told Christie. "You were the lead dog and they were smart. You got to give them credit."

"But here I am, Bob, aren't I?" Christie said.

During a stop at MJ's Restaurant in Davenport, Iowa, I sat down at a table with two women waiting for Christie to circle through the restaurant. When Christie arrived, he sat across from me and turned to the woman next to him.

"You generally have good judgment?" he asked her.

"I generally do, yes," she responded.

"Then what are you doing letting him sit in your booth!?" The governor jutted a finger in my direction.

"We're very friendly people!" she said.

"That's the only explanation. It's not an exercise in judgment."

Before I knew it, the governor was handing me an iPhone so I could snap a picture of them.

"Want a picture with Matt?" he asked.

The woman smiled. "No."

"See? I tried, Matt. I tried. I really did. But keep out on the road . . ."

He liked having us there, the local press, the familiar faces, the material for his routine.

Afterward I raced southeast from Marion toward the fairgrounds in Davenport, where the local GOP was hosting "An Evening at the Fair with Chris Christie." On the menu was whiskey-marinated pork and lemonade.

Following an awkward Bridgegate joke from a GOP congressional candidate—"All of our bridges were open coming to Davenport!"—Christie was introduced for an address covered live on CSPAN.

"We get these folks from the press following me around asking me, 'Do people in Iowa love you, Governor?' " Christie paused. The crowd cheered. "And I say, 'Heck I don't know, we just met. But the early indications are good.' "

There was an extra "o" in "good." He let it linger. It was a wonderful line, delivered melodiously.

CHRISTIE PROVED HIS worth to the party establishment as RGA chairman, increasing the number of GOP governors from twenty-nine to thirty-one. Christie was credited with deploying money into the races that needed it most, and he made himself the face of the success by taking a victory lap on five national news shows the morning after Election Day. On each, he was asked about his presidential ambitions.

Christie's RGA tenure helped to recast Christie as a "team player"—just the person who could unify the fractured Republican Party, extract money from a conservative donor base, and win in blue states. He was justifying a Christie Republican nomination to party elites.

In November 2014, the *New York Times Magazine* published a story headlined "Chris Christie Is Back." The accompanying image was a phenomenal cartoon of Christie taking a selfie with a baby. He was "back from the brink," the story declared. "Christie had charted an artful comeback, largely through the cover of his perch as chairman of the governors association."

From here, it seemed, his presidential exploratory campaign should have begun in just a few weeks, as early as January 2015. But Bridgegate lingered. Investigations continued. Documents kept getting released with less-than-flattering depictions of the inner workings of the governor's operation.

"Violating," one staffer told me, "to have that laid bare."

So to conservative talk radio hosts and at town hall meetings, Christie started to wear Bridgegate like some sort of badge of honor. Unlike Hillary Clinton, the Democratic candidate facing questions about a private email server on which she may have kept classified documents, Christie argued that he had been fully transparent during Bridgegate. "Can you imagine if I had come out and said: 'I have a private email server that I did business on as governor and that I deleted a bunch of emails and destroyed the server, but don't worry about it, there was nothing on there that was of any interest to anybody'?" Christie asked.

Thing is, Christie had his own question marks about electronic communication. Christie didn't have a private server, but he routinely used a private account for government business, as did his aides. Only one of his emails and zero of his text messages about Bridgegate or anything else at all during his entire tenure as governor had ever been released. And while the governor was said to have relied on text messages for most of his interactions, he wouldn't provide his texts in response to public records requests.

I asked him to explain why he was acting more properly than Clinton. He said only a public radio reporter would ask such a question, and then he didn't answer it.

At a private retreat for three hundred wealthy Republicans in Park City, Utah, the governor "framed the bridge scandal as a media conspiracy against him," according to what the Los Angeles Times was told by people in the room. He also played the crowd a video of a recent appearance he had made on The Tonight Show with Jimmy Fallon, where he did a skit called "Dad Dancing" for nearly three minutes, showing remarkable comfort in his recently slimmed-down but still large body as he danced with respectable dexterity in unflattering khakis pulled up to his belly button. At one point, he pulled Fallon through his legs.

This, of course, was the same Fallon who had excruciatingly mocked

Christie in a post-Bridgegate duet with Springsteen. Now, Christie was being laughed at again—but this time he was in on the joke, using self-deprecation in a way that would charm, he hoped, the masses. "Dad Dancing" quickly became the most popular YouTube video starring Christie, ever. Most important, in the appearance Fallon never asked Christie about Bridgegate. Instead, Fallon seemed to exonerate him: "You got slammed all around . . . good for you for staying in the ring and standing up."

As the GOP donors in Utah watched this skit, the hope was, they would be reminded: "Yeah, that's why I like that guy."

"Don't be so nervous," Christie told the Republican kingmakers. "I'm not that worried about [Bridgegate]. I hope none of you are worried about it, though I expect some of you are. But you'll get over it. It will be fine."

THEN CHRISTIE GOT himself in trouble again.

In January 2015, Christie jumped up and down in an orange sweater in Dallas Cowboys owner Jerry Jones's luxury box during a live telecast of a critical playoff game watched by 40 million people. The Cowboys were down by two touchdowns when they pulled off an improbable comeback for a thrilling 24–20 victory and their first playoff win in five years. After that last touchdown Christie tried to high-five Jones, but he failed. He tried to hug him, but seemed to get rebuffed amid the excitement. The scene was awkward; it's hard to look cool jumping up and down in an orange sweater while missing high-fives. The Internet love-hated the moment, sending Christie's name trending and inspiring mockeries on YouTube.

Turned out that Jones had declared Christie his personal good luck charm, and he was not only paying for Christie's tickets to several games but also, on at least one occasion, paying for the private jet that took Christie, his wife, and his four kids to a game. The governor wore an orange sweater each time. If the Cowboys win the Super Bowl, Jones declared, credit goes to Christie—and therefore "he ought to be looked at as president of the United States."

But Christie's luxury suite celebration was not deemed presidential. Christie's national polls took a hit around this time, and his advisers acknowledged the incident had a deleterious effect on his reputation because dancing with billionaires ran contrary to his brand as an everyman. Conservative talk radio host Rush Limbaugh spent two days harping on Christie's Cowboys trips and "man-hug" with Jones—and in the process reminded his audience about how Christie "side-hugged" Obama and "loves" to hang out with celebrities.

Limbaugh also brought up new revelations that Jones was part of an ownership group selected by appointees of Christie and New York governor Andrew Cuomo to operate the new observation deck at the Port Authority-owned Freedom Tower at Ground Zero.

"If Christie can close bridge lanes," Limbaugh said, "he has influence on this concession here at the top of the Freedom Tower. So it all finally comes together."

Christie explained that Jones became a friend after the contract was awarded, and so he was allowed to accept thousands of dollars in tickets—plus a flight to one game.

Ethics experts disagreed. Fortunately, the governor had formed, in the beginning of his term, an Advisory Ethics Panel to help sort through thorny issues like this one.

Unfortunately, both of the panel's members had resigned months earlier for bigger appointments.

One of those ethics watchdogs was Christie's new chairman at the Port Authority.

Everything kept coming back to that bridge.

THE DISTRACTION OF the scandal—and the loss of Christie campaign manager Bill Stepien—weakened his political operation in New Jersey, where Republicans were starting to play footsie with surprise Republican presidential candidate Jeb Bush, the former Florida governor who was the son and brother of presidents. Stepien would've been the guy to tell Republican Party county chairs in New Jersey to keep their powder dry before Christie announced his candidacy. Now, big-time Republican donors were defecting to Bush without giving Christie so much as a heads-up.

Grassroots Republicans were complaining louder and louder that their governor had abandoned New Jersey without implementing the conservative agenda that he had promised or finishing the recovery from Sandy. Christie soon lost the man who was at one point his closest ally in the legislature—Senator Joe Kyrillos, a former Christie campaign chairman and friend of twenty-five years. Kyrillos swore Christie in when he became a freeholder and spoke at his U.S. Attorney inauguration ceremony. Now, he was backing Bush.

Christie and New Jersey seemed to be moving on from each other. Gubernatorial appointments weren't being made, bills were delayed in getting signed or vetoed, and new policy proposals were rare. He was in Trenton only once or twice a week.

ONE THING CHRISTIE was doing in New Jersey was using his position as governor to plug some holes for his presidential candidacy. By late 2014, polls showed that he had become a second-tier presidential candidate, and he could not afford to run as a moderate pragmatist, as he had long envisioned. But he could use the power of his governorship, the strongest such governorship in the land, to demonstrate that he bled Republican red.

First, he changed his position on the national education standards known as Common Core, which he had adopted in New Jersey back when it was an uncontroversial Republican-backed program. Now, Common Core was viewed as an unconstitutional takeover of state educational systems, and it was therefore expected to be one of the most important issues in the GOP primary.

Just a couple of years earlier Christie called Common Core "one of the areas where I've agreed with the president more than not." He explained that others' opposition was due in part to politicians who "care more about their primaries than they care about anything else."

But as Christie's own presidential primary inched closer he told GOP gatherings that he had "grave concerns" about the way the Obama administration was implementing Common Core. He appointed a commission to study the issue.

Months later the commission hadn't even issued a report before Christie came to a conclusion on his own and announced that the Common Core standards were "not working" in New Jersey because they were being handled by "federal bureaucrats."

This confused people, because local educators were just beginning to implement the standards, and nothing significant had changed vis-à-vis "federal bureaucrats" since Christie first endorsed Common Core five years earlier.

Educators in the state were in an uproar. Were their curricula just unilaterally ripped up because the governor wanted to be president?

They needn't worry. A couple of months after Christie's denouncement of Common Core, his state Department of Education backed away from doing anything at all until yet another commission of no fewer than ninety-eight members conducted a series of listening tours and focus groups. A whole separate bureaucracy was essentially created to do, possibly, nothing at all.

CHRISTIE ALSO NEEDED to shift his rhetoric on abortion before his big campaign announcement. He was unquestionably a prolife governor, but his experience with this issue was complicated.

On a frigid day in January 2011, a year after he took office, Christie walked to the front steps of the Statehouse, sans coat, smiling as chants of "Right to life!" greeted him.

"Every life is precious and a gift from God," Christie said. ("Amen!")

"I want to thank all of you for your continued loyalty and your continued commitment to this cause!" ("Thank you!")

And he confessed: "As all of you may know this is not an issue that I always understood, nor was I always on your side. It is an issue that I began to grow and learn about in a very personal way. My daughter Sarah . . . who will turn fifteen this February, when I heard her heartbeat at three months in our doctor's office, it was at that moment that it became clear to me that being on the sidelines of this issue was not something that I could live with."

Based on when Sarah was born, this personal revelation about abortion happened some time in 1995. But well into 1996, he was still prochoice. We know that because he was a Morris County freeholder quoted in an article about partial birth abortions saying this: "I'm prochoice, but I think this procedure is reprehensible."

A former political ally from the time, Rick Merkt, claimed Christie's abortion flip-flop is bogus but can't be disproved. "It's the perfect political story," he said.

Christie described his transition to the prolife cause to me as more of an evolution. He seemed to clearly remember driving back to work from the doctor's office and thinking about that heartbeat. In the weeks that followed he said he talked to Mary Pat, who was already prolife, about the issue, and then his father-in-law, who had already been pushing him on it. Then, one day, "I just changed my position."

That he did. Shortly after he became governor he vetoed $7.5 million in funding for health services at Planned Parenthood and other family-planning clinics. The money wasn't earmarked for abortions, but he vetoed these funds every year. This led to the reduction of more than $40 million and the closure of as many as seven clinics. All along, Christie insisted he was doing this for fiscal reasons and noted that he was redirecting the money to other women's health programs.

Often, he was asked if the veto had anything to do with abortion. But both at press conferences and in his official veto statements, he cited the budget and nothing else.

Now that it was almost time to run for president, Christie suddenly changed his language. Now, he told conservatives, those vetoes of Planned Parenthood funding were evidence of his prolife beliefs.

**WHEN THE GOVERNOR** was faced with a bipartisan bill supported by almost all of his constituents, his political ambitions were put to a test. The bill banned tiny gestation crates that house pregnant pigs for pork production. The wealthy Republican donors in Iowa who ran the pork industry said the crates were needed to protect the sows from fighting, while animal rights activists said the crates were inhumane because the pigs couldn't lie down or extend their limbs.

The bill banning the crates sailed through the legislature. Then, Christie vetoed it. Pork producers in Iowa cheered; animal rights activists never forgave him.

"I guess you can't ignore the citizens of Iowa, who elected you governor of New Jersey," quipped Jon Stewart on *The Daily Show*. Iowa, of course, hosts the first presidential caucus.

Christie argued that it was unclear if any pig farmers in New Jersey even used these crates that were supposed to be banned. Christie was peeved: The state's economic outlook is bleak and its taxes are ever-rising, and yet here New Jersey legislators are trying to embarrass him with irrelevant bills? If the Democrats were going to try to force him into harming his presidential chances, he wasn't going to give them the satisfaction.

**CHRISTIE SAVED HIS** most dramatic policy shifts until the night before he announced his candidacy for president. First he shocked lawmakers by announcing an increase in a tax credit for the poor. Christie had in fact reduced this tax credit when he got into office, and every year Democrats tried and failed to restore it. Now not only was Christie restoring the Earned Income Tax Credit but he was making it even more generous than it was before he arrived in office. This meant about a half million working, poor New Jerseyans would pay $250 less in taxes a year. Democrats applauded—

and Christie could now tell conservatives that he had cut income taxes in a blue state. This was a brilliant, legacy-building surprise.

The other announcement on the night before his candidacy dealt with the hottest issue in America at the time—guns.

On guns, as with abortion, Christie began on the left. In 1993 he told the *Star-Ledger* that he was making his first bid for public office, to the state Senate, in order to preserve the state's ban on assault weapons. He then promptly dropped out of the race. But that didn't curtail his antigun beliefs. Two years after that Christie was a Morris County freeholder making an unsuccessful bid for the state Assembly when he and his running mate distributed a campaign flier that attacked their opponents for wanting to repeal a ban on automatic assault weapons. The ad read: "It's dangerous. It's crazy. It's radical. They must be stopped."

As U.S. Attorney, Christie went after guns, devoting resources to anti-violence efforts in the inner city, locking up drug kingpins, and creating an initiative to "expedite firearm identification efforts." When he indicted the owner of an Ohio gun store for selling guns to intermediaries who handed them over to Bloods in Newark, Christie said: "Enough is enough. This is our warning shot to gun dealers in other states." The guns had been used in twenty crimes in New Jersey.

As governor, Christie showed extraordinary political independence for a Republican by describing as "reprehensible" an anti–gun control ad from the powerful National Rifle Association featuring Obama's daughters. "Don't be dragging people's children into this," he said. Later, he opposed an NRA proposal to put armed guards in schools.

Christie promised to "strictly enforce" New Jersey's "aggressive" gun laws. And he bucked a Republican plan to allow other states' concealed weapons permits to be valid in New Jersey.

After the 2012 mass shooting at Sandy Hook Elementary School in Connecticut, Christie met with parents of victims for an "emotional" ninety-minute meeting. "As a father, it's difficult to hear," he told me. "But I'm glad I met with them."

Still, he rejected many of their requests. Supporting gun control in New Jersey was a political necessity, but within the national GOP it was a political liability. As Sandy Hook parents lobbied the governor to sign antigun measures, a pro-gun group in New Hampshire, home of the first presidential primary, lobbied him to veto those same bills.

At first Christie called for a "national discussion" on Sandy Hook—
"and gun control has to be part of it, too." He appointed an antiviolence
commission and endorsed a range of proposals including expanded mental
health services and a ban on the sale of Barrett .50-caliber sniper rifles. He
ultimately signed twelve largely noncontroversial bills, including increasing
the penalty for giving a firearm to a minor, forbidding those on the Terrorist
Watchlist from obtaining gun permits, and upgrading existing gun crimes
to first-degree offenses.

Christie did not, though, sign the ban on the .50-caliber gun—the very
bill he proposed. He later described this bill as "crazy." He also vetoed a
bill that would have created a background-check system to keep guns away
from criminals; in his veto statement, he scolded the legislature for focusing
too much on gun control.

Christie made these veto announcements eight months after the shooting, on a Friday night, immediately before the weekly thirty-six-hour lull in
the 24/7 news cycle. At the time, I dubbed it "Christie's Friday Night Special." It seemed to me that he wanted as few people in New Jersey as possible
to know what he had done, but wanted many conservatives to know about
it later. Monmouth University pollster Patrick Murray tweeted: "Which
governor 'announced' today that he's running for the GOP nomination in
2016? @GovChristie, of course!"

Presidential candidates often tack to their party's base before moving
to the center in a general election. Even though Christie's brand was about
saying what he thought regardless of the political consequences—a trans-
formative figure who, through the power of personality, could take positions unpopular among some conservatives—the governor was damaged
by Bridgegate and no longer held enough political capital to take such risks
on policy. He needed to be a more strident partisan in order to get his voice
heard in the crowd.

I asked Christie if politics, one way or another, affected his decision-
making on gun policy. "It's influential but not determinative," he said.
Christie also said that the .50-caliber gun veto was actually about dirty
Democratic politics—he had an agreement with leaders of the legislature
about what the ban would look like, he said, "and they decided for political
reasons to make the ban more broad." So he vetoed the bill out of principle.
"They need to understand that if they break a deal with me, there's going to
be ramifications for it."

That claim was refuted by the Democratic leader, Senate president

Sweeney. "He vetoed the bill he asked for," Sweeney said. "I was dumb-founded."

Another bill hit his desk—to lower the limit on the number of bullets in a magazine from fifteen to ten. Two parents of children killed at Sandy Hook traveled to the Statehouse with a petition of fifty-five thousand signatures in support of the measure. They believed fewer children would have died if the gunman had been forced to stop to reload his semiautomatic rifle, which had a thirty-round magazine.

But having met with Sandy Hook families the year before, Christie wouldn't sit down with them again. He argued that the bill represented a slippery slope to banning guns entirely. And so he vetoed it, late on a Friday, this time before the three-day July 4 weekend.

Then Christie took his final step. On the night before he kicked off his bid to be president, Christie signed a bill making it easier for those threatened with violence, such as domestic abuse victims, to obtain handguns. Christie also said he was creating yet another commission—this one would determine if New Jersey gun laws "infringe on New Jerseyans' constitutional rights."

For a guy who had never hunted—only target and skeet shooting for the Christies—the governor acknowledged that his recent travels in national Republican circles exposed him to different points of view. "I was young," he said of his antigun days, "and I think about it differently now."

I WAS IN Philadelphia, near my house. I had just dropped off my kids at daycare and I was on the way to get a cup of coffee when the final confirmation that I needed came over text message. Chris Christie was, finally, after six months of teases and four years of speculation and five years of buzz, going to announce his candidacy for the presidency of the United States.

In 2014 Christie indicated he'd make a decision about his political future in the first few months of 2015. January passed with rumors of an announcement but no announcement. Then February. And March. It became clear: Christie wouldn't announce his candidacy until Bridgegate indictments were handed down. That happened in May, but then Christie had to wrap up the state budget, which was due in June. Meanwhile the Republican field started coalescing, with announcements about new candidacies just about every week.

I wanted the scoop on when and where Christie would finally launch his campaign and make it official. On my walk to the coffee shop I finally got the confirmation from a third source on when, and where, the announce-ment would happen. I called my editor at WNYC, Nancy Solomon.

He's announcing on Tuesday, June 30, at Livingston High School in New Jersey, I told her. His alma mater. Of course he is.

I texted Maria Comella, who would soon be running the Christie presi-dential campaign. I told her what I was about to report.

"Nothing confirmed," Maria Comella told me. "I wouldn't do that."

Well, I thought, she didn't say I was wrong. And I was confident with my reporting. So I broke the news moments later on WNYC, calling in live on *The Brian Lehrer Show* as I sat outside the coffee shop—just as I had reported the "time for some traffic problems" email live on *Brian Lehrer* from another coffee shop eighteen months earlier.

A half hour passed before a second news outlet confirmed the scoop, but in the meantime Twitter spread the word and Christie's reps cursed me out. They wanted to break the news the way they wanted to break it. Public radio in New York wasn't part of the plan.

At a press conference the next day, though, Christie was unusually respectful. "It appears it was leaked to Mr. Katz—someone leaked some-thing," he said. "Some of you are more persuasive than others. You can get information and you do. That's your job."

THE EARLY TIP-OFF on the time and place of the announcement gave the teachers' union time to plan a protest. Organizers promised that any anti-Christie teachers who showed up at Livingston High School would get a meal voucher for the Livingston Mall food court. The protesters even had an ally in the host of the event—the Livingston Schools superintendent, who once sued the governor over a controversial cap Christie implemented on superintendent salaries. The superintendent refused to attend the announcement.

That morning, Livingston High was buzzing with security as staffers distributed posters and bumper stickers to hundreds of attendees, mostly white suburbanites dressed in business casual. The homogeneity of the crowd indicated that the coalition of nontraditional Republican voters, such as Latinos whom Christie had worked so hard to woo through his gubernatorial years, would not be coming with him on the presidential campaign trail.

Puerto Rican–born Angel Cordero, a convict-turned-activist from Camden with a huge mouth and a massive heart, was an exception. Cordero started a school for kids expelled from Camden high schools. He was a perennial Republican candidate for office, futilely fighting the Democratic machine that controls the city, and after Christie spoke at one of his school's graduations he became a Christie loyalist. Just six days after Bridgegate, Cordero showed up, in a driving snow, for Christie's second inaugural address. He stood at the front entrance holding a sign reading "Christie Strong" and "Christie 2016." He was the only supportive demonstrator there.

For Christie's Livingston High announcement, Cordero showed up ready for a rally, and the governor's advance staff made sure he had a prominent spot in the bleachers. Before the governor took the stage Cordero tried to lead call-and-response chants—"Italian . . . Stallion!" and "Tell It . . . Like It Is!" The rest of the crowd looked at him amused, but didn't join in.

The setup for the event was similar to Christie town hall meetings—a high school gym and theater-in-the-round. But there were notable differences that made the presentation less effective: Christie stood on a platform high above the crowd, Mary Pat and the kids flanked him the entire time, and he repeatedly referenced prepared remarks.

Regardless, as soon as Christie bounded onstage it was clear he was pumped up and locked in. He delivered a half-hour speech long on biography and his iconoclastic bona fides. There were elements from the stump speeches he was already giving around the country, and he fired away at President Obama. "America is tired of hand-wringing and indecisiveness and weakness in the Oval Office," he said.

Christie previewed his presidential campaign slogan, "Telling it like it is," with this: "You're going to get what I think whether you like it or not, or whether it makes you cringe every once in a while or not." He said he would not listen to his political consultants when answering questions on the campaign trail. "The truth will set us free, everybody."

And in a vestige of the pre-Bridgegate Christie—who planned to win a Republican primary on his own terms, without pandering to the base—the governor spoke of the importance of compromise in the American democracy: "If Washington and Adams and Jefferson believed compromise was a dirty word, we'd still be under the crown of England!"

NOW, THOUGH, THERE was a new king that Christie had to contend with: Donald Trump.

Suddenly, a bigger personality was on the campaign stage. Here was a king of all media, with more celebrity and a more shocking mouth who could command more attention than Christie ever could. As Trump entered the stage, Christie seemed to fade to black.

The famous New York billionaire was a longtime Christie friend. Trump sat in the front row of Christie's first inaugural mass in 2010, and the governor attended Trump's third wedding. The Trumps and the Christies often had dinner together where Trump, according to the famously loquacious Christie, did all the talking.

By the summer of 2015, Trump was drawing attention away from every other candidate, but perhaps no one suffered more from the rise of Trump than Christie. A *New York Times* analysis found that from May to August 2015, Christie lost 57 percent of his supporters to Trump. Polls showed Christie as one of the most popular second-choice candidates for Trump voters. To some conservatives, Trump sounded like a more authentic, unvarnished Chris Christie, telling hard truths that even the blunt-talking New Jersey governor would never tell.

In other words, Trump stole Christie's shtick.

In August 2015, Christie made a rare New Jersey appearance at a horse race in Monmouth County, where he had won 70 percent of the vote in 2013. Now, less than two years later, he was aggressively booed by the crowd of seventy thousand. Twice.

A few weeks later, Trump attended a golf tournament at the Plainfield Country Club in Central New Jersey. He was given a hero's welcome and a security detail of six local police officers. Eyes and iPhone cameras turned to the front-runner for the Republican nomination. They yelled "Mr. President!" *Star-Ledger* sports columnist Steve Politi wrote that it was "sheer insanity." One fan "looked like a teenage girl who turned the corner and ran into the Beatles on a New York City street in 1964."

Trump pulled Politi with him as he navigated the crowd. At one point, Trump turned to his fans, put his hand on Politi's shoulder, and shouted: "Make sure he writes well about me—if he doesn't, kick his ass!"

The crowd roared its approval. Trump double-tapped Politi on the shoulder, mischievously smiled, and moved on. The scene was a surreal dream, as if Trump had replaced Christie on the stage, nationally and at home.

Perhaps Christie peaked too soon, before the casino industry collapsed, before the state's nine credit downgrades, before operatives closed the busiest bridge in the world.

Was 2012 his time? Had we witnessed an American political implosion?

**WHEN I ARRIVED** at the Statehouse for Christie's annual State of the State speech in January 2015, I walked the hallways amid the power nexus of Trenton—lobbyists, former governors, and legislative staffers. There was a buzz in the crowd. Christie was, any day now, going to become the first New Jersey governor in a century to run for president. Trenton was at a turning point.

I ran into a prominent Republican, a regular at these things, and I asked what the word was on the gov these days. "Star fucker," he replied. Jerry Jones. Republican donors in Iowa. Springsteen and Bon Jovi. Christie had moved on, my source said, and set his sights on his famous friends and his next political gig. New Jersey was in the rearview.

I walked over toward the governor's office, where I found a scrum of reporters—friends and acquaintances I hadn't seen in some time. Someone whispered to me what was going on: These reporters were waiting to go into an hour-long, off-the-record session with the governor in advance of his State of the State address.

I texted my contact in the governor's office. Could I come?

I got no response.

Turned out, all of those reporters headed into the governor's office were from national outlets. The local New Jersey political press wasn't allowed in.

I could have tried to muscle my way into the office for the meeting. Instead, I vented on Twitter:

> *Nationally Minded: @GovChristie is holding Off The Record session with national media right now. No local press invited . . . ABC, NBC, CNN,* New York Times, Wall Street Journal, *& AP among national outlets given special Off The Record session with @GovChristie today.*

Shortly thereafter *Politico* posted a story about the incident based on my tweet. Reporters on press row, the local ones, already irritated that Christie hadn't held a press conference in New Jersey in more than three months, said this was an unprecedented dodge of the people who report for the governor's actual—current—constituents. Talking to national media is fine. But for a State of the *State* speech?

Minutes before the speech began, NJTV's Michael Aron asked me to come on TV, live, to talk about what happened. He had some time to kill before the station's simulcast of the speech began.

Aron began by asking if I was upset to be left out of the meeting.

"Forget about hurt feelings," I told him. "I don't really care about that. It's just another indication that the speech is not geared necessarily toward New Jersey. If it was, he'd want to make sure that the local reporters understand the perspective in which he was approaching the speech." I said that it appeared the speech was geared toward the Republican campaign contributors and party leaders who read the *Wall Street Journal* and watch national cable news.

"This is beginning to me to feel, as I said at the top, like the first step in the packaging of Chris Christie for a run for the White House," Aron said. "What do you think?"

"I disagree with that," I responded. "I think the packaging has been going on for years." I noted the YouTube videos emailed to national reporters and intentional leaks to favored Washington, D.C., news outlets. "He's a very compelling figure and became a national phenomenon because of that. But other parts of this are being handled and cultivated by paid government staff of the state of New Jersey to build his image as best as possible."

The speech itself was as expected. Only one new policy proposal, an extensive rehashing of the last five years of accomplishments, an eleven-minute discourse on efforts to expand drug rehabilitation, and, of course, Camden, Camden, Camden—"a city devoid of hope five years ago."

Just as he had saved Camden, was his message, he could save America. "I believe in a New Jersey renewal which can help lead to an American renewal both in every individual home and in homes around the world," he said.

TEN DAYS AFTER the speech I was at the Marriott in downtown Des Moines, Iowa, where an expansive bar in the front lobby serves as a headquarters for the press, punditry, and politicians during campaign season. At this point, Christie hadn't yet announced his candidacy, but he was expected in town for an event the next day featuring several possible candidates.

Close to midnight, I noticed an officer from Christie's security detail in the lobby.

Moments later, there he was, tie loosened, walking through the front doors of the hotel. The governor of New Jersey was carrying his own garment bag.

I caught up to him by the elevators. Drink in hand, I just wanted to say hi. After all, he was the only reason I had flown across the country for the weekend.

Christie saw me and looked disgusted. "Your pregame was terrible," he began. "Pathetic."

I had no idea what he was talking about.

Turned out that Christie had been in his office ten days earlier, psyching himself up for the State of the State speech he was about to deliver, by watching NJTV's pre-speech coverage. That's when he caught my "performance."

He was furious that I was "complaining" about local reporters getting shut out from an off-the-record session when he had recently given us our own off-the-record time at his Christmas party. I pointed out that national reporters were also at that Christmas party, and regardless, the very fact of his meeting with reporters was newsworthy because it indicated that he was moving toward a presidential run.

We went back and forth for a while as a small crowd of reporters gathered around, drinks in hand, watching a reporter and a politician go at it—democracy, Jersey-style.

Christie believed we were out to get him, that we all smelled blood and were now trying to finish him off. But he still, somehow, enjoyed the fight, even lived for it. He was complaining about a local TV news segment from more than a week earlier with inordinate intensity—but also, in his way, performing for the national journalists who were standing around.

We were fifty-three weeks before the Iowa presidential caucus, but game on. If his moment had passed, you wouldn't know it.

Christie turned away from me and walked into the elevator. "I need my beauty sleep," he said.

He then pivoted around and looked toward the other reporters.

"Oh, you're going to have fun with me," the American Governor told them, as the doors of the elevator closed. "Lots of give and take."

# ACKNOWLEDGMENTS

Covering such a notable personality has been thrilling but intense, and I would not have stayed the course without my wife and companion for life, Deborah, alongside me. She has been there to inspire, console, and cajole me; she has been there to make me laugh and smack sense into me. Through it all, she juggled two little ones while I spent far too many days and nights writing. Thank you, eternally.

Sadie Belle and Reuben Morris, you keep smiles on our faces. As we always tell you, you're the best. Sadie, it has taken me half of your life to write this book. I have a feeling you'll write your own book one day—if so, I can't wait to read it. And Ruby, thank you for keeping me company on my lap as I typed through many late nights. I'll miss that—even the typos you inserted by banging on the keyboard.

My parents put a New York *Newsday* in front of me as soon as I could read, and a *New York Times* in front of me as soon as I could comprehend. Thank you for sharing with me a respect for journalism that helped me figure out, by the age of eleven, what I wanted to be when I grew up. Your encouragement has been more meaningful than I could ever say. And thank you to my sister, Sara, who has offered me positive vibes that have meant so much, ever since I was little.

My in-laws, the Hurwitzes of New Jersey and California, provide a loving support system for our family that we couldn't do without. And my brother-in-law, Josh Hurwitz, has generously allowed me to tap into his expert inside knowledge of New Jersey politics, as if I were one of his political science students at Rutgers University or County College of Morris.

From Philadelphia to New York, Oregon, California, Utah, Tennessee, Virginia, Colorado, Indiana, Illinois, Texas, North Carolina, Louisiana, Scotland, China, Israel, and, of course, New Jersey, my friends are my life, and they've had my back in late-night texts, check-in phone calls, and unconditional love.

At *The Philadelphia Inquirer*, special appreciation to the great Mike Topel for convincing me to start covering the new governor in New Jersey; Cindy Henry, Linda Hasert, Dan Biddle, and Porus Cooper for reading and improving endless reams of Christie copy through the years; Gabe Escobar, Stan Wischnowski, and Bill Marimow for offering me continued opportunity at the paper.

*Philadelphia Inquirer* alumni Vernon Loeb and Jim Steele dished helpful advice as I set out to write.

And Inky alumna Avery Rome, my journalistic spirit guide, improved this project immeasurably, in ways tiny and enormous. She has been as compassionate an editor as she is a friend.

At WNYC, I'm grateful to Jim Schachter for including me when he boldly endeavored to create aggressive, investigative public radio journalism in New Jersey, and to Nancy Solomon, who with kindness, laughs, ceaseless support, and natural journalistic brilliance somehow turned me into a radio reporter. Andrea Bernstein, the only (and best!) reporting partner I've ever had, dug up several incredible scoops that are now part of this book, and my friends Sarah Gonzalez and Joe Capriglione have encouragingly held my hand as I've made the switch to a new medium. Thank you, WNYC. I'm also appreciative of James Rosenfeld and Yonatan Berkovits of Davis Wright Tremaine law firm for tremendous pro bono legal assistance that helped Nancy, Andrea, and I wrest information from the Christie administration.

Olivia Nuzzi, Katy O'Neill, and Jake Matlin provided important research help. And my colleagues in the New Jersey press corps, who do yeoman's work keeping the Garden State informed in the face of the pressures of modern media, produced the clips I relied on for historical perspective and the blow-by-blow of local politics.

Mitchell Ivers, my editor, has been almost unreasonably patient with me as I put this book together, as have Natasha Simons, Louise Burke, and the team at Threshold Editions of Simon & Schuster. I have deep gratitude.

Flip Brophy, my agent, believed that I had a story to tell years before it ever came to fruition. I'm lucky she is as excellent as she is at what she does.

Finally, a sincere thanks to Chris Christie, for sitting down with me, twice, for candid interviews for this book—and for being the most interesting person in American politics to cover.

# NOTES

## A NOTE ON SOURCES

*American Governor* represents the culmination of five years of reporting on Chris Christie for the *Philadelphia Inquirer* and WNYC. For this book I conducted dozens of interviews in diners, bars, coffee shops, offices, steakhouses, living rooms, and one park bench in Princeton. Several sources spoke to me on background, under the condition of anonymity. Christie's quotes were recorded in person or taken from video and transcripts.

I supplemented my reporting with tens of thousands of pages of primary source government documents, particularly related to Bridgegate. For chapters that deal with the events before, during, and after the scandal, I referenced the so-called Mastro Report, produced by lawyers hired by the office of the governor, and summaries of interviews they conducted with dozens of people in the course of their investigation. The New Jersey legislature created an investigative committee that held hearings into the matter, and I relied on its hearing transcripts, exhibits, and interim reports. I also referenced court filings in the criminal case on Bridgegate. I relied on participants' direct eyewitness accounts as laid out in these official documents to re-create events and conversations. I supplemented all this with additional reporting, but despite repeated requests several potential witnesses to Bridgegate would not speak to me for this project because of the trial scheduled for the spring of 2016.

The notes below mostly reflect information collected from books and news sources produced by hardworking journalists in Trenton and beyond.

### INTRODUCTION: MOVING THE CONES

1  Matt Katz, "Extremely Loud & Incredibly Close," *Politico*, November 25, 2013.

2  Mark Lagerkvist, "Christie's publicity blitz costs New Jersey taxpayers $5 million," *New Jersey Watchdog*, February 2, 2015.

3  Matt Katz, "The YouTube Governor, Decoded," WNYC, January 21, 2015.

4  Mark J. Magyar, "An Inconvenient Truth: State wipes out data on Christie, Corzine rebates," *NJ Spotlight*, April 11, 2014.

5  Matt Katz, "Government transparency in N.J. a murky affair," *Philadelphia Inquirer*, June 17, 2012.

6  Matt Katz, "Chris Christie's 18 State Secrets," WNYC, January 30, 2014.

7  Michael Barbaro, "Christie on Air: Undiluted and Pretty Great, If He Says So Himself," *New York Times*, January 25, 2015.

8  Melissa Hayes, "Christie Staffers Get Hefty Pay Increases as Other Areas Face Cuts," (Bergen) *Record*, May 29, 2014.

9  Emily Smith, "Watch Gov. Christie Bust a Move with Jamie Foxx," *New York Post*, *Page Six*, August 14, 2014.

10  Kate Zernike and Michael Barbaro, "Chris Christie Shows Fondness for Luxury Benefits When Others Pay the Bill," *New York Times*, February 2, 2015.

11  Bob Ingle and Michael Simmons, *Chris Christie: The Inside Story of His Rise to Power* (New York: St. Martin's Press, 2011).

12  Melissa Hayes, "Christie's travel costs for security detail tally nearly $185,000 for first part of the year," (Bergen) *Record*, June 22, 2015.

### 1: A PERENNIAL CANDIDATE

1  Frank John Urquhart, *Newark, the Story of its Early Days* (Newark: Free Public Library of Newark, 1904).

2  Matt Katz, "There But for the Grace of God Goes Christie," WNYC, November 18, 2014.

3  Robert Curvin, *Inside Newark: Decline, Rebellion, and the Search for Transformation* (Newark: Rutgers University Press, 2014).

4  Alec MacGillis, "Chris Christie's Entire Career Reeks," *New Republic*, February 12, 2014.

5  Sandra Sobieraj Westfall, "New Jersey Governor Chris Christie: A Work in Progress," *People*, June 10, 2010.

6  Susan K. Livio, "Christie Signs Law Allowing Adoptees to Get Birth Certificates 2017," *Star-Ledger*, May 28, 2010.

7  Jane Gross, "Scars From '67 Riots in Newark Are Still Visible in Central Ward," *New York Times*, July 13, 1987.

8  Brad Parks, "Crossroads Pt. 1: Before 1967, a gathering storm," *Star-Ledger*, July 8, 2007.

9  Matt Katz, "Christie brings Jersey message to GOP crowd," *Philadelphia Inquirer*, August 28, 2012.

10  Matt Katz, "When Christie was president—of his high school class," *Philadelphia Inquirer*, October 28, 2013.

11   Bob Ingle and Michael Simmons, *Chris Christie: The Inside Story of His Rise to Power* (New York: St. Martin's Press, 2011).

12   Harlan Coben, "Chris Christie Confidential," *New York Times*, November 5, 2009.

13   John Martin, "A Need to Lead, Honed by Family and Success," *Star-Ledger*, October 2, 2009.

14   Matt Katz, "Christie moves to the front of the pack," *Philadelphia Inquirer*, November 10, 2013.

15   Kathleen O'Brien, "Gov. Christie's Attitude Towards N.J. Education Bewilders, Hurts his Former Teachers," *Star-Ledger*, August 22, 2010.

16   Mark Bonamo, "The Wheels on Chris Christie's Campaign Bus Are Coming Off Before It Even Rolls," *New York Observer*, February 3, 2015.

17   Dan Piper, "DUSC Approves Budget Director," *The Review*, January 14, 1982.

18   Al Kemp, "DUSC Finances Call-In Day," *The Review*, March 5, 1982.

19   Dan Piper, "Student Trustee Bill Goes to Vote in Senate," *The Review*, May 18, 1982.

20   Marla Hirschman, "DUSC presidential candidates face the issues," *The Review*, April 29, 1983.

21   Marla Hirschman, "Few students call congressmen," *The Review*, April 15, 1983.

22   Lisa Crotty and Derrick Hinmon, "University Fails to Keep Minorities on Campus," *The Review*, October 14, 1983.

23   Richard L. Abbott, "Christie Cronyism," *The Review*, April 27, 1984.

24   Jennifer Sprouls, "Christie Evaluates DUSC," *The Review*, February 24, 2015.

25   Kevin Carroll and John Holowka, "Foster unopposed in DUSC race," *The Review*, April 20, 1984.

26   Derek Harper, "Garden State Governor Has Roots at UD," *University of Delaware Messenger*, March 26, 2010.

27   Hunter Walker, "What Christie Did to Get a Reputation as a Political Bully Even in College," *Talking Points Memo*, January 16, 2014.

28   Charles Stile, "Stile: Christie's Leadership Style Has Roots in Campus Government," (Bergen) *Record*, January 19, 2014.

29   David A. Fahrenthold, "Chris Christie Less Keen to Play Hardball as a Young Man," *Washington Post*, February 1, 2014.

30   David Kocieniewski, "New Jersey Governor's Brother: Asset and a Risk," *New York Times*, January 5, 2010.

31   Manuel Roig-Franzia, "The Human Opera Takes Center Stage," *Washington Post*, July 1, 2015.

32   John P. Martin, "Regular guy worked his way up the ladder," *Star-Ledger*, May 29, 2009.

33   Amy S. Rosenberg, "Mary Pat Christie, 'simpatico' in political and family affairs," *Philadelphia Inquirer*, April 17, 2011.

34   Elise Young, "Mary Pat Christie Juggles Roles as Political Facilitator," *Bloomberg News*, March 21, 2013.

35   Mark Leibovich, "Chris Christie Is Back," *New York Times*, November 20, 2014.

36   Mike Newall, "Christie Shows Fightin' Spirit as Fan of Delaware Blue Hens," *Philadelphia Inquirer*, January 7, 2011.

37  Olivia Nuzzi, "Portrait of the Governor as a Young Man," *Politico*, February 13, 2014.

38  Editorial Board, "For Freeholder," *Daily Record*, November 2, 1994.

39  Editorial Board, "For Assembly," *Daily Record*, May 31, 1995.

40  Editorial Board, "Cheers and Jeers," *Daily Record*, June 7, 1995.

41  Doug Most, "Assembly hopefuls' attack a swing and a miss," *Daily Record*, May 21, 1995.

42  Fred Snowflack, "Bucco, Carroll team up in fight for 25th Dist.," *Daily Record*.

43  Jason Fagone, "Feature: Is NJ Governor Chris Christie a Mad Man?" *Philadelphia* magazine, November 26, 2010.

44  Ryan Lizza, "Crossing Christie," *New Yorker*, April 14, 2014.

45  Michelle Caffrey, "What Does a Freeholder Do? 9 Things You Might Not Know About N.J. County Officials," *South Jersey Times*, November 8, 2014.

46  Gabriel Sherman, "New Jersey Nasty," *New York* magazine, October 19, 2009.

47  Michael Daly, "Remembering Ma Laureys, The Mother of 10 Christie Slandered to Win His First Election," *Daily Beast*, January 23, 2014.

48  Robert Cohen and Robert Rudolph, "Ex-Morris Freeholder to Be Tapped as a U.S. Attorney," *Star-Ledger*, September 5, 2001.

49  David M. Halbfinger, "For N.J. Candidate, First Ethics Push Was Brief," *New York Times*, August 16, 2009.

50  Dale Russakoff, "In N.J., a Crusader Confounds Skeptics; GOP Fundraiser-Turned-Prosecutor Targets Corruption in Both Parties," *Washington Post*, November 27, 2002.

51  "Freeholders Admit Wrongdoing, Apologize Over Christie Suit," *New Jersey Hills*, January 25, 2001.

52  David Kocieniewski, "Corzine's Wall Street Résumé Loses Value for Voters," *New York Times*, October 4, 2009.

53  Michael Rispoli, "Gov. Corzine, Chris Christie Trade Barbs About Lobbying Histories," *Star-Ledger*, August 25, 2009.

54  Cynthia Burton, "Christie enjoys 'a good argument,'" *Philadelphia Inquirer*, May 28, 2009.

55  William Kleinknecht, "Sondra Christie, 71, a pillar of Livingston," *Star-Ledger*, May 7, 2004.

56  Dylan Stableford, "Emotional Chris Christie Reveals 'Low Point' of His Life," *Yahoo*, August 5, 2013.

## 2: "IT'S HARD TO BE A SAINT IN THE CITY"

1  William Whitehead, *Documents relating to the Colonial History of the State of New Jersey 1631–1687, Volume 1* (*Daily Journal*, 1980).

2  The Women's Project of New Jersey Inc., *Past and Promise: Lives of New Jersey Women* (Portland: Rowman & Littlefield Publishers, Inc, 1990).

3  Bonnie Delaney, "N.J. corruption documentary has premiere," *Asbury Park Press*, October 18, 2010.

4  David Stout, "William T. Cahill, 84, Former Governor," *New York Times*, July 2, 1996.

5   Bob Ingle and Sandy McClure, *The Soprano State: New Jersey's Culture of Corruption* (New York: St. Martin's Press, 2008).

6   Cynthia Burton, "Christie enjoys 'a good argument,'" *Philadelphia Inquirer*, May 28, 2009.

7   John P. Martin, "Regular guy worked his way up the ladder," *Star-Ledger*, May 29, 2009.

8   John P. Martin, "A savvy lawyer tests his mettle as U.S. Attorney," *Star-Ledger*, February 5, 2002.

9   Laura Mansnerus, "New Jersey G.O.P. and Legal Elite Differ on U.S. Attorney," *New York Times*, August 26, 2001.

10  Ryan Lizza, "Crossing Christie," *New Yorker*, April 14, 2014.

11  Bob Ingle and Michael Simmons, *Chris Christie: The Inside Story of His Rise to Power* (New York: St. Martin's Press, 2011).

12  David Kocieniewski, "Candidate For Prosecutor Post Withdraws Name in New Jersey," *New York Times*, March 13, 2002.

13  David Kocieniewski, "Problem Arises in Candidacy for Top Aide to Prosecutor," *New York Times*, February 12, 2002.

14  John P. Martin, "U.S. Attorney drops out: Former prosecutor in political crossfire," *Star-Ledger*, March 13, 2002.

15  Ted Sherman and Josh Margolin, *The Jersey Sting: Chris Christie and the Most Brazen Case of Jersey-Style Corruption—Ever* (New York: St Martin's Press, 2011).

16  John Sullivan, "Christie Raises the Ante, and Perhaps His Profile," *New York Times*, June 1, 2003.

17  Ronald Smothers, "N.J. Law: Minding the Law," *New York Times*, March 31, 2002.

18  Beth DeFalco, "In Interview, Gov. Chris Christie Relates How 9/11 Attacks Changed His Career," Associated Press, August 22, 2011.

19  Laura Mansnerus and David Kocieniewski, "A Nation Challenged: The Attackers; A Hub for Hijackers Found in New Jersey," *New York Times*, September 27, 2001.

20  Jim Lehrer, *The NewsHour*, PBS, August 13, 2003.

21  John P. Martin, "How 2-year sting brought down missile deal," *Star-Ledger*, April 4, 2004.

22  Petra Bartosiewicz, "The Arms Trader," *This American Life*, July 8, 2005.

23  Matt Katz, "Hero Shuns Media Glare," *Courier-Post*, May 10, 2007.

24  Wayne Parry, "6 Held on Terror Conspiracy Charges in N.J.," Associated Press, May 8, 2007.

25  Josh Meyer, " 'Ft. Dix Six' Informants In Hot Seat Too," *Los Angeles Times*, October 19, 2008.

26  Murtaza Hussain and Razan Ghalayini, "Christie's Conspiracy," *Intercept*, June 25, 2015.

27  Paul Harris, "Fort Dix Five: 'If they did something, punish them. But they're innocent kids,' " *Guardian*, November 16, 2015.

28  Amanda Ripley, "Playing Tricks with the Fort Dix Six?" *Time*, January 14, 2008.

29  Jim Lehrer, "Six Men Arrested in Plot to Attack New Jersey's Fort Dix," PBS, May 8, 2007.

30  Ronald Smothers, "Paterson's Mayor Indicted On Charges of Trading City Contracts for Gifts," *New York Times*, January 25, 2002.

31  Laura Mansnerus, "A Democratic Fund-Raiser Is Charged with Extortion," *New York Times*, May 9, 2002.

32  Ronald Smothers, "Former North Bergen Official Is Charged with Corruption," *New York Times*, June 7, 2002.

33  Alec MacGillis, "Chris Christie's Entire Career Reeks," *NewRepublic.com*, February 12, 2014.

34  Laura Mansnerus, "U.S. Charges Essex Leader with Extortion," *New York Times*, October 29, 2002.

35  John Sullivan, "Christie Raises the Ante, and Perhaps His Profile," *New York Times*, June 1, 2003.

36  Lukas I. Alpert, "Sharpe Operator Nailed in Newark," *New York Post*, July 13, 2007.

37  Sharpe James interview, "Sharpe James Says His Conviction 'Made' Gov. Christie," NJTV, December 4, 2012.

38  Josh Margolin, "Christie a New Man as He Resurrects a Political Career," *Star-Ledger*, January 17, 2009.

39  David M. Halbfinger, "Christie May Have Gotten Improper Aid," *New York Times*, October 19, 2009.

40  John Sullivan, "Christie Raises the Ante, and Perhaps His Profile," *New York Times*, June 1, 2003.

41  Dale Russakoff, "In N.J., a Crusader Confounds Skeptics," *Washington Post*, November 27, 2002.

42  John Sullivan, "Christie Raises the Ante, and Perhaps His Profile," *New York Times*, June 1, 2003.

43  Cynthia Burton, "Ex-catcher is a N.J. natural," *Philadelphia Inquirer*, October 21, 2009.

44  Olivia Nuzzi, "Did Christie Go Easy on a Human Trafficker Just to Bust a Small-Time Pol?" *Daily Beast*, March 17, 2014.

45  Samantha Henry, "Easy money? Don't even think about it; Christie drives home stern warning on ethics" (Bergen) *Record*, November 15, 2007.

46  Jason Horowitz, "Prosecutor Makes a Meal of N.J. Senate Race," *New York Observer*, October 16, 2006.

47  Jeff Whelan and Josh Margolin, "Friday Feds Probe Menendez Rental Deal," *Star-Ledger*, September 8, 2006.

48  Gregory J. Volpe, "Menendez: Investigation a smear ploy," *Daily Record*, September 9, 2006.

49  Chris Mondics and Cynthia Burton, "Menendez hits U.S. Attorney over subpoenas," *Philadelphia Inquirer*, September 9, 2006.

50  David Kocieniewski, "A Governor Unindicted, but Implicated," *New York Times*, July 9, 2004.

51  Carol Morello and Carol D. Leonnig, "Chris Christie's Long Record of Pushing Boundaries, Sparking Controversy," *Washington Post*, February 10, 2014.

16 David M. Halbfinger, "Christie Failed to Disclose Loan to Federal Prosecutor," *New York Times*, August 17, 2009.

17 David M. Halbfinger, "Christie May Have Gotten Improper Aid," *New York Times*, October 19, 2009.

18 Zach Fink, "Christie Mortgage Loan," NJN, August 18, 2009.

19 Shawn Boburg and Hugh R. Morley, "Christie's Overseas Travel Funded by Firms That Do Business with N.J.," (Bergen) *Record*, January 31, 2015.

20 Rebecca Sinderbrand and Peter Hamby, "Corzine Camp Slams Christie Loan in New Ad," CNN, August 31, 2009.

21 Katherine Santiago, "GOP Gov candidate Chris Christie not issued traffic ticket after accident that injured motorcyclist in 2002," *Star-Ledger*, September 3, 2009.

22 James Ahearn, "Driving Record as Election Issue," (Bergen) *Record*, September 6, 2009.

23 Zachary Fink, "Chris Christie Accident," *Zachary Fink Blog*, September 4, 2009.

24 David M. Halbfinger and David Kocieniewski, "A Rivalry as Strained as New Jersey's Finances," *New York Times*, October 29, 2009.

25 Ken Schlager, "He's No Angel," *New Jersey*, October 13, 2009.

**4: BIG STEVE, JOE D., AND CORY B.**

1 David Kocieniewski and John Sullivan, "A Ward Boss with Influence to Spare," *New York Times*, January 16, 2006.

2 Terry Golway, "Steve Adubado, Newark's Go-To Guy," *New York Times*, March 27, 2005.

3 Ken Schlager, "He's No Angel," *New Jersey*, October 13, 2009.

4 Claire Heininger and Josh Margolin, "After victory, Christie asks for help from Democrats," *Star-Ledger*, November 5, 2009.

5 Michael Symons, "Show Me The Money," *APP.com*, November 4, 2009.

6 Guy Sterling, "Christie takes badge of honor as he leaves U.S. Attorney post," *Star-Ledger*, December 3, 2008.

7 Brian Donohue, "Ledger Live: Christie's First Move—Visiting a Democratic Stronghold," *NJ.com*, August 22, 2010.

8 Claire Heininger and Josh Margolin, "After Victory, Christie Asks for Help from the Democrats," *Star-Ledger*, November 5, 2009.

9 Michael Symons, "Show Me the Money," *Asbury Park Press*, November 4, 2009.

10 Ryan Lizza, "Crossing Christie," *New Yorker*, April 14, 2014.

11 Guy Sterling, "Christie Takes Badge of Honor as He Leaves U.S. Attorney Post," *Star-Ledger*, December 3, 2008.

12 Tom Moran, "In Essex County, politics is done Joe D.'s way," *Star-Ledger*, December 13, 2009.

13 Nikita Stewart, "DiVincenzo hires friends from Newark nonprofit," *Star-Ledger*, February 9, 2003.

14 Max Pizarro, "DiVincenzo Inevitably Part of the Struggle," *PolitickerNJ*, September 18, 2009.

15 Charles Stile, "Democrats can blame themselves for Christie," (Bergen) *Record*, May 13, 2010.

# NOTES

52 Jonathon Miller and Bruce Lambert, "Corzine Aide Resigns After Testifying Corruption Trial of a Hudson County Mayor," *New York Times*, May 1, 2008

53 Dan Eggen and Amy Goldstein, "No-Confidence Vote Sought on Gonzales," *ington Post*, May 18, 2007.

54 Steve Kornacki, "Why Bob Menendez Really Can't Stand Chris Christie," September 30, 2011.

55 Adam Cohen, "The U.S. Attorney, the G.O.P. Congressman and the Time Offer," *New York Times*, May 4, 2007.

56 Joelle Farrell, "Menendez denies opposition to appointment is political pay[ *Philadelphia Inquirer*, January 8, 2012.

57 Tom Moran, "Boss's Gift to Christie: Nearly Firing Him," *Star-Ledger*, Ma 2007.

## 3: "EVERYBODY IN NEW JERSEY WAS ARRESTED TODAY"

1 Cory Booker, *Brick City* TV series, Sundance Film Channel, 2009.

2 Josh Margolin, "Unconventional Gubernatorial Jockeying Ensues," *Star-Le* September 3, 2008.

3 David Kocieniewski, "New Jersey Governor's Brother: Asset and a Risk," *New Times*, January 5, 2010.

4 Ian T. Shearn, "U.S. Attorney's brother pumps cash into GOP," *Star-Ledger*, Sept( ber 7, 2004.

5 David M. Halbfinger, "Christie Spoke with Rove About Run, Memo Shows," *N York Times*, August 14, 2009.

6 Josh Margolin, "Christie a New Man as He Resurrects a Political Career," *NJ.c* January 17, 2009.

7 Claire Heininger, "Chris Christie Promises Change to a 'Broken' State in Campa Kickoff," *Star-Ledger*, February 4, 2009.

8 Cynthia Burton, "Christie Begins His Race for Governor: The GOP Candidat Proposals Focusing on Cities Could Be a Risk," *Philadelphia Inquirer*, February 2009.

9 Cynthia Burton, "Ex-catcher is a N.J. natural," *Philadelphia Inquirer*, October 2 2009.

10 Josh Margolin, "Chris Christie Defeats Steve Lonegan in Republican Governor Pr mary," *NJ.com*, June 3, 2009.

11 John Martin, "$52M-plus Payday for Christie's Old Boss," *Star-Ledger*, January 1( 2008.

12 Claire Heininger, "GOP Gov. Candidate Chris Christie Defends Record as U.S Attorney Before Congress," *Star-Ledger*, June 25, 2009.

13 David Kocieniewski, "In Testy Exchange in Congress, Christie Defends His Record as a Prosecutor," *New York Times*, June 26, 2009.

14 Carol Morello and Carol D. Leonnig, "Chris Christie's Long Record of Pushing Boundaries, Sparking Controversy," *Washington Post*, February 10, 2014.

15 Ted Sherman, "NJ Corruption Case Finally Ends, 5 Years After the FBI Sting Operation That Led to 46 Arrests," *Philadelphia Inquirer*, October 4, 2012.

16 Tom Moran, "Joe D's Demons and The Art of Survival," *Star-Ledger*, October 6, 2013.

17 Philip Read, "Former Essex elections official admits tampering with employee pay records," *Star-Ledger*, September 24, 2010.

18 Kimberly Brown, "DiVincenzo fights to star in the political big leagues," *Star-Ledger*, May 29, 2002.

19 Bob Hennelly, "In Hunt for Votes, Christie Amps Up Voucher Talk," WNYC, March 12, 2013.

20 David A. Fahrenthold, "Getting Chris Christie's Goat: Activists Try to Rile Up Governor, Pile Up Some YouTube Hits," *Washington Post*, December 20, 2014.

21 Josh Margolin and David Giambusso, "Facebook CEO donating $100M to Newark schools; announcement Friday on Oprah," *Star-Ledger*, September 22, 2010.

22 Josh Margolin, "Facebook CEO Zuckerberg announces $100M grant to Newark schools on Oprah Winfrey show," *Star-Ledger*, September 24, 2010.

23 John Reitmeyer, "How N.J.'s 2 Percent Property Tax Cap Plan Will Impact Residents," (Bergen) *Record*, July 12, 2010.

24 Max Pizarro, "Booker backs Christie's 2.5% hard cap," *PolitickerNJ*, June 21, 2010.

25 John Reitmeyer and Hugh R. Morley, "Closer Look at Christie's State of the State Numbers," (Bergen) *Record*, January 13, 2015.

26 Samantha Marcus, "N.J. Property Taxes Top $8,000 per Home After Rising 2.2 Percent Last Year," *Star-Ledger*, February 3, 2015.

27 Jessica Calefati and Kelly Heyboer, "$100 million, one year later: After a slow start, big grant beginning to have an impact on Newark schools," *Star-Ledger*, September 25, 2011.

28 Jessica Calefati and David Giambusso, "Consultants get big piece of Facebook pie; Records show recipients have ties to Booker and Cerf," *Star-Ledger*, October 27, 2011.

29 Lyndsey Layton, "Chris Christie's bold plan to remake public schools is running into trouble," *Washington Post*, March 3, 2015.

30 Dale Russakoff, "Schooled: Cory Booker, Chris Christie, and Mark Zuckerberg had a plan to reform Newark's schools. They got an education," *New Yorker*, May 19, 2014.

31 Dale Russakoff, *The Prize: Who's in Charge of America's Schools?* (New York: Houghton Mifflin Harcourt, 2015).

32 Matt Katz, "Christie's campaign promises to cities go largely unfulfilled," *Philadelphia Inquirer*, October 24, 2011.

## 5: CONQUERING CAMDEN

1 Claudia Vargas, "New Census Statistics Paint Grim Picture of Camden," *Philly.com*, September 22, 2012.

2 Troy Graham, "High court blocks plan for Camden fugitives," *Philadelphia Inquirer*, July 18, 2006.

3 Samantha Henry, "Fugitives surrendering at churches fuels debate," *Daily Journal*, November 3, 2010.

4 Matt Katz, "Gov. Christie goes after towns' affordable-housing money," *Philadelphia Inquirer*, August 5, 2012.

5 Alan Bjerga, "Christie Rejects Food Aid Giving $54 for Each $1 Paid," *Bloomberg Business*, September 15, 2014.

6 Susan K. Livio, "Fix N.J. Food Stamp Backlog by Hiring More Workers, Anti-Poverty Leaders Say," *Star-Ledger*, September 22, 2014.

7 Matt Katz, "Policy change in New Jersey is resulting in fewer welfare recipients," *Philadelphia Inquirer*, March 22, 2012.

8 Andrew Seidman, "Christie quietly reaps Obamacare budget benefits," *Philadelphia Inquirer*, March 2, 2015.

9 Michael L. Diamond, "What comeback? Why NJ's economy has tanked," *Asbury Park Press*, January 12, 2015.

10 Matt Katz, "Christie calls for privately run 'transformation schools,' " *Philadelphia Inquirer*, June 10, 2010.

11 Matt Katz, "Christie, Corzine, Camden, and déjà vu," *Philly.com*, June 10, 2011.

12 Matt Katz, "Backed by Norcross, Christie pushes another education initiative," *Philly.com*, June 9, 2011.

13 Claudia Vargas, "In a reversal, Camden School Board Approves KIPP Cooper Norcross Academy Renaissance School," *Philadelphia Inquirer*, November 30, 2012.

14 Matt Katz, "How Christie's school-building plan is another swing on a yo-yo," *Philly.com*, February 16, 2011.

15 Matt Katz, "Christie signs 'renaissance school' measure at Camden ceremony," *Philadelphia Inquirer*, January 13, 2012.

16 Matt Katz, "Camden letter renews fears," *Philadelphia Inquirer*, July 25, 2008.

17 Ted Sherman, "How Camden Got a New Medical School," *Star-Ledger*, January 16, 2012.

18 Richard Rys, "They Have No Choice," *Philadelphia*, May 15, 2006.

19 Claudia Vargas, "Camden board rejects four privately run schools," *Philadelphia Inquirer*, September 28, 2012.

20 Claudia Vargas, "Cooper Announces Plans For Lanning Square Renaissance Schools," *Philadelphia Inquirer*, July 29, 2012.

21 Bob Braun, "NJEA support for private management of public schools displays weakness, cynicism," *Star-Ledger*, January 9, 2012.

22 Claudia Vargas, "New Jersey school repair projects still lagging," *Philadelphia Inquirer*, March 13, 2012.

23 Steve Volk, "George Norcross: The Man Who Destroyed Democracy," *Philadelphia* magazine, March 29, 2013.

24 Kevin C. Shelly, "Donald Norcross bids for Andrews' seat," *Courier-Post*, February 7, 2014.

25 David Kinney and Joe Donohue, "State cash flows to Commerce Bank vaults," *Star-Ledger*, January 26, 2003.

26 Angela Couloumbis, "Freeholders Are Set To Transfer Accounts; Camden County Officials Cite Increased Interest Income," *Philadelphia Inquirer*, April 23, 1998.

27   Bob Ingle and Sandy McClure, *The Soprano State: New Jersey's Culture of Corruption* (New York: St. Martin's Press, 2008).

28   James Osborne and Craig R. McCoy, "Powerful Medicine: How George Norcross used his political muscle to pump up once-ailing Cooper Hospital," *Philadelphia Inquirer*, March 25, 2012.

29   Tom Turcol, "Norcross: Rise of a South Jersey power broker," *Philadelphia Inquirer*, July 7, 2002.

30   Jonathan Tamari, "Bryant trial hits at N.J. politics insider dealings and favors are on display," *Philadelphia Inquirer*, October 30, 2008.

31   Thomas Turcol, "N.J. Democrats Are Set to Choose Party," *Philadelphia Inquirer*, February 4, 1994.

32   Barbara Fitzgerald, "Up Front: Worth Noting; A Powerful New Boarder in the 'Trenton Rowhouse,'" *New York Times*, July 7, 2002.

33   Tom Turcol, "Norcross: Rise of a South Jersey power broker," *Philadelphia Inquirer*, July 7, 2002.

34   Herb Jackson and Benjamin Lesser, "Under the influence: Money in Trenton," *Record*, August 8, 2004.

35   Maya Rao, "Deal with Norcross brother makes lobbying prosper in today's Trenton environment," *Philadelphia Inquirer*, September 14, 2011.

36   Eileen Stilwell, "Lawyers take pay cuts for improvement authority work," *Courier Post*, February 9, 2007.

37   David Kocieniewski, "Power Broker Has No Post, But Big Role," *New York Times*, April 9, 2003.

38   Monica Yant Kinney, "Prosecutor's plate fascinatingly full," *Philadelphia Inquirer*, July 22, 2003.

39   John Sullivan, "Christie Raises the Ante, and Perhaps His Profile," *New York Times*, June 1, 2003.

40   Laure Mansnerus, "Again, the U.S. Attorney Is on a Statewide Blitz," *New York Times*, December 4, 2005.

41   Richard Pearsall, "Back-Room Politics on Tapes," *Asbury Park Press*, April 1, 2005.

42   Josh Benson, "In Person; the Tale of the Tapes," *New York Times*, April 10, 2005.

43   Michael Symons, "Ten Years Later, Palmyra Case Still Lives," *Asbury Park Press*, May 27, 2010.

44   Ryan Lizza, "Crossing Christie," *New Yorker*, April 14, 2014.

45   Howard Gillette, Jr., *Camden After the Fall: Decline and Renewal in a Post-Industrial City* (Philadelphia: University of Pennsylvania Press, 2005).

46   David. M. Halbfinger, "For N.J. Candidate, First Ethics Push Was Brief," *New York Times*, August 16, 2009.

47   Matt Katz and Jonathan Tamari, "State's takeover of Camden ended," *Philadelphia Inquirer*, January 19, 2010.

48   Richard Pérez-Peña, "In Camden, New Troubles on Top of Old," *New York Times*, November 12, 2010.

49   Matt Katz, "Christie grants Camden $69 million in special aid, but little to avert layoffs," *Philadelphia Inquirer*, November 25, 2010.

50  Matt Katz, "Axes fall for police, firefighters in Camden," *Philadelphia Inquirer*, January 19, 2011.

51  Matt Katz, "Christie's cuts leave Camden a big loser," *Philadelphia Inquirer*, July 3, 2011.

52  James Queally, "After heavy police layoffs in 2010, arrests plunged in Newark and Camden in 2011," *Star-Ledger*, May 1, 2012.

53  Joseph Goldstein, "Police Force Nearly Halved, Camden Feels Impact," *New York Times*, March 6, 2011.

54  Matt Katz, "Why it's so tough to rescue Camden," *Philadelphia Inquirer*, December 12, 2010.

55  Heather Haddon, "In Camden, Christie Gives and Receives," *Wall Street Journal*, October 1, 2014.

56  Matt Taibbi, "Apocalypse, New Jersey: A Dispatch From America's Most Desperate Town," *Rolling Stone*, December 11, 2013.

57  Matt Katz, "Christie says Sandy will 'dominate my life well into 2014,' " *Philadelphia Inquirer*, January 6, 2013.

58  Matt Katz, "Christie does post-budget morning new blitz, talks Camden," *Philly .com*, February 23, 2011.

59  Julia Terruso, "Camden Sent Extra Officers to Waterfront Events, Picked Up Tab," *Philadelphia Inquirer*, January 17, 2014.

60  Ailsa Chang, "Crime-Ridden Camden To Dump City Police Force," NPR, December 6, 2012.

61  Michael Boren, "In Camden, police crackdown clogs court," *Philadelphia Inquirer*, December 8, 2014.

62  Kevin Shelley, "Camden resets relationship between cops, community," *USA Today*, December 12, 2014.

63  James Osborne, "Puzzling Moves From N.J. Political Boss George E. Norcross II," *Philadelphia Inquirer*, August 22, 2011.

64  Richard Rys, "Buying the Inquirer Could Be George Norcross's Greatest Coup," *Philadelphia* magazine, April 20, 2012.

65  Robert Hennelly, "Chris Christie's Jersey Nightmare: Why his state hasn't touched the economic recovery," *Salon*, January 13, 2015.

66  John Reitmeyer, "Christie Pushes Ahead with Business-Tax Cuts, Racking up $600M in Lost Revenue," *NJ Spotlight*, March 3, 2015.

67  Jon Whiten, "Commentary: Business Tax Subsidies Need Reform," *Courier-Post*, December 18, 2014.

68  Jeff Horwitz and Geoff Mulvihill, "Christie's Camden tax breaks reward political insiders," Associated Press, March 17, 2015.

69  Matt Katz, "Camden Rebirth: A promise still unfulfilled," *Philadelphia Inquirer*, November 8, 2009.

70  John Reitmeyer, "Analysis: Despite budget gap, Christie holding firm that business tax cuts are off-limits," (Bergen) *Record*, June 15, 2014.

71  Diana Lind, "What Will an NBA Team Bring to a Struggling City? 'Not Much,' " *Next City*, June 12, 2014.

72  Julia Terruso, "N.J. Offers Sixers $82 Million in Tax Credits," *Philadelphia Inquirer*, June 12, 2014.

73  Matt Katz, "Chris Christie and America's Poorest City," WNYC, July 11, 2014.

74  Allison Steele, "Cooper, Subaru get tax deals for moving to Camden," *Philadelphia Inquirer*, December 11, 2014.

75  Matt Katz and Claudia Vargas, "Christie to announce state takeover of Camden schools," *Philadelphia Inquirer*, March 25, 2013.

76  Lydia DePillis, "Can tax breaks for big corporations turn around one of America's most dangerous cities?" *Washington Post*, December 15, 2014.

77  Matt Katz, "Coalition forming behind Christie's school takeover, but there is skepticism," *Philly.com*, March 25, 2013.

78  Matt Katz, Claudia Vargas, and Joelle Farrell, "Behind Christie's decision to take over Camden schools," *Philadelphia Inquirer*, March 27, 2013.

79  Matt Katz, "Nothing so gutsy about Christie's Camden school takeover," *Philadelphia Inquirer*, April 1, 2013.

80  Maddie Hanna, "Christie keeps a steady presence in Camden," *Philadelphia Inquirer*, June 8, 2014.

81  Matt Katz, "Chris Christie and America's Poorest City," WNYC, July 11, 2014.

82  Phil Anastasia, "Football: Camden rallies past Camden Catholic," *Philadelphia Inquirer*, October 1, 2014.

83  Matt Katz, "Gov. Christie admits his 'spontaneity' sometimes gets him in trouble," *Philadelphia Inquirer*, January 8, 2012.

84  Jenna Portnoy, "Overhauling New Jersey's university system," *Star-Ledger*, January 26, 2012.

85  Jason Method, "South Jersey power broker stepping out from shadows," *Asbury Park Press*, February 13, 2012.

86  Laura Kusisto, "City Manufacturing Takes a Hit as Brooklyn Firm Plans Move to New Jersey," *Wall Street Journal*, August 25, 2014.

## 6: "DAMN, MAN, I'M GOVERNOR"

1  David Kocieniewski, "For Christie, an Inauguration on a Budget," *New York Times*, January 18, 2010.

2  A. Matthew Boxer, "Investigative Report: Delaware River Port Authority," State of New Jersey Office of the Comptroller, March 29, 2012.

3  Tom Turcol, "Norcross: Rise of a South Jersey Power Broker," *Philadelphia Inquirer*, July 6, 2002.

4  James Ahearn, "A 'Regular Guy' as Odd Man Out," (Bergen) *Record*, October 13, 2009.

5  Josh Margolin and Chris Megerian, "Codey's Control Crumbling," *Star-Ledger*, October 1, 2009.

6  Bob Ingle, "Did Christie Blink?" *Asbury Park Press*, May 29, 2010.

7  John Reitmeyer, "$6M Fund Stake in Power Grab," (Bergen) *Record*, September 30, 2009.

8  Matt Katz, "A Fighter For people, or Power?" *Philadelphia Inquirer*, September 30, 2013.

9   Bob Ingle and Sandy McClure, *The Soprano State: New Jersey's Culture of Corruption* (New York: St. Martin's Press, 2008).

10  Matt Katz, "Gov. Christie Admits His 'Spontaneity' Sometimes Gets Him in Trouble," *Philadelphia Inquirer*, January 8, 2012.

11  Ryan Lizza, "Crossing Christie," *New Yorker*, April 14, 2014.

12  David W. Chen, "In Inquiry, It's Christie Against Prosecutor," *New York Times*, February 9, 2014.

13  Kevin Manhan, "What Would Freud Say? Is Chris Christie the Merchant of Venom or the Saint of State Street? Let's go to the couch," *Star-Ledger*, November 1, 2010.

14  Mark J. Magyar, "Analysis: What's Wrong With Chris Christie's Government?" *NJ Spotlight*, March 11, 2014.

15  Michael Symons, "Gov. Chris Christie takes ax to New Jersey budget," *Asbury Park Press*, February 11, 2010.

16  Adrienne Lu, "N.J. business embraced; others brace," *Philadelphia Inquirer*, February 14, 2010.

17  John Reitmeyer and Elise Young, "Christie orders extreme cuts," (Bergen) *Record*, February 12, 2010.

18  Caryn Shinske, "Chris Christie claims he entered office with a deficit in the billions left by Barbara Buono, Jon Corzine," *Star-Ledger*, April 28, 2013.

19  Beth DeFalco and Geoff Mulvihill, "NJ's Gov. Speaks Loudly and Carries a Big Stick," Associated Press, February 27, 2011.

20  Chris Megerian, "Gov. Christie continues 15-state political tour with appearance in Oregon stumping for former Nets player," *Star-Ledger*, October 31, 2010.

21  Jason Zengerie, "The Answer is No," *New York*, November 21, 2010.

22  Jason Fagone, "Is NJ Governor Chris Christie a Mad Man?" *Philadelphia*, November 26, 2010.

23  Richard Pérez-Peña, "Showdown Over N.J. Budget is Avoided for Now," *New York Times*, June 29, 2010.

24  David M. Halbfinger, "New Jersey Governor Proposes Deep Spending Cuts," *New York Times*, March 16, 2010.

25  Jason Method, "Christie, teachers find common goal," *Asbury Park Press*, May 27, 2010.

26  Jason Method, "Christie revises education money bid, wants performance pay," *Asbury Park Press*, June 1, 2010.

27  Mark J. Magyar, "Analysis: What's Wrong With Chris Christie's Government?" *NJ Spotlight*, March 11, 2014.

28  John Schoonejongen, "Christie Criticizes Response to Error," *Asbury Park Press*, August 25, 2010.

29  Geoff Mulvihill, "Oops! Error might have cost NJ an education grant," Associated Press, August 25, 2010.

30  Matt Katz, "Christie admits clerical error on application for education funds, blames Obama administration," *Philadelphia Inquirer*, August 26, 2010.

31  Josh Margolin and Jeanette Rundquist, "School Aid Bickering Heats Up," *Star-Ledger*, October 8, 2010.

32   Robert Hennelly, "Chris Christie's Jersey nightmare: Why his state hasn't touched the economic recovery," *Salon*, January 13, 2015.

33   Hank Kalet, "Low- and Middle-Income New Jerseyans Priced Out of Rental Market," *NJ Spotlight*, March 13, 2013.

34   Neil Haggerty, "Study Finds 16 Percent Increase in Homelessness in N.J.," *Star-Ledger*, June 9, 2014.

35   Matt Katz, "Despite Need and Funds, N.J.'s Homeowner Aid is Little Used," *Philadelphia Inquirer*, September 4, 2012.

36   Matt Katz, "Christie Administration Acknowledges Foreclosure Lapses," *Philadelphia Inquirer*, October 26, 2012.

37   "The Auditor," *Star-Ledger*, July 4, 2010.

38   Tom Moran, "Sweeney unleashes his fury as N.J. budget battle turns personal," *Star-Ledger*, July 3, 2011.

39   Charles Stile, "Handouts the Latest in Christie's Nice Guy Image Tour," (Bergen) *Record*, August 2, 2011.

40   Matt Bai, "How Chris Christie Did His Homework," *New York Times*, February 24, 2011.

41   Matt Katz, "New Jersey Joins a List of States Considering Privatizing Their Lotteries," *Philadelphia Inquirer*, April 29, 2012.

42   Matt Katz, "Christie Quietly Takes on Lottery," *Philadelphia Inquirer*, January 29, 2013.

43   James Osborne, "Christie Backs Overhaul of New Jersey's University System," *Philadelphia Inquirer*, January 6, 2012.

44   Tara Nurin, "Understanding the governing structure for the Rowan/Rutgers eds & meds partnership," *NewsWorks*, April 23, 2014.

45   Matt Katz, "No Regrets For Calling Student 'Idiot,' Christie Says," *Philadelphia Inquirer*, March 13, 2012.

46   Matt Katz, "Christie and veteran opposed to Rutgers-Rowan merger get into shouting match," *Philadelphia Inquirer*, March 9, 2012.

47   Charles Stile, "Christie Got Boost from Rival George Norcross' Power," (Bergen) *Record*, October 5, 2012.

48   Patricia Alex, "Rutgers Merger May Hike Tuition," (Bergen) *Record*, April 15, 2015.

49   Matt Katz, "Christie Grants Eminent Domain, Doesn't Realize It," WNYC, February 5, 2014.

50   Josh Margolin, "The Governor's Getaway," *Star-Ledger*, August 2, 2006.

51   Tom Moran, "Are Cory Booker and Gov. Christie Friends or Foes?" *Star-Ledger*, September 9, 2012.

52   Matt Katz, "Christie's Vetoes Rely On Her Authority," *Philadelphia Inquirer*, March 6, 2011.

53   Matt Katz, "Christie Vetoes DRPA Payment to Lobbyist," *Philadelphia Inquirer*, February 5, 2011.

54   Maya Rao, "Goof Pay and Benefits For Politically Connected At Area Utility Authorities," *Philadelphia Inquirer*, February 11, 2011.

55   Ted Sherman, "Gov. Christie Fires 71 Passaic Valley Sewerage Commissioners Employees," *Star-Ledger*, February 8, 2011.

56   Maddie Hanna, "Christie Makes Extensive Use of Vetoes Over State Authorities," *Philly.com*, April 28, 2014.

57   Maddie Hanna, "Christie Takes No Action to Replace DRPA Board," *Philadelphia Inquirer*, August 5, 2014.

58   Andrew Seidman, "Bistate Bill to Overhaul DRPA Languishing in N.J.," *Philadelphia Inquirer*, January 4, 2015.

59   MaryAnn Spoto, "Anne Patterson Sworn in as Newest N.J. Supreme Court Justice," *Star-Ledger*, September 9, 2010.

60   Matt Katz, "Confirmation Hearing Set for Christie Judicial Nominee," *Philadelphia Inquirer*, May 30, 2011.

61   Matt Katz, "Christie's Court," *Philly.com*, May 31, 2011.

62   Matt Katz, "Christie nominates a gay mayor and a Korean immigrant to Supreme Court," *Philadelphia Inquirer*, January 24, 2012.

63   Matt Katz, "In a blow to Christie, N.J. Senate panel rejects high court nominee," *Philadelphia Inquirer*, March 23, 2012.

64   Matt Katz, "Panel rejects Christie's Supreme Court nominee," *Philadelphia Inquirer*, June 1, 2012.

65   Paul Mulshine, "Chris Christie's Court Pick Has a Pro-Choice, Anti–Free Press Record," *Star-Ledger*, June 3, 2014.

66   Matt Katz, "Dems are 'Animals'—But What Party Is Christie's Court Pick From?" *Philly.com*, August 12, 2013.

67   Bob Ingle and Sandy McClure, *The Soprano State: New Jersey's Culture of Corruption* (New York: St. Martin's Press, 2008).

68   Matt Katz, "Christie released from hospital after asthma attack," *Philadelphia Inquirer*, July 29, 2011.

69   Brian T. Murray, "New freeholder agrees to trim responsibilities of sheriff's office he led," *Star-Ledger*, June 26, 1996.

70   Cynthia Burton, "Christie enjoys 'a good argument'; Raised in a household that loved politics and debate, the candidate for governor says he demands accountability," *Philadelphia Inquirer*, May 28, 2009.

71   "Chris Christie to Connie Mariano, Former White House Doctor: 'Shut Up' About My Weight," *Huffington Post*, February 7, 2013.

72   Matt Katz, "Is Christie too fat to be president? Pundits weigh in," *Philadelphia Inquirer*, October 4, 2011.

73   Andy Barr, "Christie: 'Man Up and Say I'm Fat,' " *Politico*, October 29, 2009.

74   Matt Katz, "Kimmel Makes Fat Jokes About Christie, Who Laughs Them Off," *Philly.com*, April 29, 2012.

75   Matt Katz and Joelle Farrell, "Christie Admits Weight-Loss Surgery, Denies Political Motive," *Philadelphia Inquirer*, May 9, 2013.

76   Michael Linhorst, "At Event in Princeton, Governor Christie Opens Up About His Struggle with Weight," (Bergen) *Record*, May 14, 2013.

## 7: UNION WARS

1  Ben Leach, "With pensions on the line, Gov. Christie is booed at N.J. Firemen's Convention in Wildwood," *Press Of Atlantic City*, September 18, 2010.

2  Matt Bai, "How Chris Christie Did His Homework," *New York Times*, February 24, 2011.

3  Cathy Bugman, "A Shot of Trivia," *Star-Ledger*, February 28, 2002.

4  Jarrett Renshaw, "Battle heats up between NJEA and N.J. Republicans, with new tactic: video ambush," *Star-Ledger*, February 17, 2012.

5  Matt Friedman, "Gov. Chris Christie unveils plan for legislators to be more transparent about their finances," *Star-Ledger*, September 8, 2010.

6  Winnie Hu, "Schools in New Jersey Plan Heavy Cuts After Voters Reject Most Budgets," *New York Times*, April 21, 2010.

7  Maya Rao, "Firefighters, Cops Protest at Trenton Statehouse," *Philadelphia Inquirer*, March 3, 2011.

8  Matt Friedman, "Gov. Chris Christie unveils plan for legislators to be more transparent about their finances," *Star-Ledger*, September 8, 2010.

9  Matt Katz, "Christie Details Proposals for Changes in Schools," *Philadelphia Inquirer*, April 8, 2011.

10  Jonathan Lai, "Long After Groundbreaking, 'Shovel-Ready' Campus Work Not Started," *Philadelphia Inquirer*, November 16, 2014.

11  Maya Rao, "N.J. Senate panel advances plan for public employees to pay more for benefits," *Philadelphia Inquirer*, June 17, 2011.

12  Maya Rao and Matt Katz, "New Jersey Lawmaker Disputes Christie's Account on Controversial Bill," *Philadelphia Inquirer*, September 8, 2011.

## 8: GLORY DAYS

1  Paul Mulshine, "The Ghost of Christie Past: The Guv Does the Old Switcheroo on Global Warming and Guns," *Star-Ledger*, August 3, 2015.

2  Andrew Seidman, "Christie Defends Pay Raises for His Staff," *Philadelphia Inquirer*, June 1, 2014.

3  Tom Johnson, " 'President' Christie Would Call for National Energy Policy—Details to Come," *NJ Spotlight*, February 19, 2015.

4  Matt Katz, "N.J. seeks to stop Western Pennsylvania power plant over emissions," *Philadelphia Inquirer*, February 12, 2011.

5  Tom Moran, "Gov. Christie's Towering Hypocrisy on Climate," *Star-Ledger*, April 28, 2013.

6  Salvador Rizzo, "Gov. Christie's environmental 'waiver rule' upheld by N.J. appeals court," *Star-Ledger*, March 21, 2013.

7  Maddie Hanna, "How Green is Christie's Record?" *Philadelphia Inquirer*, March 30, 2015.

8  Seth Augenstein, "DEP deputy commissioner, opposed by environmentalists, leaving for state industry association," *Star-Ledger*, September 9, 2014.

9  Bob Ingle and Michael Simmons, *Chris Christie: The Inside Story of His Rise to Power* (New York: St. Martin's Press, 2011).

10 Coral Davenport, "With Eye on 2016, Christie Resists Climate Change Plan," *New York Times*, September 18, 2014.

11 Matt Katz, "Christie Goes Jersey-Style in Tampa," *Philadelphia Inquirer*, August 27, 2012.

12 Seth Augenstein, "N.J. could lose $500M by pulling out of emissions program, environmentalists say," *Star-Ledger*, September 9, 2014.

13 Joby Warrick, "Wind Power or Hot Air? Foes Question Christie's Shift on Clean Energy," *Washington Post*, March 29, 2015.

14 Gabriel Sherman, "The Elephant in the Green Room," *New York*, May 22, 2011.

15 Gabriel Sherman, "Fox News' greatest failure: Roger Ailes, Chris Christie and the quest for a Republican president," *Salon*, January 15, 2014.

16 Chris Megerian, "Gov. Christie continues 15-state political tour with appearance in Oregon stumping for former Nets player," *Star-Ledger*, October 31, 2010.

17 Tim Murphy, "A Brief History of Chris Christie Not Running for President," *Mother Jones.com*, October 4, 2011.

18 Dan Balz, *Collision 2012: The Future of Election Politics in a Divided America* (New York: Penguin Group, 2013).

19 Elise Young, "N.J.'s Christie Used Chopper Almost Every Three Days," *Bloomberg News*, May 1, 2014.

20 Daniel Foster, "Christie, Kingmaker?" *National Review*, June 1, 2011.

21 Mike Allen, "What Chris Christie Told the Tycoons," *Politico*, July 20, 2011.

22 Mark Lagerkvist, "Travel Club: Cost of Christie Cops Continues to Climb," *New Jersey Watchdog*, April 20, 2015.

23 Ross Douthat, "Chris Christie's Cue," *New York Times*, August 14, 2011.

24 Josh Margolin, "Obama Digging Up Dirt on Potential Opponent Chris Christie," *New York Post*, May 23, 2011.

25 Josh Margolin, "Christie Seriously Considering Presidential Bid After GOP Prodding," *New York Post*, September 29, 2011.

26 Matt K. Lewis, "Top Christie Donors Told to Head to Trenton," *Daily Caller*, October 3, 3011.

27 Matt Katz, "Christie Tries to Give N.J. Lifts to Romney in N.H.," *Philadelphia Inquirer*, January 9, 2012.

28 Matt Katz, "Was Christie's Takedown Really Sexist?" *Philly.com*, January 11, 2012.

29 Matt Katz, "Gov. Christie Admits His 'Spontaneity' Sometimes Gets Him in Trouble," *Philadelphia Inquirer*, January 8, 2012.

30 Geneva Sands, "Gov. Christie Warns Iowa: 'I will be back, Jersey-Style' if Romney Loses Caucus," *The Hill*, December 30, 2011.

31 Matt Katz, "Will Christie Keep Up the Swagger?" *Philadelphia Inquirer*, September 3, 3012.

## 9: JERSEY STRONG

1 Matt Katz, "Christie Praises Obama Administration on Irene Response," *Philadelphia Inquirer*, September 6, 2011.

2   Tom Baldwin, "State unveils emergency-operations hub," *Home News Tribune*, January 25, 2007.

3   Stephanie Hoopes Halpin, *The Impact of Superstorm Sandy on New Jersey Towns and Households* (Rutgers University, 2013).

4   Matt Katz, "Christie sees 'absolute devastation,' at Shore and Beyond," *Philly.com*, October 30, 2012.

5   Matt Katz, "Christie has Emotional Ties to Twice-Stricken Seaside," *Philadelphia Inquirer*, September 16, 2013.

6   Matt Katz, "Christie: I Did NOT Hug Obama," *Philly.com*, November 25, 2013.

7   Matt Katz and Aubrey Whelan, "Obama, Christie join forces to reassure Jersey Shore residents hard hit by Sandy," *Philadelphia Inquirer*, November 1, 2012.

8   Matt Katz, "Christie Meets, Hugs Those Devastated by Sandy," *Philadelphia Inquirer*, October 31, 2012.

9   Jeffrey Goldberg, "Jersey Boys," *Atlantic*, July/August 2012.

10  Matt Katz, "Christie and the Boss: Singing Different Tunes?" *Philadelphia Inquirer*, March 28, 2012.

11  Matt Katz, "Killing with Kindness?" *Philadelphia Inquirer*, November 12, 2012.

12  Matt Katz, "Touring Battered N.J., Christie Gets Call from Springsteen," *Philadelphia Inquirer*, November 6, 2012.

13  Matt Katz, "Christie blasts Boehner for blocking Sandy relief vote," *Philadelphia Inquirer*, January 3, 2013.

## 10: FOUR MORE YEARS

1   Amy S. Rosenberg, "Mary Pat Christie, 'simpatico' in political and family affairs," *Philadelphia Inquirer*, April 17, 2011.

2   Lawrence Ragonese, "Freeholders take on emotional abortion issue," *Star-Ledger*, July 11, 1996.

3   Matt Katz, "New Jersey Likes Both Red and Blue," *Philadelphia Inquirer*, April 17, 2012.

4   Matt Katz, "Extremely Loud & Incredibly Close," *Politico*, September 3, 2013.

5   Matt Katz, "Christie, a voter, and Gay Marriage," *Philly.com*, October 8, 2013.

6   Jenna Portnoy, "Christie, confronted by Scotch Plains dad, says decision on kid medical pot bill due Friday," *Star-Ledger*, August 14, 2013.

7   Matt Katz, "Christie Brings Campaign to South Jersey," *Philadelphia Inquirer*, November 2, 2013.

8   Matt Katz, "Buono: Fierce Spirit, Overwhelming Odds," *Philadelphia Inquirer*, October 21, 2013.

9   Matt Katz, "Christie Has Emotional Ties to Twice-Stricken Seaside," *Philadelphia Inquirer*, September 16, 2013.

10  Maddie Hanna and Matt Katz, "Buono and Christie Make Points in Second Debate," *Philadelphia Inquirer*, October 17, 2013.

11  Steven Lemongello, "Christie Praises Legislative Effort to Pass Wine Bill," *Press Of Atlantic City*, January 18, 2012.

12  Sarah Maslin Nir, "A Governor and a Prince, Down at the Shore," *New York Times*, May 14, 2013.

13  Matt Katz, "Obama Joins Christie, Praises Shore Recovery," *Philadelphia Inquirer*, May 30, 2013.

14  Matt Katz, "Obama and Christie Back Together, Welcoming America to the Shore," *Philly.com*, May 28, 2013.

15  Matt Katz, "Christie uses DC stalemate to draw contrast," *Philadelphia Inquirer*, October 1, 2013.

16  Matt Katz and Joelle Farrell, "Christie Speech Focuses on Sandy—Almost Nothing Else," *Philadelphia Inquirer*, January 10, 2013.

17  Max Pizzaro, "Big Boy at the Brink: Chris Christie and the Discipline of Fear," *New York Observer*, January 14, 2014.

18  Jessica Gould, "New Jersey's New Political Party: Christiecrats," WNYC, August 1, 2013.

19  Matt Katz, "Why Do Elected Democrats Love Christie?" *Philadelphia Inquirer*, June 17, 2013.

20  Josh Margolin and Ted Sherman, "Hudson lawmaker under new scrutiny," *Star-Ledger*, March 4, 2007.

21  Jean-Pierre Mestanza, "Union City Naming New Cultural Center for Discredited Ex-Mayor," *Star-Ledger*, June 3, 2011.

22  Alec MacGillis, "The Rise and Fall of Chris Christie," *New Republic*, March 3, 2014.

23  Charles Stile, "Christie's Strategy of Wooing Key Democrats Pays Off Big," (Bergen) *Record*, November 5, 2013.

24  Matt Katz, "Christie's Complicated Relationship with Racial Issues," *Philadelphia Inquirer*, March 18, 2013.

25  Eunice Lee, "Orange Library Reopens After 9 Month Closure, Mayor Cites Funding Help from Gov. Christie," *Star-Ledger*, January 14, 2014.

26  Matt Katz, "Christie Finds Friends, Foes in Orange," *Philadelphia Inquirer*, September 26, 2013.

27  Jarrett Renshaw and Chris Megerian, "Christie Befriends Upstart Democrats in Hudson County," *Star-Ledger*, May 31, 2011.

28  Charles Stile, "Christie Divides to Conquer," (Bergen) *Record*, February 16, 2012.

29  Matt Katz, "Christie, Buono Disagree on Nearly Everything in Debate," *Philadelphia Inquirer*, October 10, 2013.

30  Matt Katz, "Christie Sets Limits on What He Will Discuss," *Philadelphia Inquirer*, August 31, 2013.

31  Matt Katz, "Why a Special Senate Election Could Be Great for Christie," *Philly.com*, June 4, 2013.

32  Rob Richie and Devin McCarthy, "The Christie Scandal Everyone Overlooked: A $12 Million Self-Motivated Political Scheme," *Salon*, February 17, 2014.

33  Kate Zernike and David W. Chen, "For Christie, Politics Team Kept a Focus on Two Races," *New York Times*, January 29, 2014.

34  Charles Stile, "Booker Praises Christie," (Bergen) *Record*, October 18, 2013.

35   Max Pizzaro, "Booker with Christie: 'I want to give some guv love,' " *Politicker NJ*, September 25, 2013.

36   Jenna Portnoy, "Christie begins re-election campaign with endorsement from major labor union," *Star-Ledger*, December 18, 2012.

37   Matt Katz, "After Cultivating Democrats, Christie Awaits Payoff," *Philadelphia Inquirer*, November 4, 2013.

38   Matthew Acro, "Republican Lawmaker Says Christie Worked With Norcross Ahead of Election," *Politicker NJ*, November 27, 2013.

39   Mark J. Magyar, "Kean Survives Ouster Vote Despite Christie Arm-Twisting," *NJ Spotlight.com*, November 8, 2013.

40   Kate Zernike, "Stories Add Up as Bully Image Trails Christie," *New York Times*, December 24, 2013.

41   Matt Katz, "After Cultivating Democrats, Christie Awaits Payoff," *Philadelphia Inquirer*, November 4, 2013.

42   Ryan Lizza, "Crossing Christie," *New Yorker*, April 14, 2014.

43   Kelly Heyboer, "In Debate, Christie Drastically Shifts Position on Tuition for Immigrants Living in the U.S. Illegally," *Star-Ledger*, October 16, 2013.

44   Eunice Lee, "Zoo Fundraiser Again Pairs Christie and DiVincenzo, Irks Dems," *Star-Ledger*, April 10, 2013.

45   Matt Katz, "Why Democrats are Smitten with Christie," *Philadelphia Inquirer*, June 17, 2013.

46   Matt Katz, "NJ Undocumented Students About to be Eligible for In-State Tuition," WNYC, December 19, 2013.

47   Matt Friedman, "Chris Christie Ends His Campaign in Union City," *Star-Ledger*, November 4, 2013.

48   Jenna Portnoy, "Christie Goes to Hispanic Stronghold Union City After Big Re-Election Win," *Star-Ledger*, November 6, 2013.

49   "Election 2013: Exit Polls," *New York Times*, November 6, 2013.

50   Gregory Giroux, "Bloomberg by the Numbers: 1,278,932," *Bloomberg Business*, December 5, 2013.

51   Kate Zernike and Jonathan Martin, "Chris Christie Coasts to 2nd Term as Governor of New Jersey," *New York Times*, November 5, 2013.

52   Matt Katz, "Extremely Loud & Incredibly Close," *Politico*, September 3, 2013.

## 11: "TIME FOR SOME TRAFFIC PROBLEMS IN FORT LEE"

1   Jeff Pillets and Melissa Hayes, "Two sides of former Christie campaign guru Bill Stepien: Highly effective but personally abrasive," (Bergen) *Record*, January 18, 2014.

2   Jenna Portnoy, "Chris Christie Bridge Scandal Takes Down Governor's Campaign Manager," *Star-Ledger*, January 9, 2014.

3   Beth DeFalco, "Town Halls Become Hallmark of Chris Christie's Tenure," Associated Press, April 10, 2012.

4   Jason Zengerie, "The Answer Is No," *New York* magazine, November 21, 2010.

5   Matt Katz, "How Christie's Office Used Government Employees to Win Endorsements," *NJ Spotlight*, April 4, 2014.

6   Matt Katz, "Playing Ball with Chris Christie," WNYC, April 10, 2014.

7   Matt Katz, "Inside Chris Christie's Permanent Campaign," *NJ Spotlight*, August 25, 2014.

8   Matt Katz, "How Christie's Office Used Government Employees to Win Endorsements," *NJ Spotlight*, April 4, 2014.

9   Mike Kelly, "Former Fort Lee Mayor Who Blew Whistle on Bribe Pulling Up N.J. Roots," (Bergen) *Record*, January 5, 2012.

10  Shawn Boburg, "Was Fort Lee Mayor a Long-Term Political Target?" (Bergen) *Record*, June 8, 2015.

11  Statehouse Bureau Staff, "List of Biggest Donors to Pro-Christie Group Includes Contractors Paid Millions by N.J.," *Star-Ledger*, December 30, 2010.

12  Mike Kelly, "GWB scandal: Fort Lee mayor now says Christie campaign courted him for endorsement," (Bergen) *Record*, February 7, 2014.

13  David Voreacos, "Christie Relationship with Fort Lee Mayor Began Over Meal," *Bloomberg Business*, February 8, 2014.

14  Kate Zernike and David W. Chen, "For Christie, Politics Team Kept a Focus on Two Races," *New York Times*, January 29, 2014.

15  "Pension Fund Bills Delayed in Jersey," *New York Times*, April 11, 1944,

16  "The Port Authority at 30," *New York Times*, April 30, 1951.

17  "Ex-Gov. W. E. Edge of Jersey is Dead," *New York Times*, October 30, 1956.

18  "Pension Fund Bills Delayed in Jersey," *New York Times*, April 11, 1944.

19  "Edge Pension Bills Passed in Jersey," *New York Times*, May 23, 1944.

20  "New Board to Plan For Jersey Tunnels," *New York Times*, June 9, 1917.

21  Kate Zernike and David W. Chen, "For Christie, Politics Team Kept a Focus on Two Races," *New York Times*, January 29, 2014.

22  Michael J. Brikner, Donald Linky, and Peter Mickulas, *The Governors of New Jersey* (New Brunswick, N.J.: Rutgers University Press, 2014).

23  "52 Are Indicted in Race Betting in Hudson, the First since Hague's Control Began," *New York Times*, August 23, 1944.

24  Nelson Johnson and Terence Winter, *Boardwalk Empire: The Birth, High Times, and Corruption of Atlantic City* (Medford, N.J.: Plexus Publishing, 2002).

25  Alex Isenstadt, "My Time with Scandal-hit Christie Aide," *Politico*, January 9, 2014.

26  Shawn Boburg, "Ex-Blogger is Governor Christie's Eyes, Ears Inside the Port Authority," (Bergen) *Record*, March 3, 2012.

27  Bryan Burrough, "Christieworld," *Vanity Fair*, August 2014.

28  Olivia Nuzzi, "Christie & The Sex Slave Ring," *Daily Beast*, March 17, 2014.

29  Olivia Nuzzi, "Christie and Wildstein: An Online Bromance," *Daily Beast*, February 14, 2015.

30  Ken Kurson, "Just How Close Was Chris Christie to David Wildstein?" *Politicker NJ*, March 13, 2015.

31  Shawn Boburg, "Was Fort Lee Mayor a Long-Term Political Target?" (Bergen) *Record*, June 7, 2015.

32  Kate Zernike, "On Blog, an Ex-Christie Ally Showed Approach to Politics," *New York Times*, February 6, 2014.

33 Kate Zernike and Matt Flegenheimer, "Even Before Fort Lee Lane Closings, Port Authority Was a Christie Tool," *New York Times*, March 11, 2014.

## 12: A BRIDGEGATE TIMELINE

1 Andrea Bernstein, "Christie, Aide Texted As Bridgegate Cover Story Unraveled," WNYC, December 8, 2014.

2 Marvin Scott, "50th anniversary of George Washington Bridge," Channel 11, October 25, 1981.

3 James W. Doig, *Empire on the Hudson* (New York: Columbia University Press, 2001).

4 John Templon, "9 Delightfully Geeky Stats About NYC Bridges and Tunnels," *BuzzFeed*, July 21, 2014.

5 Paul Vitello, "Ernesto Butcher, Who Managed Port Authority After 9/11, Dies at 69," *New York Times*, May 22, 2014.

6 Linh Tat, "For Fort Lee, Traffic Is an Everyday Challenge," (Bergen) *Record*, February 16, 2014.

7 Shawn Boburg, "GWB Scandal: In police radio recordings, officers scramble to deal with traffic jams," (Bergen) *Record*, September 12, 2014.

8 Nate Schweber, "Woman Says Lane Closings Were Not to Blame for Her Mother's Death," *New York Times*, January 9, 2014.

9 Jack Gillum and Katie Zezima, " 'Bridgegate' Gridlock Didn't Cost Lives," Associated Press, February 14, 2014.

10 Bob Ingle and Michael Simmons, *Chris Christie: The Inside Story of His Rise to Power* (New York: St. Martin's Press, 2011).

11 Shawn Boburg, "Vivid recollections show Port Authority cops' concern with GWB lane closures," (Bergen) *Record*, September 3, 2014.

12 "The Trial of Omar Abdel Rahman," *New York Times*, October 3, 1995.

13 Amanda Terkel and Sam Stein, "Days of Chaos in Fort Lee During Chris Christie Administration's Traffic Experiment," *Huffington Post*, January 1, 2014.

14 David Carr, "Local Papers Shine Light in Society's Dark Corners," *New York Times*, February 9, 2014.

15 Dustin Racioppi, Kristi Funderburk, and Larry Higgs, "Fire Consumes N.J. Boardwalk Rebuilt After Sandy," *USA Today*, September 13, 2013.

16 Matt Katz, "Christie Has Emotional Ties to Twice-Stricken Seaside," *Philadelphia Inquirer*, September 16, 2013.

17 Matt Katz, "Christie Faulted on Plan to Give Sandy Money for Seaside Fire," *Philadelphia Inquirer*, September 19, 2013.

18 John Cichowski, "Road Warrior: Closed Tollbooths a Commuting Disaster," (Bergen) *Record*, September 13, 2013.

19 Ted Mann, "Port Official: Trenton Wanted George Washington Bridge Lane Closures," *Wall Street Journal*, September 7, 2014.

20 Matt Flegenheimer, "Bridge Scandal Relegates 'Traffic Study' to Punch Line," *New York Times*, March 9, 2014.

21　Hody Nemes, "Loretta Weinberg, the Jewish Grandma Who's Making Chris Christie's Life Miserable," *Forward*, January 22, 2014.

22　Steve Strunsky, "Lawmaker Demands Answers to GWB Closure Mystery at Port Authority Meeting," *Star-Ledger*, October 7, 2013.

23　Bill Baroni with Damon DiMarco, *Fat Kid Got Fit* (Guilford, Conn.: Lyons Press, 2012).

24　Matt Katz, "Extremely Loud & Incredibly Close," *Politico*, September 3, 2013.

25　David Sirota, "Before Bridgegate, Chris Christie Used Port Authority as Political Weapon," *International Business Times*, January 8, 2015.

26　Shawn Boburg and John Reitmeyer, "Dozens of Port Authority Jobs Go to Christie Loyalists," (Bergen) *Record*, January 29, 2012.

27　Kate Zernike, "Stories Add Up as Bully Image Trails Christie," *New York Times*, December 24, 2013.

28　Tom Moran, "The Gov's Mean Streak Creates Enemies," *Star-Ledger*, March 6, 2011.

29　John Reitmeyer, "Baroni Declares Innocence, Alludes to His Previous Ethics-Reform Efforts," *NJ Spotlight*, May 5, 2015.

30　Mike Kelly, "GWB scandal: Fort Lee mayor now says Christie campaign courted him for endorsement," (Bergen) *Record*, February 7, 2014.

31　Shawn Boburg, "Port Authority official from N.Y. to testify in controversy over lane closures at George Washington Bridge," (Bergen) *Record*, December 4, 2013.

32　Mitchell Blumenthal, "Port raider: Christie claims bi-state money for Jersey roads, Albany watches," *Capital New York*, January 21, 2011.

33　David Porter, "NY-NJ port police union chief wades into GWB tiff," Associated Press, December 4, 2013.

34　William K. Rashbaum, "Head of Port Authority Police Union Questions Bridge Inquiry," *New York Times*, March 4, 2014.

35　Shawn Boburg, "Collision Course Over Lane Closures," (Bergen) *Record*, December 5, 2013.

36　N. R. Kleinfield, "A Bridge Scandal: Behind the Fort Lee Ruse," *New York Times*, January 12, 2014.

37　Joshua Alston, "NJ Lawmakers Extend Port Authority Subpoena Power," *Law 360*, February 14, 2013.

38　Steve Strunsky, "Assembly Transportation Chief Subpoenas Port Authority for Documents on Toll Increase," *Star-Ledger*, October 25, 2012.

39　Zack Fink, "See No Evil, Hear No Evil," *State of Politics*, November 16, 2015.

**13: NO SURRENDER**

1　Robert A. Caro, *The Power Broker: Robert Moses and the Fall of New York* (New York: Alfred A. Knopf, 2012).

2　Shawn Boburg, "Christie Stuck in a Jam Over GWB Lane Closings," (Bergen) *Record*, January 8, 2014.

3　Michael Barbaro, "Christie's Carefully Devised, No-Nonsense Image in Peril," *New York Times*, January 8, 2014.

4   Salvador Rizzo, "N.J. judge denies Port Authority official's request to quash subpoena in GWB bridge case," *Star-Ledger*, January 9, 2014.

5   Christopher Baxter, "In Bridge Scandal, One Lawyer Could Topple Christie," *Star-Ledger*, February 23, 2014.

6   Alan L. Zegas, "Gov. Chris Christie's attacks undermine integrity, impartiality of judiciary," *Star-Ledger*, November 27, 2011.

7   David Voreacos, "Christie Relationship with Fort Lee Mayor Began over Meal," *Bloomberg Business*, February 8, 2014.

8   Sarah Gonzalez, "Christie's Quick Trip to Fort Lee—and a Mayor's Forgiveness," WNYC, January 9, 2014.


## 14: THE CRISIS

1   David W. Chen, "In Inquiry, It's Christie Against Prosecutor," *New York Times*, February 9, 2014.

2   Bob Ingle and Michael Simmons, *Chris Christie: The Inside Story of His Rise to Power* (New York: St. Martin's Press, 2011).

3   Steve Politi, "Gov. Chris Christie Says He's Ready to Get Involved in N.J. Sports Issues," *Star-Ledger*, June 13, 2010.

4   Claire Heininger, "N.J. Gov.-elect Chris Christie Ready to Take Charge," *Star-Ledger*, January 17, 2010.

5   Brett LoGiurato, "Chris Christie Goes Scorched Earth on the New York Times and Former Ally," *Business Insider*, February 1, 2014.

6   Matt Flegenheimer, "Bridge Scandal Relegates 'Traffic Study' to Punch Line," *New York Times*, March 9, 2014.

7   Ryan Lizza, "Crossing Christie," *New Yorker*, April 14, 2014.

8   Matt Mullin, "Survey: Americans think New Jersey is the worst state," *Philly Voice*, July 3, 2015.

9   John Schoonejongen, "Chris Christie Jokes Were Plenty at White House Correspondents' Association Dinner," *APP.com*, May 4, 2014.

10   Emily Smith, "McHale roasts, then hangs out with Christie," *New York Post, Page Six*, May 4, 2014.

11   Matt Katz, "Despite, or because of, Christie's Brash Ways, N.J. Voters Still Approve," *Philadelphia Inquirer*, July 30, 2012.

12   Terrence T. McDonald, "Emails show state officials abruptly canceled meetings with Jersey City mayor," *Star-Ledger*, January 13, 2014.

13   Heather Haddon, "New Jersey Gov. Chris Christie's Aides Pressed Hard for Endorsements," *Wall Street Journal*, January 12, 2014.

14   Sarah Gonzalez, "Why a Vote for Christie Could Mean You're Voting In Guadagno as Governor," WNYC, October 31, 2013.

15   Matt Katz, "Chasing Guadagno, the Woman Who Could Be Christie," WNYC, August 5, 2014.

16   Matt Katz, "Christie's No. 2: Irrepressible, Sometimes Irascible," *Philadelphia Inquirer*, August 28, 2011.

17   Scott Gurian, "Does Chris Christie Owe Hoboken $700,000?" WNYC/*NJ Spotlight*, March 5, 2014.

18   Scott Gurian, "Investigation Reveals Sandy Energy Grant Program Riddled with Errors," WNYC/*NJ Spotlight*, March 6, 2014.

19   Scott Gurian, "New Jersey to Eliminate Inconsistencies in Sandy Aid to Towns," WNYC/*NJ Spotlight*, July 14, 2014.

20   Steve Kornacki, "Up with Steve Kornacki," *NBC News*, January 22, 2014.

21   Erin O'Neill, "N.J. Sandy energy grant program revised, leaving Hoboken with more money," *Star-Ledger*, July 11, 2014.

22   Josh Margolin, "Rockefeller Center Construction Firm Finishes Hoboken Development Plans," *Star-Ledger*, July 6, 2010.

23   Steve Strunsky, "Critics Accuse Christie of Turning Port Authority into Patronage Mill," *Star-Ledger*, February 10, 2012.

24   Andrea Bernstein, "The Incredible Sinking Port Authority," WNYC, May 6, 2014.

25   Shawn Boburg, "Top New Jersey Democratic Lawmakers Take Aim at $1B Port Authority Fund," (Bergen) *Record*, July 9, 2014.

26   Patrick McGeehan and Charles V. Bagli, "How Pressure Mounted for Development in Hoboken," *New York Times*, January 29, 2014.

27   Shawn Boburg and John Reitmeyer, "Dozens of Port Authority Jobs Go to Christie Loyalists," (Bergen) *Record*, January 29, 2012.

28   Ted Mann, "New Panel Will Consider Port Authority Reforms," *Wall Street Journal*, March 16, 2014.

29   Larry Higgs, Bob Jordan, Dustin Racioppi, and Michael Symons, "Press Investigation: Inside the Port Authority's Money Machine," *Asbury Park Press*, April 7, 2014.

30   James W. Doig, *Empire on the Hudson* (New York: Columbia University Press, 2001).

31   Ned Resnikoff, "Christie's Other Traffic Jam," MSNBC, January 30, 2014.

32   Jason Fagone, "Feature: Is NJ Governor Chris Christie a Mad Man?" *Philadelphia* magazine, November 26, 2010.

33   Ted Sherman, "N.J. Gov. Chris Christie Agrees to Reconsider Hudson River Tunnel Project," *Star-Ledger*, October 8, 2010.

34   Josh Margolin and Ted Sherman, "Frantic Behind-the-Scenes Dealings Could Resuscitate the Hudson River Tunnel Project," *Star-Ledger*, October 10, 2010.

35   Paul Mulshine, "Commuters Getting a Gift from Macy's Basement," *Star-Ledger*, February 8, 2011.

36   Kate Zernike, "Report Disputes Christie's Bias for Halting Tunnel," *New York Times*, April 10, 2012.

37   Andrea Bernstein, "How Christie's Men Turned the Port Authority into a Political Piggy Bank," WNYC, January 16, 2014.

38   Karen Rouse, "Analysis: N.J. needs new revenue source to fix roads after years of borrowing," (Bergen) *Record*, April 25, 2014.

39   Mark J. Magyar, "Transportation Crisis Puts Christie, Democrats on Collision Course," *NJ Spotlight*, April 25, 2014.

40  Cezary Podkul and Allan Sloan, "Behind Christie's budget claims, a more contro-versial legacy," *Washington Post*, April 17, 2015.

41  Elise Young, "Christie-Backed Housing to Flood Rail with Tunnel Killed," *Bloomberg Business*, June 8, 2014.

42  Linda Wolfe, *Double Life: Double Life* (New York: Reed Business Information Inc., 1994).

43  Mark J. Magyar, "Christie's Borrowing Binge Makes Transportation Trust Fund Run Dry," *NJ Spotlight*, April 3, 2014.

44  Mark Franssinelli, "Under the Pulaski Skyway: What you don't see might scare you," *NJ Spotlight*, April 8, 2014.

45  Matt Katz and Andrea Bernstein, "Bridgegate Fall Guy was Inside Man," WNYC, March 12, 2015.

46  Steve Strunsky, "Port Authority's new chairman leads with straight talk, firm hand," *Star-Ledger*, July 8, 2011.

47  Michael Powell, "Ailing Pulaski Skyway Offers a Lesson in Creative Financing," *New York Times*, April 16, 2014.

48  Shawn Boburg, "Christie's toll-money shuffle: Port Authority funds paying for repairs to state roads," (Bergen) *Record*, March 31, 2014.

49  Kate Zernike and Matt Flegenheimer, "Even Before Fort Lee Lane Closings, Port Authority Was a Christie Tool," *New York Times*, March 11, 2014.

50  John Cichowski, "Road Warrior: Pulaski Skyway's repairs latest challenge over state's worn-out infrastructure," (Bergen) *Record*, April 7, 2014.

51  Matt Flegenheimer, William K. Rashbaum, and Kate Zernicke, "2nd Bridge Inquiry Said to Be Linked to Christie," *New York Times*, June 23, 2014.

52  Steve Strunsky, "Port Authority officials: Battle over toll hikes was all for show," *Star-Ledger*, March 2, 2014.

53  Shawn Boburg, "Top Christie Port Authority appointees devised toll-hike plan to bolster image of NJ, NY governors," (Bergen) *Record*, March 3, 2014.

54  Esmê E. Deprez and Terrence Dopp, "Port Authority Raises Tolls on Bridges, Tunnels to New York," *Bloomberg Business*, August 19, 2011.

55  Peter Coy, "Think Bridgegate Was Bad? The Port Authority Is a Daily Disaster," *Bloomberg Business*, April 29, 2015.

56  "Judge and Heiress: The Rise and Fall of a Private Affair," *New York Times*, November 15, 1992.

57  Josh Barbanel, "Wachtler Charged in Indictment Detailing Harassment Campaign," *New York Times*, February 2, 1993.

58  Diana Jean Schemo, "Seeking Leniency, Wachtler Blames Adversaries," *New York Times*, September 5, 1993.

59  Andrea Bernstein, "Under Christie, Business Booms for Port Authority's Chief," WNYC, January 23, 2014.

60  Steve Strunsky, "Senate approves Christie's choice for PA chairman," *Star-Ledger*, January 26, 2011.

61  Andrea Bernstein, "How Christie Ally Profited from NJ Transit," WNYC, February 26, 2014.

62  Shawn Boburg, "New Port Authority conflict issue emerges: NJ Transit got $1 lease while a client of David Samson's law firm," (Bergen) *Record*, February 19, 2014.

63  Russ Buettner, "In a Job, Appointee Profits and Christie Gains Power," *New York Times*, March 4, 2015.

64  Ginger Adams Otis, "Port Authority Chairman David Samson unfit for role: Gov. Cuomo appointee," *Daily News*, February 25, 2014.

65  Abbott Koloff, "Analysis: Port Authority Works Under Its Own Set of Rules," (Bergen) *Record*, March 16, 2014.

66  Andrew Perez and Christine Wilkie, "Wolff & Samson, Firm At Heart Of Christie Controversy, Has Had An Ally In The Governor," *Huffington Post*, January 30, 2014.

67  Larry Higgs, Bob Jordan, Dustin Racioppi, and Michael Symons, "Press Investigation: Inside the Port Authority's Money Machine," *Asbury Park Press*, April 7, 2014.

68  Ginger Adams Otis, "Port Authority Chairman David Samson unfit for role: Gov. Cuomo appointee," *New York Daily News*, February 25, 2014.

69  Lucy Adams, "The Whisper of History," *Augusta* magazine, Fall 2014.

70  Jim Dwyer, "Broken at the Bridge, a Basic Law of Politics," *New York Times*, January 21, 2014.

71  Shawn Boburg, "Federal subpoena seeks travel records of former Port Authority Chairman David Samson," (Bergen) *Record*, February 5, 2015.

72  David Kocieniewski and David Voreacos, "The Dinner Proposal That Led United into Corruption Probe," *Bloomberg Business*, April 28, 2015.

73  Brian Murphy, "Investigations Might Sink Christie After All," *TalkingPointsMemo.com*, February 6, 2015.

74  Tom Moran, "Christie and Cuomo give bipartisanship a bad name," *Star-Ledger*, January 2, 2015.

## 15: THE INVESTIGATIONS

1  Andrea Bernstein, "Six Ways the Christie Administration Blocked Reform at the Port Authority," WNYC, March 10, 2014.

2  Matt Katz, "Meet Christie's $650-an-hour-man," WNYC, March 11, 2014.

3  Andrea Bernstein, "Six Ways the Christie Administration Blocked Reform at the Port Authority," WNYC, March 10, 2014.

4  John Shiffman and Emille Lounsberry, "Defense: City Hall case is a 'failure': Lawyers for Commerce Bank executives Glenn K. Holck and Stephen M. Umbrell gave closing arguments yesterday," *Philadelphia Inquirer*, April 12, 2005.

5  Colleen O'Dea, "Per-Pupil Costs Vary Widely in New Jersey's Schools," *NJ Spotlight*, May 16, 2014.

6  Jarrett Renshaw, "Sen. Codey: Christie Insulted the Office of the Governor," *Star-Ledger*, December 15, 2011.

7  Associated Press, "N.J. Senate Confirms 8 New Essex County Judges," (Bergen) *Record*, August 18, 2014.

8  Michael Booth and David Gialanella, "Christie Withdraws Essex Co. Judicial Nominations," *New Jersey Law Journal*, June 30, 2014.

9   Martin Bricketto, "Judicial Vacancies Plague N.J.'s Busiest Court," *Law 360*, May 3, 2013.

10  Matt Katz, "Cracks in Christie's Post-Bridgegate Ethics Reform," WNYC, March 25, 2015.

11  Matt Katz, "What We Learned at First Bridgegate Testimony," WNYC, May 6, 2014.

12  Stefanie Akin, "Questions about Christie's mouthpiece arise after he shows up in released GWB emails," (Bergen) *Record*, January 16, 2014.

13  Andrea Bernstein, "The Mystery of Christie's Deleted Bridgegate Text," WNYC, August 1, 2014.

14  Andrea Bernstein, "Christie, Aide Texted as Bridgegate Cover Story Unraveled," WNYC, December 8, 2014.

15  Patrick McGeehan, "Fort Lee School Head Calls Lane Closings an 'Act of Terrorism,' " *New York Times*, May 1, 2015.

16  Michael Symons, "Baroni, Kelly Plead Not Guilty to Bridgegate Charges," *Courier-Post*, May 4, 2015.

17  Thomas Zambito, "Bridgegate Scandal: Kelly, Baroni enter not guilty pleas in federal court," *Star-Ledger*, May 4, 2015.

18  Matt Katz, "How Christie Talks About the Bridge Thing," WNYC, May 9, 2015.

## 16: CHRISTIE LOSES HIS FLEECE

1   Matt Katz, "Christie Does Post-Budget Morning News Blitz, Talks Camden," *Philadelphia Inquirer*, February 23, 2011.

2   Dorsey Shaw, "MSNBC's 'Morning Joe' and Chris Christie: a Love Story," *BuzzFeed*, May 7, 2013.

3   Mark Finkelstein, "Morning Joe Mocks Christie with 'Govfather' Logo," *NewsBusters*, January 30, 2014.

4   Matt Katz, "Chris Christie's Greatest Weakness," *Politico*, November 14, 2014.

5   Matt Katz, "Christie Tells Sandy Protester to 'Sit Down & Shut Up,' " WNYC, October 29, 2014.

6   Russ Zimmer, "Up in the air: 1,000 days after Sandy," *Asbury Park Press*, July 24, 2015.

7   Josh Dawsey and Heather Haddon, "New Jersey Still Rebuilding After Superstorm Sandy," *Wall Street Journal*, March 10, 2015.

8   Josh Dawsey and Heather Haddon, "Ousted Firm Blames New Jersey for Sandy Ills," *Wall Street Journal*, June 13, 2014.

9   Matt Katz, "Ten Sandy Contractors Give to GOP Group Headed by Christie," WNYC, February 3, 2014.

10  Mark J. Magyar, "Analysis: What's Wrong with Chris Christie's Government?" *NJSpotlight.com*, March 11, 2014.

11  Shawn Boburg, "Debris haulers' windfall: Odd math jacks up Sandy tab," (Bergen) *Record*, April 28, 2013.

12  Matt Katz, "Contractor for Sandy Cleanup Is Focus of Hearing," *Philadelphia Inquirer*, March 9, 2013.

13  Matt Katz, "Christie's Biggest Sandy Contractor Fired," WNYC, January 23, 2014.

14 Matt Katz, "Gov. Christie's choice to distribute Sandy aid was fired from similar job in Texas," *Philadelphia Inquirer*, February 8, 2013.

15 Joseph Tanfani, "Since Sandy, a storm pattern of costly stumbles in New Jersey," *Los Angeles Times*, June 20, 2013.

16 Matt Katz, "Christie scoffs at questions about Sandy Contractor," *Philadelphia Inquirer*, February 8, 2013.

17 Karen Rouse, "NJ Transit remains silent on how it prepared for Superstorm Sandy," (Bergen) *Record*, May 13, 2013.

18 Laure Kusisto and Josh Dawsey, "Federal Sandy Funds Fall Short, Officials Say," *Wall Street Journal*, May 26, 2014.

19 Michael Symons, "How much did Sandy money reports cost?" *Asbury Park Press*, July 21, 2014.

20 Bob Jordan, "Politically Active Firm Wins N.J. Sandy Ad Contract," *USA Today*, August 4, 2013.

21 Bob Jordan, "New Documents Show Christie Office Hiding Details of Storm TV Ads," *Asbury Park Press*, January 14, 2014.

22 Matt Friedman, "Christie Used Sandy Funds for Senior Complex in Town Where Mayor Endorsed Him," *Star-Ledger*, January 28, 2014.

23 Alec MacGillis, "The Chris Christie Scandal Just Got Worse," *New Republic*, March 18, 2014.

24 Amy S. Rosenberg and Jacqueline L. Urgo, "Shore Homeowners Give N.J. Officials an Earful," *Philadelphia Inquirer*, February 13, 2014.

25 Keith Heumiller, "State recovery plan comes under fire," *The Hub*, February 27, 2014.

26 Chris Glorioso, "Sandy Funds Went to NJ Town with Little Storm Damage," NBC New York, January 31, 2014.

27 Steve Kornacki, "Sandy funds 'integrity monitors' only in place since January," MSNBC, February 1, 2014.

28 Heather Haddon, "Poll Finds New Jersey Homeowners Unhappy with Sandy Aid Efforts," *Wall Street Journal*, February 17, 2014.

29 "Sandy Aid Delays: The Biggest Scandal of All," *Press Of Atlantic City*, February 16, 2014.

30 Cezary Podkul and Allan Sloan, "Behind Christie's budget claims, a more controversial legacy," *Washington Post*, April 17, 2015.

31 "FactChecking the GOP Candidate Forum," *FactCheck.org*, August 3, 2015.

32 Steven Malanga, "The Christie Hiatus," *National Review*, March 5, 2015.

33 Kate Zernike, "Christie Broke Law with Pension Move, New Jersey Judge Says," *New York Times*, February 23, 2015.

34 Elise Young and Terrence Dopp, "Christie Cuts N.J. Pension Payments to Close Budget Gaps," *Bloomberg Business*, May 21, 2014.

35 Samantha Marcus, "Christie pension commission recommends plan for huge savings, fewer benefits," *Star-Ledger*, February 24, 2015.

36 Josh Lederman, "Gov: Pension deal to help build affordable NJ," *Bloomberg Business*, June 16, 2011.

37  Casey Tolan, "Welcome to Atlantic City, the foreclosure capital of the U.S.," *Fusion*, August 7, 2015.

38  Matt Katz, "Christie's Atlantic City plan creates tourism district, invests public money in casino," *Philadelphia Inquirer*, February 2, 2011.

39  Wayne Parry, "A.C.'s Revel starts closing after 2 years," *USA Today*, September 1, 2014.

40  Matt Katz, "Touring the Jersey Shore, Christie Pushes AC Recovery," *Philadelphia Inquirer*, August 12, 2011.

41  Josh Dawsey, "Atlantic City's Big Bet on Gambling Sours," *Wall Street Journal*, August 29, 2014.

42  Jean Mikle, "Millions spent on casinos didn't help Atlantic City," *USA Today*, June 11, 2013.

43  Hillary Russ, "Exclusive: Atlantic City recovery costs reach $1.7 million and growing," *Yahoo! News*, August 12, 2015.

44  Heather Haddon and Josh Dawsey, "Report Sees a Cloudy Future for Atlantic City," *Wall Street Journal*, November 13, 2014.

45  George Anastasia, "Detroit with a Boardwalk," *Politico*, October 20, 2014.

46  Josh Margolin and Ted Sherman, "Gov. Christie pledges to turn Atlantic City Casino District into 'Las Vegas East,' " *Star-Ledger*, July 22, 2010.

47  Josh Dawsey, "Atlantic City's Big Bet on Gambling Sours," *Wall Street Journal*, August 29, 2014.

48  Melissa Hayes and Patricia Alex, "2nd groundbreaking held at William Paterson University, with shovel reserved for Christie this time," (Bergen) *Record*, June 10, 2014.

49  Matthew Arco, "Man snapping photos of protestors at Christie town hall says he's a state policeman," *Star-Ledger*, March 3, 2014.

50  Maggie Haberman, "A More Restrained Christie Holds Court," *Politico.com*, February 20, 2014.

51  Matt Katz, "Christie Heckled at Shore Town Hall and Still Wins Over Crowd," *WNYC*, February 20, 2014.

52  Michael Barbaro, "For Christie, Awkward Return to a Setting He Once Ruled," *New York Times*, February 20, 2014.

53  Andrew Kitchenman, "Friend's Death Leads Christie to Underscore Overdose Concerns to Doctors," *NJ Spotlight*, May 19, 2014.

54  Matt Katz, "Jersey Flag Burned Over Whitney Houston Controversy," *Philly.com*, February 20, 2012.

55  Josh Dawsey, "Christie's Tack on Drug Addiction Sets Him Apart," *Wall Street Journal*, September 30, 2014.

56  The Associated Press, "Heroin Antidote Saves 5 in Ocean County," (Bergen) *Record*, April 24, 2014.

57  MaryAnn Spoto, "Gov. Christie signs bill that gives non-violent drug offenders rehab instead of jail time," *Star-Ledger*, July 19, 2012.

58  Matt Katz, "New Jersey Assembly Snubs Christie," *WNYC*, July 31, 2014.

## EPILOGUE: REBORN TO RUN

1   Michael Linhorst, "Christie meets with top Republican backers in Florida," (Bergen) *Record*, January 19, 2014.

2   Andrew Seidman, "In Tenn., Christie lists U.S. problems, proposes cures," *Philadelphia Inquirer*, June 1, 2014.

3   Peter Hamby, "On Southern road trip, Christie preaches compromise," CNN, May 30, 2014.

4   Matt Friedman, "Firms with ties to Christie gave big to Republican governors group," *Star-Ledger*, April 16, 2014.

5   Matt Katz, "Christie's New Hampshire Dress Rehearsal," WNYC, November 3, 2014.

6   Michael Barbaro, "Far From Scandal at Home, Christie Basks in Limelight on Iowa Trip," *New York Times*, July 17, 2014.

7   Thomas Fitzgerald, "Christie threatens Iowa voters," *Philadelphia Inquirer*, December 30, 2011.

8   Matt Katz, "Christie Goes to Football Game, Ignites Twitter, Draws Ethics Questions," WNYC, January 6, 2015.

9   Matt Katz, "Christie's Super Tuesday, by the numbers," WNYC, November 5, 2014.

10  Andrew Seidman, "In Tenn., Christie lists U.S. problems, proposes cures," *Philadelphia Inquirer*, June 1, 2014.

11  Philip Rucker, "Christie brushes off 'Bridgegate' in speech to Romney donors," *Washington Post*, June 14, 2014.

12  Jarret Renshaw, "National group offers Christie donors potential freedom from state laws," *Star-Ledger*, August 25, 2013.

13  Matt Katz, "Lingering Questions: Christie's Bridgegate Report Isn't Going Away Any Time Soon," WNYC, June 9, 2015.

14  Matt Katz, "Christie Sent Government Emails from Private Account," WNYC, August 27, 2015.

15  Matt Katz, "How Christie Talks About the Bridge Thing," *NJ Spotlight*, May 10, 2015.

16  Matt Katz, "How Christie Will Rely on Mouth, Money & Moxie to Run for President," WNYC, November 13, 2014.

17  Maeve Reston, "Chris Christie to GOP donors on bridge scandal: 'You'll get over it,'" *Los Angeles Times*, June 15, 2014.

18  Josh Dawsey, Andrew Tangel, and Ted Mann, "Christie Faces Scrutiny over Gifts from Cowboys Owner," *Wall Street Journal*, January 6, 2015.

19  Matt Katz, "Christie Goes to Football Game, Ignites Twitter, Draws Ethics Questions," WNYC, January 6, 2015.

20  Rush Limbaugh, "The Skinny on Christie and Jones," *Rush Limbaugh Show*, January 6, 2015.

21  John Mooney, "Christie Stirs Things Up with Call to Drop Common Core but Keep PARCC," *NJ Spotlight*, May 29, 2015.

22  John Mooney, "Chris Christie's About-Face on Common Core Standards Turns Debate Upside Down," *NJ Spotlight*, February 11, 2015.

23  John Mooney, "State Unveils Plan for Wide-Ranging Review of Common Core Standards," *NJSpotlight.com*, July 9, 2015.

24  Bob Ingle and Michael Simmons, *Chris Christie: The Inside Story of His Rise to Power* (New York: St. Martin's Press, 2011).

25  Olivia Nuzzi, "Christie's Convenient Abortion Flip," *Daily Beast*, February 2, 2015.

26  Olivia Nuzzi, "Christie Bows to Iowa's Pork Kings on Gestation Crates," *Daily Beast*, November 28, 2014.

27  Olivia Nuzzi, "Chris Christie's Faking It on Gun Rights," *Daily Beast*, July 10, 2014.

28  Samantha Marcus, "Christie Signs Low-Income Tax Credit into Law," *Star-Ledger*, July 7, 2015.

29  Matt Katz, "Christie condemns NRA Ad, Establishes Violence Task Force," *Philadelphia Inquirer*, January 19, 2013.

30  The Associated Press, "Gov. Christie Announces Plan for Curbing Gun Violence," CBS New York, April 19, 2013.

31  Matt Friedman, "Sandy Hook parents call Christie veto of NJ gun bill a 'blow to the memories of our children,' " *Star-Ledger*, July 3, 2014.

32  Herb Jackson, "Christie Opposes Handgun Leniency," (Bergen) *Record*, November 25, 2011.

33  Matt Katz, "Christie's Gun-Rules Task Force Sees Little Need for Change," *Philadelphia Inquirer*, April 12, 2013.

34  Matt Katz, "Christie's Friday Night Special," *Philly.com*, August 17, 2013.

35  Heather Haddon, "N.J. Gov. Chris Christie Says He Would Consider Revisiting State Gun Laws," *Wall Street Journal*, March 24, 2015.

36  Troy Graham, "Student gun sales armed N.J. gang, authorities say," *Philadelphia Inquirer*, December 12, 2003.

37  Matt Friedman, "Proposal reflects Christie's rightward shift on guns," *Politico*, August 26, 2015.

38  Matt Katz, "Christie Repeatedly Avoids Questions on Assault Weapons," *Philadelphia Inquirer*, January 9, 2013.

39  Jonathan Topaz, "Scarborough Slams Christie on Guns," *Politico*, July 8, 2014.

40  Maddie Hanna, "For Christie's Announcement, a Reluctant Host," *Philadelphia Inquirer*, July 1, 2015.

41  Adam Clark, "The Strange History Between Christie and Livingston's Superintendent," *Star-Ledger*, June 30, 2015.

42  John Mooney, "Not Everyone Felt Good About Christie's Feel-Good Event at His Alma Mater," *NJ Spotlight*, July 1, 2015.

43  Steve Politi, "Christie Booed Mercilessly—Twice—at the Haskell," *Star-Ledger*, August 2, 2015.

44  Steve Politi, "Donald Trump Comes to The Barclays and All Hell Breaks Loose," *Star-Ledger*, August 30, 2015.

45  Eliza Collins, "Poll: Trump has twice the support of Bush in New Hampshire," *Politico*, July 28, 2015.

46  Lynn Vavreck, "The Republican Candidates Donald Trump Has Hurt the Most," *New York Times*, September 14, 2015.

47    Allison Steele, "Camden's Story Seen as More Nuanced than Christie Narrative," *Philadelphia Inquirer*, January 15, 2015.

48    Matt Katz, "Christie's 'State of the State' Speech Nods at State of the Nation," WNYC, January 13, 2015.

49    Thomas Fitzgerald, "In Iowa, Christie basks in own awesomeness," *Philadelphia Inquirer*, January 24, 2015.

# INDEX